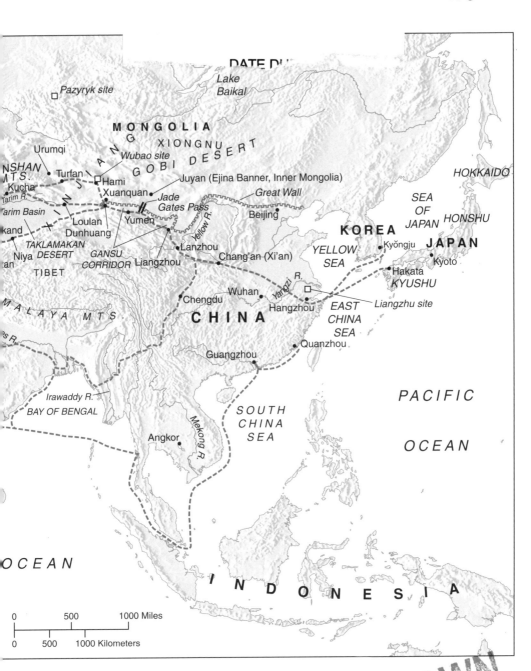

The Silk Road

The
SILK
ROAD

A NEW HISTORY

Valerie Hansen

OXFORD

UNIVERSITY PRESS

OXFORD
UNIVERSITY PRESS

Oxford University Press is a department of the University of Oxford.
It furthers the University's objective of excellence in research,
scholarship, and education by publishing worldwide.

Oxford   New York

Auckland   Cape Town   Dar es Salaam   Hong Kong   Karachi
Kuala Lumpur   Madrid   Melbourne   Mexico City   Nairobi
New Delhi   Shanghai   Taipei   Toronto

With offices in

Argentina   Austria   Brazil   Chile   Czech Republic   France   Greece
Guatemala   Hungary   Italy   Japan   Poland   Portugal   Singapore
South Korea   Switzerland   Thailand   Turkey   Ukraine   Vietnam

Oxford is a registered trademark of Oxford University Press in the UK and certain other countries.

Published in the United States of America by
Oxford University Press
198 Madison Avenue, New York, NY 10016

Library of Congress Cataloging-in-Publication Data
Hansen, Valerie, 1958–   -
The Silk Road : a new history / Valerie Hansen.
p.   cm.
Includes bibliographical references and index.
ISBN 978-0-19-515931-8 (hardcover : acid-free paper)
1. Silk Road—History. 2. Silk Road—History—Sources.
3. Silk Road—Description and travel. 4. Silk Road—History, Local.
5. Historic sites—Silk Road. 6. Trade routes—Asia—History. I. Title.
DS33.1.H36   2012
950.1—dc23   2011041804

3 5 7 9 8 6 4

Printed in the United States of America
on acid-free paper

For Jim—

who else?

Contents

Acknowledgments ix

Note on Scholarly Conventions xiii

Timeline xiv

Introduction   3

CHAPTER 1
At the Crossroads of Central Asia
The Kingdom of Kroraina 25

CHAPTER 2
Gateway to the Languages of the Silk Road
Kucha and the Caves of Kizil 56

CHAPTER 3
Midway Between China and Iran
Turfan 83

CHAPTER 4
Homeland of the Sogdians, the Silk Road Traders
Samarkand and Sogdiana 113

CHAPTER 5

The Cosmopolitan Terminus of the Silk Road

Historic Chang'an, Modern-day Xi'an 141

CHAPTER 6

The Time Capsule of Silk Road History

The Dunhuang Caves 167

CHAPTER 7

Entryway into Xinjiang for Buddhism and Islam

Khotan 199

Conclusion

The History of the Overland Routes
through Central Asia 235

Notes 243

Art Credits 291

Index 293

Color plates follow page 144

Acknowledgments

This project has been a long time in the making, and many people have provided materials, answered questions, and helped in different ways. Since the first endnote to each chapter gives a detailed account of the assistance I have received, here I would like to single out those individuals whose help far surpassed the usual expectations of scholarly collegiality:

Phyllis Granoff and Koichi Shinohara, Yale University, for wise counsel about diverse Asian religious traditions usually dispensed over delicious family meals at their house;

Frantz Grenet, Centre Nationale de la Recherche Scientifique, for imparting his knowledge of Central Asian Art and his personal collection of images, some made by the talented François Ory;

Stanley Insler, Yale University, who first encouraged me to enter this field by agreeing to teach a joint class on the Silk Road and who was always willing to answer more questions over yet another lunch at Gourmet Heaven;

Li Jian, Virginia Museum of Fine Arts, who recruited me to work on a Silk Road exhibit at the Dayton Museum and introduced me to the Hejiacun finds;

Victor Mair, University of Pennsylvania, for unceasing help since he first taught me in a graduate seminar on the Dunhuang documents thirty years ago;

Boris Marshak, Hermitage Museum, who generously gave of his knowledge in conversations about and lectures on the Sogdians before his death in 2006;

Mou Fasong, East China Normal University, who hosted my family during the academic year 2005–6 and showed by example how his advisor Tang Zhangru approached his studies;

Georges-Jean Pinault, École Pratique des Hautes Études, for his guidance on Indo-European languages, particularly Tocharian;

Rong Xinjiang, Peking University, for his unrivaled knowledge of the region and willingness to lend his personal library of books and articles;

Angela Sheng, McMaster University, for her expertise on textiles and her loyal friendship;

Nicholas Sims-Williams, School of Oriental and African Studies, University of London, and Ursula Sims-Williams, British Library, London, who both patiently corrected multiple errors in an article I submitted to the *Bulletin of the Asia Institute* and for guidance on Central Asian languages, particularly Khotanese;

Prods Oktor Skjærvø, Harvard University, who has over the years answered frequent queries, traveled to Yale to give multiple presentations, and provided copies of his own unpublished translations;

Étienne de la Vaissière, École Pratique des Hautes Études, for his unfailing generosity in answering queries about all things Sogdian and many things Central Asian, often within an hour and always within a day (even in my last weeks of revising);

Wang Binghua, Renmin University, for sharing his deep knowledge of Xinjiang archeology, particularly about the sites of Niya and Loulan;

Helen Wang, British Museum, for her command of numismatics and for close readings of multiple chapters; and

Yoshida Yutaka, Faculty of Letters, Kyoto University, for his advice on Sogdian and Khotanese language and history.

Susan Ferber, my editor at Oxford University Press, has been consistently supportive since signing this book more than a decade ago, and her careful edits improved each chapter. She answered all queries with unusual alacrity, possibly because she works harder than anyone I have ever met. Joellyn Ausanka, senior production editor, oversaw the preparation of the book with extraordinary efficiency, while Ben Sadock copyedited with a gentle touch and great acuity.

The National Endowment for the Humanities provided a year of support that allowed me to study Russian and, with the help of Asel Umurzakova, immerse myself in the Mount Mugh materials. The Fulbright Scholar Program for Faculty financed my stay at East China Normal University in Shanghai, 2005–6. The Chiang Ching-Kuo Foundation for International Scholarly Exchange (USA) provided a generous subsidy for maps and illustrations.

All the Yale undergraduate and graduate students who have taken classes on the Silk Road over the years have pushed me to clarify my arguments. Elizabeth Duggan provided an insightful reading of an early draft of the introduction. The students in my Silk Road seminar in the spring of 2010, Mary Augusta Brazelton, Wonhee Cho, Denise Foerster, Ying Jia Tan, and Christine Wight, and, in the spring of 2011, Arnaud Bertrand, read through an almost-final draft and made many valuable suggestions for revision, including starting each chapter with a document. Mathew Andrews, my research assistant, performed multiple tasks, especially the tedious preparation of images, with speed and good cheer, even as a first-year student at Yale Law School. Joseph Szaszfai and the staff of Yale's Photo + Design unit transformed many problematic images into digital files ready for publication.

Brian Vivier, now Chinese Studies librarian at the University of Pennsylvania, carefully edited all the endnotes. Jinping Wang helped to resolve multiple last-minute queries with her characteristic erudition. Alice Thiede of Carto-Graphics drew the beautiful maps, which were particularly challenging because of all the unfamiliar place-names. Pamela Schirmeister, associate dean of the Yale Graduate School, offered an incisive critique of the introduction just days before submission.

My husband, Jim Stepanek, and our children, Bret, Claire, and Lydia, have always supported my writing and teaching with good humor. No question that the best trips have been when they, either individually or collectively, were along. The final month in China before submission was an all-out family effort to proofread, prepare charts, and polish the manuscript. What will we ever talk about now that Bret, born just before I began this project, can no longer tease me about the average number of words I wrote each day?

September 30, 2011
Beijing

Note on Scholarly Conventions

The reader will encounter multiple names from different Sanskritic, Turkic, and Iranian languages. The book gives the most commonly used spelling even if at the sacrifice of consistency. Similarly, the running text does not include diacritical marks (even when quoting sources that do), which are distracting to the general reader and already known to specialists. The notes, however, do give the diacritical marks for all authors' names, terms, and titles of books and articles.

All Chinese names are given in pinyin, the romanization system in use throughout China. The pronunciation of several letters is not obvious to English-speakers: x, q, c, and zh are the most puzzling. The Tang monk Xuanzang (pronounced Shuen-dzahng) met the king of Gaochang, whose surname was Qu (pronounced like the French "tu"). Xuanzang's monastery in Chang'an was called Ci'en (pronounced Tsih uhn), and the Zhang (pronounced Jahng) family ruled Dunhuang from 848 to 914.

Personal names of Westerners are given in the usual order of given name before surname, while Chinese and Japanese names follow the Asian practice of placing the family name before the given name. In the case of some scholars who publish in multiple languages, the order of given name and surname varies depending on the language of publication.

Occasionally the text quotes from sources giving quantities of certain goods. In most cases the original term is included along with a conversion to the modern equivalent, but the reader should bear in mind that, because all units of measure in the premodern world were not standardized, the modern equivalents are only approximate.

Silk Road Timeline

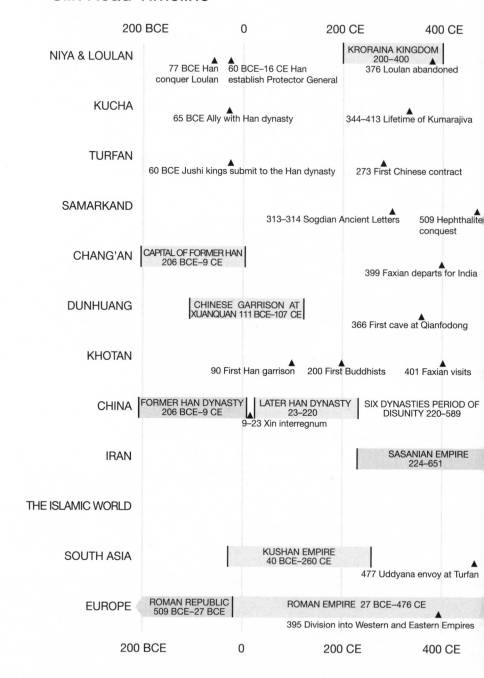

	200 BCE	0	200 CE	400 CE

NIYA & LOULAN
KRORAINA KINGDOM 200–400
77 BCE Han conquer Loulan
60 BCE–16 CE Han establish Protector General
376 Loulan abandoned

KUCHA
65 BCE Ally with Han dynasty
344–413 Lifetime of Kumarajiva

TURFAN
60 BCE Jushi kings submit to the Han dynasty
273 First Chinese contract

SAMARKAND
313–314 Sogdian Ancient Letters
509 Hephthalite conquest

CHANG'AN
CAPITAL OF FORMER HAN 206 BCE–9 CE
399 Faxian departs for India

DUNHUANG
CHINESE GARRISON AT XUANQUAN 111 BCE–107 CE
366 First cave at Qianfodong

KHOTAN
90 First Han garrison
200 First Buddhists
401 Faxian visits

CHINA
FORMER HAN DYNASTY 206 BCE–9 CE
LATER HAN DYNASTY 23–220
9–23 Xin interregnum
SIX DYNASTIES PERIOD OF DISUNITY 220–589

IRAN
SASANIAN EMPIRE 224–651

THE ISLAMIC WORLD

SOUTH ASIA
KUSHAN EMPIRE 40 BCE–260 CE
477 Uddyana envoy at Turfan

EUROPE
ROMAN REPUBLIC 509 BCE–27 BCE
ROMAN EMPIRE 27 BCE–476 CE
395 Division into Western and Eastern Empires

	200 BCE	0	200 CE	400 CE

600 CE	800 CE	1000 CE	1200 CE	

After 500 region largely deserted — **NIYA & LOULAN**

TANG RULE 648–755 **UIGHUR RULE AFTER 800** — **KUCHA**
48 Named one of Four Garrisons 755 Tang withdrawal, 790 Tibetan conquest

U FAMILY RULE 502–640 **TANG RULE** 640–755 **UIGHUR RULE AFTER 803** — **TURFAN**
755 Tang withdrawal, 792 Tibetan conquest

ISLAMIC RULE AFTER 750 — **SAMARKAND**
61–662 Afrasiab murals 709–722 Mount Mugh documents

CAPITAL OF SUI AND TANG 582–907 — **CHANG'AN**
579 Deaths of 731 Hejiacun hoard 881 Huang Chao rebels loot city
An Jia and Shi Wirkak

SUI & TANG DYNASTIES 589–786 **TIBETANS** 786–848 **ZHANG & CAO RULE 848–1002** **TANGUT RULE** 1036–1227 — **DUNHUANG**

TANG RULE 648–796 **DUNHUANG ALLY** 900–1000 **KARAKHANID RULE** 1006–1204 — **KHOTAN**
648 Named one of Four Garrisons 796 Tibetan conquest 1006 Islamic conquest

SUI DYNASTY 589–617 **TANG DYNASTY 618–907** **SONG DYNASTY** 960–1276 — **CHINA**
755–763 An Lushan rebellion

UMAYYADS 661–750 **ABBASID CALIPHATE** 750–1258 — **IRAN**
651 Islamic conquest

UMAYYADS 661–750 **ABBASID CALIPHATE** 750–1258 — **THE ISLAMIC WORLD**
570–632 Lifetime of Muhammad

SOUTH ASIA
631–643 Xuanzang studies in India

BYZANTINE EMPIRE 476–1453 — **EUROPE**
476 Fall of Rome

600 CE	800 CE	1000 CE	1200 CE

The Silk Road

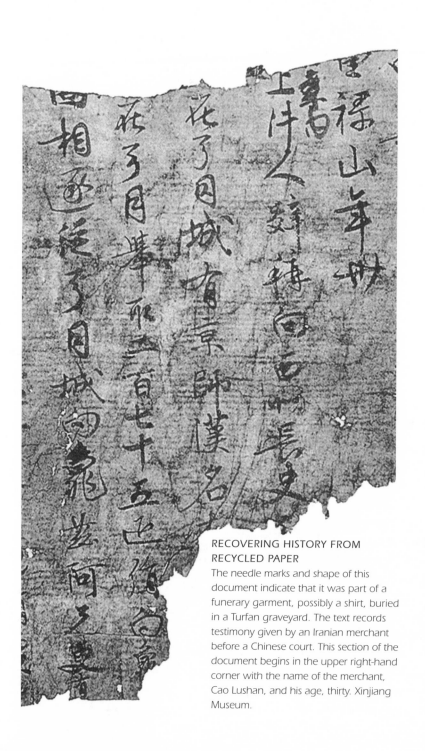

RECOVERING HISTORY FROM RECYCLED PAPER

The needle marks and shape of this document indicate that it was part of a funerary garment, possibly a shirt, buried in a Turfan graveyard. The text records testimony given by an Iranian merchant before a Chinese court. This section of the document begins in the upper right-hand corner with the name of the merchant, Cao Lushan, and his age, thirty. Xinjiang Museum.

Introduction

The document on the facing page illustrates the subject of this book. It is a court record of testimony given by an Iranian merchant living in China sometime around 670 CE. The Iranian requested the court's assistance in recovering 275 bolts of silk owed to his deceased brother. He testified that, after lending the silk to his Chinese partner, his brother disappeared in the desert on a business trip with two camels, four cattle, and a donkey, and was presumed dead. The court ruled that, as his brother's survivor, the Iranian was entitled to the silk, but it is not clear whether the ruling was ever enforced.

This incident reveals much about the Silk Road trade. The actual volume of trade was small. In this example, just seven animals carried all of the Iranian merchant's goods. Two were camels, but the other five were four cattle and a donkey, all important pack animals. The presence of Iranian merchants is notable, since China's main trading partner was not Rome but Samarkand, on the eastern edge of the Iranian world. Further, the lawsuit occurred when merchants along the Silk Road were prospering because of the massive presence of Chinese troops. This court case occurred during the seventh century, when Chinese imperial spending provided a powerful stimulus to the local economy.

Most revealing of all, we know about this lawsuit because it was written on discarded government documents, which were then sold as scrap paper, and finally used by artisans to make a paper garment for the deceased. About 1,300 years later Chinese archeologists opened a tomb near Turfan and pieced together the document from the different sections of the garment. As they connected the different pieces of paper, the testimony of the different parties was revealed.

In recent decades archeologists have reassembled thousands of other documents. What has emerged are contracts, legal disputes, receipts, cargo manifests, medical prescriptions, and the poignant contract of a slave girl sold for 120 silver coins on a particular market day over one thousand years ago. The writings are in a multitude of languages including classical Chinese, Sanskrit, and other dead languages.

Many of the documents survive because paper had a high value and was not thrown out. Craftsmen also used the recycled paper to make paper shoes, statues, and other paper mache objects to accompany the dead on their journey to the afterlife. Because recycled paper documents were used to make these funeral objects, guesswork is required to piece them together. The Iranian's affidavit, for example, was cut with scissors and then sewn to make a paper garment for the dead, leaving part of the record on the cutting room floor. Skilled historians have used the shapes of the fragments and tell-tale needle holes to reconstruct the original documents.

These documents make it possible to identify the main actors, the commodities traded, the approximate size of caravans, and the impact of trade on the localities through which goods passed. They also elucidate the broader impact of the Silk Road, particularly the religious beliefs and technologies that refugees brought with them as they sought to settle in places more peaceful than their war-torn homelands.

The communities along the Silk Road were largely agricultural rather than commercial, meaning that most people worked the land and did not engage in trade. People lived and died near where they were born. The trade that took place was mainly local and often involved exchanges of goods, rather than the use of coins. Each community, then as now, had a distinct identity. Only when wars and political unrest forced people to leave their traditional homelands did these communities along the Silk Road absorb large numbers of refugees.

These immigrants brought their religions and languages to their new homes. Buddhism, originating in India and enjoying genuine popularity in China, certainly had the most influence, but Manichaeism, Zoroastrianism, and the Christian Church of the East, based in Syria, all gained followings. The people living along the Silk Road played a crucial role in transmitting, translating, and modifying these belief systems as they passed from one civilization to another. Before the coming of Islam to the region, members of these different communities proved surprisingly tolerant of each other's beliefs. Individual rulers might choose one religion over another and strongly encourage their subjects to follow suit, yet they still permitted residents to continue their own religious practices.

Among the many contributors to Silk Road culture were the Sogdians, a people living in and around the great city of Samarkand in today's Uzbekistan. Trade between China and Sogdiana, their homeland, peaked between 500 and 800 CE. Most of the traders named in the excavated documents came from Samarkand or were descended from people who did. They spoke an Iranian language called Sogdian, and many observed the Zoroastrian teachings of the ancient Iranian teacher Zarathustra (ca. 1000 BCE, called Zoroaster in Greek), who taught that telling the truth was the paramount virtue. Because of the unusual conditions of preservation in Xinjiang, more information about the Sogdians and their beliefs survives in China than in their homeland.

Unlike most Silk Road books, which concentrate on art, this book is based on documents—documents that explain how things got to be where they are, who brought them there, and why Silk Road history is such a dazzling array of peoples, languages, and cultural cross-currents.

Not all documents discovered along the Silk Road from 200 to 1000 CE (the main focus of this book) were on recycled scrap paper. Some were written on wood, silk, leather, and other materials. They were recovered not only from tombs but also from abandoned postal stations, shrines, and homes, and beneath the dry desert—the perfect environment for the preservation of documents as well as art, clothing, ancient religious texts, ossified food, and human remains (see color plate 1).

These documents are unique because many were lost, found by accident, and written by people from a wide swath of society, not only the literate rich and powerful. These documents were not consciously composed histories: their authors did not expect later generations to read them, and they were certainly never intended to survive. They offer a glimpse into the past that is often refreshingly personal, factual, anecdotal, and random. Nothing is more valuable than information extracted from trash, because no one has edited it in any way.

Most of what we have learned from these documents debunks the prevailing view of the Silk Road, in the sense that the "road" was not an actual "road" but a stretch of shifting, unmarked paths across massive expanses of deserts and mountains. In fact, the quantity of cargo transported along these treacherous routes was small. Yet the Silk Road did actually transform cultures both east and west. Using the documentary evidence uncovered in the past two hundred years and especially the startling new finds unearthed in recent decades, this book will attempt to explain how this modest non-road became one of the most transformative super highways in human history—one that transmitted ideas, technologies, and artistic motifs, not simply trade goods.

"Silk" is even more misleading than "road," inasmuch as silk was only one among many Silk Road trade goods. Chemicals, spices, metals, saddles and leather products, glass, and paper were also common. Some cargo manifests list ammonium chloride, used as a flux for metals and to treat leather, as the top trade good on certain routes.

Another common trade item was paper, invented during the second century BCE, and surely a far greater contributor to human history than silk, which was

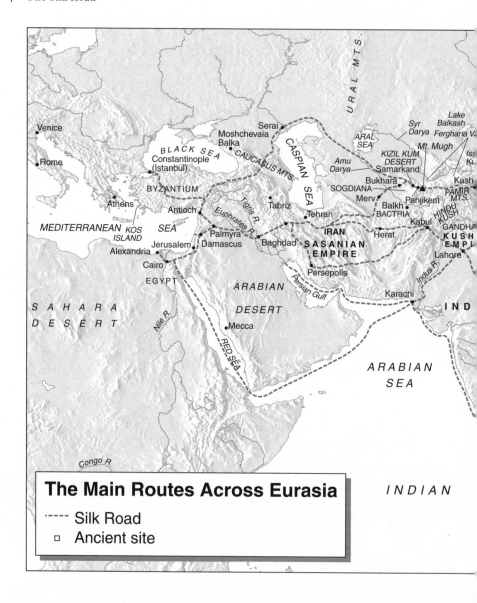

The Main Routes Across Eurasia

---- Silk Road
□ Ancient site

used primarily for garments.[1] Paper moved out of China via these overland routes first into the Islamic world in the eighth century, and then to Europe via its Islamic portals in Sicily and Spain. People north of the Alps made their own paper only in the late fourteenth century.[2]

The term "Silk Road" is a recent invention. The peoples living along different trade routes did not use it. They referred to the route as the road to Samarkand (or whatever the next major city was), or sometimes just the "northern" or "southern" routes around the Taklamakan Desert.[3] Only in 1877 did Baron Ferdinand von Richthofen coin the phrase "Silk Road." He was a

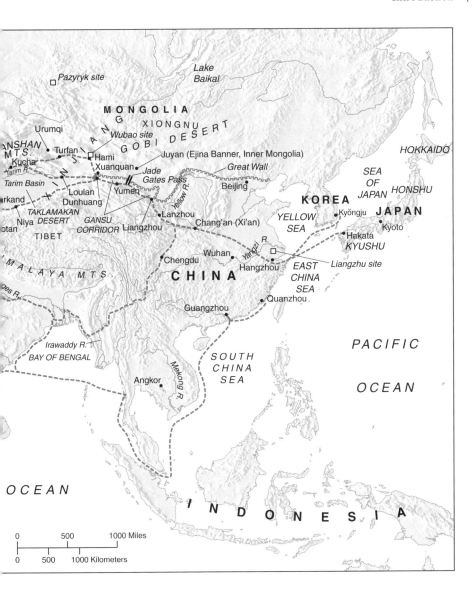

prominent geographer who worked in China from 1868 to 1872 surveying coal deposits and ports, and then wrote a five-volume atlas that used the term for the first time.

His map, reproduced in color plate 2–3, depicted the route between China and Europe in Roman times as a trunk route. Von Richthofen read Chinese sources in translation and was the first European geographer to incorporate data from the dynastic histories into a map of the region. The orange line shows information from the classical geographers Ptolemy and Marinus; the blue line, from the Chinese histories.[4] In many ways his Silk Route resembles a straight railway line cutting through Eurasia. In fact, von Richthofen was charged with designing a potential railroad line from the German sphere of influence in Shandong through the coalfields near Xi'an all the way to Germany.[5]

Gradually the term gained acceptance. Sven Hedin's 1936 book about his Central Asian explorations carried the title *The Silk Road* in its 1938 English translation. In 1948 the *Times of London* included the following question in its "Fireside Questions for the Family: A Test of General Knowledge": "From where to where do, or did," the Silk Road run? The answer: "China borders by various routes to Europe."[6] The term has shown considerable staying power as a designation for overland trade and cultural exchanges across Eurasia.

From its inception, the Silk Road was shown as relatively straight and well traveled, but it never was. Over a hundred years of archeological investigation have revealed no clearly marked, paved route across Eurasia—nothing remotely like the Appian Way of Rome—but instead a patchwork of drifting trails and unmarked footpaths. Because there was rarely a discernible route, travelers almost always hired guides to take them along a particular section, and they frequently shifted to another path if they encountered obstacles.

These meandering trails converge at oasis towns—the towns this book explores. When flying over this region today one merely has to identify the highest peaks to locate the principal sources of the streams nurturing the main Silk Road cities of ancient times. Because the documents are largely from these towns, this book is organized around seven ancient Silk Road sites—six in northwest China and one to the east of Samarkand—that form the chapters of this book.

These towns were semi-independent city states ringing the Taklamakan Desert. The rulers, whether on their own or on behalf of Chinese dynasties, strictly supervised trade and played a major role as the purchasers of goods and services. This produced a paradox: once the trade passed through totally wild regions and entered one of these oasis communities, it was suddenly highly regulated.

This was especially true when the Chinese stationed troops in Central Asia— primarily during the Han dynasty (206 BCE–220 CE) and the Tang dynasty (618–907 CE). The central government made massive expenditures to supply these armies with grain and uniforms and to pay thousands of soldiers. Bolts of silk took on another important function during the Tang dynasty, which was unable to mint enough bronze coins to cover the expenses of the central government. The authorities recognized three commodities as currency: bronze coins, grain, and bolts of silk. Since they often suffered coin shortages, and since grain rotted, most of these payments were in bolts of plain-woven silk, shown in plate 5A.

Many of the military subsidies to the northwest were paid in silk, and bolts of silk circulated widely in the Western Regions as a result. When the soldiers made many purchases at local markets, trade boomed. But when rebellion threatened the emperor and he summoned all troops back to central China, trade fell off markedly.

Even with the Chinese military presence, there was no documented traffic between China and Rome during the years of the Roman Empire. Contrary to popular belief, Romans did not exchange their gold coins directly for Chinese silk. The earliest Roman gold coins found in China are Byzantine solidus coins, including many imitations, as shown in plate 4a. They come from tombs dated to the sixth century, long after Emperor Constantine (reigned 312–37 CE) moved the empire's capital to Constantinople.

Geographically, the Silk Road goes through an astonishingly diverse landscape, much of it treacherous. Beginning in Xi'an and traveling westward, travelers first traversed the Gansu Corridor. This is a 600-mile (1,000 km) route running mainly east-west between the Qinghai Mountains on the south and the Gobi Desert of Mongolia on the north. After reaching the oasis city of Dunhuang, in Gansu Province, they had to decide whether to take the northern route or the southern route around the Taklamakan Desert, which converged in Kashgar. If both routes were impassable, those making the trip could take a central route right through one of the most inhospitable deserts on earth.

After passing through Dunhuang, travelers entered the region called Xinjiang, literally the "New Frontierlands," a term used by the Qing dynasty when it conquered this area in the eighteenth century. Before that, the Chinese called this region Xiyu, meaning "Western Regions," an area spanning parts of Uzbekistan and Tajikistan to the west and the Chinese provinces of Gansu and Shaanxi to the east.[7] Modern Xinjiang encompasses most of the Silk Road routes in western China.

Here modern tourists will see the breathtaking vistas of modern Xinjiang, and comprehend why there was not one Silk Road but multiple routes. The first daring peoples to traverse this region learned how to cross deserts in the winter when the sun was not too hot, and where to cross mountain passes in the summer when the snow was light. Above all, they learned to skirt the edge of the desert, pausing to drink, rest, and learn about the route ahead. At each oasis community they might stop for days, weeks, or much longer, in order to plan the next step.

Travel was painfully slow. In 1993 a British officer and explorer named Charles Blackmore led an expedition on foot through the Taklamakan. His men and camels managed to cover 780 miles (1,400 km) across the Taklamakan between Loulan and Merket, southwest of Kashgar, in fifty-nine days, averaging just over 13 miles (21 km) a day. Walking over the dunes in the sandy part of the desert was strenuous, and they did not always make ten miles (16 km) in a day, but walking on the flat pebbled surface, they reached as much as 15 miles (24 km) per day.[8] These rates give a good approximation of what travelers in previous centuries endured.

Once across the desert, travelers faced towering peaks separating the Taklamakan from all points west and south. It is here that the earth's largest mountain ranges crash together in a Mardi Gras of snow and ice—the Pamir Knot—where the Himalayas, Tianshan, Karakoram, Kunlun, and Hindu Kush meet. Once through, travelers descend west to Samarkand or south toward India.

Few individuals traversed all of Central Asia, covering the distance of some 2,000 miles (3,600 kilometers) between Samarkand and Chang'an. The most famous (though not the most reliable) Silk Road traveler, Marco Polo (1254–1324), claimed to have traveled all the way from Europe to China by land and to have returned home by sea. Most travelers moved on smaller circuits, traveling a few hundred miles (around 500 km) between their hometown and the next oasis and no further. Because goods were traded locally and passed through many hands, much of the Silk Road trade was a trickle trade. Long-distance caravans with hundreds of animals are rarely mentioned anywhere in the historical record—and usually only when states exchanged emissaries.

Today the region between Dunhuang and Samarkand attracts many tourists who come to see the famed ruins, including those now buried deep in the desert like the Rawak monastery outside Khotan, the walled cities of Turfan, and the caves of Dunhuang and Kucha. Local museums display artifacts found in tombs, such as silver and gold vessels and textiles combining Eastern and Western motifs in lively and exquisite designs. In a handful of places, the desert's dry climate has preserved the mundane as well as the visually striking: Chinese dumplings lie buried alongside rounds of North Indian naan flatbread baked over a thousand years ago by ancient Silk Road residents.

Before the end of the nineteenth century, no one realized that the sands of Xinjiang preserved so many documents and artifacts from the distant past. In 1890, the British officer Lieutenant Hamilton Bower traveled to Kucha, an oasis on the northern route around the Taklamakan, to investigate a murder. While there, he bought an ancient manuscript consisting of fifty-one leaves of birch bark with writing on them and announced the discovery to the Royal Asiatic Society of Bengal. Within a few years scholars identified it as a medical text from the fifth century CE, making it the oldest known Sanskrit manuscript in the world by almost one thousand years.[9] Alerted to the importance of such

DESICCATED DUMPLINGS FROM TURFAN
The dry conditions at Turfan preserved many perishable items, including food. Here we see four wontons and a single dumpling, dating to the 600 or 700s. By examining the dumplings that have cracked open, archeologists have identified Chinese chives and some type of meat, most likely pork, since Xinjiang was not yet Islamified at this time. Xinjiang Museum.

discoveries, European diplomats in Asia began to purchase various manuscripts and sent them to Europe, where scholars trained in philology could decipher them.

In 1895 the Swedish explorer Sven Hedin launched the first scientific mission to Xinjiang, the source of many of these ancient manuscripts. Departing that April from the town of Merket on the Yarkand River, Hedin entered the Taklamakan Desert in search of the source of the Khotan River. After fifteen days, he discovered that he was not carrying enough water for himself and the four men with him. Still, he did not turn back because he did not want to admit that his expedition had failed. When their supply ran out, he began a desperate search for water. As his men and camels collapsed one by one, the exhausted Hedin forced himself to crawl along a dry riverbed. On the sixth day without water, he located a stream, drank his fill, and carried back enough water in his boots to save the life of one man.

As he made his way out of the desert, Hedin encountered a caravan of four merchants and various pack animals, from which he purchased three horses, "three pack-saddles, one riding-saddle, bits, a bag of maize, a bag of wheat-flour, tea, jugs, bowls, and a pair of boots."[10] This is a revealing list. Even at the beginning of the twentieth century, just as in earlier times, almost all the goods traded in the Taklamakan were locally made necessities, not foreign imports. After leaving the desert, Hedin learned that shepherds had aided another of his men, but two others had perished.

A chastened Hedin returned to the Taklamakan in December of the same year. This time he brought along enough water for his men. Entering the desert from Khotan, one of the main oases on the southern edge of the Taklamakan, they discovered the ruins of the Dandan Uiliq site. Among the wooden posts and the remnants of walls in the sand lay several Buddhist statues. Hedin did not excavate; as he later explained, "I was not equipped to make a thorough excavation; and, besides, I was not an archeologist."[11] European newspapers carried extensive coverage of Hedin's Taklamakan explorations, which were as exotic and dangerous as space explorations are today.

One of these news reports was sent in late 1897 by a manager of a Polish coal mine to his brother, Aurel Stein, who was working as an education official in the British colonial city of Lahore in India (now Pakistan).[12] A native of Hungary, Stein had completed his doctorate in Sanskrit at Tübingen in 1883 and continued to study the language with the learned Indian scholar Pandit Govind Kaul in Lahore. Sanskrit was an enormously popular field throughout the nineteenth century; many people wanted to study the Indo-European language that was more ancient than, and closely related to, Latin and Greek. During his studies in Germany, Stein had learned the importance of obtaining the earliest and most complete manuscripts.

Immediately recognizing the implications of Hedin's discovery for the study of ancient manuscripts, Stein applied to the British archeological authorities for funding to go to Khotan. Systematic investigation of the site, he argued, would provide far more information than the pillaging that had so far occurred. He also hinted at the international competition to acquire antiquities already under way. Hedin, he reported, was bound to return to the region, and the Russians were contemplating launching an expedition too. The Government of India funded his application.

The first to locate and map many of the sites discussed here, Aurel Stein found a number of stunningly important objects and documents. Leader of four different expeditions to Xinjiang between 1900 and 1931, Stein wrote extensive formal reports as well as more casual narratives. His excavations were imperfect by today's standards; he hired workmen to dig for him and rewarded them extra pay for any finds, a widespread practice that sometimes resulted in overly rushed excavation. But few of the excavators who found documents in Xinjiang—Paul Pelliot of France, Albert von Le Coq of Germany, Otani Kozui of Japan—matched the level of detail found in Stein's archeological reports. None went to as many places as Stein or published nearly as much material.

Stein's descriptions are essential to reconstructing the original condition of each site. His explanation of the circumstances leading to the burial of the documents is also important; every subsequent scholar has relied on Stein as a point of departure even when they have updated his explanations. Stein's and other accounts from the late nineteenth and early twentieth centuries are informative because their authors, with few exceptions, traveled along the same routes, using the same means of transportation as did travelers in earlier times. Their accounts fill in many details left unmentioned by past travelers, making it possible to relive the experience of travel along the ancient trade routes.

These explorers, and many who followed, revealed what was hidden beneath the sand. First, they discovered archeological evidence showing that long-distance overland trade began long ago. Different peoples living in Xinjiang sent goods to central China as early as 1200 BCE. At the time, the kings of the Shang dynasty (1766–1045 BCE) ruled the lower Yellow River valley and wrote using the earliest extant Chinese characters. The lavish tomb of one king's consort, a woman named Fu Hao, contained over one thousand jade implements, some carved out of the distinctive milky green jade of Khotan. Large quantities of seashells found in Central Asia, particularly at the Wubao site near Hami in Gansu Province from the same period, testify to trade with coastal regions either to the east in China, to the south in India, or to the west along the Mediterranean.[13]

Secondly, they revealed that diverse ethnic groups once inhabited the area. For example, at sites in Xinjiang and Gansu dating from 1800 BCE to the early centuries BCE, the dry desert climate has preserved about five hundred desiccated corpses.[14] Many of the males measure over six feet (1.8 m) tall, much taller than their Chinese contemporaries, and the deceased often have non-Chinese—sometimes called Caucasoid—features like fair hair and pale skin. Their appearance has led scholars to propose that many of the people traveling along and settling in the different oases around the Taklamakan Desert were descended from the speakers of Indo-European languages. These peoples, linguists believe, migrated to ancient India and Iran, probably from their original homeland, possibly the Pontic steppe north of the Black Sea, sometime between 2000 and 1000 BCE.[15] Some of the corpses wear woolen textiles with plaid patterns resembling those in second-millennium BCE Ireland, further evidence for Indo-European roots.[16] Some scholars have proposed that they spoke Tocharian, an Indo-European language discussed in chapter 2. Yet because none of these tombs have produced any written evidence, we cannot know what language(s) these peoples spoke.[17]

There are also discoveries of trade with people to the north, at the site of Pazyryk in Siberia, which dates to the fifth century BCE. The residents of this site buried Chinese bronze mirrors and silk in their tombs.[18] One silk fragment bears an embroidered phoenix, most likely a Chinese motif (or a motif copied from something originally Chinese), since this had positive associations in Chinese culture. A similar textile, also from the fifth century BCE and found at Turfan, shows a beautifully embroidered phoenix on a faded yellow silk background.[19] These finds indicate that overland trade was certainly taking place in the centuries before the Common Era, but no documents reveal who was carrying these goods or why.

The first written description of the Silk Road trade concerns Zhang Qian (d. 113 BCE), a Chinese envoy from Chang'an to Central Asia in the second century BCE, during the reign of Emperor Wu of the Han Dynasty (reigned 140–87 BCE). The emperor hoped that Zhang Qian would persuade the Yuezhi people, living in the Ferghana region of modern-day Uzbekistan, to ally with the Chinese against their common enemy to the north, the Xiongnu tribal confederation, based in modern-day Mongolia. The earliest surviving account about Zhang Qian was written at least 150 years after his trip and does not provide many basic facts about his journey, such as his exact itinerary.

It is clear, though, that Zhang went through Xiongnu territory on his way to the Yuezhi. The Xiongnu imprisoned Zhang, and it took him about ten years to escape. Nonetheless, he still proceeded to visit the Yuezhi. On his return, sometime around 126 BCE, he gave the emperor the first detailed information the Chinese received about the different peoples of Central Asia.[20] Zhang Qian was extremely surprised to discover that Chinese merchants and trade goods had preceded him to Central Asia. In the markets of Bactria, in modern-day northern Afghanistan, Zhang Qian saw bamboo and cloth manufactured in the Chinese province of Sichuan, several thousand miles away. The Chinese goods must have traveled overland.

After Zhang Qian's return, the Han dynasty gradually extended its control into the northwest. By the end of the second century BCE it secured the Gansu corridor and Dunhuang. Each time the Chinese army conquered a new region, it constructed beacon towers at fixed intervals. If a disturbance occurred, the soldiers guarding the beacon tower lit torches to alert the men in the next tower, and so on down the line until the news reached the first garrison that could dispatch troops to the troubled area. In addition to the beacon towers, the Han military also established garrisons in the newly conquered territories. Documents in the form of bamboo slips recording army purchases of clothing and grain from the local people have been found at Juyan (Ejina Banner, Inner Mongolia, 90 km northeast of Jinta County, Gansu) and Shule (near Dunhuang and Jiuquan, Gansu).[21]

The largest cache of early documents from the Silk Road was excavated from just such a Chinese garrison at Xuanquan, located 40 miles (64 kilometers) east of Dunhuang.[22] A square dirt wall, 55 yards (50 meters) on each side, surrounded the complex, which had a stable for horses on its southern edge. Officials traveling on government business were entitled to get fresh mounts at the garrison, which also functioned as a postal station. On the northern and western edges of the enclosure were waste disposal areas; the western garbage pit extended 1.3 yards (1.2 m) underground at its greatest depth. The 2,650 artifacts from the site included coins, farm tools, weapons, iron cart parts, and utensils such as combs and chopsticks, as well as foodstuffs like grain, garlic, walnuts, almonds, and animal bones.[23]

There are more than 35,000 discarded documents from the Xuanquan site: 23,000 wooden slips with Chinese characters on them, and 12,000 bamboo slips trimmed to size, apparently intended for later use. About two thousand of the slips bear dates between 111 BCE and 107 CE, the years when the garrison was in use.

The slips are written on wood and bamboo because paper was just spreading to Central Asia at this time. Invented in China during the second century BCE, paper was first used as a wrapping material and not for writing. The official histories record, for example, that in 12 BCE a murderer used poison wrapped in paper.[24] Some of the earliest paper scraps found at Xuanquan, dating to the first century BCE, also bear the names of medicines, confirming the early use of paper as a wrapping material.

Not until four centuries later, in the second century CE, did paper come into widespread use as writing material in China. It took even longer for paper to replace wood and bamboo as the most common writing material along the Silk Road. Because paper was always expensive, people wrote on other materials like leather and tree bark. The documents at Xuanquan consist mostly of wooden slips tied together to form bunches (much like a placemat made from Popsicle sticks).

The documents from the Xuanquan site include much everyday correspondence among the officials stationed at the Xuanquan postal station and other nearby locations, notices of new edicts issued by the emperor, announcements of runaway prisoners, and private letters. The scribes at Xuanquan distinguished among different types of wood: they reserved higher-quality pine for imperial edicts and used poplar and tamarisk, which warped easily, for routine documents and correspondence.

Since Xuanquan was the final stop before Dunhuang on the way out of China, almost all envoys passed through it once on their journey into Han-dynasty China and again when leaving. Chinese geographic sources from the Han dynasty list more than fifty kingdoms in Central Asia. Although the Chinese documents usually refer to these rulers as kings, each domain often

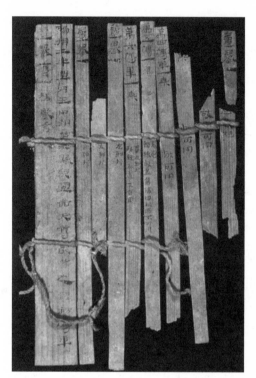

DOCUMENTS BEFORE PAPER
Even after paper spread from China to the Silk Road in the second century BCE, some documents continued to be written on wooden slips. The earliest paper was used to wrap medicine, and it was not until the third century CE that the transition to using paper for writing was complete. These slips record the carts requisitioned by a garrison. Bound together by string, they were rolled up when stored. Characters were read in columns from top to bottom and from right to left, so one began reading at the upper right-hand corner, and read vertically down the first slip, returning to the top of the second slip, and continuing in the same way until finishing at the bottom left corner.

consisted of a single oasis with a population as small as several hundred people and no larger than several thousand. These oases resembled small city-states more than kingdoms.[25]

Big or small, these different states dispatched envoys to visit the Chinese capital to present gifts to the emperor, whom they acknowledged as their superior, and to receive gifts in return. Among the most treasured gifts were the horses that grazed in the Central Asian grasslands; because they roamed free, they were always stronger than the smaller, less powerful Chinese breeds that ate fodder hand-carried to their stables. The Chinese prized the heavenly horses of the Ferghana valley, in Uzbekistan, most of all. Even in this early period, during the Han dynasty, it is impossible to distinguish between official trade, in which an envoy brought a gift (often animals such as horses or camels) and received something for his ruler in return, and private trade, in which the same envoy might present an identical animal to the Chinese and keep the return gift for himself.

The gift-bearing delegations from Central Asian kingdoms varied in size. On some occasions delegations were a thousand strong: the king of Khotan, for example, headed a single group of 1714 people.[26] More typical was a delegation from Sogdiana, in 52 BCE, that included two envoys, ten aristocrats, and an unspecified number of other followers, who led nine horses, thirty-one donkeys, twenty-five camels, and a cow.[27]

These delegations traveled on fixed itineraries and carried travel passes listing the towns, in order, they were allowed to visit. According to the law of the Han dynasty, which drew on even earlier precedents, anyone going through a checkpoint, on land or by water, needed a travel pass, called a *guosuo* (literally "passing through a place").[28]

Several of the Xuanquan documents list all the stops between Dunhuang, the first town within the empire, and the Han-dynasty capital, either Chang'an in the first century BCE or Luoyang in the first century CE. Delegations were not permitted to stray from these routes. At each stop, officials counted the people in each delegation and the animals traveling with them to ensure that the party exactly matched the one enumerated on the travel pass. Officials could emend these passes and could also issue new passes. They checked the delegations when they went through Xuanquan on their way to China and again when they left Xuanquan, usually about six months later, on their way back to Central Asia. The cooks at Xuanquan kept detailed records of their expenditures on food for each guest, whether Chinese or foreign, whom they identified by rank and direction of travel (east or west).[29]

The wooden slips from Xuanquan are remarkably detailed. One of the longest records describes a dispute occurring in 39 BCE, when four Sogdian envoys petitioned Chinese officials to protest the low prices they had received for camels. The Sogdians maintained that Chinese officials had paid them the rate for thin, yellow camels, but they had actually delivered more valuable fat, white camels. The Sogdian envoys not only had a clear sense of market values but also sufficient confidence in the predictability of the system to protest when the prices diverged from their expectations. The Sogdians also expected, as envoys carrying the appropriate credentials, to be housed and fed at each stop along the way, but ended up paying for their meals instead. The officials at Dunhuang who heard the dispute in 39 BCE concluded that the Sogdians had been appropriately compensated. One possible explanation for the harsh treatment of the envoys: the Han-dynasty officials bitterly resented the Sogdians for cooperating with their longtime enemy, the Xiongnu, so they retaliated by underpaying them.[30]

The Xuanquan documents define an entire world, a world that included oases on the far western edge of China, near the modern city of Kashgar, as well as those beyond modern China's border in Uzbekistan, Pakistan, and Afghanistan. The rulers of these different Central Asian oases participated in the systematized exchange of diplomatic envoys with the Chinese emperor of the Han dynasty, and envoys from these different points regularly traveled the Silk Road on their way to the Chinese capital.

Of the many foreign embassies that visited the Han-dynasty emperors to present tribute, only one was conceivably from Rome. An envoy from the ruler of Da Qin (literally the "Great Qin"), the official history reports, arrived by sea in 166 CE. Da Qin sat on the western edge of the world known to the Chinese and displayed many characteristics of a utopia; only in some instances does the term refer specifically to Rome. The Da Qin emissary presented ivory and rhinoceros horn, typical products of Southeast Asia. Many suspect that this envoy was an imposter who claimed to be from a distant, barely known place in order to receive permission to trade. This single mention is intriguing but hardly conclusive.[31]

As the Xuanquan documents and other materials reveal, the Han dynasty initiated regular trade along the routes around the Taklamakan for purely strategic reasons—they sought alternative routes to Central Asia so that they could bypass the Xiongnu, their constant enemy. Official envoys might occasionally engage in private trade, but always as a sideline to their official business. Their movements were never spontaneous but took place along carefully planned and recorded itineraries. For all their detail about Chinese trade with the Central Asian oases, the Xuanquan documents make no mention of any place west of the Kushan Empire (in northern Afghanistan and Pakistan) and certainly not of Rome itself.

Unfortunately, no documents with a level of detail comparable to the Xuanquan documents have been excavated on the European side, so analysis of Europe's trade must rely on known Greek and Latin texts. One of the most informative sources is the *Periplus of the Erythraean Sea*, a book written sometime in the first century CE by an anonymous merchant living in Egypt who wrote in Greek.[32] After describing the various ports of east Africa, Arabia, and India, the *Periplus* concludes with an account of the lands lying beyond the known world:

> Beyond this region [an island in the sea to the east of the port at the mouth of the Ganges], by now at the northernmost point, where the sea ends somewhere on the outer fringe, there is a very great inland city called Thina from which silk floss, yarn, and cloth are shipped by land . . . and via the Ganges River. . . . It is not easy to get to this Thina; for rarely do people come from it, and only a few.[33]

Thina? The spelling makes sense, given that ancient Greek had no letter for the sound "ch" and the letter theta was probably pronounced something like *ts* in ancient Greek. The author did his best to record the unfamiliar name he heard from Indian traders. In Sanskrit, China was pronounced Chee-na (named for the Qin dynasty, 221–207 BCE); the Sanskrit word is the source of the English word "China." In subsequent centuries, Roman geographers like Ptolemy (ca. 100–170 CE) learned more about Central Asia, but scholars are still struggling to reconcile their descriptions with the actual geography of the region.[34] The author of the *Periplus* is certain of only one kernel of information about the Chinese: they produced silk in the form of floss from cocoons, spun thread from that floss, and wove cloth from the thread.

The Chinese were indeed the first people in the world to make silk, possibly as early as 4000 BCE, if an ivory carving with a silkworm motif on it, from the Hemudu site in Zhejiang, constitutes proof of silk manufacture. According to the Hangzhou Silk Museum, the earliest excavated fragment of silk dates to 3650 BCE and is from Henan Province in central China.[35] Skeptical of such an early date, experts outside of China believe the earliest examples of silk date to 2850–2650 BCE, the time of the Liangzhu culture (3310–2250 BCE) in the lower Yangzi valley.[36]

In the first century CE, when the *Periplus* was written, the Romans did not know how silk was made. Pliny the Elder (CE 23–79) reported that silk cloth had made its way to Rome by the first century. Pliny misunderstood silk production: he thought silk was made from a "white down that adheres to . . . leaves," which the people of Seres combed off and made into thread. (His description more accurately describes cotton.) Yet in another passage he wrote about silkworms.[37] Modern interpreters often translate Seres as China, but, to the Romans, it was actually an unknown land on the northern edge of the world.

China was not the only manufacturer of silk in Pliny's day. As early as 2500 BCE, the ancient Indians wove silk from the wild silk moth, a different species of silkworm than the one the Chinese had domesticated. In contrast, the Indians collected broken cocoons that remained after the silk worms had matured into moths, broken through their cocoons, and flown away.[38] Similarly, in antiquity, the Greek island of Cos in the eastern Aegean produced Coan silk, which was also spun from the broken cocoons of wild silk moths. Early on, the Chinese had learned to boil the cocoons, which killed the silk worms, leaving the cocoons intact and allowing the thread to be removed in long, continuous strands. Even so, Chinese silk cannot always be distinguished from wild silk, and it is possible that Pliny may have described Indian or Coan, not Chinese, silk.[39]

Because Chinese and Coan silk resemble each other so closely, analysts must identify motifs unique to China in order to determine the origins of a piece of silk. Yet since any motif can be copied, the most reliable indicator of Chinese manufacture is the presence of Chinese characters, which only the Chinese wove into their cloth. Textiles found in Palmyra, Syria, from the first to third centuries CE were among the earliest Chinese silks to reach west Asia from China.[40] The Chinese emperor routinely sent envoys to the Western Regions to bestow textiles on local rulers, and they in turn probably sent them further west.

Still, most of the beautiful silks found in Europe that are labeled "Chinese" were actually woven in the Byzantine Empire (476–1453 CE). One scholar who examined a thousand examples dating between the seventh and thirteenth century found only one made in China.[41]

Silk in particular drew Pliny's ire because he simply could not understand why the Romans imported fabric that left so much of the female body exposed: "So manifold is the labor employed, and so distant is the region of the globe drawn upon, to enable the Roman matron to flaunt transparent raiment in public."[42] He railed against other imported goods as well—frankincense, amber, and tortoiseshell, among others—because consuming them, in his opinion, weakened Rome.[43]

Had the trade between China and Rome been as significant as Pliny contended, some Roman coins would presumably have been found in China. Yet the earliest European coins unearthed in China are from Byzantium, not Rome, and date to the 530s and 540s.[44] Vague rumors to the contrary, not a single Roman coin has turned up in China—in contrast to the thousands of Roman gold and silver coins excavated on the south Indian coast, where Roman traders often journeyed.[45] Historians sometimes argue that coins made from precious metals could have circulated between two places in a given period but might not survive today because they were melted down. But the survival of so many later non-Chinese coins in China undercuts this argument. Many Iranian coins made of silver and minted by the Sasanian Empire (224–651) have appeared in quantities as large as several hundred (see the example in plate 4B).

In sum, the absence of archeological or textual evidence suggests surprisingly little contact between ancient Rome and the Han dynasty. Although Pliny the Elder offered a confident critique of the silk trade, no one in the first century CE collected any reliable statistics about Rome's balance of trade.[46] If Romans had bought Chinese silk with Roman coins, some remnants of Chinese silk might have surfaced in Rome. Starting in the second and third centuries, a few goods managed to make their way between Rome and China. This is the period of the Palmyra silks and also when Romans began to pin down the location of Seres.

The art-historical record in China also confirms intermittent contacts between Rome and China that accelerate in the second and third centuries CE. In the Han dynasty, only a few rare examples of Chinese art display foreign motifs. But by the Tang dynasty much more Chinese art incorporated Persian, Indian, and even Greco-Roman motifs.[47] The Tang dynasty marked the high point of Chinese influence in Central Asia and also the height of the Silk Road trade.

This book starts with the first perceptible contacts between China and the West in the second and third centuries CE and concludes in the early eleventh century, the time of the latest excavated documents from Dunhuang and Khotan. Proceeding in chronological order, each chapter examines a different Silk Road site, chosen for its documentary finds. Niya, Kucha, Turfan, Dunhuang, and Khotan are in northwest China. Samarkand lies in Uzbekistan, while the nearby site of Mount Mugh is located just across the border in modern Tajikistan. The seventh, Chang'an, the capital of the Tang dynasty, is in Shaanxi Province in central China.

Chapter 1 begins with the sites of Niya and Loulan, because they have produced extensive documentary evidence of the first sustained cultural contacts among the local peoples, the Chinese, and a group of migrants from the Gandhara region of modern-day Afghanistan and Pakistan. These migrants introduced their own script and imported a technology for keeping written records on wood; they were also among the first Buddhists to enter the Western Regions. Even though Buddhist regulations, or *vinaya*, prescribed celibacy for monks and nuns, many of these Buddhists at Niya married, had children, and lived with their families, not in celibate monastic communities, as is so often thought.

Kucha, the subject of chapter 2, was home to one of China's most famous Buddhist translators, Kumarajiva (344–413), who produced the first understandable versions of Buddhist texts in Chinese. Kumarajiva grew up speaking the local Kuchean language, studied Sanskrit as a young boy, and learned Chinese after being held captive in China for seventeen years. The Kuchean documents have excited a century of passionate debate among linguists trying to solve the puzzle of why a people living in the Western Regions spoke an Indo-European language so different from the other languages of the region.

The Sogdians were the most important foreign community in China at the peak of the Silk Road exchanges. Many Sogdians settled permanently in Turfan on the northern route, the site discussed in chapter 3, where they pursued different occupations, including farming, running hostels, veterinary medicine, and trading.[48] In 640, when Tang-dynasty armies conquered Turfan, all the residents came under direct Chinese rule. Turfan's extremely dry conditions have preserved an unusual wealth of documents about daily life in a Silk Road community.

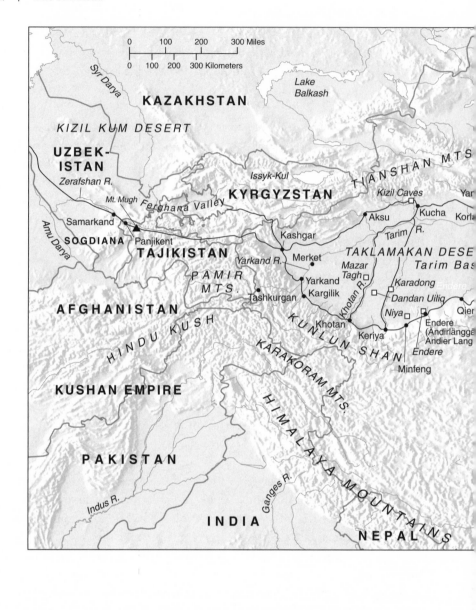

Chapter 4 focuses on the Sogdian homeland around Samarkand in modern-day Uzbekistan and Tajikistan. While China has gained a reputation as a country that does not welcome outsiders, large communities of foreigners moved to China in the first millennium, particularly after Samarkand fell to Muslim forces in 712.

Some of the most exciting archeological finds in recent years have been the tombs of foreigners resident in the Tang-dynasty capital at Chang'an, or modern Xi'an, discussed in chapter 5. The Sogdian migrants from the Iranian world

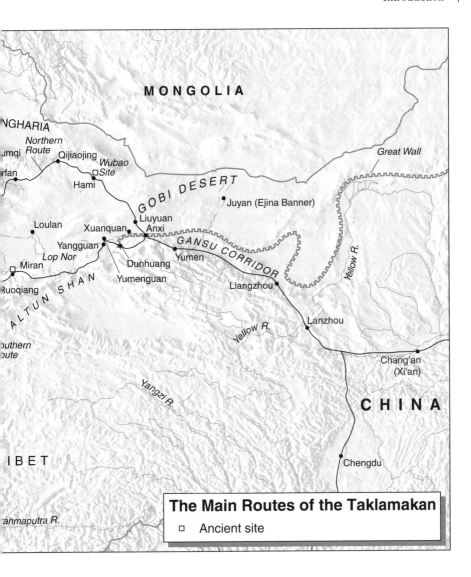

MONGOLIA

DZUNGHARIA

Northern Route

Urumqi

Qijiaojing

Wubao □Site

Turfan

Hami

GOBI DESERT

Juyan (Ejina Banner)

Great Wall

Liuyuan
Anxi

Loulan

Xuanquan

Yangguan

Lop Nor

Miran

GANSU CORRIDOR

Yumen

Dunhuang

Yumenguan

Liangzhou

Ruoqiang

ALTUN SHAN

Yellow R.

Lanzhou

Yellow R.

Chang'an
(Xi'an)

Yangzi R.

CHINA

TIBET

Chengdu

Brahmaputra R.

The Main Routes of the Taklamakan

□ Ancient site

brought their Zoroastrian beliefs with them; they worshipped at fire altars and sacrificed animals to the gods. After they died, their kin prepared them for the next world by leaving the corpses exposed to predators who cleaned the bones of flesh—thought to pollute the earth—before burial. Although most Sogdians subscribed to Zoroastrian teachings, several Sogdians living in Chang'an at the end of the sixth and in the early seventh century opted for Chinese-style burials instead. These tombs portray the Zoroastrian afterlife in far more detail than any art surviving in the Iranian world.

Some 40,000 documents from the library cave at Dunhuang, covered in chapter 6, form one of the world's most astounding collections of treasures, which includes the world's earliest printed book, The Diamond Sutra. A monastic repository, the library cave contained much more than Buddhist materials, because so many other types of texts were copied on the backs of Buddhist texts. The cave paintings at Dunhuang are certainly the best preserved and most extensive of any Buddhist site in China; they testify to the devotion of the local people as well as the rulers who commissioned such beautiful works of art. Even as they created these masterpieces, Dunhuang residents did not use coins but instead paid for everything using grain or cloth, as was true of all the Western Regions after the withdrawal of Chinese troops in the mid-eighth century.

The rulers of Dunhuang maintained close ties to the oasis of Khotan, the focus of chapter 7, which lies on the southern Silk Road just west of Niya. Almost all surviving documents are written in Khotanese, an Iranian language with a huge vocabulary of words borrowed from Sanskrit; they were found at the library cave in Dunhuang and in towns surrounding Khotan. Oddly, none of these early documents have surfaced in the oasis of Khotan itself. These documents include language-learning aids showing how Khotanese students learned Sanskrit, the language used in most monasteries, and Chinese, a language spoken widely in the Western Regions. Conquered in 1006, Khotan was the first city in today's Xinjiang to convert to Islam, and, as visitors today observe, Xinjiang is still heavily Muslim. The chapter concludes by surveying the history and trade of the region since the coming of Islam.

In sum, this book's goal is to sketch the main events in the history of each oasis community, describe the different groups who resided there and their cultural interactions, outline the nature of the trade, and ultimately tell the flesh-and-blood story of the Silk Road, a story most commonly written on recycled paper.

CHAPTER 1

At the Crossroads of Central Asia

The Kingdom of Kroraina

In late January 1901, even before Aurel Stein arrived at the site of Niya, his camel driver gave him two pieces of wood with writing on them. Stein, to his "joyful surprise," recognized the Kharoshthi script, which was used to write Sanskrit and related vernacular Indian languages in the third and fourth centuries CE.[1] One of these two documents appears on this page—part of a historic cache proving that the Silk Road played a paramount role in transmitting languages, culture, and religion, which is why this book begins with a chapter about the ancient lost city of Niya.

DOCUMENTARY EVIDENCE OF CULTURAL EXCHANGE ON THE SILK ROAD
This wooden document represented an entirely new writing technology that migrants from northern Afghanistan and Pakistan introduced around 200 CE to the residents of northwest China, who had no writing system of their own. Using two pieces of wood, they crafted a base (shown here) with a top that slid over it like a drawer and protected the contents. These wooden documents written in the Kharoshthi script of their homeland, which include contracts, royal orders, letters, and rulings in legal disputes, make it possible to reconstruct this early encounter of people from radically different backgrounds. The upside-down label gives the date and name of the site, Niya, where the wooden slip was found. Courtesy of the Board of the British Library.

The wooden documents from the site and others nearby confirmed the existence of a small oasis kingdom stretching 500 miles (800 km) along the southern Silk Road route—all the way from the site of Niya to the salt lake of Lop Nor in the east. The Kroraina Kingdom flourished from around 200 CE to 400 CE. The native inhabitants spoke a language that was never written down and is totally lost (except for their names as recorded by outsiders).

The only reason we know anything about these people is due to the arrival of immigrants from across the mountains to the west—immigrants who did have a writing system, Kharoshthi. They used this script to record land deeds, disputes, official business, and thousands of other important events. The Kharoshthi script is the key unlocking the history of the Kroraina civilization and in particular the lost cities of Niya, where most documents were found, and a site even deeper in the desert, Loulan, that was the capital of Kroraina for part of the kingdom's history. Supplementing these documents are valuable Chinese texts dating from the Han dynasty that shed light on the kingdom's relations with early Chinese dynasties.

The immigrants came from the Gandhara region of modern-day Afghanistan and Pakistan. The script they had learned to write on wooden documents is the first proof of sustained cultural exchanges on the Silk Road in the late second century. These immigrants gave the kingdom its name, Kroraina; the Chinese name for it was Shanshan. Around 200 CE, the immigrants seem to have arrived in small waves of one hundred people or less. Apparently, they assimilated and never attempted to conquer the local people or overthrow the Kroraina Kingdom. The refugees intermarried with the local people, introduced their script to them, gained employment as scribes, and taught local officials to make wooden documents. The migrants brought Buddhist teachings from India, too, but they interpreted them far more flexibly than the wording of Buddhist regulations suggest; these early Buddhists married and lived at home with their own families.

The kingdom encompassed a desolate region of China that today is a former nuclear testing zone, off limits to almost everyone but professional archeologists. Yet this remote area was inhabited as early as 4000 BCE, and was home to several oasis states during the Han dynasty (206 BCE–220 CE). Sometimes maintaining garrisons in the region, the Han exercised only intermittent control.

Stein's discoveries in Niya confirmed his view that Chinese Turkestan (the term he and his contemporaries used for modern Xinjiang) "served as the channel for that interchange of the early civilizations of India, China and the Hellenized west of Asia."[2] When Stein had first applied to the British Government of India for financial support in 1897, he promised tangible evidence of cultural exchange in ancient times. The wooden tablets buried in the sands of Niya were exactly what he had hoped for.

Although roughly the size of the United Kingdom, Kroraina was largely a wasteland when Stein visited. Agriculture existed only along the beds of the rivers flowing north from melting glaciers of the Kunlun Mountains. Everything we know about Kroraina comes from the two most important sites that have yielded documents—Niya and Loulan—and two sites preserving artworks and textiles—Miran and Yingpan. All are deep in the desert, and inaccessible except by camel or a four-wheel-drive jeep. Because the desert has expanded, today these sites lie fifty to one hundred miles (80–160 km) north of the modern highway that runs along the current southern edge of the Taklamakan.

The ancient kingdom of Kroraina is certainly among the least accessible places on earth, but within months of each other Sven Hedin and Aurel Stein both reached the kingdom. In March 1900 Hedin marched along the course of the Kongque (Peacock) River, with its clear, peacock-blue water.[3] He traveled west from Lop Nor and surveyed Loulan for a single day before continuing his journey.

Months later, Stein came from Khotan to make his first visit to Niya in January 1901; in 1906 he returned to the site and also traveled to Loulan. In these initial forays, Hedin and Stein unearthed the lion's share of the region's artifacts and documents, although subsequent investigations, notably a Sino-Japanese joint expedition in the 1990s, also made significant discoveries.[4]

Stein raised a most intriguing question: How did hundreds, maybe thousands, of people living in the Gandhara region (including the modern cities of Bamiyan, Gilgit, Peshawar, Taxila, and Kabul in modern Pakistan and Afghanistan) travel nearly one thousand miles (1,600 km) over the highest mountain passes on earth?

Stein followed the same route from India to the Taklamakan Desert region that the immigrants had taken nearly two thousand years earlier. He began his trek in the Indian town of Kashmir. From there he crossed a region with over thirty mountains more than 25,000 (7,600 m) tall, the Pamir Knot, which includes the treacherous Nanga Parbat, one of the fastest growing mountains on earth, rising 0.28 inches (7 mm) per year.[5]

These mountains were formed some fifty million years ago when the continent of India collided with the Eurasian landmass, creating a spiral galaxy of massive peaks radiating clockwise into the Karakorum, Hindu Kush, Pamir, Kunlun, and Himalayan mountain ranges.

Stein used a new route through the town of Gilgit that the British had opened only ten years earlier. He timed his crossing of the Tragbal Pass (11,950 feet, or 3,642 m) and Burzil Pass (13,650 feet, or 4,161 m) to occur in the summer after the snow had melted. Once through the two passes, Stein followed the course of the Indus River past Chilas, where he saw the Nanga Parbat peak towering above. The Indus River led to the Gilgit River, and the Gilgit River, in turn, led to the Hunza River valley.

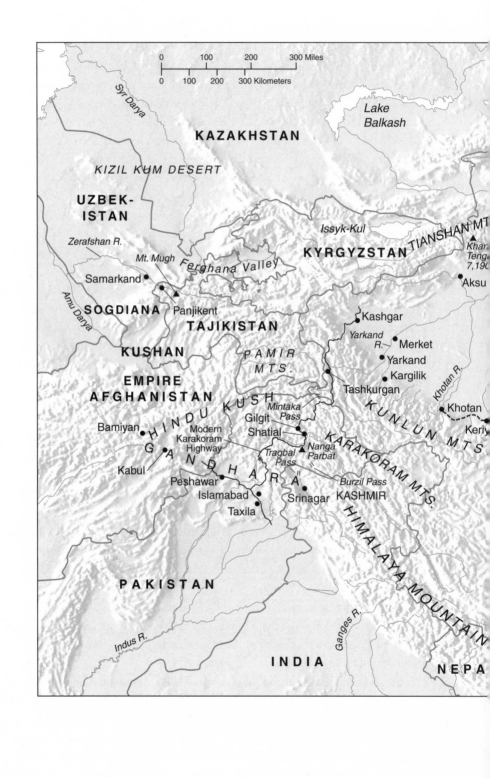

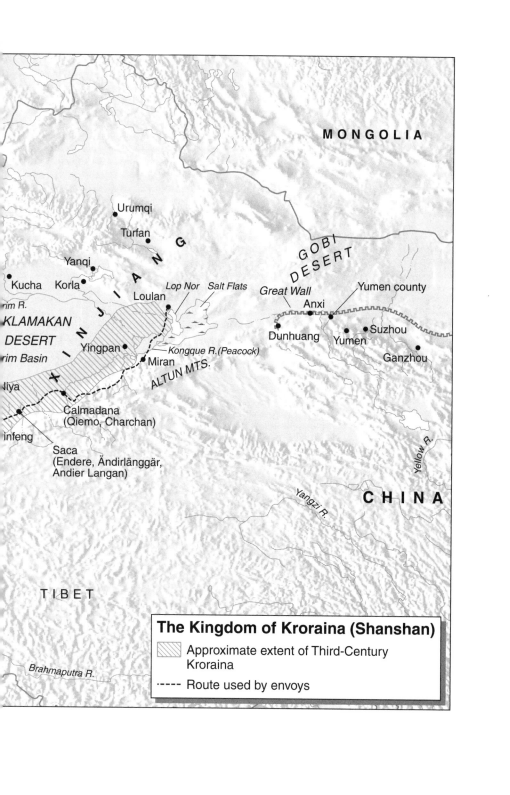

MONGOLIA

Urumqi

Turfan

N

G

Yanqi

Kucha   Korla

Lop Nor   Salt Flats

GOBI
DESERT

Great Wall

Yumen county

Loulan

Anxi

rim R.

KLAMAKAN

Dunhuang   Yumen   Suzhou

DESERT

Yingpan

Kongque R.(Peacock)

Ganzhou

rim Basin

Miran

X

I

N

J

I

A

N

ALTUN MTS.

Jiya

Calmadana
(Qiemo, Charchan)

infeng

Saca
(Endere, Ändirlänggär,
Andier Langan)

Yangzi R.

Yellow R.

CHINA

TIBET

Brahmaputra R.

The Kingdom of Kroraina (Shanshan)

Approximate extent of Third-Century
Kroraina

----- Route used by envoys

The going was not easy. Stein and his party had to stay on treacherous paths cutting through steep gorges hundreds of feet above icy rivers. They inched along cliff faces by walking on man-made supports, called rafiks, consisting of branches and rock slabs stuck in cracks on the face of the mountains. He used human porters, as no pack animal could negotiate these tortuous trails. After crossing into China at the Mintaka Pass (15,187 feet, or 4,629 m), they proceeded north to Kashgar and from there to Khotan and then Niya.

On some sections of the Gilgit Road, one can still see drawings and inscriptions left behind by ancient travelers on the rock walls. Travelers often had to halt for several months before they could proceed; like Stein, they had to wait for the snow to melt in the summer and could take desert routes only in cooler winter weather. During these lulls, they used sharp tools or stones to rub off metallic accretions and etch extremely short messages or simple sketches directly on the surface of the rock.[6]

Stein noticed the graffiti carved into stone along his path, yet not until 1979, when the Karakorum Highway linking China with Pakistan was completed, were many able to see for themselves what was left behind. Since then a team of scholars has transcribed and photographed the over five thousand inscriptions and drawings done along the route.[7]

The first identifiable drawings on the Karakorum Pass, made in the first to third centuries, show a round burial mound, called a stupa, with a ladder reaching up to them. Followers of Buddha, who died circa 400 BCE, walked clockwise around mounds containing his remains. These mounds changed shape over the centuries, becoming taller and more like columns; ultimately they took the form of pagodas in China and Japan. Early Buddhist art did not portray the Buddha, but drawings made in the seventh and eighth centuries depict different scenes in the historical Buddha's life, as well as other buddhas and bodhisattvas, who were believed to have turned back at the moment of attaining nirvana to help their fellow Buddhists still on earth. Zoroastrians, who adhere to the teachings of the Iranian prophet Zarathustra, made other sketches depicting fire altars.

Early travelers also left messages and graffiti in two Indic scripts: one thousand in Kharoshthi, the script used at Niya, and four thousand in Brahmi, which replaced Kharoshthi throughout Central Asia around 400 CE. The use of Kharoshthi script indicates that many of the travelers came from Gandhara.[8] Since the fourth century BCE, when Alexander of Macedon conquered the Gandhara region, it was home to a cosmopolitan population with roots in Greece, India, and East Asia. A series of recently excavated manuscripts written in Kharoshthi script in the Gandhari language from Afghanistan indicate that the Dharmaguptaka school of Buddhists was active in the region during the early years of the first century CE.[9]

BUDDHIST GRAFFITI ON THE KARAKORUM HIGHWAY
This inscription stands in a giant field of boulders near the town of Hodur, which is on the
northern bank of the Upper Indus River in the Gilgit-Baltisan Province of Pakistan. It shows a
Buddhist burial mound, or stupa, flanked by two buddhas. It is one of the later images from the
Karakorum Highway, dating to the sixth to eighth centuries CE. To the right, one can see graffiti
left by travelers going between China and what is now Pakistan. Courtesy of Rock Art Archive,
Heidelberg Academy of Sciences.

Although numbering in the thousands, most of the inscriptions on the Karakorum Pass are frustratingly formulaic. The vast majority simply say "son of a,
b, arrived" or a Buddhist variation, "b, son of a, pays homage."[10] Some of the
writers recorded the name of the reigning king, but these local kings are all
unknown. Accordingly, scholars can date the inscriptions only by analyzing the
shape of certain letters, an approximate method at best, which puts them
between the first and eighth centuries.[11]

In addition, at the Shatial site, some 30 miles (50 km) downstream from Chilas,
550 inscriptions are in Sogdian, the language used by the residents of Samarkand.
One of these inscriptions reads: "I, Nanai-vandak the son of Narisaf have come here
on the tenth day and asked a boon from the spirit of the sacred place K'rt that . . . I
may arrive in Tashkurgan more quickly and see my brother in good health with
joy."[12] This text is one of the few along the Gilgit route that states the traveler's destination, namely, Tashkurgan, a mountain fortification just to the west of Kashgar,
from where travelers entered Xinjiang. A handful of inscriptions are in other Iranian
languages, Chinese, and Tibetan. One of the latest, in Hebrew, records the names of
two men, evidence that Jewish merchants also used the Karakorum Highway.[13]

Stein was certain that the migrants from India who traveled to the Kroraina in the second and third centuries crossed the mountains along the same routes—following the Indus, Gilgit, and Hunza rivers—that he had followed. At the end of the Hunza River, they had a choice of several routes leading into Xinjiang.[14] Jason Neelis, an expert on the inscriptions, refers to these as "capillary routes," to convey the complex network of main roads, like veins and arteries, and the many side paths, like capillaries, that led through the mountains to Xinjiang. In the late nineteenth and early twentieth centuries, travelers usually entered China at the Mintaka Pass, as Stein did, but nowadays they follow the Karakorum Highway, which crosses into China at the Khunjerab Pass to the southeast.

The surviving inscriptions do not reveal why the migrants left Gandhara. At the time, the Kushan Empire was in its waning years. The Kushans ruled much of north India (including modern-day Pakistan and Afghanistan) in 40–260 CE, and peaked in the early second century CE during the reign of the great ruler Kanishka (ca. 120–46).[15] The official history of the Later Han dynasty, written by the Chinese in the mid-fifth century, records that the Kushan Empire sent troops into Xinjiang several times.[16] In 90 CE, it reports, the Kushan ruler dispatched seventy thousand soldiers to the Western Region. Although these huge numbers cannot be taken at face value, the Kushan dynasty was clearly powerful enough to send troops to western Xinjiang.

Most Chinese records say little about these migrations from India, but one biography of Zhi Qian, a Buddhist teacher of Indian descent, explains: "He came from the Great Yuezhi Kingdom (viz. the Kushan empire). Led by his grandfather Fadu, hundreds of his countrymen immigrated into China during the reign of Emperor Ling Di [ca. 168–189 CE] and Fadu was offered an official post."[17]

This conclusion—that the Gandhari-speaking residents of Niya came from Pakistan and Afghanistan—consciously rejects the account in the Chinese official histories that the Kushans (Yuezhi in Chinese) originally lived in Gansu Province, near Dunhuang, but that the rise of the Xiongnu around 175 BCE forced them to abandon their Chinese homeland and move west. According to the official histories, the Greater Yuezhi were one of the five nomadic groups who subsequently formed the Kushan Empire around 23 CE.[18] There are several good reasons to doubt the account of the Yuezhi migration out of Gansu as given in the dynastic histories. The compilers of the histories, writing many generations later, recorded received wisdom and legends about non-Chinese peoples. They almost always ascribed Chinese homelands to foreign peoples, including the Xiongnu, the Japanese, and, most implausibly of all, the residents of Da Qin, the mythical empire on the western edge of the known world. Finally, and most convincingly, no archeological evidence for such a migration exists.[19]

The most plausible explanation is the simplest: multiple nomadic groups moved across vast stretches of territory in the third and second centuries BCE, but we cannot trust Chinese observers writing three centuries later to give an accurate account of these migrations. Although the Chinese ascribed a Chinese homeland to the Yuezhi, we can only be certain that the Yuezhi were in Bactria (the lands between the Hindu Kush and the Oxus River in north central Afghanistan, with its capital at Balkh) in 138 BCE, because that is where Zhang Qian encountered them. Any claims about their earlier movements must remain speculative.

Following the same arduous route through the mountains that the ancient migrants had taken, Stein finally entered Xinjiang. He visited a series of oasis towns—Yarkand, Khotan, Keriya, Niya—strung along the southern edge of the Taklamakan Desert like beads on a necklace. Most were a day's travel apart; travelers had to prepare enough water and supplies for those legs of the journey that were longer. In Keriya, a "respectable old" farmer named Abdullah told Stein about seeing old ruins in the desert. The Niya ruins were 75 miles (120 km) north of the modern town of Niya, now called Minfeng, which lies on today's Khotan-Minfeng highway. When Stein arrived in Minfeng, his camel driver met an "enterprising young villager" named Ibrahim who tried to sell him the wooden tablet with Kharoshthi writing shown in the photo at the beginning of the chapter.

Stein immediately hired Ibrahim to guide Stein's work crew north along the Niya river to the last inhabited village, the site of an active shrine to a revered Muslim teacher, Imam Jafar Sadik. There the river ended. Stein and his men followed the dry riverbed north for another 24 miles (39 km) to the ancient site of Niya. The site consisted of the ruins of many wooden houses lying in the sand and a Buddhist brick tower, or stupa, shown in color plate 6.

Characteristically, Stein recorded his first impressions of the site in great detail:

> Shrivelled trunks of ancient fruit-trees appeared rising from the low sand. Moving on northward for less than two miles I soon sighted the first two "old houses," standing on what looked at first sight like small elevated plateaus, but which closer observation proved to be merely portions of the original loess soil that had escaped the erosion proceeding all round. . . .
>
> Marching about two miles further north, across broad swelling dunes, I arrived at the ruined structure of sun-dried bricks of which Abdullah had already spoken at Keriya. . . . It proved, as I expected, to be the remains of a small Stupa, buried for the most part under the slope of a high conical sandhill. . . .
>
> As I retired to my first night's rest among these silent witnesses of ancient habitations my main thought was how many of the precious

documents on wood, which Ibrahim declared he had left behind at the ruin "explored" by him a year before, were still waiting to be recovered.

Drawn by the direct evidence of connections among civilizations, Stein visited ancient Niya four times—for fifteen days in 1901, eleven in 1906, five in 1916, and a week in 1931. Each time he unearthed new houses, Buddhist remains, and documents on wood.

The Fourth Expedition did not go as smoothly as the first three.[20] By the 1930s, the Chinese authorities had passed laws stipulating that only excavations jointly conducted by foreigners with Chinese collaborators could remove artifacts from the country. Working closely with British authorities, Stein thought that he had obtained permission to excavate in Xinjiang, but when he arrived in Kashgar, the local authorities assigned guards to make sure that he did not take anything. At Niya, Stein wandered around the site trying to distract his keepers, while his assistant, Abdul Ghafar, looked surreptitiously for documents. When they returned to Kashgar, Stein had somehow managed to collect 159 packets of materials.

Yet his expedition failed: the Chinese authorities did not allow Stein to ship anything out of the country, and the artifacts have since disappeared. All that remain from that expedition are Stein's meticulous notes and photographs. From Kashgar, a disconsolate Stein wrote to his friend Percy Stafford Allen: "I said farewell for the last time to that favorite ancient site where I could live more than anywhere else in touch with a dead past."[21]

Even before he arrived at the site for the first time, Stein realized that he had to identify the ancient Chinese name of the site before he could tap the extensive geographical information in the Chinese official histories. *The History of the Han Dynasty* and its sequel, *The History of the Later Han*, give capsule descriptions of all the different kingdoms of the northwest: their distance from the capital, their population (total number of households, individuals, and "those who could bear arms"), and an overview of their history. Established around 60 BCE and dismantled in 16 CE, the office of the protector general, the Han-dynasty official in charge of the Western Regions, provided this information to the history office in the central government.[22]

A century later, the staff of the history office drew on this information to describe the various oasis states of the northwest.[23] They wrote that the Shanshan Kingdom (using the Chinese name for Kroraina) was located 6,100 *li* (approximately 1,550 miles, or 2,500 km) from the Han-dynasty capital of Chang'an.[24] (The actual distance from Loulan to Chang'an is 1,120 miles, or 1,793 km). The distances given in the official histories were probably calculated by approximating how far an animal could travel in a day and then multiplying that rate by the number of days it took to reach the destination. These distances are not exact, but they do indicate the positions of the different oasis kingdoms in relation to each other.

In 1901, Stein found a wooden seal with four characters that said "edict of the king of Shanshan," which the Han dynasty, or a later dynasty, had bestowed on the local ruler with whom they had diplomatic relations.[25] Stein believed that Niya was too small to have been the capital of Shanshan. He uncovered only about fifty dwellings at the site. (According to Stein's numbering system, "N.xiv.i.1" referred to "N" for Niya, the 14th house he discovered, room 1, and the first item discovered in room 1, whether an artifact or document.) Since then archeologists have unearthed one hundred more structures, far too few for the 14,100 people living in 1,570 households mentioned in the official history. In *Serindia*, published in 1921, Stein identified the ancient site of Niya as the seat of the Jingjue Kingdom, which reportedly had 480 households and 3,360 individuals.[26] Even these figures are too large for the site. Some say that more houses lie still undiscovered under the sand, but it is also possible that the Han-dynasty population figures for the distant kingdoms of the northwest were not accurate.

While most scholars accept Stein's identification of Niya as Jingjue, his view that the archeological site of Loulan was the capital of the Shanshan Kingdom remains controversial. Like Niya, the site of Loulan has a single brick stupa, the wooden remains of houses, and a few wooden carvings in Gandharan style. Loulan was the Chinese transliteration of "Kroraina," which denoted both the name of the kingdom and its capital in the Kharoshthi documents.[27]

Since 108 BCE, *The History of the Han* records, the Han dynasty had occasionally sent armies to attack Loulan but had never conquered the city, which was the capital of a small kingdom, also called Loulan. For several decades, the ruler of Loulan had tried to maintain amicable relations with the two rival states of the Han dynasty and the Xiongnu peoples living in modern-day Mongolia by sending princes as royal hostages to each of these empires.

The strategy failed in 77 BCE, when the brother of the reigning Loulan king informed the Han officials that the king favored the Xiongnu. The Chinese sent an emissary who first feigned friendship, then invited the king to his tent and killed him. Han armies then invaded Loulan, and the Chinese renamed the kingdom Shanshan. The Han dynasty established a new capital for Shanshan at Endere (modern Ruoqiang), and stationed the official charged with overseeing all Han-dynasty activities in the Western Regions in Loulan.[28]

The histories report that Loulan was occupied for more than five centuries, starting in 77 BCE, but few finds suggest such a long period of occupation. The most direct evidence of Chinese presence is newly minted coins, most likely from a Chinese garrison, outside of Loulan. Stein discovered 211 round bronze coins with square holes, distributed evenly over an area some 30 yards (27 m) long and 3–4 feet (ca. 1 m) wide.[29] The coins, apparently freshly minted, were of the *wuzhu* (literally "five-grain," a measure of weight) type and dated from 86 BCE to 1 BCE.[30] Stein explained:

> It was clear that all these coins had dropped from a caravan moving in the very direction in which I had supposed the ancient route to lie. They must have got loose from the string which tied them and gradually dropped out unobserved through an opening in their bag or case. The swaying movement of the camel or cart in which this receptacle was carried sufficiently explains why the line marked by the scattered coins had the width above indicated.[31]

About 50 yards (ca. 45 m) away from the last coin, one of Stein's workmen found a pile of unused arrowheads, surely part of the same shipment of military supplies as the *wuzhu* coins. The coincidence of coins and arrowheads suggests that in Han China, payments to soldiers constituted a major source of fresh coins in a given region.[32]

A small number of Chinese documents from Niya, and probably dating to this early period, suggest a nonmilitary Chinese presence during the Han dynasty as well. House 14 had two rooms in addition to a large hall measuring 56 feet (17 m) by 41 feet (12.5 m).[33]

Inside the hall, Stein's men dug through a refuse heap and found eleven wood slips with Chinese characters on both sides; eight were legible. Each records the name of the giver and the recipient—the king, his mother, his wife, the heir apparent in the royal family, and a courtier.[34] The front side of one, for example, says "Minister Chengde bows his head to the ground and sincerely presents this piece of jade. He bows again to ask," while the reverse gives the name of the recipient, in this case, "the great king."[35] These tags suggest that a Chinese advisor, who visited, or lived at, the Jingjue court sometime early in the first century CE, taught the ruler to attach them to gifts. Three of the wood slips from room 14 use the distinct language of the usurper Wang Mang (reigned 9–23 CE), who founded the Xin ("New") dynasty, a fourteen-year-long interregnum between the Former and Later Han dynasties.[36] Several other Chinese documents from the refuse pit in Niya house 14 mention envoys: "The seat of the envoy of the King of Ferghana [Dayuan]; below him on the left, the Great Yuezhi."[37] These various documents all indicate that the Chinese must have had some type of outpost at Niya before and after the start of the Common Era.

According to Chinese laws, every time a traveler arrived in a new place within China, he had to present his *guosuo* travel document to local officials who verified that he was the person whose name appeared on the pass. Travel passes found at

Niya, which date to the third century, state whether or not the traveler was a free man, give a physical description, and specify his destination. One, for example, describes a thirty-year-old traveler "of medium build, black hair, big eyes, with moustache and beard." They also list the itinerary of the travelers, who had to keep to a predetermined route. Two of the wood slips instruct officials what to do if someone's pass was missing, but do not reveal what actually happened when local officials discovered the problem. Did the border officials simply issue a new pass? Or did they punish the errant merchants? Regardless, Chinese officials at Niya were clearly aware of existing regulations about travel passes.[38]

Assessing Chinese power in the region during this early period has direct political implications for today. The Chinese government's legitimacy in Xinjiang rests partially on the precedent of Han-dynasty control. But that claim seems weaker if local rulers were largely independent and simply hosted Chinese garrisons and received the occasional advisor or envoy, as surviving documents indicate.

HOUSE 26 AT NIYA

After he finished excavating house 26 at Niya in 1906, Stein asked his workers to place the double wooden bracket that provided support for the main room's ceiling on a pillar so that it could be photographed. Typically Gandharan, the carved wooden bracket shows a vase with fruit and flowers at the center and a mythical animal with wings, a dragon's head, and a horse's body. Measuring 9 feet long and 1.5 wide (2.74 m by .46 m), the bracket was too large to transport. Stein's men sawed it into pieces and hollowed it out so that it could be shipped to London. Courtesy of the Board of the British Library.

Whatever they suggest about the Chinese presence at the turn of the Common Era, the wooden slips from house 14 at Niya reveal little about the lives of those who lived at the site. Fortunately, material evidence supplements these early Chinese documents. Niya's ancient residents joined several wooden beams together to form a foundation and slotted vertical poles into the floor beams to make walls. They then packed the walls with grasses and mats to protect occupants from the wind. They crafted roofs from beams, too. The houses ranged from small dwellings with just one room to larger houses with multiple rooms with walls over 16 feet (5 m) long. Stein and Hedin found a few elaborate carvings at Niya and Loulan; their designs matched wooden objects made in the Gandhara region, confirming that their makers had come to Xinjiang from Pakistan and Afghanistan.

The extreme dryness of the Niya and Loulan sites has preserved about one hundred ancient corpses of the residents. At Loulan Stein found one corpse with "fair hair," while another had a "red moustache." Both he and Hedin sensed that these desiccated corpses did not look either Chinese or Indian. All subsequent excavators in the region have marveled at the excellent state of preservation of corpses whose light skin, fair hair, and heights nearing six feet (1.8 m) mark them as Caucasoid. It seems most likely that the original inhabitants of the Kroraina Kingdom, like many others living in Central Asia, originally came from somewhere on the Iranian plateau.[39]

Burials at the Niya and Loulan sites have much to tell us about the lives of those interred there because they carried their most precious articles with them to the afterlife. In 1959 a team of ten archeologists from the Xinjiang Museum entered the desert on camels (lacking desert vehicles) and walked seven days before reaching the site where they discovered the graves. They found a huge coffin measuring 6.5 feet (2 m) long with four wooden legs, which they dated between the second and fourth centuries CE.[40] The coffin held the corpses of a man and woman and two wooden staffs for carrying their possessions. The man carried a bow and four arrows in an arrow holder, while the woman had a makeup box along with combs and other female grooming articles. Although the clothing of the deceased couple had decayed wherever it touched their skin, the archeologists managed to recover pieces from more than ten different textiles, some cotton, some silk. The presence of the two fabrics testified to Niya's location midway on the overland routes linking China with the West.

While the knowledge of how to raise silkworms and to spin silk originated in central China and traveled west, cotton traveled east to Niya from West Asia. This and another tie-dyed piece of cotton are the earliest cotton textiles unearthed in China to date.[41] A Chinese encyclopedia reports that in 331 CE the king of Ferghana (in western Uzbekistan) gave cotton cloth and glass to a north Chinese ruler, confirming the introduction of cotton from the west.[42]

COTTON TEXTILE FROM NIYA
A distinctive printed cotton textile from the tomb had different squares showing a checkerboard pattern, a Chinese dragon, a goddess holding a cornucopia, and the tail and two paws of an animal whose body has been cut off. The dragon motif is clearly of Chinese origin, but the goddess is Tyche, the Greek city guardian who frequently appears in the art of Afghanistan. Because Tyche is often paired with Hercules, it is likely that the paws and the tail are those of Hercules's lion.

The Niya site also produced cocoons and seeds from mulberry trees, the main foodstuff of silkworms. The residents knew how to spin silk thread and how to make a simple tabby weave (one thread over, one under—a basket weave), but they did not have the sophisticated looms required to make the elaborate silk brocades found in the coffin. Those found in 1959 included gloves and socks for the man and a pillow for the couple, all cut from the same bolt of cloth with seven Chinese characters woven into the design: "increased longevity over the extended years and multiple sons and grandsons." These twin goals—a long life and many male descendants—date back to the earliest times in China. These textiles, which closely resemble one of the brocades found at Palmyra, were clearly of Chinese manufacture, as was a mirror found with them. Four characters along the rim of bronze mirror urged the deceased tomb owner: "You should be a high official."[43] While it is unclear if the deceased couple could read Chinese, the placement of the inscribed textiles and mirror in the coffin indicate that these were valued items.

A 1995 expedition to Niya unearthed eight more burials, three in rectangular coffins, five in boat-shaped coffins made from poplar trees that had been hollowed out after being set on fire. The coffin in the largest tomb (M3) contained the desiccated bodies of a man and a woman that were remarkably well preserved (shown in color plate 7). As in the tomb found in 1959, gender roles were apparent. The man was buried with bows, arrows, a small dagger, and a knife sheath; his wife had

CHINESE SILK FROM NIYA
Artfully woven into the fabric were Chinese characters saying "kings and lords shall be married for thousands of autumns and tens of thousands of years; it is right that they bear sons and grandsons." This is one of thirty-seven textiles found in a single burial at Niya, making it one of the most important finds along the Silk Road. Courtesy of Wang Binghua.

a makeup box, a bronze mirror of Chinese manufacture, combs, a needle, and small bolts of cloth. Knife marks stretching from the man's ear to his neck are from the wound that caused his death, while his wife's body was unscarred, suggesting death by suffocation so that she could be interred at the same time.

The couple lay underneath a single-layered coverlet of blue silk brocade with a pattern of stylized dancers in red, white, and brown. The deceased wore complete sets of clothing.

A slightly later tomb, numbered M8, also contained a deceased couple, as well as some textiles with Chinese characters on them and a simple clay vessel with the Chinese character for king on it.[44] The use of the words "king" and "lord" in the textiles from tombs M3 and M8 suggests that these are gifts from the Chinese central authorities to a local king. At some point after 48 CE the Shanshan Kingdom "incorporated" the Jingjue Kingdom, we learn from the *History of the Later Han*.[45] And so the Niya site, which had served as the capital of the Jingjue state, became part of the larger Shanshan Kingdom.

A contemporaneous burial from the site of Yingpan (southwest of Loulan) contrasts sharply with the Niya burials, because the corpse was buried in wool, not cotton or silk.[46] The deceased man wears a red woolen robe with an elaborate design composed of pairs of facing pomegranate trees, animals, and human figures. Naked cherubic figures brandish swords and lassos as they confront one

YINGPAN BURIAL

Interred in a painted wooden coffin, the deceased wore a white mask, made of layers of hemp glued together, with a rectangle of gold foil on the forehead above the eyes. He was buried with two miniature sets of clothing (for use in the afterworld?): one at his left wrist, the other on his stomach. Grave M15, excavated 1995. Courtesy of Wang Binghua.

another in a combat stance. With two interwoven layers, this textile is too complex to have been made by local weavers. It was probably made in Bactria, far to the west, where local artisans modified the Greco-Roman motifs first introduced to the region by the armies of Alexander of Macedon in the fourth century BCE.[47] Archeologists have speculated about the identity of this beautifully dressed corpse. The former director of the Xinjiang Archaeological Institute, Wang Bing-hua, suggests the he may have been a ruler of yet another small oasis kingdom mentioned in the official histories, the Kingdom of Shan (literally "The Hill King-dom"), whose southeastern border abutted the Shanshan Kingdom.[48]

Whether or not the deceased in Niya tomb M3 or the Yingpan tomb were actually local kings (still the most likely possibility), they certainly were among the wealthiest people living at these settlements, and their tombs offer a vivid picture of the local economy. The region's inhabitants buried the dead with grains such as millet, barley, and wheat, and fruits grown in orchards like grapes, pears, peaches, pomegranates, and dates. They viewed a whole leg of lamb as the ultimate treat, the centerpiece of a feast in the next life, and garments made from imported textiles as the most suitable clothing for that life.

Most analysts concur that the material evidence from the Niya, Yingpan, and Loulan sites dates to somewhere between the second and fourth centuries but are not sure exactly when. In contrast, the written evidence from Loulan is clear: documents in both Chinese and Kharoshthi reveal that Chinese armies were stationed at Loulan in the late third and early fourth centuries CE.

Most of the documents in Chinese from Loulan date to 263 to 272, with a few remaining examples from 330.[49] This was the time when the Shanshan Kingdom ruled the region from Niya to Loulan and when the different Chinese dynasties based in north China who succeeded the Han dynasty, primarily the Wei (220–65) and the Western Jin (265–316), stationed garrisons in Loulan. Loulan produced about fifty Kharoshthi-script documents, but over seven hundred Chinese documents, either short texts (usually no more than ten characters) on wood slips or on tiny scraps of paper.[50] The Chinese often recorded private transactions on paper, while garrison officials tended to use wooden slips for their records, an indication that private individuals used paper before government officials did.[51]

Like their Han-dynasty predecessors, the Loulan garrison belonged to the Chinese system of military colonies whose inhabitants were expected to grow their own food while they stood ready to serve in the army. The soldiers in Chinese employ used draft animals, like cows and horses, to plow the land on which they raised wheat, barley, and millet. They were not necessarily Chinese; the Chinese military recruited from among the local people as well. The farmer-soldiers also introduced agricultural techniques, most notably irrigation for watering crops. They experimented with cattle-drawn ploughs, and they used new types of iron spade and sickle, the first metal tools employed in the region.[52]

Chinese government regulations stipulated that each soldier was entitled to 1 peck (*dou*) 2 pints (*sheng*) (approximately 2.6 quarts [2.4 L]) of grain each day—but local officials could not always provide the stipulated amount, and the rations sometimes dipped as low as half that.[53] When the grain grown by the farmer-soldiers ran short, Chinese officials, surviving documents reveal, bought extra grain from the local people using coins and colored silk. The Loulan garrison received funds, in both coin and silk, from military units based to the east in the city of Dunhuang or possibly Wuwei, both in Gansu. The silk came in various colors and in two lengths, long and short. One bolt of plain tabby silk found by Stein at Loulan in 1901, shown in color plate 5A, is the only surviving example of silk used as money from such an early period.[54]

Many documents give the exchange rates for conversions among three different types of currency: coins, colored silk, and grain. Officials used silk to buy grain and horses for their men, and the soldiers themselves also exchanged silk and grain for shoes and clothing. They regularly converted prices from one currency to another.[55]

The Loulan documents mention a few much larger transactions as well. One wood slip, dated 330, reports that the Sogdians, traders originally from the Samarkand region, presented ten thousand piculs (each picul was approximately 1/2 bushel, or 20 L) of something (the word is missing), most likely of grain, and two hundred coins (*qian*) to the authorities.[56] Although the back of the slip has the seals of two Chinese officials, the document does not explain why the Sogdians made these payments. This was either a tax payment or one of an ongoing series of transactions to provide the Chinese troops with food. Another fragment records a large payment of 319 animals in exchange for 4,326 bolts of colored silk.[57] This, too, appears to be a payment by Sogdian merchants to the Chinese authorities, and we know from fragments of two Sogdian-language documents found by Stein that Sogdians were active at Loulan at this time.[58] In later centuries, Sogdians played a key role in supplying Chinese armies, and it is quite likely they had already begun to do so in the early fourth century CE at Loulan.

The Chinese documents found by Stein and Hedin at Loulan come from only a few spots.[59] Still, they give the overwhelming impression that the transactions at Loulan exclusively involved the garrison collectively or soldiers individually, using grain, silk, and coins to obtain grain, horses, clothing, and shoes from the local people. In sum, the indigenous subsistence economy occasionally supplied the Chinese garrison with locally produced commodities. As Ito Toshio, who teaches at Osaka Kyoiku University, has concluded after a thorough survey, the documents do not mention any profit-seeking activities.[60] The only evidence of merchants—and it is highly fragmentary—indicates Sogdian merchants who worked for the military authorities.

The Kharoshthi-script documents from Niya and Loulan are much richer than the Chinese-language documents. They portray a broader range of society, from the lowliest cultivators to the ruler himself, involved in a host of activities, some utterly mundane. Accordingly, they make it possible to glimpse life along the Silk Road in a way that the Chinese documents do not.

Some of the Kharoshthi documents give the name of the current king, the year of his reign, and occasionally the name of his predecessor or successor. In 1920, using such clues, Rapson and his collaborators drew up a list of five kings who ruled for a total of some ninety years. Yet no one knew exactly when those local kings had ruled. In 1940 Thomas Burrow produced a comprehensive translation of all those Kharoshthi documents whose meaning could be understood, but they still remained undated.

Then, in 1965, John Brough announced that he had found the key to dating the Kharoshthi documents: the Chinese title *shizhong*, literally meaning "palace attendant," corresponded to the term *jitumgha*. In 263, the Kroraina king Amgoka used the new title for the first time. He may have received it from the ruler of the Western Jin dynasty (265–316), a regional Chinese dynasty based in Luoyang city, Henan Province, but this was two years before the Western Jin decisively defeated the dynasties that preceded it. The forms of address for the rulers also changed: before the seventeenth year of Amgoka's reign, letter writers used long strings of titles for kings; after that year, the titles became noticeably shorter and include the word *jitumgha*.[61]

The year 263 was the seventeenth of King Amgoka's reign. Once this single year was fixed, it was simply a matter of assigning calendar years to all the kings' reigns. Brough's original chronology has since been extended slightly because of the subsequent discovery of Kharoshthi documents naming other kings.[62] Not everyone accepts Brough's dating, but there is general agreement that the Kharoshthi documents date from the mid-third to the mid-fourth century, give or take twenty years. This period overlaps with the Chinese documents from Loulan, which date to 263–330. And because the Kharoshthi documents refer to no specific external event, there is little chance of dating them more precisely.

Since the local inhabitants lacked their own written language, the Kharoshthi script served to record people's names, very strange-sounding names indeed. The approximately one thousand proper names and 150 loanwords that appear in the Kharoshthi documents indicate that the local language of Niya was not Chinese and totally unlike the language spoken by the refugees from Gandhara. Writing in 1935, Thomas Burrow suggested that the indigenous Niya language was related to Tocharian, an Indo-European language spoken on the northern route, but his suggestion has not been widely accepted, nor has it prompted further study.[63] It appears that, before the arrival of the immigrants, the indigenous peoples had their own language but no means of writing it, which is why they adopted the Kharoshthi script.

While rulers tend to have names of local origin like Ly'ipeya, many scribes have names of Sanskritic origin like Buddhasena, meaning "The one whose lord is the Buddha." As we often see today, names are not always a reliable indicator of someone's ethnic background; immigrant parents do sometimes draw the names of their children from the culture of their new home. Yet often the only identifying trace that survives of a given individual living along the Silk Routes is his or her name.

In reconstructing the migration of the technologically more sophisticated Gandharans to Niya, one might expect the migrants to overthrow the local rulers and found their own states. Interestingly, the names of the rulers and the scribes indicate that, while many scribes were Gandharan, the rulers continued to be local men. The scenario of refugees from north India, migrating in groups of no more than a hundred at a time, seems likely.

The Kharoshthi documents do not record what happened when the first migrants from India arrived. A later ruler instructed local officials to receive refugees, "who are to be looked after as if they were your own." He also stipulated that the refugees be given land, houses, and seeds "so that they can make copious and plentiful cultivation."[64] Not all refugees fared so well; some were assigned to work as slaves for the residents. The later treatment of migrants is important because it suggests how the migrants from Gandhara may have been treated on their arrival.

The refugees taught the indigenous peoples how to write their script and to store their documents in archives, the first of which Stein and a man named Rustam, whom Stein called "the most experienced and most reliable of my old diggers of 1901," discovered in 1906. The two men returned to room 8 of house 24, because, as Stein explained:

> Already during the first clearing I had noticed a large lump of clay or plaster near the wall where the packets of tablets lay closest. I had ordered it to be left undisturbed, though I thought little of its having come to that place by more than accident. Rustam had just extracted between it and the wall a well-preserved double-wedge tablet, when I saw him eagerly burrow with his hands into the floor just as when my fox terrier "Dash" was at work opening rat holes. Before I could put any questions I saw Rustam triumphantly draw forth from about six inches [15 cm] below the floor a complete rectangular document with its double clay seal intact and its envelope still unopened. When the hole was enlarged we saw that the space toward the wall and below its foundation beam was full of closely packed layers of similar documents. It was clear that we had struck a small hidden archive.[65]

The marking of the site with a lump of clay or plaster, Stein felt, showed that the original owner had been obliged to leave the village in a hurry, but with the intent to return.

This single find produced nearly eighty documents, of which twenty-six were "double rectangular tablets" with their seals intact.[66] Stein used this term for a specific type of document: like a shallow drawer, the upper piece of wood slotted into the bottom rectangular piece of wood, and the two pieces of wood were tied together with string and sealed.

Local officials archived these documents and retrieved them when needed. In one instance, a monk sold a plot of land to a man named Ramshotsa for three horses; twenty years later, when someone encroached on Ramshotsa's land,

EAST MEETS WEST ON A KHAROSHTHI DOCUMENT

This wooden document from Niya survives intact: the upper drawer has been slotted into the lower holder, and cords have been wrapped around both pieces of wood through notches and then sealed with clay. The seal on the left is in Chinese; that on the right shows a Western-looking face, most likely a Greek or Roman deity, which are often shown on Gandharan seals. These double rectangular tablets record the exchange between two parties of various types of property—slaves, livestock, and land—and give the names of the officials who recorded the transaction.

officials consulted the earlier rectangular tablet before deciding that the land indeed belonged to Ramshotsa.[67] In all, over two hundred double rectangular tablets were excavated at Niya, most ending with a statement of the penalty to be charged should either party challenge the terms of the exchange, and a variation of the assertion that the document's "authority is a thousand years, as long as life."[68]

Suspecting that the different shapes of documents had distinct purposes, Stein proposed that a second type of document, "wedge-shaped tablets," was for royal orders or policy decisions. He found nearly three hundred documents of this type. The wedge-shaped documents consisted of two pieces of wood of the same size, 7–15 inches (18–38 cm) long and 1.13–2.5 inches (3–6 cm) wide, that were placed face to face, tied together with string, and then sealed. The seals portrayed Greek gods like Athena, Eros, and Heracles, who were familiar to the migrants from the Gandhara region, who had worshipped them for centuries.[69] The outside piece of wood gave the name of the recipient, and on the inside were the king's orders, most of which followed the same opening formula:

To be given to the cozbo Tamjaka.

His majesty the king writes, he instructs the cozbo Tamjaka as follows:[70]

These official orders came from the king of Kroraina to the highest-ranking local official, or cozbo, the equivalent of governor.[71] Assisted by a group of lower officials, the cozbo heard and adjudicated local disputes.

This wedge-shaped tablet was addressed to Tamjaka, the cozbo of Cadh'ota, the name used in the Kharoshthi documents for the settlement at Niya. The king asked the cozbo to investigate a complaint from a resident of the town that soldiers from a neighboring district had stolen two of his cows. They had eaten one, he claimed, and returned the other. The royal orders often addressed intensely local concerns like this.

If the king had a more urgent order, he wrote it on leather. Only a few of this type of document survive. Other shapes of documents from Niya were used for private correspondence or for lists. The Japanese scholar Akamatsu Akihiko, who teaches Indic languages at Kyoto University, has suggested that the different types of Kharoshthi documents had their origins in the bureaucratic system of the Mauryan dynasty of northern India (ca. 320–185 BCE) as recorded in the *Arthashastra*.[72] This text, while it may be based on earlier texts, dates to the second to fourth centuries CE.[73] Attributed to Kautilya, the *Arthashastra* is a prescriptive text packed full of instructions about how to govern. Presuming that the ruler will issue written orders to his subordinates, it lists "the characteristics of a good edict" and "the defects" of bad edicts. It also gives the sources of law as dharma (a Sanskrit term usually understood as meaning correct conduct according to law or custom, but sometimes specifically indicating the teachings of the Buddha), evidence, custom, and royal edicts. Since the royal edicts are assumed to coincide with dharma, they take precedence over the other sources of law.

The *Arthashastra* lists nine types of royal edicts (some with subtypes) that do not correspond one-to-one with the Niya documents, but the overlap is noticeable. Many of the Kharoshthi documents from Niya, for example, seem to fit the category of "a conditional order," which instruct the recipient, "If there is any truth to this report, then the following shall be done."[74] The resemblance is not surprising: people familiar with South Asian bureaucratic norms in the third and fourth centuries CE wrote both the *Arthashastra* and the Kharoshthi documents.

Earlier scholars took the presence of so many documents in an Indic language as evidence that the Kushan Empire actually occupied Niya (after conquering it with the forces described in the official histories). More recent interpretations hold that a group of migrants from the Gandhara region could just as easily have introduced this system of document keeping to the local residents and that Niya did not come under direct rule of the Kushans.[75] The persistence of so many rulers with indigenous—and not Indic—names supports the migration scenario.

Migrants and indigenous peoples alike farmed and tended herds. They often exchanged animals, rugs, and grain for livestock—horses, camels, cattle—or slaves, a distinct social group. Children put up for adoption constituted a group between slaves and free people. Sometimes the adoptive parents made a payment, usually a horse, called a "milk payment." If they did so, then the new family member joined the family as an equal. But if no milk payment was made, then the adopted child was treated as a slave.[76]

Women participated fully in this economy. They initiated transactions, served as witnesses, brought disputes to the attention of officials, and owned land. They could adopt children and give them away, too. One woman put her son up for adoption and received a camel as milk payment. When she discovered that her birth son's master was treating him as a slave, she took her son back and sued his adoptive father in court. The court found in her favor yet returned her son to his adoptive father, stipulating that the father henceforth had to treat the boy as his son and not a slave.[77]

The residents of the village paid taxes to the Kroraina king but often fell into arrears. On one occasion, the people in one district submitted pomegranates, cloth, grain, cattle, ghee, sacks, baskets, sheep, and wine, all in order to pay back taxes. The list of goods is ample evidence that villagers made payments in a wide variety of agricultural products and locally made handicrafts.[78] They recorded payments and debts in units of grain, a clear indication that it functioned as a type of money.[79]

The few coins that circulated in the Kroraina Kingdom indicate that the Niya economy was only partially monetized. The Kroraina rulers did not mint their own coins but used those from neighboring Khotan and the Kushan Empire. The Kushans issued a gold coin called a stater (the soldiers of Alexander the Great originally introduced this Greek coin to the Gandhara region in the fourth century BCE), and some bronze stater coins have been found in Khotan, the oasis 150 miles (240 km) west of Niya. In addition, the Khotan kings minted their own bronze coins in imitation of the stater (with Chinese on one face, Kharoshthi on the other), which are called Sino-Kharoshthi coins.[80] The different coins circulating in Niya show that the oasis's primary trading partners were the Khotanese and the Kushan Empire, not Rome as is sometimes thought.

Those who came to Niya from the capital tried to collect taxes in staters but did not always succeed in doing so. In a report describing the various taxes paid by the people in one district, one official cited a specific instance: "On another occasion the queen came here. She asked for one golden stater. There is no gold. Instead of it we gave carpet (*tavastaga*) thirteen hands long."[81] When gold coins were not available, the residents of Niya sometimes used solid gold that had not been minted into coins. In one case, someone paid off a debt with a gold necklace.[82] In another, a Chinese man paid two gold staters and two silver drachma coins as compensation for a slave he received from the Supis, a raiding people living south of Khotan. This is the only transaction recorded at Niya involving silver coins, which indicates that silver coins were even less common than gold ones.[83]

The residents of Niya preferred to use grain or to exchange animals rather than risk using coins, since they faced constant political instability and must have feared that any other currency might lose its value. Officials frequently allude to the losses of warfare, including cavalry attacks and plundering by the Khotanese and raids by marauding outsiders, the Supis, who are usually labeled as "dangerous." Raids occurred so often that the local officials repeatedly refused to hear property disputes about lost items: "The established law here," the king explained in one order, "is that what has been given or received before the plundering of the kingdom by the Khotanese cannot be the object of a legal dispute."[84]

The Kharoshthi documents mention only a handful of Chinese who lived in Niya and the surrounding villages, who owned land and were given runaway cows.[85] One royal order explicitly refers to the Chinese. The king issued a wedge-shaped tablet that ordered:

> At present there are no merchants from China so that the debt of silk is not to be investigated now. . . . When the merchants arrive from China, the debt of silk is to be investigated. If there is a dispute, there will be a decision in our presence in the royal court.[86]

Clearly the authorities associated the use of silk as currency with the Chinese and sought their expert advice. They had to wait for the Chinese merchants to arrive before they could settle the dispute about the silk, which must not have been used to make payments very often. If it had, they would have known its value.

Usually only outsiders who did not live in the village used silk as money. In one instance, a man, most likely an official, returned from the capital with different rolls of silk, one specifically designated as "royal silk."[87] Royal laws and monastic rules drafted in the capital specified penalties in silk for violating legal procedures. The villagers of Niya converted payments in silk into the equivalent amount of grain, rugs, or animals. The coexistence of these different currencies meant that anyone buying something in the village had to decide whether to pay with coins, gold bullion, or silk or to make a barter exchange using something else.

Even in these unstable times, the rulers of Khotan and Kroraina continued to dispatch and to host diplomatic envoys. These envoys carried gifts for local rulers. Although the documents do not specify what they were, they were probably luxury textiles like those found in tombs M8 and M3. Niya was one stop on the route from Khotan to Loulan. Diplomats were entitled to transport, usually by camel, guides, and provisions including food, meat, and wine. From Calmadana (modern Qiemo) to Saca (Ändirlänggär), and from Saca to Nina (the site of Niya), one emissary had received a guard, but the authorities at Niya had failed to give him a guard on the final leg from Niya to Khotan.[88] The king ordered that he be compensated for his out-of-pocket expenses.

In addition to envoys, others traveled the route between Khotan and Kroraina. The Kharoshthi documents regularly use the word "runaway" to refer to the people displaced by these raids and counter raids.[89] Reports of thefts show which goods these little-documented travelers carried, and, by extension which goods best retained their value in those uncertain times. One robbery victim, identified as a "runaway," reported the theft of "four roughly woven cloths, three woolen cloths, one silver ornament, 2,500 masha [possibly Chinese coins], two jackets, two somstamni [most likely some kind of garment], two belts and three Chinese robes."[90] Although a "runaway," he was demonstrably better off than the penniless refugees who arrived and had to depend on the authorities for assistance.

Another robbery report specifies that "seven strings of pearls (mutilata), one mirror, a lastuga made of many-colored silk, and a sudi ear ornament" were stolen. Most pearls came from modern-day Sri Lanka, where divers dived into the ocean to find them, while mirrors and multicolored silk were made in China. In this case, the thief confessed, but claimed to have received no payment for the goods, which he no longer possessed. Despite his denials, he must have fenced the listed goods, which were all portable and easily resold.[91]

The Kharoshthi documents number more than a thousand, but they use the word "merchant" only once (for the Chinese merchants who knew the price of silk).[92] They mention a few robbery victims, who may or may not have been merchants. Does this mean there was minimal overland trade in a Silk Road town of the third and fourth centuries?

The unusual circumstances leading to the preservation of excavated documents mean that only a tiny portion of the original evidence survives. Still, the finds from Niya and Loulan do not consist of a single accidental find but multiple groups of documents, some deliberately buried, some carelessly discarded. These different caches of documents, with only one mention of "merchants," and the limited use of coins do indicate that the Silk Road trade of the third and fourth centuries CE in this area was indeed minimal. These documents clearly attest to the migration of people to Xinjiang from the Gandhara region of modern-day Pakistan and Afghanistan. They also show how often local kings dispatched envoys to neighboring kingdoms. But the evidence of private commerce is slight.

Read and analyzed as a group, the Kharoshthi documents illuminate the most important groups in Niya society in the third and fourth centuries. The local people, who farmed the land and maintained herds, recorded transfers of property witnessed by the cozbo and other officials. The king, living in Kroraina's capital, frequently wrote to the cozbo with instructions to investigate a wide range of matters. Other groups—Supi raiders, refugees from Khotan, runaways, envoys—came to the settlement, and officials tried to resolve the various conflicts that arose. The main innovation brought by the refugees from Gandhara—the technology for writing on wooden documents—allowed local officials to record a wide variety of disputes and property transfers, hardly any involving long-distance luxury trade.

In addition to their writing system, the refugees introduced Buddhist teachings, a religion new to the area that subsequently had an enormous impact on all of East Asia. The Gandharan migrants who arrived in Niya in the third and fourth centuries were already Buddhist devotees, many with Buddhist names. The documents refer to them using the standard Buddhist term *shramana*, usually translated as "monk." According to Buddhist *vinaya* law, all shramana should have adhered to vows of celibacy. But clearly the shramana at Niya did not. They lived with wives and children, and they engaged in the same kind of disputes over milk fees and the status of adopted children that embroiled ordinary people. Many of these Buddhists, even if called shramana, lived at home with their families.

Some Buddhists lived in distinct communities. One royal order records a set of rules issued to the "community of monks" at Niya by the "community of monks" in the capital, who appointed two elders to "be in charge of the monastery (viharavala)" to enforce these rules. The new rules concerned the *posatha* ceremony, on the first and fifteenth day of each lunar month, during which Buddhist rules were explained to the monastic community. Fines, in bolts of silk, were stipulated both for failing to attend the ceremony and for wearing "householder's dress." Such a regulation implies that members of the Buddhist order only wore Buddhist robes when attending group ceremonies.[93] Other documents confirm that the community of monks met as a body and constituted a legal entity that could witness the transfer of property and decide disputes.

Much of the evidence concerning Buddhism at Niya comes from house 24, the location of Rustam's archive. This was a big home, with ten rooms, one measuring 25 feet (8 m) by 19 feet (6 m), and clearly the residence of a well-off person. House 24 produced four documents not in Gandhari but in a form of hybrid Sanskrit that combined classic Sanskrit grammar and vocabulary with more vernacular forms. The four documents include a list of syllables used to memorize certain teachings, a fragment of the great Sanskrit epic the Mahabharata, a *pratimoksha* text listing rules for monks, and a long wooden plaque promising tangible benefits, including "a good complexion" and "a sweet-smelling body," and the ultimate promise of all Buddhist teachings, "an end of birth and death" to those who wash the image of the Buddha.[94] Clearly members of the Buddhist order participated in ceremonies like the bathing of the Buddha. House 24, with its large meeting room and additional nine rooms may have served as the main place for Buddhists to meet, and for some to reside on a full-time basis. Other Buddhists put on their lay clothing and returned to their families once the ceremonies had ended.

One tantalizing Kharoshthi letter has attracted the interest of many researchers because it uses the term "Mahayana," the Sanskrit word meaning Greater Vehicle. Adherents of the Greater Vehicle believed that even lay people could attain salvation. They applied the derogatory label Hinayana, or Lesser Vehicle, to these earlier teachings that limited the attainment of nirvana to only those who joined the monastic order. Historians of Buddhism have recently revised their earlier assessment of the black-and-white division between Hinayana and Mahayana.[95] Individual monks identified themselves as members of given school depending on the vows they took at ordination. These varied slightly among the different schools, of which the Sarvastivadins and Dharmaguptakas were the most active in Central Asia in the third and fourth centuries. Once ordained, some members of a given school chose to study Mahayana teachings, while others did not, with the result that followers of Mahayana teachings lived alongside those who did not accept the teachings.

The letter using the term "Mahayana" begins, as many letters do, with several phrases praising the virtues of the recipient, in this instance a local cozbo official named Shamasena: "At the feet of the great cozbo Shamasena, beloved of men and gods, honoured by men and gods, blessed with a good name, who set forth in the Mahayana who is of infinitely pleasing aspect, the tasuca . . . makes obeisance, and sends the health of his divine body, much, immeasurable." The phrase "set forth in the Mahayana" appears in at least two other inscriptions: one, written in the mid-third century, at Endere, praises the ruler of the Shanshan Kingdom, while the other, praising the Kushan ruler Huvishka, the successor of Kanishka, appears in a fourth-century manuscript from Bamiyan, Afghanistan.[96] The use of the phrase, though, does not reveal how Mahayana beliefs affected local Buddhist worship at Niya. Nor do the surviving materials indicate which schools of Buddhism were active at Niya.

Evidently stupa worship constituted an important focus for Buddhist worship at Niya, as it had for the migrants from Gandhara who left so many

SQUARE STUPA AT NIYA
This Buddhist stupa, square in shape, was unearthed in the 1990s. It measured 6.5 feet (2 m) on a side and was surrounded by a passageway for circumambulation 3.6–4.6 feet (1.1–1.4 m) across. The walkway was originally decorated with paintings, whose remnants are visible on the upper left-hand outer wall. Courtesy of Wang Binghua.

drawings of stupas along the Karakorum Highway. The site's most prominent ruin was a square-based stupa with a bowl-shaped top made from earthen bricks and grass-filled mud, shown in color plate 6. Located in the center of the settlement, it stands 23 feet (7 m) tall, with a base 18 feet (5.6 m) tall. Even in Aurel Stein's time robbers had emptied its central chamber—where Buddhist relics and sometimes objects of value given to the Buddhist order were placed—so that it slumped over slightly.

The Niya site contained a second Buddhist stupa, square in shape, whose remains were excavated by the Sino-Japanese expedition near house 5. Similar square structures have been found at other places along the southern Silk Road, including the site of Keriya, upriver from Khotan.[97] Buddhist devotees worshipped at these sites by walking clockwise around the perimeter of the square to express their devotion. The paintings in the passageway around the stupa at Niya portrayed individual buddhas, as is the case at Keriya, and no narrative scenes.

Stein found much more elaborate Buddhist structures, including a monastery, at the site of Miran, which lay to the east, about halfway to Loulan.[98] The use of the Brahmi script alongside Kharoshthi suggests that the site dated later than Niya, most likely to sometime after 400 CE. There Buddhist devotees walked around covered circular stupas, whose central pillar contained relics of the Buddha and whose walls portrayed different Buddhist scenes. The roofs of these round buildings had collapsed, so Stein and his men had to remove the sand to reach the original passageway where worshippers left offerings so long ago.

In one ruin, Miran 3 (M3), they uncovered a cloth landscape, illustrated with flowers of silk and cotton sewn onto a background (possibly by individual believers), and also scraps of cloth with Kharoshthi script on them, praying for the continued health of the donors' relatives. The wall paintings Stein found were particularly striking; on the lower edge of wall, below waist level, were paintings of sixteen winged figures, with distinctly Western-looking faces (shown in color plate 5B). The paintings above them survived only partially, but Stein was able to make out a Buddha and his disciples. The paintings formed a narrative depicting different scenes from the Buddha's life. Such narratives came from a later period than the individual portraits of the Buddha found at Niya.

Another building some 200 feet (60 m) away was, like M3, a round covered stupa with a painted corridor around it. More of the paintings survived at M5 than at M3, allowing Stein to identify a scene from the life of the Buddha, who appears while still a young prince riding a horse and leaving his father's palace. The artist signed his name "Tita" in Kharoshthi script and recorded the amount he had been paid. Stein, always quick to detect Western influence, concluded that Tita was the localized name of a Roman painter originally named Titus; even if the artist was really a Central Asian with a foreign name, the iconography of the painting, particularly the lower band showing cherubs among undulating wreaths, uses motifs borrowed from Roman art, perhaps brought by artists who came from the eastern edge of the Roman Empire in Syria or copied from sketchbooks.

The Kroraina Kingdom's residents continued to live in the harsh conditions of the desert kingdom until sometime in the fifth century. Surviving documents do not explain why the residents abandoned the sites of Loulan, Miran, and Niya. While some sites along the southern Silk Road, like Keriya, show clear signs of environmental degradation at the time they were abandoned, at Niya archeologists have found healthy petrified trees, some large enough to cut down for timber, dating to the third and fourth centuries.[99]

The Niya site gives every indication that the residents expected to return. They left a considerable amount of millet in different places, and they carefully buried documents and marked the holes so that they could find them again. They had sufficient warning to pack before leaving the site; Stein observed that they had left almost nothing of intrinsic value behind. Perhaps an attack by the Khotanese or the Supis prompted the residents to leave, and they were never able to return.

All we have to tell us about when the end came is a Chinese-language source by the famous Chinese monk and Buddhist pilgrim Faxian. In 401, he passed by Kroraina and wrote these subdued lines:

> The land is uneven and infertile. The clothing of ordinary people is coarse and the same as in the land of the Han people. The only difference is in felt and coarse cloth. Their country's king worships the dharma. It is possible that there are over four thousand monks; all are adherents of Hinayana. The ordinary people of various countries and the shramana all carry out the dharma of India, but to a greater or lesser degree.[100]

It is not clear exactly which city he visited, since the city of Loulan was abandoned in 376, when one regional dynasty replaced another that had been based there. Chinese official histories mention the Shanshan Kingdom in the first half of the fifth century; this was a period when a non-Chinese dynasty, called the Northern Wei, gradually conquered different regional dynasties in north China. The Shanshan rulers submitted to the Northern Wei in 450. Twenty years later, a Central Asian confederacy of tribes from north of the Gobi Desert, called the Rouran, occupied the Shanshan Kingdom.

The fifth century was a time of great turbulence in Central Asia, and traffic across the Taklamakan came to a halt. After the year 500 the Chinese histories no longer mention the Shanshan Kingdom as a destination, and most travelers shifted to the northern route around the Taklamakan, the subject of the next chapter.[101]

CHAPTER 2

Gateway to the Languages of the Silk Road
Kucha and the Caves of Kizil

As a meeting place for peoples of multiple nationalities, the Silk Road was a site of sustained language exchange in an era long before the development of modern learning aids like dictionaries and textbooks. Among the most dedicated language teachers were Buddhists who hoped to convey their sophisticated teachings as originally expressed in Sanskrit to potential converts. The residents of the prosperous oasis of Kucha on the northern route around the Taklamakan enjoyed an advantage over other language learners along the Silk Road, since their native language of Kuchean (a Kuchean document is shown on the opposite page) belonged to the same Indo-European language family as Sanskrit. Kucha (this is the Uighur pronunciation; the Chinese say Kuche) provided a natural gateway for the entry into China of Buddhist teachings. The oasis also afforded Buddhist teachers the opportunity to meet with multilingual travelers who came to Kucha—then the largest and most prosperous settlement on the northern Silk Road, rivaled only by Turfan.

Kucha's most famous native son, Kumarajiva (344–413), produced the first understandable translations of Buddhist works from Sanskrit into Chinese, greatly facilitating the subsequent spread of the new religion into China.[1] He was the lead translator of some three hundred different texts from Sanskrit into Chinese, of which the most famous is the Lotus Sutra. (Sutra is the Sanskrit term for a work credited to the Buddha; in fact, many took shape long after his death around 400 BCE.) Even though subsequent translators tried to improve on Kumarajiva's work, many of his translations, prized for their readability, continue to be used even today.

Kumarajiva was an unusually talented linguist, who, like many of Kucha's residents, had mastered multiple Central Asian languages including his native Kuchean, Chinese, Sanskrit, Gandhari, and possibly Agnean and Sogdian as well. Kumarajiva's father spoke Gandhari in his homeland of Gandhara, as did the immigrants to Niya. Sogdian prevailed in the area around Samarkand,

A SILK ROAD TRAVEL PASS

This travel pass in the Kuchean language, measuring 3 ¼ inches (8.3 cm) by 1 ¾ inches (4.4 cm) and written in Brahmi script, gives the name of the official inspecting a party of travelers going through a border station, the official to whom he is sending the report, and the name of the person carrying the pass. Over one hundred such passes have been found, which usually continue by listing the people and the animals traveling together, information missing from this document. Written with ink on notched poplar wood, these passes originally had a cover tied with twine and sealed, but no intact examples survive. Courtesy of Bibliothèque Nationale de France.

and Agnean was used along a stretch of the northern Silk Road centered on the settlement of Yanqi, roughly 250 miles (400 km) to the east of Kucha. Yanqi is the Chinese name; the Uighur is Qarashahr. Kumarajiva and his colleagues used the Brahmi script to read and write Kuchean and Sanskrit, and they may also have studied the Kharoshthi script, which stopped being used around 400.

This chapter will discuss these languages, especially the immense intellectual effort to understand the lost languages of Kuchean and Agnean after 1892. Scholars around the world spent almost one hundred years translating Kuchean, not only to decipher the language but also to understand how it differed from the closely related Indo-European language Agnean. The effort proved most worthwhile.

In Kumarajiva's lifetime, work began on building the world-famous caves of Kizil, located 42 miles (67 km) to the west of Kucha. The caves are one of the most appealing tourist sites in Xinjiang, and can be visited today by taking a car, train, or plane to Kucha or Korla, and then by ground transportation to the

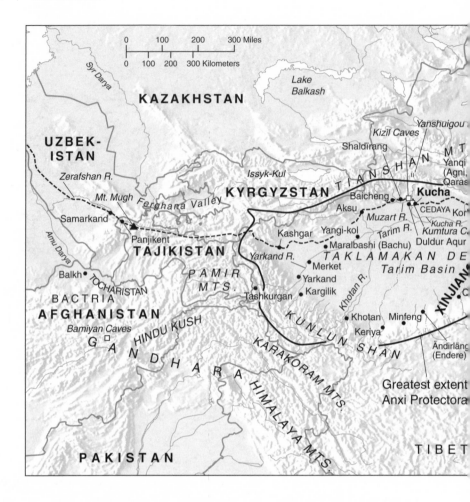

valley where the caves are located. But in the past, until about a century ago, almost everyone came by boat, down the many rivers fed by glacial runoff that flowed through the Taklamakan Desert. The largest river, the Tarim, runs along the northern edge of the desert, and two of its tributaries are near Kucha, the Kucha River and the Muzart River, which passes directly in front of the Kizil caves. The heavy demand for water in northwest China means that these rivers now carry much less water than they did in the past. Today, if one wants to cross the desert by boat, it has to be done in the early spring, when the water levels are at their highest. A century ago these rivers were navigable most of the year, except when blocked by ice.

To understand how dramatically different the Kucha region was just a century ago, one only has to read the splendid account by Sven Hedin of Sweden. In the fall of 1899 he purchased a barge 38 feet (12 m) long with a shallow draft

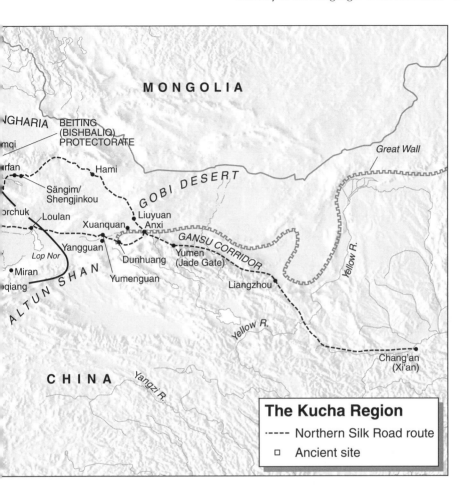

The Kucha Region

---- Northern Silk Road route

□ Ancient site

of just over a foot (30 cm). The deck accommodated Hedin's tent, his dark-room, and a clay fire pit for cooking. Alerted that the river would narrow near Maralbashi (modern-day Bachu), he bought a second boat "less than half the size" of the barge, and the two boats traveled together (see color plate 10).

Hedin began his voyage in the far western corner of Xinjiang in Yarkand, just southeast of modern Kashgar. He vividly depicted his departure on September 17, 1899, from the Lailik pier in Yarkand: "The wharf presented a lively scene. Carpenters were sawing and hammering, smiths were forging, and Cossacks [guards hired by Hedin] supervised the whole scene." On that day, Hedin recorded the width of the river at 440 feet (134 m) and the depth at 9 feet (3 m).[2]

After six days, Hedin reached the point where the Yarkand River divided into several smaller streams, each with its own perils.

The river-bed narrowed. We were carried along at breakneck speed by the current. The water seethed and foamed around us. We flew down a rapids. The passage was so narrow, and the turns so abrupt, that the boats could not be steered off; and the big boat struck the shore so violently, that my boxes were nearly carried overboard. . . . The water swirled all the way; and we moved so swiftly, that the barge nearly capsized when we struck the ground violently.

Suddenly the rapids ended, trapping the larger barge in the mud. It took thirty hired men to carry the barge overland so that the trip could resume.

Continuing down the river, Hedin followed the Yarkand River north to where it met the Aksu River, entering from the north, forming the start of the Tarim River. Hedin continued through the Taklamakan Desert, floating east. For leisure, he would go sailing on the smaller craft, while the larger barge followed behind. The river continued to flow at a vigorous pace of some 3–4 feet (1 m) per second, but the chunks of ice in it became larger and larger until, after an eighty-two-day trip that had taken him nearly 900 miles (1,500 km), Hedin called an end to his river journey at Yangi-kol, three days' travel from the oasis of Korla.[3] Had Hedin departed earlier in the summer, he could have gone the full distance to Kucha, still slightly more than 200 miles (300 km) away.

Hedin's exploration aroused great interest in Europe, leading to the organization of British, French, and German expeditions. The Germans launched three expeditions in quick succession. After literally tossing a coin, the leader of the third expedition, Albert von Le Coq, decided to go north to Kucha and arrived at the Kizil caves in 1906. He found one of the most beautiful religious sites in all of China, with a total of 339 caves carved into a hillside along a one-mile (2 km) stretch.[4] Some caves are small, while others range from 36 to 43 feet (11–13 m) in height and are 40 to 60 feet (12–18 m) deep. The Muzart River flows four miles (7 km) to the south. An oasis in front of the caves creates a lovely natural setting, where one can occasionally hear a cuckoo—a rare sound in modern China.

The Kizil hillside is composed of conglomerate, a rock so soft that caves could be easily carved out. It also made the caves fragile, so the original diggers often left a central pillar in the middle of caves for support. Over the centuries, earthquakes have done grave damage to the site, causing the outer rooms to collapse, leaving the interior rooms sometimes totally exposed to the elements. Le Coq described such an earthquake he and Theodor Bartus and their crew experienced in March, 1906:

A strange noise like thunder was followed quite suddenly by a great quantity of rocks rattling down from above. . . . The next moment—for everything happened with amazing speed—I saw Bartus and his workmen hurrying down the steep slope, and a procession of my Turkis [Uighurs], screaming after! I followed them, too, and in a flash we were down in the plain, pursued by great masses of rock, tearing past us with terrifying violence, without a single one of us being hurt—why or how I cannot understand to this very day!

I turned my eyes in the direction of the river and saw its waters in wild commotion—great waves beating against its banks. In the transverse valley, farthest up the stream, there suddenly rose an enormous cloud of dust, like a mighty pillar, rising to the heavens. At the same instant the earth trembled and a fresh roll, like pealing thunder, resounded through the cliffs. Then we knew it was an earthquake.[5]

Despite the precarious situation of the caves and the removal of many paintings by Le Coq and others, many paintings still remain at the site where today's visitors can view them. Several other sites in the immediate vicinity of Kizil contain caves with paintings, such as those at Kumtura, which are the most extensive and well worth visiting.

Many of the Kizil caves share the same structure: a room with a central stupa pillar for devotees to circumambulate. Since the time of the Buddha's death, devotees expressed their devotion by walking clockwise around his buried remains in north India, and they circumambulated the stupas in the Western Regions as well. Unlike the stupas at Niya and Miran, the central pillars built along the Silk Road did not contain relics of the Buddha. Instead, a niche in the pillar originally held a statue of the Buddha, most of which are now missing.

Cave 38 at Kizil, dated to 400 CE, is certainly one of the earliest and possibly the most visually appealing of all the caves.[6] The back wall of cave 38 shows the Buddha lying on his deathbed attended by the kings of different countries who came to offer their respects to him. Standing at the central pillar and looking back to the cave entrance, one views the Maitreya Buddha, the Buddha who presides over a future paradise, over the doorway.

Along the central spine of the arched ceiling of cave 38 are the Indian gods of the sun, moon, and wind, as well as two flaming buddhas and a two-headed Garuda, the legendary Indian bird who protects Buddhist law. Distinctly Indian in style, these were most likely painted by either artists from India or based on sketches brought from India. Le Coq calls the paintings "frescoes," but because

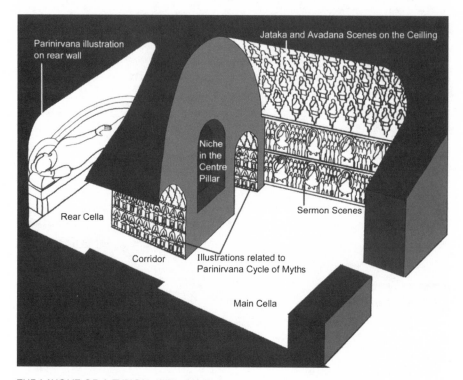

Parinirvana illustration on rear wall

Jataka and Avadana Scenes on the Ceilling

Niche in the Centre Pillar

Rear Cella

Sermon Scenes

Corridor

Illustrations related to Parinirvana Cycle of Myths

Main Cella

THE LAYOUT OF A TYPICAL KIZIL CAVE

Many caves at Kizil originally had the same structure. Visitors passed through an anteroom and entered the main room through a door. They demonstrated their devotion by walking around the central stupa pillar, which held a statue of the Buddha and was decorated with rocks and boughs of wood to represent Mount Sumeru, the mountain at the heart of the Buddhist cosmos. Often, only the holes that originally held these decorations are still visible. The back wall showed a painting of the Buddha on his deathbed. Courtesy of the Freer Gallery of Art and Arthur M. Sackler Gallery, Smithsonian Institution, Washington, DC.

they were painted on dry plaster, they are not technically frescoes, a term reserved for paintings done on wet plaster. The cave construction techniques themselves came from India, adopted from the magnificent caves at Ajanta, outside Bombay, and other sites built by early Buddhists.

On each side of the central ridge of cave 38 are rows of diamond-shaped lozenges with postage-stamp edges fitting neatly into one another. The rows alternate *avadana* stories with *jataka* stories, which recounted the previous lives of the Buddha. Avadana stories, also called cause-and-effect stories, show a seated Buddha with a figure alongside; these allegorical tales about the Buddha taught listeners the relationship between their behavior in this life and its long-term effects in future lives.

Usually jataka tales reinterpreted preexisting Indian folk tales to teach Buddhist values. The tale of the monkey king, for example, told of a band of monkeys

KIZIL CAVE PAINTING

This detail from the barrel roof of a Kizil cave shows the characteristic postage-stamp lozenges local artists used to depict scenes from the Buddha's earlier lives. Each lozenge portrays a major event from a single jataka tale, affording local storytellers an opportunity to tell the whole story for the entertainment of visitors to the caves.

who stole fruit from a king's garden. The king's guards chased the monkeys to a wide river, and their leader made his body into a bridge so that they could cross. Then he fell into the river and died. This traditional folktale, according to the Buddhist explanation, illustrated the willingness of the Buddha, here the monkeys' leader, to sacrifice himself for others.

Another jataka tale, shown in several caves, particularly appealed to merchants. It told of a group of five hundred merchants traveling at night. When it became so dark that they could no longer see, their leader—the Buddha in a previous existence—wrapped his arms in white felt, which he drenched with butter, lit like torches, and lifted up to illuminate the merchants' path. In this tale, too, the Buddha sacrificed for the sake of others. Devotees who listened to monks tell these jataka tales understood nirvana as something that only the Buddha and few other eminent monks could attain, a key teaching of the early Buddhists.

Today the biggest cave at Kizil (no. 47) stands empty. Fifty-five feet (16.8 m) tall, it originally held a large statue of the Buddha, which would have been visible from far away to travelers coming to the site along the Muzart River. This kind of monumental Buddha cave did not originate at Kizil; the Bamiyan caves of Afghanistan contained similar giant statues, which the Kizil cave builders must have known about. Five rows of holes for wooden posts on both sides of this large cave suggest they originally supported platforms for smaller Buddha figures flanking the larger image. Other caves at Kizil held large Buddha images, no longer in place, and a visiting Chinese monk reported that two Buddha figures, each more than 90 Chinese feet (roughly 90 feet, or 28 m) high, stood outside the western gate of the city and were worshipped at a major festival every five years.[7]

Even the most casual visitor to the Kizil caves today notices the many gashes in the cave walls where sections were removed. All the world's major collections of East Asian art contain paintings displaying the still-fresh deep lapis lazuli blues and malachite greens of Kizil art; most were removed before the outbreak of World War I in 1914. The German holdings in Berlin are particularly extensive.

Le Coq pioneered a new technique for removing the fragile paintings, which he proudly described:

> The process of cutting away the frescoes is somewhat as follows:
>
> The pictures are painted on a special surface-layer, made out of clay mixed up with camel dung, chopped straw, and vegetable fiber, which is smoothed over and covered with a thin layer of stucco.
>
> To begin with, the picture must be cut round with a very sharp knife—care being taken that the incision goes right through the surface-layer—to the proper size for the packing cases. The cases for transport by carts may be large, somewhat smaller for camels, and smallest for horses. . . .
>
> Next, a hole must be made with the pickaxe in the wall at the side of the painting to make space to use the fox-tail saw; in the excavated

rock-temples, as we have said, this space often has to be made with hammer and chisel in the solid rock, which fortunately is very soft.[8]

This step-by-step description has a chilling effect, as one can easily imagine the damage inflicted on the art. Some Europeans thoroughly disapproved of removing the paintings. Le Coq's colleague Albert Grünwedel felt, instead, that the sites should be sketched and carefully measured so that, if desired, replicas could be made in Europe. His was the minority view at the time.

A year after the arrival of the Third Expedition, the French scholar Paul Pelliot came to Kucha for an eight-month stay in 1907 when he collected many important documents in the local language of Kuchean. He also devoted one month to exploring the routes north through the Tianshan Mountains. Following the Muzart River north out of Kizil, he found two routes that connected the Tarim Basin with the grasslands to the north.[9] These grasslands, spanning the northern half of Xinjiang (Zungharia), modern-day Kazakhstan, and neighboring Uzbekistan, were home to a succession of nomadic peoples, who posed a continuous threat to successive Chinese dynasties over the centuries.

Kucha's location on the route to the grasslands of Central Asia led to its earliest appearance in official Chinese histories. When, at the end of the second century BCE, the emperor Han Wudi sent the general Li Guangli to visit the ruler of the Ferghana kingdom in modern-day Uzbekistan, he traveled via Kucha.[10] Like the rulers of the Loulan kingdom, the rulers of Kucha did their best to maintain good relations with both the Han dynasty and its enemy, the Xiongnu confederation, which controlled the grasslands of modern Mongolia. Between 176 and 101 BCE, the rulers of Kucha acknowledged the superiority of the Xiongnu by sending their sons to live with them. It was customary for subordinate kingdoms to send their crown princes to live with their most important allies so that they could learn their language and familiarize themselves with their customs.

But when the Xiongnu weakened, the rulers of the Kucha kingdom shifted their allegiance to the Han dynasty in the first century BCE.[11] The king of Kucha and his wife traveled to the Han-dynasty capital in Chang'an in 65 BCE, where they stayed for a year. In 60 BCE, the Han dynasty appointed a governor general, its official in charge of the Western Regions, to oversee its operations in Central Asia. This was the office that supplied the center with the information about different oasis kingdoms of the northwest, which is recorded in the dynastic histories. The official history of the Han dynasty gives the population of Kucha as 81,317, making it the largest oasis on the northern route.[12] Little evidence of Han rule survives in the region itself. The Chinese headquarters were in modern-day Cedaya (Luntai County, Kucha), where the ruin of a Han-dynasty settlement has been found.[13] In 46 BCE Kucha fell to the neighboring oasis state of Yarkand.

The constant jockeying for power among the different Central Asian states meant that the Han dynasty was able to keep control of its garrison only intermittently. The Han general Ban Chao was named governor general in 91 CE, and managed to reestablish Chinese control in Kucha and place members of the Bai family on the throne. But less than twenty years later, in 107, several oasis kingdoms rose up against Chinese rule, and the Chinese again lost control of the garrison. Starting at this point, and continuing in later centuries, the Bai family regained power and ruled Kucha, sometimes in their own right, sometimes after submitting to a neighboring power.

By the fourth century, when Kumarajiva was born, Kucha was an established center for Buddhist studies. Several translators with the family name Bai, most from the royal family of Kucha, participated in the translation effort. In the third century, the earliest dated evidence of Buddhism in Kucha,[14] many were active in the Sarvastivadin school, which subscribed to Hinayana teachings.[15] The residents of Kucha learned about Buddhism from Indian missionaries. The third and fourth centuries marked the peak of Indian influence, as illustrated by the ease with which Kumarajiva and his parents traveled between India and Kucha.

Kucha provided the perfect environment for the future translator to grow up in. The oasis kingdom had extensive ties with Gandhara, because the rivers across the Taklamakan led to the southern oases of Yarkand and Khotan, from where travelers crossed through the mountains to reach Gandhara. Kumarajiva's father was an Indian prince, the son of a high minister, who left Gandhara so that he could pursue his studies of Buddhism at Kucha. When the king of Kucha pressured him to marry his younger sister, Kumarajiva's father reluctantly assented to the match. The child of this union, Kumarajiva grew up speaking Gandhari and the indigenous language, Kuchean.

Kumarajiva's mother was a devout Buddhist who did not want to live a married life. When Kumarajiva was seven years old, she requested permission to join a Buddhist order, but her husband refused. After she went on a hunger strike of six days, her husband gave in, and she entered a nunnery, taking Kumarajiva with her. Kucha was one of the few places outside India where women could take vows; one Buddhist text lists four nunneries at Kucha with between 50 and 170 nuns each.[16]

After studying in Kucha, Kumarajiva traveled with his mother to Gandhara to study texts with a Hinayana teacher. Kumarajiva then moved to what is now Kashgar for further study with a Mahayana teacher. He later returned

COMMEMORATING KUMARAJIVA

An imposing bronze statue of Kumarajiva greets all visitors to the Kizil caves, evidence of the translator's fame even today. In fact, we have no idea what Kumarajiva actually looked like. Since no portraits survive, the sculptor based this entirely on his imagination. Courtesy of Takeshi Watanabe.

to Kucha, where he converted some monks to Mahayana teachings. Although later Buddhist sources assert a sharp division between Hinayana and Mahayana teachings, the situation was much more fluid during Kumarajiva's lifetime. When a young man entered the Buddhist order, he took vows from a monk ordained in a given Buddhist lineage. Membership in a lineage, like the Sarvastavadins, did not determine whether one followed Hinayana or Mahayana teachings. One could begin by studying Hinayana texts, as Kumarajiva did, and then study Mahayana texts. Monks who identified with the two schools lived side by side in the same monasteries and apparently saw no problem in doing so.[17]

Yet in practice some differences between Hinayana and Mahayana teachings were obvious. Where Hinayana monks believed that it was acceptable to eat meat as long as an animal had not been killed expressly to feed them, Mahayana monks refused all meat. One later traveler noticed that Kuchean monks ate meat, scallions, and leeks—all banned by Mahayana orders—and concluded that Kucha must be predominantly Hinayana.[18]

In 384, when Kumarajiva was around forty years old, his home city of Kucha fell to the armies of a general named Lü Guang. A description of the city at this time survives:

> The city wall had three overlapping enclosures and was equal in area to Chang'an. The pagodas and temples inside numbered in the thousands. The palace of the Bai kings was imposing and lovely like the residence of the gods. The non-Chinese of the city lived luxurious and rich lives. Their homes had stores of grape wine verging on a thousand piculs [about 500 gallons, or 2,000 L] that did not spoil even after ten years. The soldiers drowned themselves in the wine of the successive households that stored it.[19]

After his forces took the city, Lü Guang sent Kumarajiva to his capital at Liangzhou (now Wuwei, Gansu) as an expression of his piety. Although Kumarajiva had taken a vow of celibacy, he was, the general believed, too great a teacher not to father his own children. Accordingly, the general made him drink too much and then tricked him into sleeping with a young woman. This is the first of three occasions on which according to Kumarajiva's biographers he violated his vows.

Kumarajiva was kidnapped a second time, and was sent to modern-day Xi'an in 401 on the order of Yao Xing, the ruler of a regional dynasty called the Later Qin (reigned 394–416). Hoping that Kumarajiva would father his own "dharma seeds," the king encouraged Kumarajiva to establish a household outside the monastery where he lived with multiple concubines. In a third incident, recorded in the official histories, Kumarajiva, of his own volition, requested a woman and fathered twins by her.[20] Because of the strong conventions shaping Buddhist biographies, and the variations among surviving biographies of Kumarajiva, scholars are not certain whether these three incidents actually occurred. Still, these variant accounts, they concur, do show that around the year 400 CE laypeople were not surprised when Buddhist monks broke their vows of celibacy.[21]

Kumarajiva's transgressions did not diminish his prominence as a Buddhist teacher. In 401, when Kumarajiva came to Chang'an, the ruler Yao Xing named him head of a translation bureau, which he directed until his death in 413. Kumarajiva's lasting legacy was his translations of Buddhist texts from Sanskrit to Chinese.[22] The best-known text of all of Kumarajiva's translations was the Lotus Sutra, a Mahayana text that disparaged earlier Hinayana teachings and promised salvation to everyone who recited even a single verse.[23]

Although earlier translators had produced Chinese translations of Sanskrit originals, many of their texts contained so much technical vocabulary that only the few Chinese who had studied Sanskrit could comprehend them. Most of these early Buddhist translations were done in the same way: a Buddhist teacher, usually from India, recited a text he had memorized and explained its contents orally. His disciples then recorded what he had said in Chinese. The early system of translation caused many errors: the teacher could not read what his students wrote, and they could not be certain that they had understood him.[24]

Making translation particularly difficult, Chinese and Sanskrit belong to two different language families; Sanskrit, like other ancient Indo-European languages, is highly inflected. Verbs and nouns take a wide variety of forms, depending on their role in the sentence. A member of the Sino-Tibetan language family, Chinese is grammatically much simpler; nouns and verbs do not change form, with the result that the meaning of a sentence hinges on word order, with much resulting ambiguity. In 400 CE the best a language student could hope for was a bilingual text that gave the same sentence side by side in different languages.

Kumarajiva's great innovation was to found a translation bureau whose staff could check the Chinese translations against the Indian originals. Their translations, credited to Kumarajiva, are famous for their readability. Even Chinese who did not know any Sanskrit could understand them, and the language flowed so beautifully that many Chinese readers preferred Kumarajiva's fluent versions to subsequent, more accurate texts.

The successes of Kumarajiva and other translators made thousands of Buddhist texts accessible to Chinese readers, and they developed a system, still used today, of assigning certain Chinese characters and their sounds to represent each syllable of foreign words. This is the basis of the modern Chinese spelling system of pinyin, which renders Coca Cola as *Kekou kele* and McDonald's as *Maidanglao*. Kumarajiva's name was pronounced something like Kuw-ma-la-dzhip.[25] Due to changes in Chinese over the centuries, his name today is rendered in pinyin as Jiumoluoshi.[26]

The significance of this practice—of writing Chinese that incorporated elements of the spoken language to better capture the sense of the Sanskrit originals—caused Chinese itself to change. Victor Mair, professor of Chinese at the University of Pennsylvania, estimates that the vocabulary of Chinese expanded by as many as 35,000 words—not just Buddhist terms like the Sanskrit word for "sagacity" (*prajna*) but also secular words like "moment." The encounter with Sanskrit also helped the Chinese to better comprehend the phonology of their own language. The Chinese, for example, did not realize their language was tonal, something first-year students of Chinese learn on day one. It was only at this time that they came to a systematic understanding of the tonal properties inherent in their speech.[27]

During the same centuries that Kumarajiva and his colleagues were working in Chang'an, other translators throughout Central Asia were engaged in the same long-term enterprise of making Buddhist texts originally written in Sanskrit available in local languages. One of the most important local languages was Kuchean, different in important respects from the indigenous language spoken in nearby Yanqi, called Agnean. Like so many research endeavors involving the Silk Road, the process of discovery has been fraught with setbacks, massive intellectual detours, and controversy. It required almost a century of scholarly work around the world to finally understand the relationship between these two languages.

The first hint that a lost language we now know to be Kuchean existed came in 1892. In that year, the Russian consul living in Kashgar purchased a document written in the familiar Brahmi script, known to scholars of Sanskrit, but in a language that was definitely not Sanskrit. The meaning of the text frustrated scholars for years. First, even after more texts in the same language were subsequently discovered, there was frustratingly little material to study: most of what survives today consists of individual leaf-shaped sheets of paper from different texts and some business and administrative documents on wood. Moreover, almost all of these texts are undated.[28]

Yet by 1908 two German scholars, Emil Sieg and Wilhelm Siegling, had deciphered the unknown language using a bilingual text giving the same school exercises word for word in Sanskrit and the unknown language. Sieg and Siegling did not know of any document giving the name of the language, so they chose one for it on the basis of a short colophon. (A colophon is a passage giving the name of each chapter of a text, the title of the full text, and the name of the text's author and/or copyist. In addition it may give the date on which the text was copied and the name of the donor who paid for the text to be copied by hand.)

The colophon was for a Uighur, or old Turkic, Buddhist text entitled the Maitreyasamiti (Meeting with the Maitreya). Uighur is a Turkic language spoken by the peoples living in the grasslands of what is now Mongolia who moved into the Tarim Basin in the mid-ninth century.[29] The colophon recorded that the text had been translated from the "Indian language" into "Twghry" and from "Twghry" into Uighur.[30] "Twghry," Sieg and Siegling concluded, had to be the Uighur name for the unknown language. Since the Maitreyasamiti text existed only in Uighur and the newly discovered language, it was a brilliantly plausible identification.

Sieg and Siegling went on to argue that Twghry was the Uighur spelling of Tocharian, the language of the Tocharoi, the ancient people known to the Greeks who lived the Bactrian region of Afghanistan, around the city of Balkh in today's Pakistan. Further, they identified the Tocharoi with the Yuezhi, one of the tribes who founded the Kushan dynasty. Sieg and Siegling accepted the traditional Chinese account that, around 200 BCE, the Yuezhi broke into two groups, the Lesser Yuezhi in Gansu and the Greater Yuezhi in the Ferghana valley. Still, Sieg and Siegling could not explain why all the documents in the new language had been found on the northern route, far from either the putative homeland of the Yuezhi in Gansu Province or where they settled in the Ferghana valley of modern Uzbekistan.[31]

Later commentators have struggled to reconcile the account of Yuezhi migrations in the dynastic histories with more recent discoveries. One has suggested that, despite the wording in the histories, the original Yuezhi homeland was not limited to the Dunhuang region but extended across all of Xinjiang and Gansu.[32] Another has proposed that the Yuezhi left Gansu speaking Tocharian but then switched to the Iranian language of Bactrian when they got to Afghanistan.[33] Still, when the descendants of the Yuezhi arrived at Niya, they were speaking yet another language, Gandhari, which is an Indic, not an Iranian, language. All of these proposals cast further doubt on the traditional Chinese description of the Yuezhi migrations and on the accuracy of the name Tocharian.

In 1938 W. B. Henning offered a different, more persuasive explanation for Twghry. He noticed that the term "Four Twghry" (sometimes without the final y) appeared in a handful of documents in Sogdian, Middle Persian, and Uighur, composed sometime in the early ninth century.[34] The term "Four Twghry" referred to a region spanning Beiting (Beshbaliq in Uighur), Turfan, and Yanqi, but not Kucha. Henning proposed that the Twghry language was originally spoken across the northern edge of the Taklamakan from Turfan and Beiting in the east to Yanqi in the west, but that it died out first in Turfan and Beiting, and then finally in Yanqi, where it was ultimately replaced by Uighur, the language still spoken throughout Xinjiang.[35] Henning's proposal has not been universally accepted, but it has the great virtue of accounting for the geographic distribution of documents in the Twghry language.

In fact, we know that the Yuezhi used Bactrian, an Iranian language written in Greek characters, as an official language.[36] For this reason, Tocharian is a misnomer; no extant evidence suggests that the residents of the Tocharistan region of Afghanistan spoke the Tocharian language recorded in the documents found in the Kucha region. Although Sieg and Siegling were mistaken in linking the Twghry language with the Tocharoi peoples of Afghanistan, their name for the new language caught on.

Sieg and Siegling divided the surviving manuscripts into two dialects, A and B, separate languages now known as Tocharian A and Tocharian B. The two languages belong to the Indo-European family of languages: like Sanskrit, both were highly inflected, with a complex system of verbs and nouns that changed endings depending on their role in each sentence. Tocharian A and Tocharian B shared many vocabulary items, an indication that both diverged from an unknown common source language.

The eminent twentieth-century American linguist George Sherman Lane felt that the differences between the two languages were so great that the languages must have developed independently of each other for perhaps one thousand years, and certainly five hundred.[37] Since Tocharian A and Tocharian B were in fact quite different, as different as French and Spanish are today, a speaker of one could not understand someone speaking the other.[38]

Given the region in which they were used—the northern route of the Taklamakan—it was logical to assume that the two Tocharian languages would share many elements with the Indo-Iranian branch of the Indo-European languages spoken in the neighboring regions of Iran and India. But the two Tocharian languages turn out to have much more in common with German, Greek, Latin, and Celtic than with any Iranian or Sanskritic languages. A professor of English at University of Idaho, Douglas Q. Adams, proposes that "it is possible, on the basis of these relationships with Germanic, Greek, etc., to 'place' Tocharian geographically in the late Proto-Indo-European world in some manner, say, between the Germanic (on the 'north'?) and Greek (on the 'south'?)."[39] Adams's tentative phrasing suggests that sometime in the distant past, probably between 3000 and 2000 BCE, the language that would develop into Tocharian A and B calved off from the mother language of Proto-Indo-European at a time between when German speakers and when Greek speakers left the Proto-Indo-European population. Given how little we know of ancient migrations, and the risks of using linguistic evidence to reconstruct migrations, we cannot identify a homeland for the ancient speakers of Tocharian before they moved to the Tarim basin. It is also possible that other Indo-European languages more similar to Tocharian A and B were spoken in Central Asia but that no material in these lost languages survives.

One conclusion is certain, though: the peoples living in Central Asia were always moving, and the languages spoken in a given region often changed as a result. Chinese-language records document the successive displacement of peoples resulting from the Xiongnu expansion in the second century BCE, with the rise of the Turks (a people the Chinese called Tujue, who were distant ancestors of the modern Turks of Turkey) in the sixth century, and the migration of the Uighurs (who also spoke a language in the Turkic language family) into Xinjiang in the ninth century.[40] Similar displacements could easily have occurred with the migration of different tribal peoples in the distant past, before any records survive. The norm in Central Asia was linguistic change, not linguistic continuity.

Since the time of Sieg and Siegling, linguists have clarified the relationship between the two languages they called Tocharian A (more accurately called Agnean) and Tocharian B (now recognized to be Kuchean). In 2007, a scholar at the Austrian Academy of Sciences, Melanie Malzahn, did a census of all extant manuscripts in Agnean. She put the total number of extant leafs and fragments at 1150.[41] The complete leafs total no more than fifty.[42]

Of the Agnean manuscripts, 383 came from a single scriptorum at Shorchuk, southwest of Yanqi on the road to Korla.[43] None of the surviving documents gives the name of the language itself, but since almost all were found near Yanqi—the town called Agni in Sanskrit—scholars prefer to call this language Agnean, the term we will use henceforth.[44] The surviving manuscripts hint that the residents of Yanqi (Agni) and Turfan may have spoken Agnean in the early centuries of the Common Era, when Iranians living to the west first introduced the teachings of Buddhism.

The longest manuscript in Agnean has twenty-five consecutive leafs with no significant gaps—unlike the individual leafs that survive in most cases. It is a jataka story with many of the same plot elements as the classic Coppélia tale. It tells of a prince named Punyavan, a Sanskrit name meaning "Possessing Merit," who competes for the throne of his country against his four brothers (Possessing Virile Force, Possessing Technical Skill, Possessing Good Looks, and Possessing Sagacity). In the Agnean version of this text, which differs both from the Sanskrit original and later Chinese and Tibetan versions, the contest among the princes occupies only two of the seventeen leafs. The rest of the text is devoted to long speeches in which each prince describes his own attribute.

In the story Possessing Sagacity tells, a young painter falls in love with a mechanical doll created by an artisan, who left the doll in the painter's room overnight. When the painter reaches for her, she breaks into pieces, and the painter responds by hanging himself from a cord connected to the wall. After the artisan discovers the artist's suicide, he summons the neighbors and the authorities. As they arrive, he prepares to cut the cord from which the corpse hangs. At that moment, the painter emerges from behind the wall and says to the artisan: "A painting is one thing, a painter another." The artist's trompe l'oeil painting of himself hanging was his response to the animated doll, which utterly lacked sagacity.[45] This memorable story taught the advantages of sagacity to its audience, most likely students in a monastery.

A manuscript found by the Germans at Sängim (Shengjinkou in Chinese), just outside of Turfan, illustrates the different uses of the two Tocharian languages most clearly. The text is in Agnean, with nineteen explanatory notes in Kuchean and two in Uighur. As Lane explains, "It should be abundantly clear that we are dealing with the glossing of a Tocharian A [Agnean] text by a newcomer whose monastery language, at least, was dialect B [Kuchean], and to whom the 'old' monastery language of the area was not familiar. His own native speech may have been Turkish [Uighur]."[46] By the sixth, seventh, and eighth centuries, then, Agnean had become almost entirely a written language used exclusively by Buddhists inside monasteries. Surviving Agnean texts display no regional differences, another sign that the language had largely ossified. Outside the monasteries, most of the people living in the region of Yanqi and Turfan were speaking either Chinese or Uighur.

Kuchean and Agnean differ in important ways. The Kuchean language displays regional variants, the product of evolving use over time in different places, as well as clear stages of development: archaic, classical, late, and colloquial.[47] In 1989 the leading scholar of Tocharian, the French scholar Georges-Jean Pinault, calculated the total number of documents in Kuchean to be 3,120.[48] He has since revised his count upward to 6,060 to include newly available fragments from Berlin. Still, the total number of intact leaves remains no more than two hundred.[49]

At the beginning of the twentieth century, Pelliot collected some two thousand of these fragments, most in the immediate vicinity of a monastery in Duldur Aqur, 12 miles (20 km) south of Kucha.[50] Unlike the texts in Agnean, these texts give the name of the language in which they are written as Kuchean.[51] Kuchean was used in a broader geographic region, all along the northern edge of the Taklamakan, with the core area in Kucha, but extending as far east as Turfan, and overlapping with the Agnean core area of Yanqi.

Many of the Chinese and Kuchean materials came from a single library, Pelliot's notes suggest, where a wall had collapsed, preserving the contents, and where a subsequent fire heavily damaged the documents. Pelliot unearthed the surviving records from more than one place. The religious documents were from the sanctuaries and stupas inside the monastery, while the administrative documents must have come from the edge of the monastery.[52]

At the end of the fifth century, when the inhabitants of Kucha were speaking Kuchean, Central Asia entered a particularly unsettled period as various tribal confederations, including the Rouran (also known as the Ruirui and Ruanruan in China and as the Avars in Europe) and the Hephthalites, vied for control of the major trade routes. After conquering both Kucha and Yanqi, the Avar confederacy eventually broke apart, only to be succeeded in 552 by the Turks (Tujue in Chinese), who formed another powerful confederacy that conquered Kucha and Yanqi, leaving the local rulers in place. After 552, the brother of the founder of the Turkish confederacy led a series of successful military campaigns to the west, conquering parts of Xinjiang and lands extending all the way to the Black Sea. The two brothers eventually formed a dual Turkic kaghanate in which the founder retained control of eastern territories, while his brother, the leader of the Western kaghanate, accepted a subordinate role. Over time, this relationship grew more formal, and by 580 distinct Eastern and Western kaghanates had taken shape.[53] Recognizing the Western kaghan as their overlord, the rulers of Kucha paid tribute to them and provided troops when asked.

The Bai-family kings continued to rule Kucha in the sixth through the eighth centuries, the official Chinese histories confirm. Frequently repeating the contents of earlier histories, the compilers of the histories concur that the kingdom was wealthy and sent valuable tribute to the Chinese. The official history of the Wei dynasty, composed 551–54, is the first to report that the people of the kingdom paid their taxes using silver coins: "The customs of the local people are licentious. They have established a market where women are sold and officials collect the coins that men pay." The same official history also reports the existence of an unusual natural resource: "In the middle of the mountains to the northwest is a river formed from an ointment-like substance that travels some distance before it enters the soil. It is like clarified butter and has a foul odor. When applied to hair or teeth that have fallen out, it makes them grow back, and the sick who take it are all cured." This mysterious substance has been identified as petroleum.[54] Today Korla is one of China's most important oil fields.

The official history of the Northern dynasties, written about a century later, reports that those cultivating the land paid their tax in grain while everyone else paid in silver. It lists different products from Kucha: fine carpets, copper, iron, lead, deer skins (used to make boots), ammonium chloride (an important flux used in metallurgy and textile dying), felt wall coverings, white and yellow powder used for makeup, incense, fine horses, and cattle.[55] When a Chinese monk visited the kingdom in 629, he reported that the people used gold, silver coins, and small copper coins.[56]

Although these sources all say that silver coins were used in Kucha, to date only bronze coins have been excavated, most likely because anyone who uncovered silver coins in later generations would have melted them down. Pelliot found a clay vessel holding 1,300 coins, of which 1,105 are now held in the Cabinet des Médailles in Paris. These include coins from the Han and the successor dynasties of the third century but none from the Tang. The curator of the collection, François Thierry, dates the horde to somewhere between the third and seventh centuries, preferring a date in the sixth or seventh century.[57] Finds of molds for coins and even two copper foundries confirm that the Bai-family kings of Kucha had everything they needed to mint bronze coins locally.

Surviving accounts written in Kuchean that give the expenditures, receipts, and balances of Buddhist monasteries show that the monasteries spent bronze coins.[58] These accounts list cash expenditures for sugar and for alcohol for musicians who performed at a ceremony. Monasteries also bought supplies, like oil, for ceremonies and paid millers to grind grain.

The monasteries also received some goods in kind. Certain donors gave foodstuffs for the support of monks as well as the dependents who lived on and worked the monastic lands. Villagers paid sheep and goats to the monastery, on some occasions to clear debts. Kuchean had a rich vocabulary for describing sheep and goats, whether male or female, that were young, middle-aged, or old (literally "with a large tooth," since the mature animals had permanent central incisors).[59] In one transaction, the elders exchanged two goats for 250 pounds of barley and a sheep for 200 pounds of grain; the measures of barley and grain functioned as money, and there is no mention of coins of any kind. These monastic accounts mention only goods that were produced within the oasis itself, giving the impression that the monasteries were largely self-sufficient and did not participate in any long-distance trade.

The Kuchean language in the sixth through eighth centuries was clearly still a living language used by monastic officials for accounts, kings for royal orders, historians for their chronicles, travelers for graffiti, and devotees to label their offerings to monasteries. In addition, storytellers used Kuchean to tell Buddhist narratives. Like later transformation texts in Chinese, these tales alternate prose passages with poetry. The poetry sections are preceded by the name of a musical tune, which indicated to the storyteller how they should be sung.[60] Three phrases—"here," "after that," and "anew"—occur in manuscripts recounting the well-known story of the Buddha's birth, luxurious childhood, departure from the palace, discovery of human suffering, and eventual enlightenment. These same phrases appear in boxes underneath narrative scenes in the caves of Kizil (cave 110) and Kumtura (cave 34), serving there as captions to the illustrations. When the storytellers told the narratives shown in the paintings, they would point to a certain scene and say, "This the place where . . ."[61] Kuchean was still spoken at a time when Agnean had largely died out, but, after 800, Kuchean also fell from active use.[62]

Some Kuchean documents dwell not on Buddhism but on the far more prosaic subject of trade. A fascinating series of Kuchean texts found by Pelliot and also published by Pinault describe the caravan traffic in and out of Kucha. In January 1907 a local person brought Pelliot a half-dozen wooden tablets with Brahmi script on them from the Buddhist ruins some distance from the pass of Yanshuigou.[63] Pelliot then went to a still-functioning tax station near Shaldïrang, a small place in the mountains north of Kucha, on the pass through the mountains to Baicheng. On top of a cliff among the ruins of a guard tower, Pelliot found a total of 130 travel passes 8 inches (20 cm) beneath the snow.

The Kucha king's officials issued these travel passes to caravans after recording a headcount of the individual members of each caravan—first human, then animal. They did not write down the goods that each caravan carried. At each station, the caravans handed in their current passes and received new ones, which is why Pelliot found over one hundred discarded passes at Yanshuigou.

Even though paper was widely available in Kucha and was used for monastic accounts and letters, officials made the passes from wood slips cut from poplar trees, which were cheaper than paper. Averaging about 4 inches (10 cm) long and 2 inches (5 cm) high, the passes show considerable variation in size (shown in the photo at the beginning of the chapter). Like the Kharoshthi documents on wood found at Niya, these Kuchean documents consisted of two parts that fitted together. An outer wooden envelope partially covered an interior wooden slip (sometimes slips) so that the contents could not be seen from the outside: only the name of the official at the postal station was visible.[64]

Although the size of the passes varied, the contents followed a fixed format: they recorded the name of the sending official, the receiving official's name and address, an introductory greeting, and the name of the traveler carrying the pass. A list of the members of the party followed: first men, then women, then donkeys, horses, and cattle. The use of the unabbreviated forms of numerals indicates that these were formal administrative documents. The documents close with an exhortation: "Let them pass. If their party is more than what is listed here, do not allow them to pass." Finally, the documents give the year of the king's reign, the month, and the day, as well as a statement of verification by a witness. These documents all date to 641–44, the closing years of the reign of the Kuchean king Suvarnadeva (reigned 624–46), and they document the close government scrutiny under which caravans proceeded from one permitted destination to the next.

Pinault has provided a helpful chart of all those passes listing the people and animals in each caravan. Of the thirteen instances in which the number of men with each caravan is given, nine caravans had fewer than ten men, while the

TABLE 2.1 COMPOSITION OF CARAVANS IN KUCHA, 641–644

Document No.	Men	Women	Donkeys	Horses	Cattle
1	20	–	3	1	–
2	–	–	–	–	4
3	2	–	–	–	–
5	10	–	–	5	1
12	–	–	–	3	–
15	–	–	–	3	–
16	4	–	–	–	2
21	3	–	15	–	–
25	5	1	–	–	–
30	6	10	4	–	–
31	–	–	–	–	5
33	32	–	–	7	–
35	3	–	12	–	–
37	2	–	2	–	–
44	3	–	–	4	–
50	8	–	–	17	–
64	–	X	X	3	–
79	–	–	–	–	2
80	40	–	–	–	–
95	–	–	–	10	–

Source: Georges-Jean Pinault, "Épigraphie koutchéenne: I. Laisser-passer de caravanes; II. Graffites et inscriptions," in *Mission Paul Pelliot VIII. Sites divers de la région de Koutcha* (Paris: Collège de France, 1987), 78.

largest four consisted of ten, twenty, thirty-two, and forty men. The highest number of animals is seventeen horses, who traveled with eight men. Because pass no. 80 is damaged, we do not know how many animals accompanied the party of forty men. As is still true of modern Xinjiang, donkeys were an important means of travel; some caravans consisted of only men and donkeys. Two travel passes listed accompanying children, and two others listed "monastic attendants," who were permitted to do tasks forbidden by the Buddhist vinaya regulations for monks.[65] One caravan (pass no. 64) consisted entirely of women except for a male caravan leader; the number of women (and donkeys) is illegible. Conceivably these women were on their way to be sold at the market for women at Kucha mentioned in the official histories. While the travel passes do not reveal what goods the caravans carried, they do show that the Kucha kings closely monitored the caravans going in and out of Kucha and ensured that they stayed on their prearranged routes.

These documents are important because few sources detail the size of caravans. The dynastic history of the Zhou dynasty (557–81), which was composed around 629, tells of a caravan going to Wuwei, Gansu, that consisted of 240 non-Chinese merchants, with six hundred camels who carried 10,000 bolts of multi-colored silk.[66] This was before the Sui reunified the empire, when travel was difficult; merchants formed large groups, often hiring guards, to ensure their own safety. The Kuchean travel passes indicate a routinization of caravan travel in the seventh century: because the roads were safe, travelers could move in smaller groups.

These different sources—the official Chinese histories, coin finds, and the Kuchean-language documents—portray a thriving local economy in which a money economy in coins coexisted side-by-side with a subsistence economy. In 648 the Tang-dynasty armies conquered Kucha. The Bai-family rulers went from being vassals of the Western Turkish kaghanate to subjects of the Tang dynasty. Kucha was the site of the headquarters that administered the "Four Garrisons of Anxi" (Kucha itself being one of the four). The Tang maintained only intermittent control for most of the following century; the other three garrisons were Khotan, Kashgar, and Yanqi (between 679 and 719 Tokmak replaced Yanqi).[67] Like the Han dynasty before them, the Tang established garrisons in the Western Region, but with one crucial difference: they used the same administrative system for the Western Regions as for the traditional core areas of China. The prefecture of Kucha was structured exactly like a prefecture within central China. Prefectures were divided into counties, which were divided into villages in rural areas and quarters in urban areas.

Our best information about the Chinese occupation comes from a severely damaged group of documents that Pelliot found at the Duldur Aqur monastic site just south of Kucha: 214 scraps of paper, many of them damaged by fire and highly fragmentary, with Chinese on them. The earliest ones date to fifty years after the Tang conquest, the 690s, a time of much political turmoil. At the end of the seventh century, the peoples living in Tibet formed a powerful expansionist empire that challenged Tang control of Central Asia in 670, and the Tang managed to reassert control in Kucha only in 692.[68] Then, after fifty years of stable Chinese rule, a rebellion led by a part-Sogdian, part-Turkish general named An Lushan almost brought down the Tang dynasty, which defeated the rebels only in 763 after hiring mercenary troops.

Although the Tang dynasty was much weakened and Tang armies withdrew from Central Asia, Chinese military colonies, under the rule of the Anxi Protectorate, continued to exist in Kucha. Between 766 and at least 781, a Chinese official named Guo Xin served as the highest official in the Anxi Protectorate, based in Kucha, but had no contact with the Tang court in Chang'an.[69] In 781 Guo Xin reestablished contact with the Tang by sending envoys but continued to govern on his own. The Tibetans conquered the region in 790, although they have left minimal traces in the archeological record, and the Uighurs took over Kucha in the early ninth century and remained in power until the coming of the Mongols in the thirteenth century.[70]

The Chinese documents from Duldur Aqur start in the 690s, when the Tang was still powerful, and continue through 792, when the Chinese finally lost control of Kucha.[71] Unlike the Kuchean religious texts and monastic accounts, the Chinese materials cover secular matters too. Written by Chinese soldiers stationed in Kucha, they include letters home as well as three funeral notices praising the deceased for their military prowess. One contrite believer lists various violations of Buddhist proscriptions committed while in military service: drinking alcohol, eating meat, breaking a vegetarian fast, damaging monastic property, and harming sentient beings.[72] These materials document a range of activities: monks reciting sutras in a monastery, women writing letters, the size of agricultural plots, the number of banners used in Daoist religious ceremonies, and an evaluation of an official's performance.[73] These documents point to a separate Chinese settlement, possibly a garrison staffed by soldiers living with their dependents.[74]

These materials, like the Kuchean-language travel passes, document the movement of caravans, which various letter writers used to send their correspondence. One letter writer, apparently en route himself, writes so quickly that he repeats certain phrases, in order to finish his letter in time to give it to a group of colonists returning to Kucha.[75]

The main item of trade mentioned in these documents is horses, which the Chinese bought from the nomadic peoples north of Kucha in exchange for one thousand catties (roughly 1,300 pounds, or 600 kg) of steel or roughly 1,000

Chinese feet of cloth. One account gives the amount and type of grain (crushed grain with soy, bran, or barley) given to government officials for the horses in their care.[76] The militia and different expeditionary armies used horses, as did the postal and relay stations.[77] One letter is from a horse merchant who reports the illness of a horse that subsequently recovered. Other sources confirm that Sogdians, either immigrants from Samarkand and its environs or their descendants, played an important role in supplying the Tang army with horses, and the Duldur Aqur scraps contain a few faint traces of Sogdian presence.[78] Like the documents from the garrison at Loulan, these documents point to the existence of trade, but it is a trade carried out by Chinese officials purchasing what they need: mostly horses. Fragmentary and difficult to interpret, they document the existence of government-sponsored trade above all else.

Consistent with this picture of government-sponsored trade is the frequent mention of coins in Duldur Aqur documents. They document a monetized economy in which certain individuals spend considerable amounts in individual transactions. One person without an official rank paid a tax of one thousand coins to be exempted from a labor obligation; another paid 1,500 coins. A list of debtors gives the amount of money paid by the people whose names appear: 4,800 coins, 4,000 (possibly more) coins, 2,500 coins.[79] Archeologists have found eleven Chinese-language contracts at other sites in Kucha. Three of the best-preserved Chinese contracts are for loans of one thousand coins each; the borrower agrees to pay back the loan in installments of two hundred coins.[80]

Who minted all these coins, and why? Where some historians of Rome have identified the state as the most likely producer of coins, since it paid soldiers, others point out that if local markets had not existed, soldiers would not have needed coins.[81] The Tang state collected taxes and made payments in three types of currency: coins, measures of grain, and cloth (usually bolts of a fixed length of silk). Their extensive payments to their armies resulted in ample supplies of coins circulating throughout Kucha.

In 755, with the An Lushan rebellion, the Tang dynasty withdrew its forces from Kucha and the flow of coins into the region came to a sudden halt. The authorities at Kucha responded by minting their own inferior copies of Tang coins. Using a coin from the Kaiyuan (713–41) era to make a mold, they replaced the two characters for Kaiyuan with the name of the new eras proclaimed by the Tang emperor (Dali, 766–69; Jianzhong, 780–83). Cruder than the original characters, the new characters include some mistakes. These Kucha-issued coins have other signs that they were not minted by the central government: their central holes are sometimes octagonal instead of rectangular (because the molds were not aligned properly). The metal in these coins was also a redder copper than used in central China, another sign of local manufacture. One thousand coins of this type have been found in Xinjiang, of which eight hundred came from the Kucha region. Only two were found in central China.[82] Clearly these coins circulated primarily in Xinjiang. Even though Kucha was cut off from the Tang, the different local rulers still had to pay their troops, and they needed coins to do so.

Undeniably, the Chinese-language materials from Duldur Aqur are limited. Totaling only 208 documents, many of them consisting of a few characters, they touch on a surprising range of activities. The historian who has translated these documents into French, Éric Trombert, summarizes their content: "One other characteristic of the Chinese materials from Duldur Aqur—collected by Pelliot and Ōtani—is the absence of identifiable commercial documents. No lists of goods destined to be commercialized. No travel documents like the many travel passes for caravans found near the postal station at Yanshuigou. Few contracts, which seem to be mostly transactions among peasants."[83] Yet for all their variety, they do not mention anything that looks like the conventional portrait of the Silk Road trade—no private merchants carrying vast quantities of goods across long distances. Trombert believes that Kucha was a center of commerce, but that the merchants traveling there stayed within the city or outside the oasis—not at Duldur Aqur, which is why no commercial documents survive.

Yet, like Duldur Aqur, the much-better-documented sites along the Silk Road also lack documents about long-distance trade. The body of materials from Kucha in Agnean, Kuchean, and Chinese, the focus of this chapter, is certainly the most piecemeal and damaged of any site discussed in this book. All the Chinese and Kuchean materials from the Kucha region combined total under ten thousand scraps; of these, only several hundred documents are preserved well enough to be read and understood. There was trade in Kucha, but, as the travel passes show, government officials supervised it closely, and, as the materials from the Chinese garrison at Duldur Aqur reveal, the Chinese army's demand for horses constituted a major component of that trade. Even in the late 700s, when military conflict was endemic, local rulers continued to mint coins—an indication of how closely tied the trade was to the presence of armies.

The surviving evidence from Kucha, as partial as it is, suggests an alternative to the standard picture of the fabled Silk Road trade: rather than a long-distance trade initiated and staffed by private merchants, these materials indicate that the Chinese military contributed significantly to the Silk Road economy. When Chinese armies were stationed in Central Asia, money—in the form of coins, grain, and cloth—flowed into the region. When the Chinese troops withdrew, small-scale trade resumed, largely maintained by local travelers and peddlers.

CHAPTER 3

Midway Between China and Iran

Turfan

Located on the northern route around the Taklamakan Desert, Turfan bridged the Chinese and Iranian worlds. Even today, Turfan retains some of its cosmopolitan feel. Vendors on every corner sell naan, the leavened flatbread like that eaten in Central Asia and north India. At a conference I attended there in the mid-1990s, one Norwegian professor of Iranian languages cheerfully greeted everyone at breakfast, explaining that it was the first time he had woken up to the sound of braying donkeys since being in Iran before the 1979 revolution. In town, one sees many Uighur and Chinese faces, and the proprietors at the bazaar—even Chinese speakers say *"baza'er"* and not the Chinese word for "market"—proffer rugs, glistening jeweled knives, and always a glass of tea to potential customers.

Historically, Turfan had a mixed population. Migrants from China and Sogdiana, the region around Samarkand, formed the largest communities. After the fall of the Han dynasty in 220 CE the Chinese migrated in large numbers to the northwest. Turfan and Kucha were the two largest settlements on the northern route around the Taklamakan. The Chinese residents of Turfan listened to Iranian music as they, man and woman alike, performed the Sogdian swirl, a wild twirling dance that was all the rage, shown in color plate 14. To the Sogdians, Turfan felt so Chinese that they called it Chinatown.[1]

The Sogdians and the Chinese overshadowed the indigenous residents, some of whom originally spoke Kuchean. Turfan's residents had already started using Chinese characters in 273, the date of the earliest excavated document found so far at the oasis. The sources from Turfan are particularly significant because the inhabitants recycled paper with writing on it to make shoes, belts, hats, and clothing for the dead. The records preserved in this way form a random, unedited sample that offers an unparalleled glimpse of life on the Silk Road during its peak.

When the southern route fell into disuse after 500, many travelers opted for the northern route that went through Turfan. One such traveler was a Chinese monk named Xuanzang (ca. 596–664) who decided in 629 to go to India

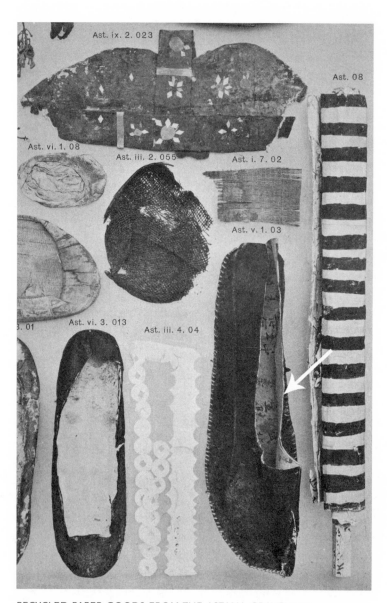

Ast. ix. 2. 023

Ast. 08

Ast. vi. 1. 08

Ast. iii. 2. 055

Ast. i. 7. 02

Ast. v. 1. 03

3. 01

Ast. vi. 3. 013

Ast. iii. 4. 04

RECYCLED PAPER GOODS FROM THE ASTANA GRAVEYARD

To save space in his archeological reports, Aurel Stein labeled similar items from a single site and photographed them together on the same page. This photo shows some of the paper goods he found at the Astana graveyard in Turfan: a hat decorated with flowers, a rolled-up flag, a string of coins, and, most typically, shoes. Craftsmen cut paper documents into shoe soles and covers, sewed them with thread, and then blackened the exterior. The arrow marks the writing still visible inside one of the shoes. By disassembling such items and reconstructing the original documents, archeologists have learned much about life along the Silk Road.

to study the original Sanskrit versions of several Buddhist texts whose Chinese versions did not make sense.[2] His timing could not have been worse, since an imperial ban on travel beyond the borders of the new empire was then in effect.

We know about his trip because Xuanzang dictated a detailed account of his harrowing journey to his disciple Huili (615–ca. 675) in 649 after he returned to China.[3] As Huili relates, Xuanzang was born near Luoyang, Henan, entered a monastery while a teenager, and left the city in 618 when the Sui dynasty collapsed. For eleven years he read Buddhist texts, first in the Tang capital of Chang'an (modern Xi'an, Shaanxi) and then in Sichuan Province. In preparation for his trip, he studied Sanskrit, the Buddhist liturgical language that was also spoken in monasteries.[4]

To travel the 350 miles (550 km) between Dunhuang and Turfan, visitors today can choose between an overnight train ride and a one-day car trip. The ease of travel nowadays, however, obscures the genuine perils the journey posed in the past. The first leg of the trip took Xuanzang to Liangzhou, modern Wuwei in Gansu Province, an important city where "merchants and monks from the different countries east of the Pamirs came and went without pause."[5] Wuwei was the last city inside Tang-dynasty China of any importance; from there one could join caravans going west.

The city's top-ranking official, the prefect, urged Xuanzang to abandon his plan to leave China. But a local Buddhist teacher helped him to proceed to Guazhou, where the local prefect tore up an imperial order for Xuanzang's arrest and urged him to depart as soon as possible. (Xuanzang did not pass through Dunhuang, only nearby Guazhou.) At Guazhou, Xuanzang learned of the obstacles on the way to Hami, the first major stopping point beyond the Chinese border: the rapids of the Hulu River, five successive watchtowers to the north that kept a lookout for unauthorized travelers, and, finally, the Mohoyan (Gashun Gobi) Desert. Retracing Xuanzang's footsteps in 1907, Aurel Stein estimated the distance Xuanzang covered at 218 miles (351 km).[6] He found Huili's account remarkably accurate, with one exception; Huili omitted two days of walking between the first and fourth watchtowers, probably to speed up the narrative.

Since there was no clearly marked road, Xuanzang hired a guide, Shi Pantuo, to take him to Hami. The guide's last name, Shi, indicated that his family had originally come from the region of Kesh, or Shahrisabz, outside Samarkand, Uzbekistan, while his given name, Pantuo, was the Chinese transcription of Vandak, a common Sogdian name meaning "servant" of a given deity.[7] Vandak introduced the young monk to an elderly Sogdian who had already made the trip to Hami fifteen times and urged Xuanzang to trade his horses

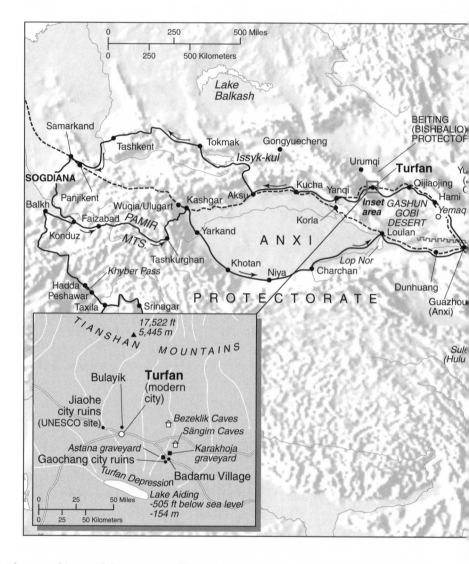

for the monk's aged horse. Recalling the prediction of a fortune-teller in Chang'an that he would ride on a thin, red, old horse, Xuanzang agreed to the trade.

Sometime after midnight Vandak and Xuanzang set off. They followed the Hulu River north until they reached a shallow ford where the river could be crossed. Vandak cut down some Chinese parasol trees to make a simple bridge so that the two men and their horses could get to the other bank, where they lay down to sleep. In the middle of the night Xuanzang thought he saw Vandak advance toward him carrying a knife—could this have been a nightmare?—but he prayed to the bodhisattva Guanyin for help, and the crisis passed.

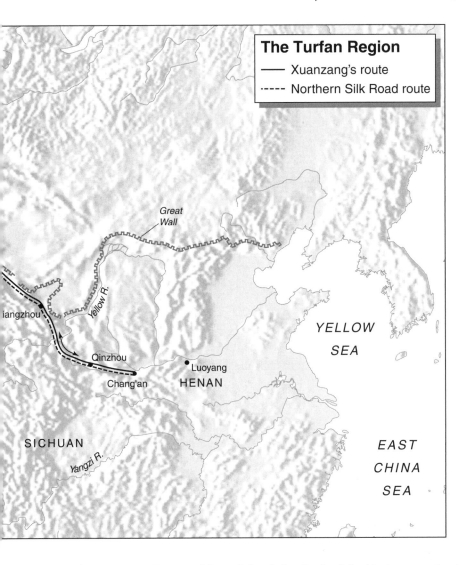

The Turfan Region

——— Xuanzang's route

----- Northern Silk Road route

Great
Wall

Yellow R.

iangzhou

Qinzhou

Luoyang

Chang'an   HENAN

YELLOW

SEA

SICHUAN

Yangzi R.

EAST

CHINA

SEA

The next morning Vandak explained that he had decided to turn back: "I think the road ahead is dangerous and far, with neither water nor grass, and the only water is by the five towers. One must reach these at night so that one can steal water and keep going, but discovery means certain death." He and Xuanzang agreed to part ways. Xuanzang gave him a horse as a gift and then set off alone through the desert.

Huili describes the terrors of his master's solo journey vividly. Following a track through the gravel marked only by the horse dung and dried bones of earlier travelers, Xuanzang hallucinated and saw mirages in which hundreds of soldiers in the distance constantly changed their appearance. When he arrived at the first tower, he hid in a ditch until nightfall. Then, as he was drinking his fill and replenishing his water bag at a water tank, several arrows whizzed past, just missing his knee. He stood up and cried, "I am a monk who has come from the capital. Don't shoot me." A watchman opened the door to the tower, and the captain invited him inside to spend the night. The captain promised that a relative of his would help Xuanzang at the fourth gate. There, too, arrows showered Xuanzang until he again explained who he was, and the guards allowed him to pass. The guard-tower captain urged him to proceed directly to the Wild Horse Spring (Yemaquan), about 30 miles (50 km) away, the nearest source of water.

Continuing alone and on foot, Xuanzang traveled a long way without finding the spring. At one point, when he stopped to take a drink, his water bag slipped through his fingers, and all his water drained out. Discouraged, he started back but then decided: "It would be better to go west and die than to return to the east and live!" Wandering in the desert for a full five days and four nights, Xuanzang prayed again to the bodhisattva Guanyin before his horse finally led him to a spring in the desert. He recovered from dehydration and proceeded to Hami, where three Chinese monks received him in a local monastery. He had made it out of China.

Occupying less than a chapter, the account of Xuanzang's trip from Chang'an to Turfan is only one episode in Huili's hagiography, whose primary purpose was to record the different miracles Xuanzang had performed. Like all hagiographers, Huili exaggerated the perils of the trip in order to document his master's piety. Still, the modern reader cannot help wondering about some of the details. Would any Chinese official have torn up a writ of arrest in the presence of the person he was supposed to detain? Why would Xuanzang give a horse to a guide who had menaced him at knifepoint and then left him to travel the most difficult leg of the journey alone? How could the unaccompanied Xuanzang have survived his desert journey? Would two separate watchtower captains have allowed a fugitive, even a Buddhist monk, to pass? Could he have lived five days and four nights in the desert with no water? (Admittedly, Hedin survived six days and five nights without water in 1896.)[8]

Huili's account makes it sound as though the one act that violated imperial orders—leaving China in spite of the travel ban—Xuanzang did entirely on his own. Even though Xuanzang must have originally intended to go directly to see the kaghan of the Western Turks, the main rival of the Tang for control of Central Asia, Huili altered his account so that Xuanzang became a loyal Tang subject who left China on his own and decided only after leaving China to visit the kaghan.[9]

Whatever the circumstances of his departure were, Xuanzang's experience differed significantly from that of ordinary travelers on the northern route. On the Guazhou to Turfan leg of the trip he traveled alone, but almost everyone traveled in caravans. When no travel bans were in effect, caravans applied at the border for a travel pass. Guides would have led travelers on difficult-to-find routes through the desert, and, barring the disasters that befell those whose skeletons lay along the path, they would have survived the trip. Xuanzang's itinerary underscores the important place of Turfan on the Silk Road. Along with Kucha, it was one of the largest cities in the Western Regions.

As Huili tells it, once Xuanzang left the Tang Empire, his fortunes shifted. Qu Wentai, the king of the Gaochang state, which was based in Turfan, the next oasis after Hami on the northern route, sent an envoy to greet him. Proceeding in the dark, the monk and his guide arrived at the palace at midnight, and the king and his retinue, carrying torches, came out to greet him. The king kept Xuanzang up all night talking, and the next morning, while the monk was still asleep, the royal couple waited outside his door so that they could show their devotion by being the first to greet him in the morning. Xuanzang then moved to a monastery for ten days before deciding to resume his journey.

THE RUINS OF ANCIENT GAOCHANG CITY
The dirt walls of Gaochang City near Turfan are among the few genuine above-ground ruins in all of China. Visitors can see where the residents dug into the ground to make dwellings that would remain cool in the summer and piled earth into high walls. Here two dirt towers stand above the other buildings of Gaochang; it is quite likely that Xuanzang preached from one of them after he ended his hunger strike in 629. Author photo.

The king tried to convince him to stay:

> From the time I heard the name of the Master of the Law my body and soul have been filled with joy, my hands and feet have danced.
>
> I propose that you stay here, where I will provide for your wants to the end of your life. I will order the people of my realm to become your disciples. I hope you will instruct the clerics here, who, although not numerous, number several thousand.

Xuanzang demurred, the two men argued, and the king threatened to send him back to China. When Xuanzang insisted on leaving, the king locked him in the palace and each day personally delivered his meals. For three days Xuanzang refused all food and drink. On the fourth day the king gave in. The two men negotiated a compromise: Xuanzang would stay an additional month in Turfan, where he would teach a Buddhist text entitled The Scripture of the Benevolent Kings while the king prepared gifts for his journey.

At the end of the month, the king assigned four newly ordained monks and twenty-five attendants to accompany Xuanzang and provided them all with face masks, gloves, boots, and socks. He also gave the monk enough money and cloth to cover his travel expenses for an estimated twenty years: one hundred ounces of gold, 30,000 silver coins, and five hundred bolts of damask and silk. Gold, silver coins, and silk: all served as currency on the Silk Road of the seventh century. Even more important were twenty-four letters of introduction the king provided to the kaghan of the Western Turks and twenty-three subordinate kings who, like the Gaochang ruler, were the kaghan's allies.[10]

Xuanzang's route allowed him to stay in the territory controlled by the Western Turks and their allies as long as possible. For the kaghan, whose capital at Tokmak lay on the northwestern edge of Lake Issyk-kul in what is now Kyrgyzstan, the Gaochang king sent two cartloads laden with five hundred bolts of damask silk and delicious fruit, probably dried. Although the Gaochang kings had ice houses so that they could enjoy fruit in the winter, fresh fruit could not have survived the long trip to the kaghan's camp. Xuanzang left Turfan in the winter, most likely in the twelfth month of 629.[11]

The king's family had been in power since 502.[12] Although probably not ethnically Chinese, the Qu-family rulers adopted many Chinese ways. The original inhabitants of Turfan, the Jushi people, "lived in felt-tents, kept moving in pursuit of water and grass for grazing, and had a fair knowledge of farming," the official history of the Later Han dynasty reports.[13] The graves of the Jushi kings, with rectangular pits for their human retainers and circular pits for their horses, confirm their nomadic ways.[14] In 60 BCE, when the Xiongnu confederation weakened, the local Jushi rulers submitted to the Han dynasty. The Chinese then established a garrison in the town of Jiaohe, and various Chinese dynasties retained control for most of the time until 450 CE. Jiaohe has a dramatic setting at the meeting of two rivers. Guided by labels on different buildings, tourists walk through the ruins on paved paths provided by UNESCO.[15]

During the centuries of Chinese control, numerous Chinese migrants settled in Turfan, and many local people learned Chinese. In the third and fourth centuries, as in Niya and Kucha, few coins circulated. The earliest Chinese contract from Turfan, dated 273, records the exchange of a coffin for twenty bolts of silk, which the residents used as currency.[16] The contract specifies that the silk was degummed, meaning that the external coating of the silk thread had been removed by boiling so that the silk absorbed dye more easily. The residents of Turfan retained their preference for degummed silk for centuries, and also used rugs and measured amounts of grain as media of exchange.

The Qu-family rulers, who came to power in 502, embraced Chinese cultural norms, and, like many Chinese rulers, patronized Buddhism. Structuring their bureaucracy on the Chinese model, they used Chinese as the language of administration, and their walled capital had gates with the standard Chinese names. Students studied Chinese-language classics in school, the dynastic histories record, but they translated them into a local language, possibly Kuchean or Sogdian.[17]

After 640, when a Tang army defeated the Gaochang army and conquered the oasis, Turfan became even more Chinese. The tenth and last Gaochang king, Qu Wentai (reigned 620–40), who had hosted Xuanzang, collapsed from fright, his son surrendered, and the Chinese established direct administration over the oasis. Jiaohe became the headquarters for the Chinese, who created the Protectorate General of Anxi, which oversaw affairs in the Western Regions.[18]

Since Turfan was a prefecture exactly like the three hundred other prefectures in the Tang Empire, officials implemented redistribution of land as stipulated by the regulations of the equal-field system, which was in effect throughout the empire. They were required to update household registers every three years. The household registers listed the head of each household, all family members and anyone else living in the same house, and their tax obligations. Each able-bodied male was obliged to pay three types of taxes—corvée labor, grain, and cloth. The registers also listed the young, the elderly, the handicapped, and women, who had lower obligations or were exempt.

In exchange, each household headed by an able-bodied male was entitled to 20 *mu* (three acres, or 1.2 hectares of permanent holding land) and 80 mu (12 acres, or 4.8 hectares) of personal share land.[19] The authorities hoped to encourage long-term investment (like the planting of mulberry trees, whose leaves silk worms ate) on permanent holding land; personal share land, redistributed every three years, was for ordinary farming.

Drawing up registers for each household in 640, officials counted 37,700 people living in 8,000 households in Turfan.[20] (One hundred years later the number of households had increased to 11,647.)[21] Since land was scarce in the oasis of Turfan, the land registers list both how much land each household received (usually around five mu, .75 acres, or .3 hectares) and how much was still owed. Although the authorities realized that they would never have enough land to allocate the still-owed allotment, this accounting fiction demonstrated their compliance with the Tang Code. This flexibility at the local level made Tang law successful; officials could adjust all regulations to suit local conditions.

We know that the Tang officials in Turfan recorded the amount of land still owed because the people of Turfan had the burial custom of outfitting the dead in clothing, hats, boots, and belts made from recycled paper. It seems likely that the Chinese living in other regions also buried their dead with similar paper clothes, but the fragile garments have since disintegrated.[22] The living may have believed that paper had a quality that would allow it to ascend to the afterworld, since Buddhists conceived of heavenly realms somewhere above the earthly realm. One shoe sole dating to the early fifth century from Turfan has a single character meaning "rise" written on the bottom in blue ink.[23]

Because paper was expensive, the residents of Turfan used discarded paper, sometimes official documents, to make these clothes for the dead. The Chinese official histories record that the officials of the Gaochang Kingdom disposed of all documents once a given matter was settled; the only documents they did not throw away were household registers. After 640 Turfan came under Tang rule, and all Gaochang Kingdom documents became obsolete. In addition, to mini-mize the space taken up by documents, Tang regulations prescribed that all doc-uments be thrown away after three years.[24] Sometimes those making funeral clothing also recycled private materials including letters, contracts, poems, medical prescriptions, and school exercises. The Turfan documents are fasci-nating precisely because of the enormous variety of materials recovered from funerary garments.

Turfan's arid climate helps to preserve the paper and other fragile matter, like textiles. The oasis lies in an unusually low depression formed millions of years ago when the Indian subcontinent collided with Eurasia and formed the Himalayas. The lowest point in Turfan is the dried up bed of Lake Aiding at 505 feet (154 m) below sea level; this is the second lowest place on earth, after the Dead Sea. Turfan is dry and hot, so hot that the Chinese sometimes called it the prefecture of fire, or Huozhou. Summer temperatures regularly reach 140 degrees Fahrenheit (60 degrees Celsius), an unbearable temperature for humans without air-conditioning (although indigenous dwellings dug into the ground remain cool) and perfect for Turfan's famous melons and grapes. In addition to paper documents, Turfan's dry climate has preserved over one hundred desiccated human corpses, and also artificial silk flowers, shown in color plate 1.

When Aurel Stein visited the Astana graveyard, just outside the walls of the city of Gaochang, in January 18, 1915, the graves had already been thoroughly ransacked. A local digger named Mashik assured Stein that he and his father had personally examined every grave on the site:

> Mashik, our special cemetery assistant, whom long practice in searching the dead had relieved of all scruples, by breaking the jawbones of the skull recovered from the mouth's cavity a thin gold coin. . . . Mashik claimed the distinction of having been the first to learn by experience to look for coins of gold or silver placed in the mouths of the dead, though his search was but rarely rewarded.[25]

In the Astana and Karakhoja graveyards, Stein found different artifacts, including some coins Mashik pried out of the mouths of the dead, but he and the other excavators who followed him to the site did not realize how many documents the graveyard contained.

Today the Astana graveyard is open to tourists, who can walk down stairways into two tombs and view the wall paintings they contain. The site is impressive only if one considers the enormity of the graveyard—it runs 1.5 miles (2.4 km) east to west and is up to three-quarters of a mile (1.2 km) wide—and how much information historians have pieced together from the recovered documents.

Local archeologists realized that the Astana graveyard, though severely disturbed, still contained many artifacts, but no one excavated systematically until 1958. This was the year that the Communist Party launched the Great Leap Forward, an intensive mass campaign intended to raise China's economy to the level of England's. Everyone—every farm, every factory, every work unit—was required to increase production by meeting quotas, many of which were artificially high and impossible to achieve. In many regions the forced collectivization and neglect of agriculture resulted in a terrible famine in which forty-five million people died.[26]

The Xinjiang archeologists also had quotas, set in thousands of artifacts.[27] They tried test pits in a few different places, but the most productive were those at Astana. When the archeologists ran short of money to pay workers to dig, the local authorities agreed to let them excavate alongside work crews digging roads and irrigation channels, saving them the cost of hiring laborers. The archeologists found even more tombs. Local archeologists in Turfan today describe the truckloads of artifacts taken to the Urumqi Museum in the same tone that others describe the removal of artifacts by the camel trains of the early twentieth-century European explorers. The archeologists reached their quotas, and excavations at the site continued until 1975. These years saw many tumultuous political campaigns, particularly during the Cultural Revolution from 1966 to 1976. The emphasis was always on the quantity of artifacts recovered, and, accordingly, the level of reporting is often poor.[28] It is not always possible to determine, on the basis of published reports about these hurried excavations, which artifact came from which tomb.

The documents from the site have fared much better. Under the farsighted leadership of a professor of history from Wuhan University, Tang Zhangru, the government sponsored a group of scholars who met in Beijing to analyze the documents from the site. In some cases they dismantled different items of clothing made from recycled paper and reconstructed the original documents. Each of these reconstituted documents has been published with an expert transcription in modern Chinese characters accompanied by a clear photograph. Since 1959 archeologists have excavated 465 tombs at Astana and Karakhoja, 205 of which contained documents.[29] To date, about two thousand documents have been recovered, of which over three hundred are contracts.[30]

These documents offer unparalleled insight into the life of ordinary people living in a Silk Road community between 273, the date of the earliest Chinese document, and 769, the date of the last. During the years before the establishment of the Gaochang Kingdom, the different rulers of Turfan participated in the same exchange of envoys as the rulers of Niya and Kucha. In 477 one document lists the expenses of hosting envoys from the Rouran peoples of central Asia (known in Europe as the Avars), the Karghalik Kingdom on the southern edge of the Tarim basin; the Song dynasty (420–479) whose capital was in Nanjing, China; the Uddyana Kingdom in north India, and the "Brahman country," most likely a reference to south India.[31]

This particular list of envoys reveals the neighboring kingdoms with which the rulers of Turfan maintained diplomatic relations, but it does not identify their most important trading partner. Other coins and documents from Turfan indicate a consistent and unmistakable pattern: the Iranian world, especially the eastern Iranian world around Samarkand—not Rome—was the most important trading partner of first the independent Gaochang Kingdom and then, after the 640 conquest, Tang China.

As early as the year 300 the residents of Turfan used silver coins minted by the Sasanian Empire based in western Iran. Famed for their purity (between 85 percent and 90 percent silver), Sasanian coins are distinctive.[32] The face of each coin shows the profile of the reigning ruler, each identifiable by his characteristic crown, and his name in Middle Persian, while the reverse shows two attendants tending a fire altar that represents the state religion of Zoroastrianism, shown in color plate 4B. The earliest Sasanian coins found anywhere in China date to the fourth century and have been found in hoards buried in the dirt ruins of Gaochang City. Many of these early coins show little wear, because they did not circulate widely.[33] Confirming this impression of limited use, the fourth-century documents from Turfan record payments in bolts of cloth.

The first document that specifically mentions silver coins, a list of goods placed in the grave, dates to 543. It lists one hundred silver coins, one hundred gold coins, and 100,009,000 cubits of "climbing-to-heaven silk."[34] (A cubit measured roughly 10 feet, or 3 m.) Although this grave inventory does not specify where the silver coins were minted, Chinese coins at this time were cast from bronze, so the silver coins must have been Sasanian. The elevated amounts of textiles and coins indicate that facsimile textiles and coins were placed in the tomb, not actual goods.

The earliest certain mention of real silver coins appears in a contract dating to 584 for the rental of a field of one mu for five silver coins. Similar contracts continue until 677; people used silver coins to rent land, trees, oxcarts, or homes and to buy land, hire people to staff beacon towers in their place, make loans, and pay taxes.[35] Confirming the information from Chinese-language contracts, the one surviving Sogdian-language contract from Astana records the sale in 639 of a female slave for 120 "very pure" silver coins.[36]

The documentary record indicates that the Turfan residents used silver coins from the late 500s to the late 600s, a pattern supported by coin finds. Archeologists have unearthed 130 Sasanian silver coins in the ruins of Gaochang City and thirty in the Astana cemetery, many wrested from the jaws of the dead by Stein's assistant Mashik.[37] Sasanian silver coins continued to circulate after the Chinese conquest of 640, and even after the Sasanian Empire fell to invading Islamic armies in 651, when the conquerors shifted to Arabo-Sasanian coins minted by Arab governors. The Arabo-Sasanian coins, like their precursors, weighed about four grams; mints replaced the portrait of the Sasanian emperor with that of the Arab governor and added an Arabic inscription to the face of the coin.[38]

Some 1,300 Sasanian coins have been excavated in China. Of those, the vast majority have been found in Xinjiang.[39] In the modern town of Wuqia (Ulugart in Uighur), far to the west of Turfan on a tiny side road outside of Kashgar, archeologists found the largest cache of silver coins anywhere in China. In 1959 a road crew using dynamite to widen a road uncovered 947 silver coins, many fused together, along with thirteen gold bars that had been hidden in a rock crevice. The hill was near the main route between Turfan and the capital of the Western Turks just northwest of Lake Issyk Kul in today's Kyrgyzstan. The findspot, on the side of a hill, is so remote that someone—perhaps a merchant? an envoy? a bandit?—must have left the money for safekeeping and never managed to return.[40] The 947 coins included both Sasanian and Arabo-Sasanian coins. The presence of Arabo-Sasanian coins dated the hoard to after the fall of the Sasanian Empire to caliphate armies in 651, and the presence of Chinese copies of Sasanian coins, possibly as much as a quarter of the hoard, underlines the continuing appeal of silver coins to the residents of the Western Regions.[41]

What was the purchasing power of 947 silver coins in the late seventh century? Documents recovered from the Turfan tomb of a moneylender named Zuo who died in 673 offer some clues. The tomb contained a folded-up letter from a servant to the deceased that denied responsibility for the theft of five hundred silver coins six years earlier in 667. The servant, like many Chinese, believed that courts in the underworld meted out justice both to the dead and to the living. His letter indicates that a prosperous member of the community might have as much as five hundred coins on hand at any given time.

The fifteen intact contracts buried in the moneylender Zuo's tomb record that he usually made smaller loans: between ten and forty silver coins or between three and thirty bolts of degummed silk. Government regulations specified that purchasers should use bolts of silk for large purchases, such as of slaves and livestock, and coins for less valuable items, probably because coins were often in short supply. In line with these regulations, the moneylender Zuo purchased a slave girl for six bolts of degummed silk in 661, and paid 450 silver coins for ninety bundles of hay in 668. Eight contracts record loans of silk or silver coins, while five contracts record the rental of fields, at least once to someone who had borrowed money from him. Unlike so many of the other Turfan documents, the contracts were placed intact in his tomb, probably because Zuo had not managed to collect on them during his life but hoped to do so after his death.[42]

The contracts buried in his tomb consistently charge interest of between 10 and 15 percent each month. The rate seemed high even to contemporaries: the Tang Code limited interest to 6 percent each month.[43] Ordinary people who fell into debt for a variety of reasons came to the moneylender to borrow money to tide them over. We do not always know what happened to these people, but it is certain that they never paid back the loans, because if they had, the moneylender would have destroyed his copy of the contract as was customary on receiving the final repayment.

While people in Turfan were using silver coins, people in central China used the same bronze *wuzhu* coins that they had been using since the second century BCE. The distinct currency spheres, silver in Turfan and points west, bronze in China, persisted after the 640 conquest of the oasis. Only sometime around 700 did people in Turfan shift to bronze coins, which they often strung together in bunches of a thousand, called strings. The latest Astana document to mention silver coins, a tax receipt dated 692, specifies the equivalent value in bronze coins: two silver coins were worth sixty-four bronze coins.[44]

The use of silver coins in Turfan during the sixth and seventh centuries reinforces the point that China's main trading partner at the height of the Silk Road trade, when the Tang stationed massive armies in the northwest, was the Iranian world, not Rome. Recall that no coins minted by the Roman republic (507–27 BCE) or the subsequent principate (27 BCE–330 CE) have been found—so far—anywhere in China. The most thorough survey by Luo Feng, the leading archeologist in Ningxia Province, identifies the earliest Byzantine solidus coins found in China (there are two) as minted in the reign of Theodosius II (409–50) and buried sometime in the early sixth century, and the latest in the mid-eighth century.[45]

The period of these Byzantine coins overlaps with that of the Sasanian silver coins, and the two were often found together. Far fewer gold coins have surfaced in China than silver coins: eleven in Xinjiang and thirty-seven in central China for a total of forty-eight (versus more than 1,300 silver coins).[46] These coins all appear to be solidus coins. First minted by Constantine (reigned 306–37), and containing 1/72 of a Roman pound's worth of gold, or 4.55 grams, they show the reigning Byzantine emperor on the face and have an image of the Cross or Christ on the back.[47] When Muslim troops conquered large chunks of the Byzantine Empire after defeating the Sasanians, Islamic mints removed all Christian elements from the solidus coins, just as they had removed Zoroastrian elements from the silver coins.

On close inspection, many of the Byzantine gold coins turn out to be fakes.[48] Sometimes they weigh less than the standard weight of genuine coins, or the iconographical details of the emperor's portrait are wrong, or the lettering on the inscription is incorrect.[49] Many have holes punched in them, an indication that they were sewn onto clothing, most likely for use as protective talismans (one is shown in color plate 4A).

The largest number of gold coins found together in China is five, and it is far more common to unearth a single coin.[50] Archeologists have not uncovered anything comparable to the hoards of silver coins from Wuqia and Turfan, yet another indication that the Byzantine gold coins were used for ceremonial purposes and did not circulate as a genuine currency, either in Turfan or in central China.[51] None of the Astana documents record a transaction using gold coins, and those that have been excavated from tombs were often used as talismans. The Wuqia hoard, with its 947 silver coins and thirteen bars of gold, confirms this basic pattern: it shows that silver circulated in the form of coins while gold was used as bars.

As the widespread use of silver coins indicates, Turfan lay halfway between the Iranian and Chinese worlds. During the years of the Silk Road trade, Turfan absorbed many foreign immigrants, none more numerous than the Sogdians who came from Samarkand. Sogdians came to settle in Turfan during the fourth, fifth, and sixth centuries, and the pace of migration heightened considerably after the fall of the Sasanian Empire in 651 and the Islamic conquest of Samarkand in 712.

Although the Sogdians were famous traders, the Sogdians living in Turfan pursued a wide variety of occupations including cultivating the land, serving as soldiers, running inns, painting, working leather, and selling iron goods.[52] When local officials, either under the Gaochang Kingdom or the Tang dynasty, drew up household registers, they did not label which residents were Sogdian and which were not. As a result, modern scholars must identify Sogdians by analyzing their family names and given names. Although the Chinese generally referred to the Sogdians as the people of the "nine jeweled surnames," most Sogdians adopted one of seven Chinese family names: Kang, used by those coming from Samarkand; An, from Bukhara; Cao, from Kabudhan, north of the Zerafshan River; He, from Kushaniyah between Samarkand and Bukhara; Mi, from either southeast of the Zerafshan River or Panjikent; Shi, from Kesh, modern-day Shahrisabz; and Shi (written with a different character), from Chach, modern-day Tashkent.[53] In recent years two Japanese scholars of the Sogdian language, Yoshida Yutaka and Kageyama Etsuko, have reconstructed forty-five different Sogdian given names from their Chinese translations.[54] Many of the original Sogdian immigrants who moved to Turfan used these names, while those who lived in China for generations tended to give their descendants traditional Chinese names—in much the same way that immigrants often choose American-sounding names for their children.

In addition to naming, the Sogdians who migrated to Turfan gradually modified their burial practices, bringing them in line with Chinese practices.[55] Because Zoroastrians believe that flesh pollutes the pure earth, they traditionally exposed the dead to scavengers and buried the cleaned bones in ossuaries. Two ossuaries have been found in Turfan.[56] Zoroastrians sacrificed animals to the major Zoroastrian deities, including tree, rock, and mountain gods; the god of wind; and the supreme deity, Ahura Mazda.[57] It is likely that the political and religious leader of the Sogdian community, a man who bore the title *sabao*, led these sacrifices.[58]

Many of the Sogdians living in Turfan adopted Chinese burial practices, including burying wooden slips to represent servants to serve the dead in the next world.[59] Recent excavations of a graveyard to the northeast of Gaochang City in Badamu Village have found more than eighty graves of Sogdians, as indicated by their family names written on Chinese-style epitaphs.[60] These naming patterns make it possible to identify Sogdians who appear in different documents, whether household registers recording the names of each member of the household or other materials.[61]

Sometime around 600 officials of the Gaochang Kingdom recorded the names of forty-eight merchants who paid a tax, called a scale fee, on the goods they sold to one another.[62] After the goods were weighed, the tax was assessed in silver coins. This much-studied document survives as ten paper shoe soles cut from four different sections of the original register. Offering a series of snapshots of individual transactions over the course of a single year in the early seventh century, it is the single most informative document about the commodities exchanged in the Silk Road trade. These documents embody all the joys and the frustrations of the documents pieced together from the Astana graveyard: they give more information than any other materials available, but missing sections of the documents—where they were cut to make shoe soles—mean that they are incomplete.

Even so, these records highlight the dominant role played by Sogdians in the Silk Road trade. Of the forty-eight names mentioned either as purchasers or sellers of a given good, fully forty-one are Sogdian.[63] The scale-fee records suggest a relatively low frequency of trade—a handful of transactions each week—with many weeks in which no tax was collected.[64]

Officials recorded all the sales by each day and then twice a month tallied up the total number of coins they collected. The rate of taxation was two silver coins (weighing 8 grams) on two Chinese pounds (*jin*) of silver, less than one percent. Scholars do not know how much a jin weighed in the year 600: either 6 ounces (200 grams) in the older system or about 1 pound, 3 ounces (600 grams) in the newer one. The lower weight is more likely, but the accompanying chart uses the original units of jin and *liang* (a Chinese ounce, with sixteen to a jin) because of the uncertainty.[65]

The scale-fee register lists thirty-seven transactions over the course of a single year. Brass, medicine, copper, turmeric, and raw sugar traded hands only once, while other goods appear more often: gold, silver, silk thread, aromatics (the term *xiang* refers broadly to spice, incense, or medicine), and ammonium chloride. The one unfamiliar item on the list, the chemical ammonium chloride, was used as an ingredient in dyes, to work leather, and as a flux to lower the temperature of metals. These documents list ammonium chloride six times, in

TABLE 3.1 SCALE-FEE TAX RECEIPTS FOR ONE YEAR AT ONE CHECKPOINT NEAR TURFAN, CA. 600 CE

Commodity	Weight	Last Name of Seller (probable ethnic background)	Last Name of Buyer (probable ethnic background)	Date	Tax paid
Silver	2 jin	Cao (Sogdian)	He (Sogdian)	1st month, 1st day	2 coins
Silver	2 jin 5 liang	Cao (Sogdian)	Kang (Sogdian)	1st month, 1st day	2 coins
Gold	9.5 liang	Di (Gaoju peoples)	missing	1st month, 2nd day	missing
Silver	5 jin 2 liang	He (Sogdian)	An (Sogdian)	1st month, 3rd day	5 coins
Fragrance	572 jin	Di (Gaoju peoples)	missing	1st month, 3rd day	missing
Brass	30+ jin	missing	missing	1st month, 3rd day	missing
Medicine	144 jin	Kang (Sogdian)	Ning (Chinese)	1st month, 5th day	missing
Silk thread	50 jin	missing	Kang (Sogdian)	missing	7.5 coins
Gold	10 liang	missing	Kang (Sogdian)	missing	
Missing	5 jin	missing	missing	missing	70 coins
Missing	missing	missing	missing	missing	42 coins
Ammonium chloride	172 jin	An (Sogdian)	Kang (Sogdian)	1st month, 15th day	missing
Fragrance	252 jin	Kang (Sogdian)	Kang, He (Sogdian)	missing	missing
Ammonium chloride	50 jin	Cao (Sogdian)	An (Sogdian)	1st month, 22nd day	missing
Copper	41 jin	Cao, He (Sogdian)	An (Sogdian)	1st month, 22nd day	missing
Silver	8 jin 1 liang	Di (Gaoju peoples)	He (Sogdian)	missing	missing
Gold	8.5 liang	[He] (Sogdian)	Gongqin (Turkish)	missing	2 [coins]
Missing	missing	missing	An (Sogdian)	missing	14 coins
Missing	71 jin	missing	He (Sogdian)	[3rd month]	missing

Commodity	Weight	Last Name of Seller (probable ethnic background)	Last Name of Buyer (probable ethnic background)	Date	Tax paid
TABLE 3.1 (CONTINUED)					
Turmeric	87 jin	Kang (Sogdian)	Ju (Jushi peoples)	[3rd month]	1 coin
Gold	9 liang	Cao (Sogdian)	He (Sogdian)	3rd month, 24th day	2 coins
Fragrance	362 jin	Zhêmat Vandak (Sogdian)	Kang (Sogdian)	3rd month, 24th day	15 coins
Ammonium chloride	241 jin	Zhêmat Vandak (Sogdian)	Kang (Sogdian)	3rd month, 24th day	
Ammonium chloride	11 jin	Bai (Kucha)	Kang (Sogdian)	3rd month, 25th day	missing
Silver	2 jin 1 liang	Kang (Sogdian)	He (Sogdian)	4th month, 5th day	missing
Silk thread	10 jin	Kang (Sogdian)	Kang (Sogdian)	4th month, 5th day	1 coin
Missing	missing	missing	missing	missing	17 coins
Missing	missing	missing	missing	missing	1 coin
Silver	2 jin	missing	He (Sogdian)	[4th month]	2 coins
Fragrance	800 jin	missing	missing	[4th month]	missing
Muscado sugar	31 jin	missing	missing	[4th month]	22 coins
Silk thread	80 jin	He (Sogdian)	missing	[4th month]	8 coins
Silk thread	60 jin	Ju (Jushi peoples)	Bai (Kuchean)	5th month, 2nd day	3 coins
Silk thread	missing	Ju (Jushi peoples)	missing	5th month, 12th day	1.5 coins
Ammonium chloride	251 jin	Kang (Sogdian)	Shi (Sogdian)	6th month, 5nd day	6 coins
Fragrance	172 jin	missing	He (Sogdian)	missing	4 coins
Missing	missing	Kang (Sogdian)	missing	7th month, 16th day	missing
Missing	missing	Cao (Sogdian)	missing	7th month, 22nd day	missing
Missing	missing	missing	missing	missing	8 coins

(continued)

TABLE 3.1 (CONTINUED)					
Commodity	Weight	Last Name of Seller (probable ethnic background)	Last Name of Buyer (probable ethnic background)	Date	Tax paid
Missing	missing	An (Sogdian)	missing	7th month, 25th day	missing
Gold	4 liang	Kang (Sogdian)	Ju (Jushi peoples)	8th month, 4th day	[.5 coins]
Fragrance	92 jin	missing	Kang (Sogdian)	8th month, 4th day	2 coins
Missing	missing	Cao (Sogdian)	missing	9th month, 5th day	missing
Gold	missing	Kang (Sogdian)	Cao (Sogdian)	10th month, 19th day	4 coins
Fragrance	650+ jin	Kang (Sogdian)	Kang (Sogdian)	12th month, 27th day	21 coins
Ammonium chloride	210 jin	missing	missing	missing	
Fragrance	52 jin	missing	missing	missing	1 coin
Fragrance	33 jin	An (Sogdian)	An (Sogdian)	missing	8 coins

amounts from a low of 11 Chinese pounds to a high of 251 Chinese pounds. Fragrance, similarly, was traded in both small and large amounts, with a low of 33 Chinese pounds and a high of 800 Chinese pounds—the largest single amount recorded on the list. Gold, as one would expect, appears in small amounts ranging from a quarter to more than half a Chinese pound, and the largest amount of silver did not exceed 8 Chinese pounds. Surprisingly, these documents do not mention bolts of silk cloth, but, since their value was determined by width and length, they would not have been subject to a tax by weight.[66]

The scale-tax documents do not list all the inventory of a given merchant, just individual sales, but even the largest quantity mentioned—800 Chinese pounds—could have been carried by several pack animals.[67] We glimpse the same low level of trade in a series of affidavits given during the legal dispute mentioned in the introduction between a Chinese merchant and the brother of his business partner.[68] The plaintiff's Chinese name was Cao Lushan, a clear indicator that he was Sogdian; Cao was one of the nine jeweled surnames, and Lushan was the transcription of Rokhshan, a Sogdian name meaning "bright," "light," or "luminous," cognate with our Persian-derived name Roxanne.

Appearing before a Chinese court sometime around 670, the younger brother sued a Chinese merchant for the return of an unpaid loan. The Chinese merchant had violated Tang-dynasty contract law, in effect since the 640 conquest of Turfan, the Sogdian contended. As his brother's heir, he was entitled to 275 bolts of silk. He brought the suit in Turfan, which served as the headquarters of the Anxi Protectorate between 670 and 692.

At the time of the brother's death, both he and his Chinese partner, like many merchants of the time, maintained households in the Tang capital of Chang'an and traveled the long route to the Western Regions when business required it. The brother had met his Chinese partner in Gongyuecheng (modern-day Almaligh, Xinjiang, near the Chinese border with Kazakhstan) and lent him 275 bolts of silk, which could be carried on several pack animals. Since the two men did not have a common language, they spoke through an interpreter.

As this case demonstrates, plain silk—undyed with a simple basket-weave pattern—served as a currency alongside bronze coins during the Tang dynasty. Silk had many advantages over bronze coins. The value of the coins fluctuated wildly while the price of silk was more stable. The dimensions of a bolt of silk held remarkably steady between the third and the tenth centuries at 1 Chinese foot, 8 inches (22 inches, or 56 cm) wide and 40 Chinese feet (39 feet, or 12 m) long.[69] Also, silk was lighter than bronze coins; the standard unit of one thousand coins could weigh as much as nine pounds (4 kg).[70]

After making the loan the Sogdian went south to Kucha, leading two camels, four cattle, and one donkey. These seven pack animals carried his goods, which included silk, bows and arrows, bowls, and saddles. The Sogdian never made it to Kucha; one witness in the trial speculated that he had been killed by bandits who stole his goods. Even though the surviving brother did not have a copy of the original loan agreement, he was able to present two witnesses, both Sogdians, to the signing of the contract. According to Tang law, their oral testimony constituted sufficient proof of the original agreement. The Chinese court ruled in favor of the living Sogdian brother and against the Chinese merchant, ordering him to repay his debt.

The deceased Sogdian brother had traveled with seven pack animals carrying his goods. Other caravans were about the same size, as we learn from twelve surviving travel passes found at Turfan. Like similar documents from Niya and Kucha, these record the members of each party—both people and animals—proceeding together from one destination to another and all the places to which they were allowed to go. At the beginning of his trip, each traveler applied for a travel pass that listed his ultimate destination, a few intermediate points, and the people and animals traveling with him. In addition, each time he entered a new prefecture, he received a document verifying the people and animals traveling with him.

At every guard station, both within and between prefectures, local officials checked that all the people—classified as relatives of the primary traveler, servants (*zuoren*), or slaves—and all the draft animals rightfully belonged to him. Tang-dynasty law prohibited the enslavement of people to repay debts; the only legal slaves were those who were born to slave parents or who had been purchased with a contract registered with the authorities and who had the proper market certificate to show for it.[71] Tang law was equally strict about animals: a traveler could bring a donkey, horse, camel, or cow by a checkpoint only if he carried a market certificate for any purchased animals. Like officials at Kucha, Turfan officials did not record what cargo each caravan carried. Still, the travel passes do give the size of caravans, which usually included four or five people and about ten animals.[72]

One merchant, named Shi Randian (in Sogdian, Zhemat-yan, "Favor of the god Zhemat"), appears in several documents, so it is possible to track his movements in the years 732 and 733 and to grasp the level of government supervision. With his household registered in Turfan, Shi carried a travel pass allowing him to proceed from Guazhou to Hami via Dunhuang and then all the way west to Kucha, on a route similar to Xuanzang's. Surviving documents record the approval of four different officials on the leg from Guazhou to Dunhuang. The caravan was checked two times on the nineteenth day of the third month, once on the twentieth day, and again on the twenty-first day.[73] On his first trip, Shi traveled with two servants, a slave, and ten horses, but on his way back he had purchased an additional horse (for eighteen rolls of silk) and a mule.[74] Since he carried the necessary market certificate demonstrating he had purchased them legally, he was allowed to proceed. A small-scale trader, Shi carried his wares on ten horses, and bought and sold individual animals from time to time to augment his income.

Officials did stop those caravans whose papers were not in order. In 733, one resident of Chang'an, Wang Fengxian, was returning from a trip supplying the army in Kucha. He applied for a new travel pass, because he had diverged from his permitted route to pursue a debtor who, he said, owed him three thousand bronze coins. Local officials apprehended him in a town to which he had not been given permission to travel. When he explained that he had fallen ill, and others verified his account, they allowed him to proceed.[75] The Turfan travel passes, like those from Niya and Kucha, confirm that all travelers were subject to the intense scrutiny of the authorities and could not diverge from their itineraries without official permission.

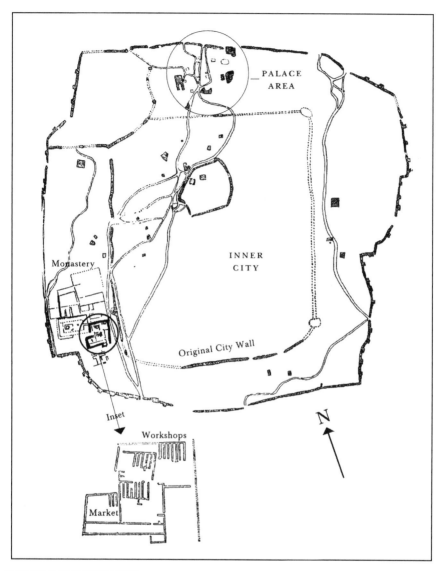

MAP OF GAOCHANG CITY

By carefully examining the roads and buildings in the ruins of Gaochang, archeologists have identified distinct neighborhoods in the city. The Tang authorities divided Gaochang City into different wards, just as in the cities of central China, and these wards continued to be used under the Uighurs. The commercial district in the southwest of the city housed workshops where craftsmen made handicrafts sold at the local market. The authorities divided vendors of different goods into groups, each with its own row of stalls at the market, and visited regularly to record prices.

Once a caravan passed through the official checkpoint into a new town, its members could find innkeepers, who also stored their wares for them, doctors, who treated their illnesses, and prostitutes, who, as today, have left little documentary evidence of their activities.[76] The caravans visited the markets in each town they stopped in. Tang-dynasty law required certain designated officials, known as market supervisors, to inspect markets every ten days and record three prices—the high, the low, and the medium—of all commodities on sale.[77] Such a register, in 121 fragments, for the main market in Turfan survives and is dated 743; some sections are dated to the fourteenth day of a certain month, others to the twenty-eighth, an indication that officials collected the data on two separate occasions.[78] Chinese markets were divided into rows, where merchants sold related goods; the Turfan register lists over 350 goods divided into over ten different rows.

As informative as it is, the price list does not reveal everything about the market. Some of the high-medium-low pricing sequences—6/5/4—seem suspiciously regular, for example, and the register gives the same prices for livestock, regardless of age or overall health. Nor does the register reveal how much of any single item is for sale or how many different stalls offer that particular item.

Like markets all over China today, the Turfan market offered a wide variety of flours and grains, in addition to vegetables like onions and scallions. Other daily-use items, like cauldrons and pots, as well as livestock, including horses, camels, and cattle, were all for sale. One could even buy a cartload of human excrement used as fertilizer for 25/22/20 coins.

The market also offered a variety of goods imported from the Iranian world. Many of these overlap with those in the scale-fee records: ammonium chloride, aromatics, sugar, and brass. The market register lists more than seventy different kinds of medicine. Many of the imported goods are small and light, because they had to be carried overland, but there are some heavier items, including brass-inlaid high-quality iron swords for 2,500/2,000/1,800 coins, which were for sale alongside much cheaper, locally made knives, which went for 90/80/70 coins. The largest goods from the west were animals: gelded Turkish steeds and Persian camels, which could have been walked to Turfan and would have found ready customers among the officers in the Tang armies stationed there. The horses sold for 20/18/16 rolls of silk; the camels for 33/30/27 rolls of silk.[79] The different textile stalls offered specialized silks made in Sichuan, Henan, and other interior Chinese provinces, which were precisely the tax silks paid to soldiers.

The market register portrays a market supplied by small-scale traders traveling in small caravans of ten to twenty animals, the same level of commerce documented by the scale-fee documents and the *guosuo* travel passes. The major player in the Central Asian economy—which diverges from the prevailing image of the Silk Road trade—was the Tang government. Starting in the 630s with the campaigns against the Western Turks, the Tang administration poured funds into the Western Regions to support its military efforts. To finance their campaigns, the Tang state collected bolts of cloth in central China and then shipped them to Wuwei and Qinzhou (modern Qin'an), also in Gansu Province, and from there to places farther west, closer to the frontier.[80] Over twenty examples of this type of tax cloth originating from central China have been found in Xinjiang.[81]

Immediately after the 640 conquest, the Tang forces in Turfan probably numbered several thousand. Although we speak of Tang armies, many of the soldiers were not Chinese but local.[82] The losses of territory in the northwest, including Kucha, to the Tibetans from 670 to 692 resulted in ever-increasing military expenditures in the eighth century. Du You (735–812), the author of the first comprehensive institutional encyclopedia, put the costs of defending the frontier at two million strings of coins in 713, ten million strings in 741, and fourteen to fifteen million strings in 755. Tang officials combined strings of coin, piculs of grain, and bolts of cloth to create an aggregate accounting unit whose value eludes anyone who has tried to make sense of the internally contradictory figures that survive.[83]

However one understands these figures, the outlays by the Tang state are staggering. Even individual payments dwarf all the transactions recorded in the Turfan documents. In the 730s or 740s, the central government sent 900,000 bolts of silk each year to four military headquarters in the frontier regions of the Western Regions: Hami, Turfan, Beiting, and Kucha. By 742 some five thousand Tang soldiers were stationed in Turfan, yet the tax receipts from local inhabitants covered only 9 percent of their expenses.[84] The Tang state's subsidy for the military injected vast sums of money, in the form of silk, into the local economies of the Silk Road oases.

These massive expenditures by the Tang central government came to a sudden halt with the An Lushan rebellion. The rebellion forced the Tang dynasty to withdraw from Central Asia and nearly brought the dynasty down. Born to a Sogdian father and a Turkish mother, the leader of the rebellion, An Rokhshan, worked his way up from buying horses for the Chinese army to being the general in charge of three different originally separate military commands.[85] (An's given name, Lushan, was the Chinese transcription of the Sogdian "Rokhshan.") Fearful that his own troops might join the rebels, the emperor Xuanzong (reigned 712–56) accepted their demand that he strangle his consort Yang Guifei, rumored to be romantically involved with An Rokhshan, and then abdicated his throne to his son Suzong, who reigned from 756 to 762. With the largest provinces in central China under the rebels' control, the tax receipts of the Tang state plummeted after 755, forcing the Tang military to cease payments to the armies in the northwest.[86] The Tang emperor had no choice but to hire Uighur mercenaries to fight the rebels. Only in 763 did the much-weakened dynasty succeed in putting down the rebellion.

During the Tang campaign to regain control from the mutineers, Uighur mercenaries occupied Luoyang in 762. There, in a fateful encounter with far-reaching implications for Turfan, which came under Uighur rule fifty years later, the leader of the Uighurs encountered a Sogdian teacher who introduced him to the basic teachings of Manichaeism.[87] Manichaeism, a religion founded in Iran by the prophet Mani (ca. 210–76), held that the forces of light and darkness were engaged in a perpetual battle for control of the universe. The Uighur kaghan adopted Manichaeism as the official religion of his people and recorded his decision in a trilingual inscription (in Sogdian, Uighur, and Chinese) on a stone tablet.[88] This was the first—and the only—time in world history that any state named Manichaeism its official religion.

The Tibetan Empire seized on this moment of Tang vulnerability during the rebellion to expand its power. During the 780s Tibetan armies moved into Gansu, conquered the Beiting (Beshbalyq) Protectorate immediately to the north of Turfan in 786, and in 792 took Turfan as well. In 803 the Uighurs wrested control of Turfan from the Tibetans. The Uighurs in Mongolia were then defeated by the Kirghiz in 840, and some of these Uighurs withdrew to Turfan. There, between 866 and 872, they established a new state called the Uighur Kaghanate, with its capital at Gaochang City.[89] A second Uighur kaghanate was based to the east in Ganzhou (Zhangye, Gansu).

Under the Uighurs, the local people of Turfan continued to record their purchases and sales of land, slaves, and animals in contracts, but they used Uighur, not Chinese, as their written language.[90] The thirteenth- and fourteenth-century contracts from Turfan in Uighur show that the economy returned largely to barter, with people exchanging animals and land for fixed measures of grain or cloth, often cotton, which replaced silk as a currency.

The documents in the Uighur language reveal much about the religious life of the community. Under the Tang dynasty, the residents of Turfan had worshipped Buddhist, Daoist, and Zoroastrian deities as well as local ones. Under the Uighurs, devotees of two new religions worshipped in Turfan as well: Christianity and Manichaeism.

Evidence of Christianity was discovered in the early twentieth century by the second German expedition to the region. Outside the eastern walls of Gaochang City, archeologists found a small Christian church, from which they salvaged one mural showing Palm Sunday worship. At Bulayik, a site to the north of Turfan,

MANICHAEAN WALL PAINTING FROM BEZEKLIK

A tree of life heavily laden with fruit, with three intertwined trunks, dominates this large painting from cave 38 at Bezeklik, which stands 5 feet (1.5 m) high, 8 feet (2.4 m) wide, making it one of the world's largest surviving Manichaean artworks. The Uighur-language prayers at the base of the tree give the name of the donor, who requests the protection of guardian deities. The female donor wears an unusual bird headdress and kneels at the right of the tree; two guardian deities stand behind her, and three others kneel next to her. The opposite side of the painting shows her husband, partially effaced, wearing a similar headdress. This copy was made in 1931, when the mural was already severely damaged.

they excavated Christian manuscripts in Syriac, Sogdian, Middle Persian, modern Persian, and Uighur. One manuscript even gave a line in Greek before translating a psalm into Sogdian. Syriac was the primary language of worship, but some psalters and hymn collections have Sogdian headings in them. These Sogdian headings indicate that the Christians of Bulayik were mainly Sogdian speakers, though the presence of Turkish names and linguistic features in the Sogdian texts suggests that they were gradually giving up Sogdian in favor of Uighur. The dating of these manuscripts is uncertain; most likely they date to the ninth and tenth centuries, when Turfan was the capital of the Uighur Kaghanate.[91]

Like most Christians in Central Asia, the Christians at Turfan belonged to the Church of the East, which was based in Mesopotamia, and the liturgical language was Syriac, a dialect of Aramaic. The teachings of the Church of the East held that Christ had two natures—divine and human—and, furthermore, that Mary was the mother of the human Jesus but not the divine Christ. Their opponents sometimes called them Nestorians in an effort to associate them with Nestorius (ca. 381–ca. 451), a Syrian patriarch in Constantinople from 428 to 431, who had been expelled from the church, but members of the church do not refer to themselves as such.[92]

After the kaghan's conversion, Manichaeism was the official religion of the Uighur Kaghanate. One charter, 125 lines long, specifies how a Manichaean monastery should be run, and most likely dates to the ninth century. It is not clear whether the Uighur government of Turfan or the monastery's own leaders issued the document, which charges different monastic officials with supervising fields, vineyards, and the monastery storehouse. Some of the titles, like "elect," are unique to Manichaeism, but the monastery's structure closely resembled that of Buddhist monasteries. Dependent workers tilled the fields and supplied the monastery's residents with grain and clothing. The clergy conducted feasts and were responsible for the spiritual lives of the congregation, whose main obligation was to supply them with vegetarian food that they would eat and so increase the amount of light in their bodies.[93]

Albert von Le Coq, the German excavator who was so active at Kucha, found some of the most interesting documents about Manichaeism in two buried monastic libraries dating to the period of Uighur rule. Texts of many Manichaean hymns survive: some in the liturgical language of Parthian, which Mani spoke, some in Uighur, the local language of Turfan by the year 1000. These hymns often celebrate the victory of the forces of light over the forces of darkness:

> All beings of Light, the righteous [elect] and the auditors, who have
> endured much suffering, will rejoice with the Father. . . .
> For they have fought together with Him, and they have overcome and
> vanquished that Dark One who had boasted in vain.[94]

Hymns like this have permitted scholars to reconstruct the major tenets of Manichaeism, which would otherwise be unknown, since so few Manichaean texts exist anywhere in the world.

Some of the texts Le Coq found were beautifully illustrated but so severely damaged by water that all the pages stuck together and could not be separated. One such fragment survives in the Museum of Indian Art in Berlin, which holds all the material brought back by the four German expeditions that survived the bombing during World War II. This miniature depicts the Bema festival, the most important holiday of the Manichaean year, in which the clergy, or elect, sang hymns, read aloud Mani's teachings, and ate a meal, shown in color plate 11A.[95]

Although Manichaeism was the official state religion of the Uighur Kaghanate, little Manichaean art survives onsite at Turfan. Only one cave painting at Bezeklik, all scholars concur, is definitely Manichaean.[96] The mural has suffered great damage since 1931 when the copy shown on page 109 was made, and those managing the site rarely show it to visitors.

Why does so little Manichaean art survive at Turfan and the surrounding cave sites? Sometime around the year 1000 the rulers of the Uighur Kaghanate chose to patronize Buddhism and not Manichaeism.[97] Several surviving caves in Turfan, including cave 38 at Bezeklik, bear witness to this shift: close examination of the cave walls shows that the caves had two layers, often a Manichaean layer (not always visible) lies beneath a Buddhist layer. The Uighur court's decision to support Buddhism apparently ushered in a new era in which only one religion was tolerated.

In 1209 the Mongols defeated the Uighur Kaghanate of Turfan but left the Uighur kings in place. In 1275 the Uighurs sided with Khubilai Khan. When defeated by one of his rivals, the Uighur royal family fled and settled in Gansu in 1283. Although peasant rebels overthrew the Mongol rulers of China and established the Ming dynasty in the fourteenth century, Turfan remained outside of the borders of China and under the rule of the united Mongols and, later, the Chaghatai branch of the Mongols. In 1383 Xidir (Xizir) Khoja (reigned 1389–99), himself a Muslim, conquered Turfan and forced the inhabitants to convert to Islam, the prevailing religion of the region today.[98] The region remained independent of China until 1756, when the Qing dynasty armies invaded.[99]

The history of Turfan falls into three distinct periods: before the Tang conquest of 640, Tang rule (640–755), and after 803, when the Uighur Kaghanate was based in the oasis. In the periods both before and after Chinese rule, the economy was largely self-sufficient. Most of the documented movement along the overland routes was either by envoys or refugees. The high point of the Silk Road trade coincided with (because it was caused by) the presence of the Chinese troops. The Tang government injected vast amounts of both cloth and coin into the local economy, which resulted in high interest rates on loans even for poor farmers. But when the Chinese forces withdrew after 755 the local economy reverted to a subsistence basis. As coming chapters will show, much information about the spending patterns of the Tang government survives in other oases (particularly Dunhuang), but the overall pattern is clear. The Silk Road trade was largely the byproduct of Chinese government spending—not long-distance commerce conducted by private merchants, as is so often thought.

A LETTER TO SAMARKAND

One of eight folded pieces of paper from an abandoned mailbag, this letter was written on a sheet of paper and then folded into a small silk bag and labeled "Bound for Samarkand." These letters, dating to 313 or 314, are among the most important surviving documents about the Silk Road trade, because they are written by private individuals, including businessmen, and not by government officials. Courtesy of the Board of the British Library.

CHAPTER 4

Homeland of the Sogdians, the Silk Road Traders

Samarkand and Sogdiana

In 630, when the Chinese monk Xuanzang left Turfan, he took the most traveled route west. After stopping in Kucha, he crossed the Tianshan Mountains, visited the kaghan of the Western Turks on the northwestern edge of Lake Issykkul in what is now Kyrgyzstan, and then proceeded to Samarkand in modern Uzbekistan. From Samarkand, travelers could go west to Syria, return to the oasis states of the Taklamakan, or proceed south to India, as Xuanzang did. Samarkand was then the major city of the Sogdians, the Iranian people who played such an important role in the Silk Road trade and who formed China's largest and most influential immigrant community during the Tang dynasty.[1] The Sogdians spoke a Middle Iranian language called Sogdian, a descendant of which is still spoken in the remote Yaghnob Valley in nearby Tajikistan (see the document on the facing page in Sogdian).

In Samarkand, Xuanzang entered the cultural sphere of the Iranians, whose languages, religious practices, and customs, although equally old and equally sophisticated, differed profoundly from those of the Chinese. The modern traveler following in Xuanzang's steps crosses a different kind of border, just as distinct, between China and the former Soviet Union. Jokingly referred to as the "Steel Road" by Chinese, this treacherous highway is strewn with overturned trucks and metal debris from dismantled Soviet-era factories being carted off to China.

The seventh-century route posed real dangers. After waiting two months for the snow to melt, Xuanzang left Kucha and headed toward the Tianshan Mountains. Provided with camels, horses, and guards by the Kucha king, Xuanzang traveled only two days before encountering more than two thousand Turk (Tujue) robbers on horseback. They did not rob Xuanzang, his disciple and biographer Huili explains, since they were too busy dividing previously looted goods among themselves.

The travelers then reached the towering Tianshan Mountains, where Mount Ling made a profound impression on Xuanzang:

The mountain is dangerous and precipitous, so steep that it rises up to the sky. Since the road was first opened, the icy snow accumulates in places where it remains frozen, not melting in either the spring or summer. Huge expanses of ice meet and join the clouds. The snow is so blindingly white that one cannot see where it ends and the clouds begin. The icy pinnacles fall and lie across the road. Some are a hundred feet high, some several cubits [*zhang*, roughly 10 feet, or 3 m] across.

The trip was extremely arduous, Huili continues:

It is difficult to proceed on the rough, narrow paths. Add the snowy wind flying in different directions, and even fur-lined garments and boots cannot prevent a battle with the chill. Whenever one wants to sleep or eat, there is never a dry place to stop, so the only thing to do is to hang up a cauldron and cook, and to lay one's mat out on the ice and sleep.

After seven days the survivors in Xuanzang's group finally left the mountains. Three or four out of every ten people in the group had died from hunger or cold, and the losses among the horses and cattle were even greater.[2]

These fatalities were unusually high, prompting some to wonder whether Xuanzang and his companions were caught in an avalanche unmentioned by his biographer.[3] Due to the extraordinarily dry climate, ice formed only at the mountaintops of the Tianshan Mountains, far above the timberline, with the result that a band of dirt and sand lay immediately below the ice. When chunks of ice broke off, they hurtled down dirt, not ice, creating truly terrifying avalanches. Avalanche or not, this was certainly the most perilous crossing of Xuanzang's entire trip to India.[4]

After crossing the Tianshan Mountains, Xuanzang and his companions arrived at Lake Issyk-kul in Kyrgyzstan. Issyk-kul means "hot lake" in Turkic, and the sea is fed by warm springs that prevent it from freezing over. The Chinese also called Issyk-kul the "warm sea."[5] Near the modern town of Tokmak, at a site called Ak-Beshim, near the lake's western edge, Xuanzang met the leader of the Western Turks, the kaghan, who wore a fine green silk robe and wrapped a ten-foot-long silk band around his head, allowing his long hair to fall down his back.[6]

At the time, in 630, the kaghan headed a confederation of Turks that controlled the territory all the way from Turfan to Persia. He did not rule directly but left local rulers, like those in Turfan, Kucha, and Samarkand, in place as long as they paid him tribute, provided troops when requested, and obeyed

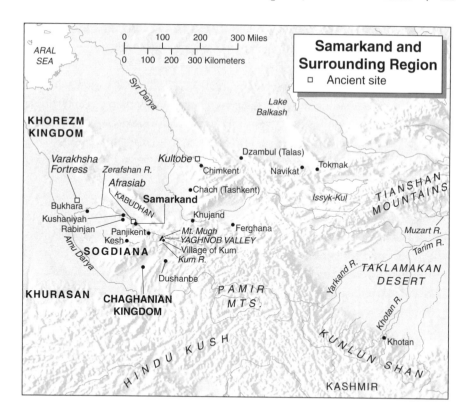

his commands. For several days the kaghan, like the Gaochang king, tried to persuade Xuanzang to stay at Tokmak and not go on to India. When Xuanzang did not consent, the kaghan finally gave in and provided the monk with an interpreter, fifty pieces of silk for travel expenses, and letters of introduction to the various rulers who accepted him as their overlord. From the town of Tokmak, Xuanzang and his party traveled westward, going through lovely mountain pastures, and then across the barren Kizil Kum desert before reaching Samarkand.

In his *Record of Travels to the West*, a detailed account of the different countries of the Western Regions, Xuanzang sketched the basic traits of the Sogdians.[7] They did not write characters; instead they used an alphabet of some twenty letters in various combinations to record a broad vocabulary. Their clothing was simple, made of fur and felt, and, like the Turkish kaghan, the men bound their heads with cloth and shaved their foreheads. This struck Chinese observers as unusual, because they viewed hair as an integral part of the body, a gift from one's parents that should not be cut.

Xuanzang gives voice to a widely held Chinese view of the Sogdians: "Their customs are slippery and tricky, and they frequently cheat and deceive, greatly desiring wealth, and fathers and sons alike seek profit."[8] The compilers of the official history of the Tang dynasty echoed this prejudice in their description of how the Sogdians raised their sons to be merchants: "When they give birth to a son, they put honey on his mouth and place glue in his palms so that when he grows up, he will speak sweet words and grasp coins in his hand as if they were glued there. . . . They are good at trading, love profit, and go abroad at the age of twenty. They are everywhere profit is to be found."[9]

Unfortunately, few Sogdian-language sources are available to correct these stereotypes. The climate in and around Samarkand is not as dry as that of the Taklamakan Desert, the soil is more acidic, and many materials were destroyed after the Islamic conquest of the early eighth century. Only two important groups of Sogdian-language documents survive: the first, the eight Sogdian "Ancient Letters" from the early fourth century, was found by Aurel Stein outside Dunhuang, while the second, nearly a hundred documents from a castle under siege, is from the early eighth century and was discovered in the 1930s outside Samarkand. Other Sogdian-language materials are limited to inscriptions on silver bowls or textiles, captions on paintings, and the many religious texts found at Turfan, which say little about the history of the Sogdians.[10]

The first traces of the Sogdians in the archeological record come from the earliest levels of habitation at Samarkand, which date to the seventh century BCE. Writing several centuries later, the biographers of Alexander of Macedon commented on the ferocious resistance of the inhabitants of Marakanda, the Greek name for Samarkand, who ultimately surrendered to Alexander. After Alexander's death, various dynasties took power, and, for much of the time, a confederation based in what is now Tashkent controlled the city.[11]

Until recently, scholars have thought that the abandoned mailbag that Aurel Stein unearthed near Dunhuang in 1907 was the earliest surviving body of Sogdian-language materials, but between 1996 and 2006 archeologists working at the site of Kultobe (near Chimkent on the river Aris) in southern Kazakhstan found ten scraps of baked brick plaques with Sogdian letters on them. After careful examination of these materials, Nicholas Sims-Williams, the world's leading expert on the Iranian languages of Central Asia, has determined that they predate the mailbag letters. At least four Sogdian city-states existed at the time this wall was built, but the texts are so fragmentary that it is difficult to learn much from them.[12]

The eight Sogdian-language letters found by Stein are largely intact and thus far more informative. Stein discovered the abandoned mailbag 56 miles (90 km) northwest of Dunhuang. One of the letters was addressed to a resident of Samarkand, an indication that the letter carrier was on his way to Samarkand when the letters were lost. In 1907 Stein's men unearthed the letters while exploring a series of watchtowers, spaced two miles (3.2 km) apart, built by different Chinese dynasties to defend the frontier. Twenty feet (6 m) or more high, these guard towers often were attached to small dwellings for the guards.[13] At one tower, which Stein numbered T.XII.A (T for Tun-huang, a variant spelling of Dunhuang), Stein noticed nothing special and assigned a team to clear out the passageway while he went to explore another tower. When he returned in the evening, the workmen showed him what they had discovered: some colored silks, a wooden case, Chinese documents dating to the early first century CE, a piece of silk with Kharoshthi script on it from before 400 CE, and "one small roll after another of neatly folded paper containing what was manifestly some Western writing."[14] The script resembled Aramaic, and Stein remembered that he had found other similar examples at Loulan. Only later was the unfamiliar script identified as Sogdian.

These eight sheets of paper proved to be extraordinarily revealing, even though the letters are difficult to decipher and many words are missing. The handful of the world's scholars who can read Sogdian continue to debate the meaning of each sentence, even now still occasionally explicating a phrase that has puzzled everyone for the past century. Four of the five intact letters have been translated into English.[15] Stein's excavation methods were advanced for his day, but not perfect; his workmen did not record which materials they found at which level in the collapsed tower, a real problem, given that the letters were undated.

Crucially, one letter provides a clue to the time of composition: "And, sirs, the last emperor, so they say, fled from Luoyang because of the famine and fire was set to his palace and to the city, and the palace was burnt and the city destroyed. Luoyang is no more. Ye [Zhangde fu, Henan] is no more!"[16] Attacks on Luoyang occurred in 190, 311, and 535. Most scholars of Sogdian concur that the letter refers to the events of 311 and was written in either 313 or 314.[17] The author of the letter refers to the invading army as "Huns," and indeed their leader, Shi Le (274–333), belonged to one of the peoples in the Xiongnu confederation. This is one of the main pieces of evidence linking the Xiongnu with the Huns of Central Asia who invaded Europe in the late 300s.[18]

The eight letters were not in envelopes but "folded up into neat little convolutes," as Stein called them, measuring 3.5–5 inches (9–13 cm) long, 1–1.25 inches (2.5–3 cm) across. Although originating in different Chinese towns, the letter paper had similar dimensions, of roughly 15.5–16.5 inches (39–42 cm) by 9.5–9.75 inches (24–25 cm), suggesting that even then sheets of paper were made in standardized sheets—a rather rapid development given that paper came into widespread use in China only in the third century CE. Three letters were placed in individual silk bags; a fourth, letter 2 (shown at the beginning of this chapter), was in a silk bag with a linen covering that said "bound for Samarkand" but with no return address. The other letters were not addressed, suggesting that the person delivering them may have known the recipients for whom they were intended. Letters 1 and 3 were written by a woman living in Dunhuang to her mother and husband who probably lived in Loulan, while Letter 5 was sent from Wuwei.

Already in the early fourth century, the letters reveal, Sogdian communities existed in Luoyang, Chang'an, Lanzhou, Wuwei, Jiuquan, and Dunhuang. The second letter mentions settlements of forty Sogdians in one place and one hundred "freemen" from Samarkand in another (both locations unfortunately illegible); the Luoyang settlement included both Sogdians and Indians. As soon as a community of Sogdians reached a certain size, perhaps forty, they erected a fire temple. The *sabao* performed ritual functions, namely tending the fire altar and presiding over Zoroastrian festivals, and as headman adjudicated disputes.

In Iran Zoroastrianism evolved toward monotheism, with Ahura Mazda as the supreme deity, but in Sogdiana its adherents worshipped many deities, including Ahura Mazda.[19] Zoroastrian teachings forbade both Chinese burial in the ground and Buddhist cremation since both were polluting: burial polluted the earth, and cremation polluted fire. Instead, the Zoroastrians exposed the corpses of the dead, allowing scavenging animals to clean the meat from the bones before burying them in clay urns, called ossuaries.

Miwnay, the Dunhuang woman who wrote letters 1 and 3, was abandoned by her husband and saddled with his debts. The list of the men she approached for assistance provides a capsule sketch of Sogdian society in exile. Miwnay turned to a councilor (apparently an official who collected taxes), a relative of her husband's, and then to a third man, apparently a business associate. Each refused to help on the grounds that it was her husband's obligation, not theirs. Finally, she approached the "temple-priest," who promised a camel and a male escort.

Miwnay vents her frustration forcefully in her letter to her husband: "I obeyed your command and came to Dunhuang and did not observe my mother's bidding or that of my brothers. Surely the gods were angry with me on the day when I did your bidding! I would rather be a dog's or a pig's wife than yours!"[20] A postscript written by her daughter reports that the two poverty-stricken women were reduced to tending sheep. Stuck in Dunhuang for three years, Miwnay had five opportunities to leave with caravans but not enough money to pay the twenty staters she needed for her passage.

Scholars are not certain of the value of a stater. Did it weigh .42 ounces (12 grams), as some of the stater coins circulating at the time did? Or was it a much lighter coin of .02 ounces (.6 grams) of silver circulating in Samarkand? (This is just one of the many conundrums still facing Silk Road researchers.)

Far richer than Miwnay was the business agent who reported the fall of Luoyang. He had sufficient funds in Samarkand for him to authorize merchants handling his affairs to "take 1,000 or 2,000 staters out of the money" to assist an orphan in his care. In his letter, the business agent wrote to his boss in Samarkand about the different people he had hired in the Gansu towns of Jiuquan and Wuwei. His letter documents three levels in the company: the boss (a father and son in Samarkand); the agent (author of the letter), who supervises a network of weavers who work for them; and the weavers themselves.

Letter 2 also mentions some of the commodities being traded at the time, namely woolen cloths and linen. The agent reports that he has sent 32 "vesicles"—a unit of uncertain value—of musk to Dunhuang. Musk, processed from the glands of the musk deer, was used as a scent and as a fixative. According to Étienne de la Vaissière, a prominent historian of the Sogdians, the musk probably weighed 1.75 pounds (.8 kg), an enormous amount of pure musk.[21] The second letter also mentions woolen cloths and linen but gives no quantities.

The fifth letter, from a more local level of commerce between Guzang and Dunhuang, is addressed to the caravan leader. It mentions much smaller amounts of money: the author claims that he received only four and a half staters from the twenty he was owed. He describes several goods being sent by caravan from Guzang to other destinations, most likely Loulan, some 900 miles (1,400 km) away: "white," most likely ceruse, a cosmetic with a white lead base; pepper; silver; and "rysk," a term whose meaning is not clear. Certain goods traveled great distances: pepper (letter 5) and camphor (letter 6) could be purchased only in Southeast Asia or India, while musk (letter 2) came from the Tibetan border with Gansu. In the sixth letter, only sections of which survive, the author asks the recipient to buy something, possibly "derived from the silkworm," meaning silk cloth or thread. If this is not available, then the recipient is to purchase camphor instead. This is apparently the only mention of silk in the Sogdian letters.[22] None of the quantities given in the Sogdian letters is certain, but most scholars concur that the amounts are small, most likely between 3.3 pounds (1.5 kg) and 88 pounds (40 kg).[23] An animal, or a few animals, could easily have carried these amounts, suggesting that the Silk Road trade was a trade limited in scope, in what some scholars have called a "petty" trade.[24]

Source: Étienne de la Vaissière, *Histoire des Marchands Sogdiens*
(Paris: Collège de France, Institut des Hautes Études Chinoises, 2002), Map 3.

The Sogdian Ancient Letters are significant because they are among the only Silk Road documents written by merchants, not by the authorities overseeing or taxing trade. They depict a diasporic group of Sogdians living peacefully as merchants, farmers, and even servants in lands still engaged in commerce and long-distance trade at a time when China was in chaos, with one dynasty having just fallen and another struggling to take over.

In the following centuries the Sogdians continued to speak their own language but modified their clothing and hairstyles to conform with the demands of their new, nomadic conquerors—the Huns, Kidarites, Hephthalites, and Turks, who gained control of Samarkand, sometimes with the assistance of the Sasanian empire (224–651), far to the west with their capital at Ctesiphon, near modern-day Baghdad. In 509 Samarkand fell to the Hephthalites, a confederation of Iranian and Turkic peoples who are occasionally called the White Huns and who

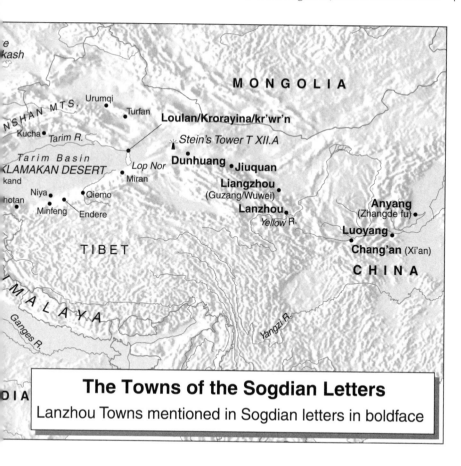

The Towns of the Sogdian Letters

Lanzhou Towns mentioned in Sogdian letters in boldface

lived in northern Afghanistan.[25] Later, around 560, the Sasanians allied with the newly formed Turkish confederation to defeat the Hephthalites.[26] After 565 Samarkand came under the rule of the Western Turks, which is why Xuanzang continued on to Samarkand after meeting the kaghan at Tokmak. Although the Turks developed a written language of their own in the eighth century, they often wrote in Sogdian, and cultural ties between the Turks and Sogdians were close.

During these centuries of frequent political shifts, the Sogdians gradually expanded out from Samarkand and Bukhara. In the fifth century and later, Sogdians put up Sogdian-style buildings and irrigation works as they designed new settlements around the Zerafshan River. Economic growth accelerated in the fifth century, and by the sixth and seventh century, Sogdiana had become the richest country in Central Asia, as demonstrated by the ever larger houses and more elaborate paintings found by archeologists at Panjikent.[27]

Panjikent, 37 miles (60 km) east of Samarkand in Tajikistan, is one of the most important archeological sites on the Silk Road, as first Soviet and now Russian archeologists from the Hermitage Museum in St. Petersburg have been excavating the site every summer since 1947.[28] Unlike many of the excavations in China, archeologists are not digging up individual tombs but painstakingly excavating a small city, house by house, quadrant by quadrant.

The excavations at Panjikent have so far uncovered about 15–17 acres (6–7 hectares), or one-half of the small city. Built sometime in the fifth century, the city reached its largest size in the seventh century. Panjikent fell to Arab armies in 722, revived briefly in the 740s, and then was completely abandoned between 770 and 780.[29] Between five and seven thousand inhabitants lived there, surrounded by a city wall dating to the fifth century. Their city contained several streets, alleyways, two bazaars, and two temples, one with a side fire altar, the other with images of at least ten different deities.[30] This temple had a room with a separate entrance that housed a statue of the Indian god Shiva sitting on a bull holding a trident. His trident and erect penis conformed to Indian prototypes, but his boots were Sogdian.

Commercial granaries and bazaars show that a retail trade existed in Panjikent. Although archeologists have not found evidence of permanent buildings to house caravans, called caravanserai in Persian, anywhere in Sogdiana, some modern historians believe that the caravanserai originated in the region. The geographer Ibn H. awqal described the ruin of a giant building that could house up to two hundred travelers and their animals, with food for all and room to sleep as well.[31] Several Panjikent houses had courtyards large enough to house a caravan, and the word "hotel" in Sogdian (*tym*) was borrowed from the Chinese word "inn" (*dian*).[32]

Caravans passed through Panjikent, since it was on the road between Samarkand and China, which crossed the Ammoniac Mountains, a major source of ammonium chloride in the Tianshan Mountains between modern-day Tajikistan and China.[33] Yet few artifacts found in Panjikent can be identified as coming via the caravan trade; small glass vessels dating to the seventh century are one important exception. Local production of glass began only in the mid-eighth century.[34]

More evidence of trade lies in the thousands of bronze coins found in the city, many apparently loose change discarded or mislaid at the market place. Silver coins, from the Sasanian Empire, also circulated during the sixth century in smaller quantities. The earliest locally minted coins date to the second half of the seventh century. Apparently the central authorities granted local workshops the right to make coins. In the seventh century, the period of greatest contact between Sogdiana and China, the residents of Panjikent used bronze coins with the same shape as Chinese coins—round coins with a square hole—some with Chinese characters on them, some without.

As at Turfan, residents sometimes used gold coins. Between 1947 and 1995, archeologists found two genuine gold coins from the Byzantine Empire and six extremely thin imitations. Five, found in houses, indicate that the coins and the imitations were used as currency.[35]

Similarly, imitation gold coins also served as burial goods. Two of the gold coins (and possibly a third) were found inside *naus* structures the Sogdians built to house the dead, usually members of the same family. These buildings were small, square, and made of mud brick; they held the cleaned bones in ossuaries.[36] Zoroastrian texts do not mention naus buildings, which first appear in the Samarkand region—but not in central Iran—in the late fourth or fifth centuries.

Motifs on some of the ossuaries document the belief that Ahura Mazda would use the bones of the deceased to reconstitute them on the Judgment Day.[37] The burial of coins with the dead shows that the living thought they would benefit from having a gold coin, or an imitation gold coin, near them. The practice does not seem to have been limited to the wealthy; one of the deceased buried with such coin was a potter.[38]

Not all the dead were buried in Zoroastrian ossuaries; one graveyard in Panjikent included tombs with fully extended bodies, apparently Christian-style

ZOROASTRIAN BURIAL IN SAMARKAND

This clay ossuary, found in the village of Molla-Kurgan outside Samarkand, held the bones of the deceased after they had been cleaned. The lid of the box shows two woman dancers wearing transparent robes. Since there is no evidence of priestesses in the Samarkand region, they may be mourners at a funeral, or perhaps beautiful young women coming to greet the newly dead in the afterlife. The base shows a fire altar flanked by two Zoroastrian priests, who wear padam face masks and head coverings to keep any bodily substance or hair from polluting the fire. Courtesy of Frantz Grenet.

burials. One corpse wore a cross made from bronze.[39] A writing exercise in Syriac has been found, most likely copied by a Sogdian student studying the liturgical language of the Church of the East.[40]

The houses excavated so far, numbering over 130, include the dwellings of ordinary people as well as the very rich.[41] The large houses all have a fire altar in one room, the room for family prayers. Smaller, portable fire altars were kept in reception halls; these held religious images as well as pictures of worshippers, themselves often family members. The widespread presence of fire altars throughout the city indicates that most of the town's residents were Zoroastrians, but the Sogdians were open to other religious beliefs as well.

Different Sogdian households chose a deity that they worshipped in their own houses and whose pictures they placed on the walls of their reception rooms. These deities, with varying iconographical attributes, have not all been identified. Clearly Nana, an originally Mesopotamian goddess, had many devotees.[42] A deity shown sitting on a camel or holding a small camel figurine was also venerated by travelers.[43] One house owner placed a small image of the

PANJIKENT STREET SCENE

The wealthiest urban residents lived in multistoried dwellings with large halls, which could seat a hundred, complete with elaborate wall paintings and lavish carvings (4). Their homes were located close to shops and craftspeople's workshops (7) and a forge (8). Their poorer neighbors lived in smaller houses, often of two stories and sometimes with several rooms decorated with small paintings (9). Their occupants produced the crafts and staffed the shops where the rich purchased these items. From Guitty Azarpay, *Sogdian Painting: The Pictorial Epic in Oriental Art*, University of California Press, 1981 © The Regents of the University of California.

Buddha in a separate room in his house; although not as big as the paintings of the God of Victory and Nana in his house, the image demonstrates his willingness to accept a non-Sogdian deity.[44]

The houses of the wealthiest have wall paintings extending from the ceiling to the floor divided into different levels. On the highest part of the wall, facing doorways, are large portraits of deities, with donors—the householders themselves—below. The middle section paintings, roughly one yard (1 m) high, portray well-known folk tales from other countries: the Iranian epic Rustam, Aesop's fables, and Indian tales from the Panchatantra. In the bottom frame, usually about 20 inches (.5 m) high, are scrolls showing scenes in sequence that would have been narrated by a storyteller. As the page-sized format makes clear, these were copied from book illustrations.[45]

Although the residents of Panjikent commissioned paintings with many different types of subject matter, almost no paintings show commercial activity. Archeologists have identified one house with a painting of a lavish banquet as the house of a merchant who lived immediately next to one of the bazaars. The sole indication that the guests are merchants—and not nobles—is that, instead of the usual sword, one guest wears a black bag attached to his belt.[46]

Merchants are also absent from the large and beautiful set of murals from the Afrasiab site in Samarkand, which provide a visual introduction to the political situation of Samarkand. The realistic subject matter of the Afrasiab paintings distinguishes them from other Sogdian wall paintings depicting legends and deities found at Panjikent and the Varakhsha fortress outside Bukhara. They were painted between 660 and 661 during the reign of the Sogdian king Varkhuman, a name that appears in the official Chinese histories, because the Chinese emperor Gaozong (reigned 649–83) awarded him the title of governor of Sogdiana. In 631, an earlier Sogdian king made a similar request for an alliance with the Chinese, but the emperor Taizong turned him down on the grounds that Samarkand was too distant and that the Chinese would be unable to send troops if they were needed.[47]

Now located in the Afrasiab History Museum, these paintings were salvaged in 1965 after a bulldozer digging a new road removed the room's ceiling. The Afrasiab wall paintings stand over 6.5 feet (2 meters) tall and 35 feet (10.7 m) long and fill the four walls of an imposing square room in the house of a wealthy, aristocratic family. As the top section of the paintings on three of the four walls was bulldozed away, archeologists are uncertain of the paintings' original height.[48]

The Afrasiab paintings deserve careful study because they illuminate how the Sogdians viewed the larger world.[49] A few different figures, including a goose and a woman, bear labels written in small black Sogdian script that

PANJIKENT HOUSE

Many of the houses of the wealthy in Panjikent had a large reception room like this with high columns that displayed a painting of a deity. This family worshipped the originally Mesopotamian deity Nana, but other Panjikent houses had paintings of other deities as well. Note the multiple tiers of painting on the wall behind the goddess; Panjikent artists typically divided wall paintings into horizontal sections like this. From Guitty Azarpay, *Sogdian Painting: The Pictorial Epic in Oriental Art*, University of California Press, 1981 © The Regents of the University of California.

identify their owner as Varkhuman, who was probably acquainted with the owners of the house. One enters the room with the paintings through the heavily damaged eastern wall, which shows scenes from India, but it is difficult to make much out.[50]

The western wall facing the viewer portrays ambassadors and emissaries from different countries, who march in an impressive procession. Bulldozed away, the top figure presiding over the scene is missing. On the left-hand side of the western wall, a headless figure, the second from the left, is wearing a white robe with a long inscription in Sogdian on it. This inscription, the only long text on the painting, records the speech of an envoy from Chaghanian, a small kingdom just south of Samarkand near the modern city of Denau, Uzbekistan, as he presents his credentials to Varkhuman:

> When King Varkhuman Unash came to him [the ambassador] opened his mouth [and said thus]:
>
> "I am Pukarzate, the chancellor of Chaganian. I arrived here from Turantash, the lord of Chaganian, to Samarkand, to the king, and with respect [to] the king [now] I am [here]. And with regard to me do not have any misgivings: about the gods of Samarkand, as well as about the writing of Samarkand I am keenly aware, and I also have not done any harm to the king. Let you be quite fortunate!"
>
> And King Varkhuman Unash took leave [of him].
>
> And [then] the chancellor of Chach opened his mouth.[51]

This inscription presents one part of a protocol, and it probably continued with the speech of the envoy from Chach (modern Tashkent). The Chaghanian emissary claims knowledge of both the language and the gods of Samarkand. Although only the Chaghanian's speech is visible now, it is likely that the speeches of all the envoys were originally written in different places on the wall painting.

Here the artist's desire to depict a world order with Samarkand at its center is at its most obvious. Five Chinese, wearing typical Chinese black caps and robes, stand in the center and carry rolls of silk, skeins of silk thread, and silk in cocoons. Shown in a stance of deference, the Chinese come bearing gifts like other emissaries, although in actuality the ruler of Samarkand depended on them for military support. The Chinese are more significant than the other emissaries, and so they are placed in the focal point of the composition. On the upper left are four seated men whose long braids and swords mark them as Turks, probably mercenaries.

On the right-hand edge of the picture stands a wooden frame on which two flags hang down diagonally; drums with vivid monster faces are propped up in front. Two men wearing feathered headdresses stand with their hands in their

THE WORLD OF THE SOGDIANS

Forty-two figures, all representatives of the major powers, appear in the original wall painting of the ambassadors from Afrasiab, Samarkand. This reconstruction shows the surviving parts on a white background and the artist's reconstruction on gray. The western wall illustrates the genuinely cosmopolitan world in which the Sogdians lived. Their immediate neighbors from what is now southern Uzbekistan and Tashkent appear, as do those from much more distant places like China and Korea. © 2010 F. Ory-UMR 8546-CNRS.

sleeves; they are Korean, quite possibly from the state of Koguryo, which ceased to exist in 669.[52] These figures so closely resemble contemporary Chinese paintings that they may, in fact, be based on Chinese models, and not portraits from life.[53] They stand observing the figures to the left, whose simple clothing and headdresses contrast with the others' robes. One has an animal skin over his arm. These mountain people listen to an interpreter whose finger is pointed up in the air.[54]

The importance of the Chinese is also clear from the northern wall, which shows Chinese women on a boat and a hunting scene.[55] To the right of the empress's boat is a vigorous hunting scene in which Chinese huntsmen spear leopards. The oversized figure on the right has to be the Chinese emperor, for Sogdian artistic convention portrayed only deities and monarchs as larger than life-size.[56]

The southern wall depicts a Zoroastrian ceremony complete with sacrificial victims (the four geese), two Zoroastrian dignitaries carrying clubs on camel-back, and a horse led by a Zoroastrian priest wearing a face-mask. This face mask, called a *padam* in Pahlavi, was a veil covering the nose and mouth to protect the fire altar from contact with body fluids. The ceremony could well be the Nauruz festival described by the calendrical expert al-Biruni, himself a native of Khorezm, the region northwest of Samarkand.[57] (Even though it is non-Islamic, Nauruz is still today a major holiday across Central Asia and the Caucasus, and even in Iran.) Writing in the year 1000, several centuries after the Islamic conquest of the city, he recounts that the Persian king led his people in a six-day ceremony to celebrate the coming of spring and that the Sogdians celebrated the same festival in the summer. The southern wall offers a parallel composition to the northern, but some of the figures in the procession have been effaced. Opposite the Chinese emperor is a white elephant, which probably carried the no-longer-visible Samarkand queen, while the figure on horseback at the end of the procession is the ruler of Samarkand, Varkhuman himself.

The Afrasiab paintings give paramount importance to interactions with the outside world, especially envoys. These diplomats are shown engaging in trade-like activities, but they are actually presenting real-life commodities such as silk cloth and silk thread. In the middle of the seventh century Varkhuman portrayed the peoples belonging to the Sino-Turkish alliance.[58] His painters gave the Chinese pride of place, as befitted their role as the most important ally of the Sogdians.

But the political orientation of Samarkand—and all of Central Asia—was about to undergo a seismic shift. Following the death of Muhammad in 632, the Arabs under the leadership of the Rightly Guided Caliphs and then the Umayyad Caliphate (661–750) conquered north Africa, southern Spain, and Iran. After defeating the Sasanians in 651, they continued to move east through Central Asia, and targeted Samarkand. They took the city for the first time in 671, and in 681 an Arab governor was able to spend his first winter in the region.[59] Between 705 and 715, the Arab general Qutayba ibn Muslim campaigned in Sogdiana and in 712 conquered Samarkand.

The largest group of Sogdian-language documents found in Sogdiana— and not in western China—date to this period. In 1933 Soviet archeologists uncovered an extraordinary cache of nearly one hundred documents at Mount Mugh, 75 miles (120 km) east of Samarkand in Tajikistan.[60] These documents offer a unique account of the Islamic conquest from the vantage point of the conquered—and not the conquering—peoples. In capturing one ruler's desperate negotiations with Turks, Chinese, and other local rulers in his last-ditch efforts to keep the Islamic armies at bay, they remind us that the Islamic conquest of Central Asia was slow and uncertain, and the Chinese of the Tang dynasty played a difficult-to-discern role in the region's politics in the early eighth century.

The documents at Mount Mugh were found by local people, not by a foreign expedition. In czarist times, the residents of the village of Kum, some 4 miles (6 km) away, knew that the hilltop held some kind of treasure. In the spring of 1932 a few local shepherd boys visited the site. They dug around in a pit, unearthed several documents on leather, put the others back, and brought the most complete piece back to their village.[61] The local Communist Party secretary, Abdulhamid Puloti, who had studied history in Tashkent, got wind of the find and promised a villager a job as a policeman in return for help in finding the documents. When Puloti was finally taken to a villager's house, the host reached into a hollow section between the wall and a door post and pulled out a document. Puloti alerted his superiors, who in turn informed the cultural authorities, and the document, later numbered 1.I, was transferred to Dushanbe, the capital of Tajikistan.[62] The document was confiscated by the first secretary of the Communist Party in Tajikistan, D. Husejnov, and disappeared after 1933 when he was purged.[63]

Like many Asian peoples, the Sogdians dated documents by the reign year of a given ruler; many of the Mugh documents were dated between the first and fourteenth years of the ruler Devashtich (a more technical romanization is Dēwāštīč). But because the years of Devashtich's reign were unknown, scholars could not assign a precise date. Of the ninety-seven documents found at Mount Mugh, ninety-two are written in Sogdian, three in Chinese, one in Arabic, and one in Runic script in a language not yet identified.[64] One of the Chinese documents was dated 706, suggesting that the documents probably dated to the early years of the eighth century.[65]

The sole Arabic document proved to be the key to dating the documents, as the great Soviet Arabist I. Y. Kratchkovsky (1883–1951) explains in his memoirs.[66] In the letter, Devashtich writes to the Arab governor of Khurasan, al-Jarrah in perfect Arabic, which suggests that he hired a scribe. Identifying himself as a *mawla*, or client, of the governor, he offers to send the two sons of Tarxun, the previous ruler of Samarkand, to the governor for safekeeping.[67] When he read the letter, Kratchkovsky remembered that the great historian al-Tabari had written about a landed noble (*diqhan*) from Samarkand named Divashni, who had resisted the Islamic conquest between 721 to 722.[68] Divashni, Kratchkovsky realized, was a scribal error for Divashti, one of several Arabic renderings of the name Devashtich. That crucial identification made it possible to date the Mount Mugh documents to 709–22.

In response to the news of the discovery, the Academy of Social Sciences in Leningrad sent an expedition to Tajikistan headed by A. A. Freiman (1879–1968), the leading Soviet scholar of Sogdian. For two weeks in November 1933, Freiman led a team from the Academy of Sciences who excavated the site.[69] It was the ideal location for a fortress: the Kum and Zerafshan rivers surrounded it on three sides, and the residents had constructed inner and outer walls for further protection.

The fortress held only a few large clay pots to store water, a clear indication that its residents depended on the people of the nearby village to carry water a quarter of a mile (0.5 km) from the nearest creek. Too small to house an army unit, the citadel was designed to be the home of the ruler who lived inside with

THE SITE OF THE MOUNT MUGH FORTRESS

Mount Mugh is a small, remote peak that stands 5,000 feet (1,500 m) above sea level in Tajikistan just across from the border with Uzbekistan. Surrounded by water on three sides, it made the perfect refuge for about a hundred families fleeing the invading Muslim armies in the early 700s. Courtesy of Frantz Grenet.

a few family members and servants, but, when necessary, its large rooms and courtyard could temporarily house one hundred families.

After examining the artifacts found at the site, archeologists were able to determine the use of the different rooms within the small five-room fortress. The four rectangular rooms measured 57 feet (17.3 m) long and between 6 and 7.2 feet (1.8–2.2 m) wide, with a ceiling only 5.5 feet (1.7 m) above the ground. The building was not luxurious. The rooms received light only from the south, where a wall, no longer preserved, had originally contained windows.

To the surprise of the excavators, almost nothing of value was left at the site. The terrace was a garbage pit covered by a 20-inch- (.5 m) thick layer of little pieces of bone, clay, and fabric. Room 1 had a 39-inch- (1 m) thick deposit consisting of nine distinct layers of animal manure separated by clay-heavy loess soil, suggesting the citadel had been occupied for nine to ten years. Because it also contained wood scraps, the excavators concluded room 1 had been a wood workshop that had doubled as a barn during the winters. Room 2, the kitchen, held the bulk of household utensils: clay pots, fragments of dishes, reed baskets, small clay cups, beans, and barley seeds, along with traces of fire. Since room 3 was almost entirely empty except for some small glass bottles and a hair comb, the archeologists concluded that it served as a granary. Room 4 had the most artifacts, including three clay jars, many household utensils, three coins (one of silver), metal arrowheads, pieces of clothing, and a belt buckle. All these artifacts were from the upper floor, which had collapsed on top of the lower level.[70]

The northern part of room 4 contained a big clay jar lying on its side. Scattered near it were twenty-three willow sticks with writing on them, as if the sticks had fallen from the opening of the clay jar. These sticks contain the records of household expenditures compiled by the steward for his lord and kept in this compact local archive.[71] He used willow sticks as a writing material—not paper or leather—because they were cheaper and more readily available.

Since the steward recorded the dates on which different amounts of wine and wheat were consumed in hosting various visitors, his ledgers offer a sketch of the local economy. On several occasions people from nearby villages brought cartloads of grain to the fortress, which they gave to the lord, perhaps as a tax paid in kind, and the steward's accounts report that they received grain from him as well. Herding animals was a major economic activity: people ate sheep and goats, and they made suits from animal skins, sometimes from as many as fifty, but usually from a smaller number. One such document (A17) lists various expenditures: 200 dirhams for a horse; 100 dirhams to build a roof; 50 dirhams to the Zoroastrian priest; 15 dirhams for both a doctor and a wine pourer; 11 for a cow to be eaten at a New Year's dinner; 8 dirhams for a document drafter; 8 dirhams for paper, silk, and butter; and 5 dirhams for an executioner. Although scholars are not certain what kind of coin circulated in Samarkand, the dirham was the main unit of silver currency at the time throughout the Arabic-speaking world and had superseded Sasanian silver coins. Almost all the goods appearing on the willow-branch accounts, with the important exceptions of paper and silk, both from China, were produced locally, giving the impression that the local Sogdian economy, at least during these years of conflict, functioned largely through barter.

In addition to the willow sticks, the site produced nearly sixty documents on paper and leather that had originally been stored on the second story and were scattered among the remains of the collapsed ceilings of the first and second stories of rooms 2 and 3.[72] A third findspot for leather documents was the basket the shepherd boys had unearthed.

Among these ninety-seven documents were three legal contracts written on trapezoidal pieces of leather. They reveal a sophisticated legal apparatus for that time. Although leather may seem like a cumbersome writing material, it was used throughout the entire Arabic-speaking world (Europeans were using parchment, also made from treated sheepskin, in the same centuries), and experienced scribes could record detailed agreements on it. By far the lengthiest, and so the most informative, text from Mount Mugh is the marriage contract and the accompanying document, labeled "the bride's script," or copy, in which the husband restates his obligations to the bride's family. Both were found in the basket Puloti handed over to the authorities.[73]

The marriage contract and the bride's script are dated to the tenth year of King Tarkhun's reign, or 710. Together, the two documents run a full ninety lines on two pieces of leather, respectively 8 inches (21 cm) and 6 inches (15.5 cm) long. These documents specify the terms of the exchange of the Sogdian woman Chat from her guardian, Cher, the ruler of Navikat (a Sogdian city in the Semirech'e region of modern Kazakhstan), to her new husband Ot-tegin, whose name clearly marks him as a Turk. Because her father's name is mentioned even though he plays no role in the arrangements, it seems that Chat was the ward of Cher.

This pre-Islamic contract is striking for what it reveals about the strict reciprocity of obligations in this society: just as a husband can end the marriage under certain circumstances, so too can a wife end the marriage under those same circumstances. The Sogdian contract invokes the legal term for a special kind of marriage that granted husband and wife equal rights in a number of respects.[74] The agreement begins by explaining that the husband is obliged to provide "food, garments, and ornaments," as his wife is "a lady possessing authority in his own house, the way a noble man treats a noble woman, his wife." She, in turn, "must always conform to his well-being and obey his orders as befits a wife, the way a noble woman treats a noble man, her husband."[75]

Then, much like a modern prenuptial agreement, the contract outlines what will happen should things go wrong. If the husband should take "another wife or concubine, or keep another woman that does not please [his wife] Chat," he promises to pay her a fine of "thirty good, pure dirhams of [the type] Den" and send the woman away. If he decides to end the marriage, then he may do so, but he must provide his wife with food and return her dowry and all the presents that she gave to him when they were married. Neither husband nor wife will owe the other any compensation. The husband will then be free to remarry. Notably, the wife, too, is entitled to end the marriage, but only after returning her husband's gifts; she is to retain her own property as well as a payment from him. Should the marriage end, neither party will be responsible for the other's crimes, and only the criminal party shall be obliged to pay any penalties.

The contract confirms the fluidity of Sogdian social divisions. Should either the husband or the wife become the "slave, hostage, prisoner, or dependant," of someone else, his/her former spouse will not be responsible. Clearly some people in this society are better off than others, and those signing contracts with 30-dirham penalties are among the better off, but they, just like the less privileged, faced the real prospect that, if their fortunes changed, they, too, could be reduced to slavery.

The statement of the husband's obligations in the wife's script repeats much of this information but adds a few new clauses. Ot-tegin begins by saying, "And, Sir, by god Mithra! I shall neither sell her nor pawn her."[76] Mithra, the guardian of truth and contracts, was one of the three most important gods of the Zoroastrians and ranked just below the supreme deity, Ahura Mazda, to whom the word "God" would ordinarily refer. Ot-tegin promises to return Chat to her guardian in the event that the marriage ends, at either his or her instigation. In addition, if "someone, from my side or from the enemies' side takes her or detains her," he will obtain her immediate release. He promises, too, that he will pay a fine of one hundred dirhams if the marriage ends but he fails to return her unharmed to Cher's family. If he does not make the payment promptly, he will pay a 20 percent late penalty on the unpaid balance. Much of this document spells out the procedures by which the guardian can obtain payment; for instance, it names a guarantor whom the guardian can seek out. The entire population is enjoined to monitor the agreement, which was signed in a "Foundation Hall" in front of witnesses.

The two other contracts from Mount Mugh, one for the rental of mills (B-4), and the other for the sale of a burial plot (B-8), share the same overall structure as the marriage contract, though they are much shorter. Both give the date (the year of the king's reign, the month, and the day), the names of the parties involved, the item to be transferred, the conditions of transfer, and the names of the witnesses and of the scribe.

The contract for the lease of three mills to a man by Devashtich specifies an annual rental of 460 units of flour.[77] Like the willow-branch documents, this contract requires payment in kind, here in flour. But this contract goes beyond a simple statement of rent. Forty-two lines long, it is a sophisticated legal instrument specifying the time within which the lessee must pay the ruler and the consequences should he fail to make complete payment.

The third contract is for the rent of a burial place for 25 dirhams.[78] The contract sets the terms by which two sons rent a mud-built "eskase" location for burial from two brothers. It may mark a truce between two feuding families—the family of the brothers renting the plot and that of their enemies whom they fear may disturb their mourning. Zoroastrians disposed of their dead first by placing them in a structure outside, called a Tower of Silence by modern Zoroastrians, where animals of prey could eat the flesh, and then placing the cleaned bones in a well, called an eskase in this contract.[79] Yet, because no such burial wells have been found yet in the region of Sogdiana, others suggest the word may refer to a naus structure for the remains of the dead like those found in Panjikent.[80]

The Mount Mugh contracts help us understand that the fortress contained more than just the personal archive of the ruler Devashtich. Certain documents, like the agreement specifying the amount to be paid to him as rent for his mills, clearly belonged to him. But why would he have kept a copy of the contract giving the complicated terms of the marriage between a Turk and his Sogdian bride? Or the document leasing the burial place?

Quite possibly the residents of Mount Mugh, including the bride Chat, brought all their important legal documents with them for safekeeping, perhaps during the final siege of the fortress. They may have hoped to recover their documents after the Arab threat had been eliminated. But the contracts remained in the fortress of Mount Mugh—untouched—until the shepherd boys found them in 1932. If this is what happened, it explains why the Mount Mugh documents included the correspondence of not just the ruler Devashtich but also the letters of several other lower-ranking lords who also took refuge in the citadel.

By combining information in al-Tabari's detailed chronicle with that from the Mount Mugh documents, we can reconstruct the events leading to the fall of the Mount Mugh fortress.[81] The chronicles record that a new Arab governor, nicknamed "the Lady," fought the Sogdians between the autumn of 720 and the spring of 722. The Sogdians were allied with the Turgesh, a people who had originally been the subjects of the Western Turks but who, between 715 and 740, gained control of some of Western Turks' territory.[82] In 721, Devashtich, who had been the local ruler of Panjikent for some fourteen years, was officially crowned as "king of Sughd, lord of Samarkand."[83]

Devashtich claimed to be the successor of Tarxun, the last ruler of Samarkand. Tarxun had surrendered to Qutayba in 709, but following a local revolt he either committed suicide or was executed in 710. A man named Ghurak took over as his successor. Qutayba, claiming to avenge Tarxun's death attacked the city again and gained control in 712. When Ghurak surrendered, he signed a treaty promising a onetime payment of 2 million dirhams and then 200,000 dirhams each year thereafter.[84] Qutayba and some local lords accepted Ghurak's claim to succeed Tarxun, but others who lived to the southwest of Samarkand supported Devashtich. For a decade the two rivals coexisted, but not much is known about this period.

In 719 Devashtich wrote to the Arab governor of Khurasan deferentially as though he was his subordinate, but by the summer of 721 he was optimistic about his chances of defeating the Arabs. At this time, he wrote a letter (document V-17) to Afshun, a lord of the town of Khakhsar, 8–10 miles (12–16 km) southwest of Samarkand, in which he described a "large army come down, both of Turks and Chinese." Apparently the Turgesh, some Chinese, and the king of Ferghana to the east had formed an alliance against the Islamic forces. The

Mount Mugh letters provide the only evidence of Chinese involvement in these events, and another letter (document V-18) mentions a "Chinese" page (the word for "page" is uncertain). The word "Chinese" may refer to someone ethnically Chinese from the Western Regions—not necessarily forces sent by the central government in Chang'an.[85]

The documents reveal that a year later, most likely in 722, the circumstances have completely changed. A messenger reports that the "Turks" are nowhere to be found, while another, possibly a postmaster, describes the fall of Khujand in Ferghana to the Muslim forces and the surrender of 14,000 people.[86] The chronicler al-Tabari reports that the Sogdians divided into two groups. The larger, consisting of at least 5,000, went to Ferghana, where they were denied entry, and a Muslim army slaughtered them.[87] A much smaller group, of perhaps one hundred families, sided with Devashtich and fled to the fortress of Mount Mugh.[88]

During the final massacre by the Arab forces, only the merchants in this larger group could afford to pay a ransom to the invading forces in exchange for their safety. Taxation was a major issue for the newly conquered peoples of Central Asia, who hoped to avoid heavier taxes by converting to Islam and thereby becoming eligible for the preferential tax rates for Muslims. During the eighth century, however, the caliphate desperately needed all revenues for its war effort, and individual governors did not always grant their new converts the preferential rates. Many Sogdians fled to the Turkish lands or to China as a result.

Devashtich and his followers, who numbered perhaps only a hundred men and their families, moved to the Mount Mugh fortress (called Abghar by al-Tabari).[89] They sent a small force outside the fortress to fight the Muslim forces, who drove them back to the fortress and defeated them after laying siege. Following his defeat, Devashtich requested a safe conduct from Said al-Harashi, who initially granted his request. The one hundred families remaining in the citadel surrendered the contents of the fortress in exchange for their freedom. The Arab army commander, al-Tabari reports, then auctioned off the contents of the fortress, leaving a fifth for the state treasury, as Islamic law prescribes. That is why the fortress was nearly empty when the Soviet archeologists excavated the site in 1933. Everything of any value had already been removed, and the paper and leather documents must have escaped notice.

Although the Arab commander had promised Devashtich safe conduct, he reneged on his word. Al-Tabari describes his grisly end. The commander "slew al-Diwashini [Devashtich], crucifying him on a [Zoroastrian] burial building [naus]. He imposed upon the people of Rabinjan the obligation to pay one hundred [dinars] if the body were removed from its place. . . . He sent al-Diwashini's head to Iraq and his left hand to Sulayman b. Abi al-Sari in Tukharistan."[90] The method of killing suggests that Devashtich was an important figure. Because

Devashtich represented Sogdian resistance, the Arab commander chose an extreme method to dispose of his body.[91] (He was subsequently dismissed for having used such a gruesome punishment.)

Devashtich's death was just one chapter, and a minor one at that, in the Islamic conquest of Samarkand. Within a few decades Muslim troops had secured the region, and over time Persian displaced Sogdian and Islam replaced Zoroastrianism. At the 751 battle of Talas, which took place at what is now Kazakhstan, Muslim troops defeated a Chinese army largely because the forces of a nomadic people, the Qarluqs, defected to the Islamic side. Four years later General An Lushan rose up against the Tang dynasty, and the dynasty was forced to withdraw its troops from Central Asia to suppress the mutiny. These two events in rapid succession meant that, after the mid-eighth century, the city of Samarkand and the surrounding region of Sogdiana no longer looked east to China. The Islamicization of Sogdiana prompted many of the Sogdians living in China to settle there.

The Mount Mugh documents predate both the Islamicization of Central Asia and the spread of paper-making technology to the region. The different materials used to write the Mount Mugh documents show that local rulers were willing to pay for Chinese paper because of its durability and convenience, but the residents of Central Asia continued to use leather for important documents, like the single letter in Arabic that Kratchkovsky deciphered, and reserved willow sticks for less important matters like household accounts.

A rare indicator of long-distance trade at Mount Mugh is the Chinese paper found there. Three Chinese-language documents were pieced together from eight fragments, all on recycled paper originating in China. No one at Mount Mugh actually wrote Chinese. One of the documents originated as an official document written in Wuwei, Gansu, a thriving city on the Chinese silk route to the east of Dunhuang. After it was discarded and sold as paper (the reverse side was blank and could still be used), Silk Road traders brought it west some 2,000 miles (3,600 kilometers) to Mount Mugh.[92]

In the eighth and ninth centuries, Chinese paper reached far into Central Asia, as far as the Caucasus Mountains, to the site of Moshchevaia Balka, literally "ravine of the mummies/relics." The site, consisting of burials either on limestone terraces or dug out of the hillside, near the northeast edge of the Black Sea is the farthest location from China where Chinese paper has been found to date. In the early twentieth century, excavators unearthed a few scraps of paper with Chinese writing on it. The most complete document, 6 inches (15 cm) by 3 inches (8 cm), contained a few lines in running hand that give the date and then the amount of various expenditures (2,000 coins, 800 coins). Although extremely fragmentary, it appears to be a ledger of expenses.[93] The site produced other items, all clearly of Chinese origin: a piece of silk with a design showing a Buddhist deity on it as well as a man riding a horse (the prince Siddhartha before he left the palace?), a scrap of paper with a Buddhist text, and a fragment of an envelope from some paper mache object. These items clearly demonstrate that at least Chinese paper and silk paintings—and possibly even Chinese merchants—had reached the Caucasus region sometime between the eighth and ninth centuries.[94]

During the eighth century people living in Central Asia learned how to manufacture paper. An Arab account reports that at the 751 Battle of Talas the Abbasid Caliphate won a resounding victory over the Chinese and brought back prisoners of war to their capital at Baghdad. Some of the POWs taught their captors how to make paper.[95]

As with other legends about technological transfer, this one is not necessarily credible.[96] The techniques of making paper—beating a mixture of organic material and rags to a pulp and drying it on a screen—were not difficult to replicate. The technology steadily spread out from central China, reaching Central Asia by the eighth century. After the year 800, paper gradually replaced leather as the primary writing material of the Islamic world. Paper had many advantages over leather: low in cost and quickly produced, it was far more convenient than leather and much more available than papyrus, which grew only in Egypt. Paper entered Christian Europe through its Islamic portals at Spain and Sicily, in the late eleventh and early twelfth centuries.

There is no question that the Chinese invention of paper—unlike silk—transformed the societies it touched. Silk, however great its allure in the premodern world, was used primarily for clothing or for decorative purposes. If not available, other textiles could easily replace it, and in Central Asia cotton often did. Paper, by contrast, marked a genuine breakthrough. With the introduction of cheap paper, books went from being luxury items to a commodity that many could afford, and educational levels rose accordingly. Unlike parchment or leather, paper absorbed ink, so it could be used for printing. The world's major printing revolutions—whether with woodblocks in China or moveable type in Europe—could not have occurred without paper.

The different scholars who have worked on the Sogdian Ancient Letters, the Panjikent excavations, the Afrasiab murals, and the Mount Mugh letters concur that they contain surprisingly few depictions of trade. The Ancient Letters, though written by merchants, document mostly small-scale purchases. Similarly, excavations at Panjikent have produced few trade items, and the city's wall paintings hardly ever show merchants and never actual commerce. The same is true of the Afrasiab murals. A French archeologist with extensive experience digging at Samarkand, Frantz Grenet has summed up the situation trenchantly:

"In the whole of Sogdian art there is not a single caravan, not a single ship, except in the pleasure boats of the Chinese empress" at Afrasiab.[97] Many paintings have been found on the walls in the over 130 houses excavated so far at Panjikent, yet they do not show business dealings. Similarly, the Mount Mugh documents all involve locally made goods, except for silk and paper. And the technologies for making those two items were moving west out of China into Central Asia at just this point.

The evidence at hand makes it clear that Silk Road commerce was largely a local trade, conducted over small distances by peddlers. Technologies, like those to make silk and paper, and religions, like Zoroastrianism and later Islam, moved with migrants, who brought the technologies and religious beliefs of their motherland with them to their new homes, wherever they settled.

DOCUMENTS TURN UP IN UNUSUAL PLACES

If you look closely, you can see paper sticking out from the wrists of this tomb figurine, which was excavated in Turfan and dates to the 600s. Her arms are made from rolled-up recycled paper, which was then twisted into shape. Figurines like this have been steamed apart, revealing various types of documents, including pawn tickets, one of which, with a big black cancelation mark in the shape of a 7, is shown here. The pawn tickets mention place names in Chang'an, a crucial clue to identifying the place of manufacture. Courtesy of Xinjiang Museum.

CHAPTER 5

The Cosmopolitan Terminus of the Silk Road
Historic Chang'an, Modern-day Xi'an

The modern city of Xi'an offers more archeological attractions than any other Chinese destination. The famous terra-cotta warriors are only an hour's drive away, and the Silk Road has left many traces in the city. Many non-Chinese minority peoples inhabit the city, which was similarly diverse during the Tang dynasty when the city was called Chang'an. The elegant figurine on the facing page, who wears an outfit combining Chinese and Sogdian elements, was made in Chang'an. Chang'an was so big that only in the past ten years has modern Xi'an expanded beyond its Tang-dynasty boundaries. With a population of over ten million, it is certainly the largest city in the northwest.

As the city's residents often remind visitors when composing toasts, the city served as the capital of ten dynasties. Seven of these dynasties were short-lived and controlled only the immediate region. Three major dynasties that governed a unified China designated Chang'an as their capital: the Former Han (206 BCE–9 CE), the Sui (589–617), and the Tang (618–907). While a political center, the city also served as a point of departure for those who, like Xuanzang, traveled west on the Silk Road. Before setting off, Xuanzang visited the city's Western Market, home to many Sogdians, because the city's residents could provide him with better advice than anyone else in China.

This inland city was also a starting-off place for those traveling by sea from China to points west. These ocean voyagers proceeded overland (the Yellow River was not navigable) to different ports on the Yangzi River or directly to China's coast. At these ports, they caught boats sailing along the world's most frequented sea route in use before 1500: that linking the Chinese coastal ports with Southeast Asia, India, the Arabian world, and the east African coast.[1]

The city received visitors traveling overland and by sea throughout the first millennium, the peak centuries of Silk Road traffic. After the fall of the Han dynasty in 220 and before the reunification of China by the Sui dynasty in 589, different dynasties led by nomadic peoples ruled the various regions of China, which was never united during that long period. In the north, the Northern Wei

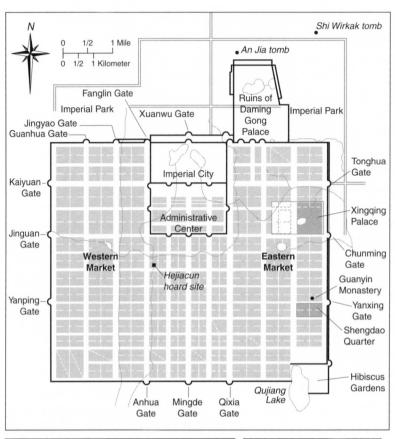

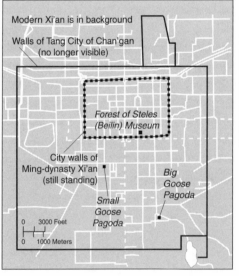

Chang'an, the Tang Capital, Then and Now

Walled quarter

—— Walls

⌣ Gate

⌢ Water course

(386–534) was the longest-lived dynasty, and two brief dynasties, the Northern Qi (550–77) and Northern Zhou (557–81), succeeded it.

Modern Xi'an contains many traces of the past. Chinese law requires that the archeological authorities be notified each time that a bulldozer unearths something ancient, a frequent event in a city like Xi'an, where each year archeologists uncover several hundred tombs from both the Han and Tang dynasties.[2] During the Northern Zhou, a graveyard for high-ranking officials was located in the northern suburbs of modern Xi'an. Some of the newest evidence about overland migration comes from the recent discovery of several tombs of Sogdians who moved to Chang'an and other northern Chinese cities in the late sixth and early seventh centuries.

Two Sogdian tombs in particular have excited much attention since their discovery: that of An Jia (d. 579), unearthed in 2001, and of Shi Wirkak, discovered in 2004. In the fall of 2005 Xi'an archeologists also excavated the tomb of the first Indian buried in the city. His epitaph identified him as a Brahman, meaning someone from India, not necessarily of high caste, with the Chinese name Li Cheng.[3] Sogdian tombs have also been found in other Chinese cities, including Guyuan, Ningxia, and Taiyuan, Shanxi.[4]

These tombs show how immigrants to China, mostly Sogdian, adjusted to—and modified—Chinese cultural practices. While the traditional method of burial in Sogdiana was to expose the bodies of the deceased before placing them in either an ossuary or an aboveground naus structure, the Sogdian tombs found in Xi'an are Chinese in style, with a sloping walkway leading to an underground chamber, and often hold a Chinese-language epitaph giving a brief biography of the deceased.

Yet these tombs retain distinctly Sogdian elements. In place of Chinese coffins, the Sogdian tombs contain either a stone bedlike platform or a miniature stone house. In some cases the remains of the dead were placed on the platform or inside the house, but in others—most notably that of An Jia—they were not.[5] Like ossuaries, the stone houses are decorated on the outside; in contrast, the stone beds have partitions with decorations facing in, as if an ossuary has been "turned inside out."[6] Unlike ossuaries, the stone beds show scenes from the life of the deceased, never the subject of traditional Sogdian ossuary art. The extremely realistic scenes clearly draw on the life experiences of the deceased; they may depict this world or possibly the next.

Named one of the top ten archeological discoveries of 2001, the tomb of An Jia is the only tomb of a Sogdian that had not been previously disturbed when archeologists uncovered it. The vast majority of tombs in China have been opened previously, often multiple times, by grave robbers. An Jia's tomb had a sloping walkway 9 yards (8.1 m) long leading to a door (see color plate 15).

Outside the door was an epitaph for the deceased. Typical of Chinese epitaphs, the text was carved on a low, square base and then covered with a lid, both made of stone. According to Chinese burial practices, An Jia's remains should have been placed in a coffin that rested on top of this stone bed. But the bones were scattered outside the tomb door on the ground, not on the stone bed inside where the Chinese would have placed them—a practice that has defied all explanation, since neither Zoroastrian nor Confucian custom sanctioned such a burial. Everything near the epitaph, including the walls, had smoke marks, as if a fire had occurred at some point.[7]

An Jia, his epitaph reports, was descended from a Sogdian family from Bukhara (in modern Uzbekistan) who had migrated to Liangzhou, what is now Wuwei, the important Gansu town on the road between Chang'an and Dunhuang where Xuanzang also stopped.[8] An Jia was born in 537 to a Sogdian father and probably a Chinese mother from a local Wuwei family.[9] The epitaph claims that his father held two government positions, one in Sichuan, but this seems unlikely given the distance from Sichuan to Wuwei; much more likely, these were honorary positions granted to the father posthumously because of his son's success.[10] An Jia was indeed successful. First serving as sabao in Tongzhou (modern-day Dali, Shaanxi, north of Xi'an), he was given the highest rank a sabao could achieve.[11]

Starting in the Northern Wei dynasty (386–534) dynasties in central China began to appoint headmen for the Sogdian communities, and they adopted the originally foreign word for the position in the Chinese bureaucracy. As a result, sabao took on a new meaning: an official appointed by the Chinese to administer the residents of a foreign community. An Jia received such an appointment under the Northern Zhou, the dynasty in power in Chang'an before his death at the age of sixty-two in 579. An Jia's tomb combines Chinese and Sogdian motifs. The painting above the door shows a Zoroastrian fire altar on a table borne by three camels, an attribute of the Sogdian God of Victory.[12]

The funeral chamber measured 12 feet (3.66 m) square, 10.83 feet (3.3 m) tall, and held the stone funeral platform with stone panels on the sides and along the back. The craftsmen who made them first carved shallow reliefs into the stone and then painted the figures, buildings, and trees with red, black, and white pigments and filled in the background with gold paint. There are twelve scenes in all (three each on the left and right sides, six at the back).[13] On the center of the back wall, a plump An Jia appears seated next to a woman, probably his wife, wearing Chinese clothes in a Chinese-style building with a bridge in front. The Sogdian funeral beds and houses found in China almost always depict the Sogdian swirl, a dance performed by both

PLATE 1. DRIED SILK FLOWERS FROM THE ASTANA GRAVEYARD, TURFAN
Excavated from a tomb in 1972, these brightly colored artificial silk flowers, 12.6 inches
(32 cm) high, testify to the extraordinary conditions of preservation at the oasis of Turfan,
Xinjiang, in northwestern China. With less than an inch (2.5 cm) of rain each year, the dry
soil preserves many items that survive nowhere else in China and in only a few places in
the world. Archeologists found a few strands of hair among the stems, suggesting that the
flowers were part of a headdress worn by a dancer welcoming the spring in the 600s or
700s CE.

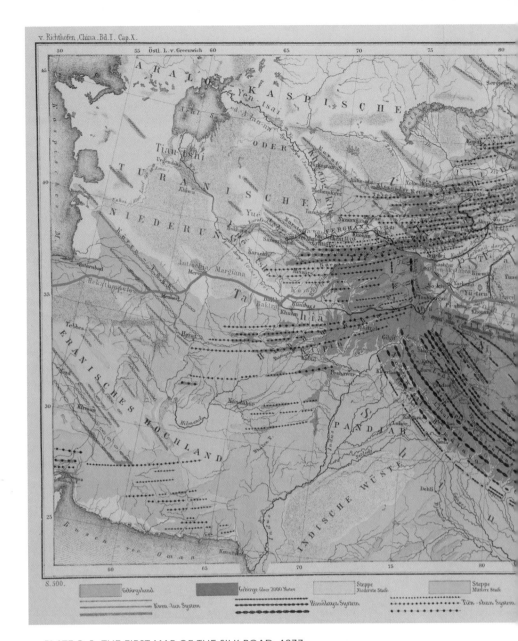

PLATE 2–3. THE FIRST MAP OF THE SILK ROAD, 1877

The German geographer Ferdinand von Richthofen coined the term "Silk Road" with the publication of this map. An orange line, highlighted here, marks the Silk Road. Charged with finding the ideal railroad route from Germany to China, von Richthofen conceived of the ancient trade route as a single line.

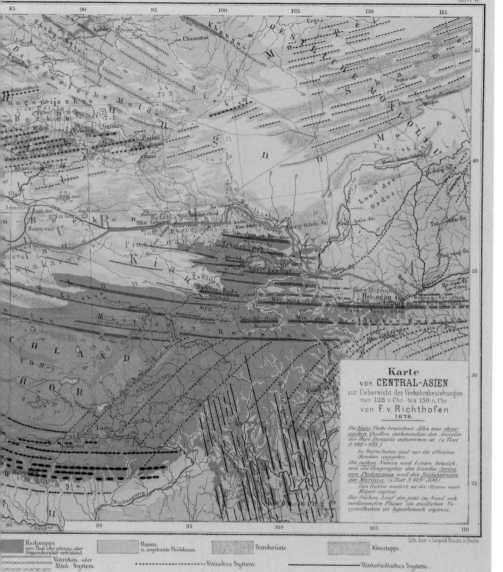

Karte
von CENTRAL-ASIEN
zur Uebersicht der Verkehrsbeziehungen
von 128 v.Chr. bis 150 n.Chr.
von F. v. Richthofen
1876.

Die blaue Farbe bezeichnet Alles was chinesischen Quellen, insbesondere den Annalen der Han-Dynastie entnommen ist. (s. Text S. 905–976.)

Im Tarym-Becken sind nur die östlichen Strassen angegeben.

Die rothen Namen und Linien bezeichnen die Geographie des Landes Serica von Ptolemaeus und die Seidenstrasse des Marinus. (s. Text S. 479–500.)

Von Baktra westlich ist die Strasse nach Rogart ergänzt.

Der frühere Lauf der jetzt im Sand sich verlierenden Flüsse im südlichen Tarym-Becken ist hypothetisch ergänzt.

Lith. Anst. v. Leopold Kraatz in Berlin.

Hochsteppe zum Theil sehr gebirgig, aber Steppencharakter vorwaltend	Oasen u. angebaute Thalbecken	Sandwüste
		Kiessteppe

Kuenlun - oder Altai - System

Sinisches System.

Hinterindisches System.

PLATE 4A. IMITATION ROMAN COIN USED AS A BURIAL OFFERING

Contrary to the popular view that the Silk Road trade linked Han-dynasty China with Rome, the earliest Roman coins found in China date to the 500s CE, long after Emperor Constantine moved the capital from Rome to Byzantium in 330 CE. To date fewer than fifty gold Roman coins have surfaced in all of China, and many are imitations. This coin, with a diameter of .63 inches (1.6 cm) and weighing .03 ounces (.85 grams), is stamped from a sheet of gold and has a raised front and a concave back like a bottle cap. Genuine gold solidus coins weighed more than five times as much. The Chinese used gold coins like this as protective talismans, not as money. © The Trustees of the British Museum.

PLATE 4B. GENUINE SASANIAN SILVER COIN FROM THE ASTANA GRAVEYARD, TURFAN

Starting in the late 500s and continuing into the 600s CE, the residents of the northwest frequently made loans and purchases using silver coins minted by the Sasanian Empire of Iran (224–651 CE). This example, with a diameter of 1.22 inches (3.1 cm) and weighing .15 ounces (4.28 grams), shows the Sasanian emperor Khusraw II (reigned 591–628), wearing his identifying winged crown on the face and a Zoroastrian fire altar flanked by two attendants on the back. More than a thousand such coins have surfaced in northwest China, testifying to their circulation all the way from the Sasanian capital of Ctesiphon (near modern Baghdad) to the Chinese capital of Chang'an. © The Trustees of the British Museum.

PLATE 5A. SILK AS CURRENCY

Before it snapped in half, this bolt of silk, from the third or fourth century CE, measured 20 inches (.50 m) in length and was used to pay the expenses of Chinese soldiers stationed in the garrison in Loulan. A bolt of silk weighed much less than its equivalent in coins and was easier to ship overland. Much of the silk used on the Silk Road functioned as currency, not as a luxury good, which is why this bolt is a plain basketweave (one thread over, one thread under) with no design. This is the only surviving example of currency silk from the third and fourth centuries. © The Trustees of the British Museum.

PLATE 5B. ROMAN-STYLE WINGED FIGURE MOTIF FROM MIRAN

In Rome, the god Eros was often depicted as a handsome young man with wings. This figure, though, is one of sixteen Aurel Stein found in a Buddhist context at Miran, a site lying between Niya and Loulan. Artistic motifs like this were easily transported along the Silk Road, whether made by live craftsmen traveling far from home or copied from sketchbooks.

PLATE 6. NIYA'S ANCIENT BUDDHIST STUPA
After 1700 years, Niya's stupa, standing some twenty-three feet (7 m) tall, is the site's major landmark. Worn by the centuries, its outer layer has been stripped away, revealing the bricks underneath. Even when Aurel Stein arrived on January 28, 1901, looters had already forced open the repository at the base and removed the relics of the Buddha stored there. The rest of the site lay buried under the sands, where Stein found over one hundred dwellings and more than a thousand wooden slips with writing on them.

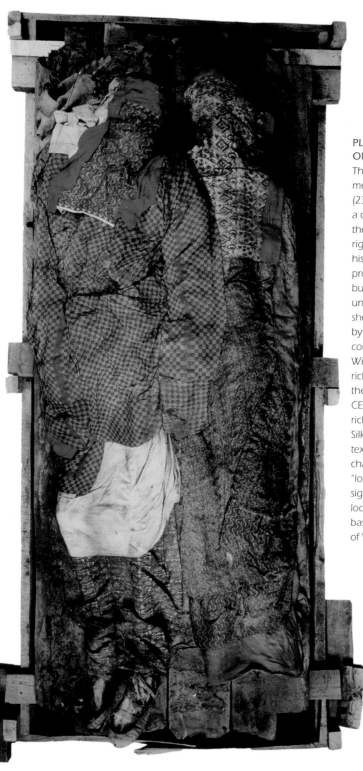

PLATE 7. JOINT BURIAL ON THE SILK ROAD

This Niya coffin, measuring 7 feet 6 inches (230 cm) in length, holds a couple: the man on the left, his wife on the right. Knife wounds on his neck point to the probable cause of death, but his wife's corpse is unmarked, indicating that she was most likely killed by suffocation so that they could be buried together. With a total of thirty-seven richly woven silks dating to the third or fourth century CE, the tomb is one of the richest textile finds at any Silk Road site. Some of the textiles have the Chinese characters for "king" and "lord" in their designs, a sign that they were gifts to local rulers from dynasties based in China. Courtesy of Wang Binghua.

PLATE 8. THE HEIGHT OF SILK ROAD FASHION

Crafted in the seventh century in the Tang capital of Chang'an, this Chinese beauty has typical Tang-dynasty hair and makeup, including flowers painted above her eyebrows. Her outfit combines the best of Central Asian fashion: a shirt with facing birds surrounded by pearls—and Chinese: a shawl and a striped skirt with a gauze overskirt. When this figurine was on display at the Metropolitan Museum of Art, the staff nicknamed her "Tang Barbie" because she was the same height (11.6 inches, or 29.5 cm) as the doll and every bit as fashionable. Courtesy of Xinjiang Museum.

PLATE 9. BUDDHIST CAVES AT BEZEKLIK

This once-remote Buddhist retreat is now a major tourist destination for those visiting Turfan. The Bezeklik Caves, like almost all Buddhist cave sites in Xinjiang, were dug into the fragile conglomerate of the hillside overlooking a river valley. Many of the original wall paintings in the Buddhist caves (on left) are now on display in Berlin where they were taken early in the twentieth century. Still, one priceless Manichaean mural remains on site under lock and key, and few tourists manage to see it. The brick house for drying raisins (lower center) is a typical sight in the Turfan countryside. Author photo.

PLATE 10. SVEN HEDIN TRAVELS ACROSS THE TAKLAMAKAN DESERT BY BOAT

Most riverbeds in the Taklamakan Desert today are bone dry, but in 1899 the Swedish explorer Sven Hedin used this 38-foot (12 m) boat to explore the waterways of the region. Starting north of Yarkand, he traveled 900 miles (1500 km) in eighty-two days and stopped three days' journey away from Korla because of large blocks of floating river ice. Hedin's watercolor shows that the deck was large enough for his tent, a small wooden building that served as his darkroom, and a clay firepit where his men prepared meals.

PLATE 11A. NEW LIGHT ON A LOST RELIGION

Before the discovery of the Turfan documents, the little we knew of Manichaeism came from Augustine's critical description in his *Confessions*. Manichaeism was an Iranian religion founded by the prophet Mani (ca. 210–276) who told of the struggle between light and dark. This brilliantly colored detail from an eighth- or ninth-century book found at Turfan shows the Bema festival, the high point of the Manichaean ritual year. It depicts the transformative process that lies at the heart of Manichaean doctrine—lay people offer melons, grapes, and loaves of bread shaped like the sun and moon, to the "elect" (clergy), who eat the food and so transform it into light particles. When the ruler of the Uighurs converted to Manichaeism in 762, he became the only ruler in world history to name Manichaeism his official state religion. Bildarchiv Preussischer Kulturbesitz/ Art Resource, NY.

PLATE 11B. PROCESSION OF AMBASSADORS FROM SAMARKAND

Dating to the mid-600s CE, this wall painting from the Afrasiab site in Samarkand shows three envoys bearing gifts for the ruler of Samarkand, then the center of Sogdiana, the Sogdian homeland. These three ambassadors from nearby kingdoms, each wearing a beautifully patterned robe, are among over forty figures—Turks, Chinese, Koreans, and other Sogdians—who illustrate the range of the world's cultures known to the Sogdians and document the importance of envoys in Silk Road exchanges. Courtesy of François Ory.

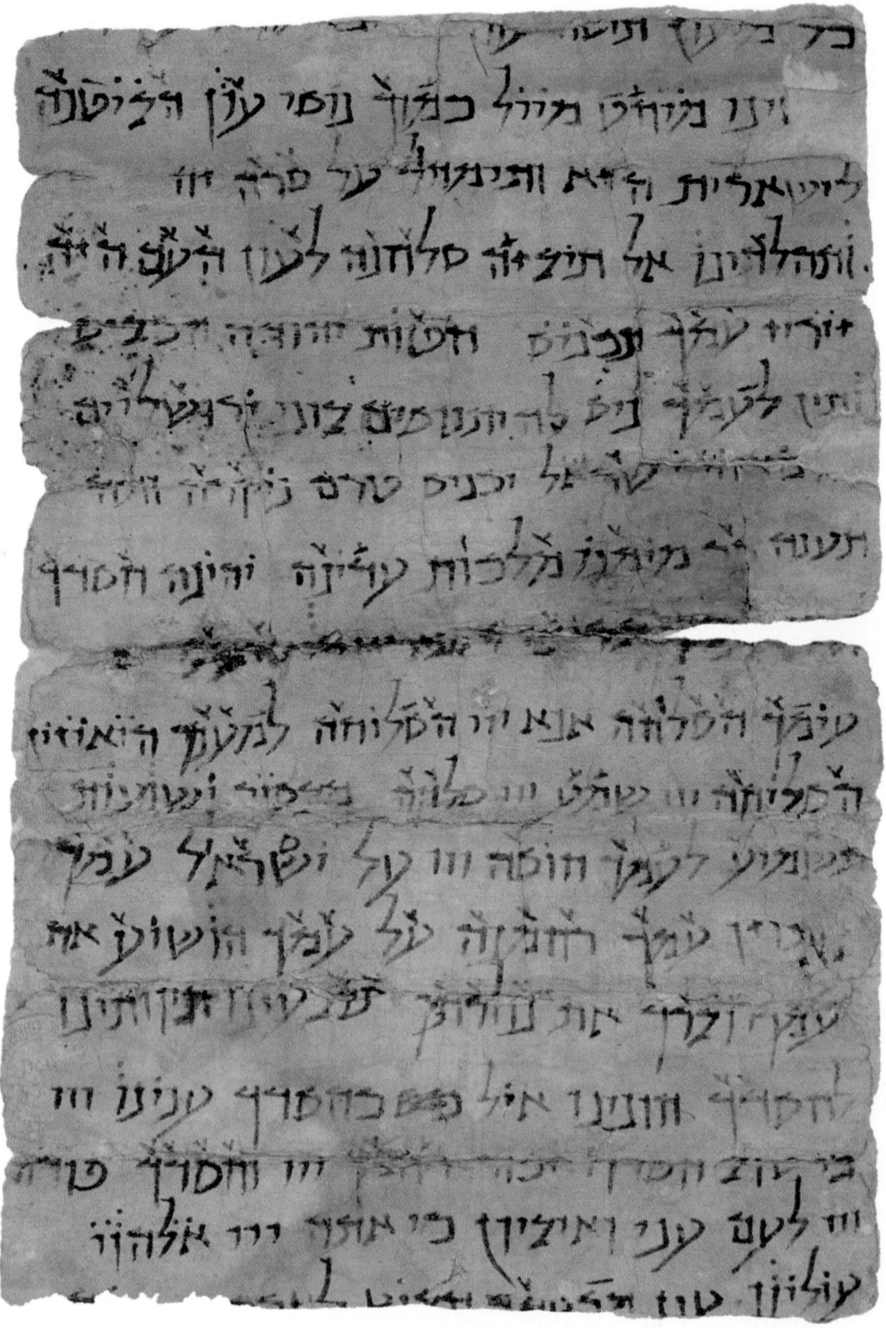

PLATE 12. HEBREW PRAYER FOUND IN THE LIBRARY CAVE AT DUNHUANG
The library cave at Dunhuang contained some forty thousand documents, the lion's share in Chinese and Tibetan. The materials in other languages—Sanskrit, Sogdian, Uighur, Khotanese, and Hebrew—intrigue scholars because they document the presence of other peoples about whom we would otherwise know nothing. This, the sole Hebrew document in the cave, contains an eighteen-line prayer composed of individual lines from the Psalms. Folded over several times and placed in a pouch, it most likely served as a protective talisman carried to China from Babylon. Courtesy of Bibliothèque Nationale de France.

PLATE 13. WOOLEN PANT LEG FROM KHOTAN

This woolen trouser leg was woven locally but features a classical Greek centaur with a warrior shown below. Found at the Shanpula site outside Khotan, these motifs traveled first with Alexander the Great's army to northern Afghanistan and Pakistan and from there to northwestern China. The centaur's cape and the flower/diamond motif on the warrior's lapel are central Asian modifications to the original motifs. The exact date of the pantleg from this heavily looted site is unknown, but Shanpula contains materials from the third century BCE to the fourth century CE.

PLATE 14. SILK ROAD DANCE PARTY FROM THE AN JIA TOMB, XI'AN
The swirl dance, introduced by the Sogdians, was performed all along the Silk Road by men and women alike and described by contemporaries as fast-paced and exciting, This painted stone panel comes from a funerary couch in the tomb of a Sogdian headman in Xi'an who died in 579 CE. This is one of twelve different panels containing shallow reliefs painted in red, black, and white on a gold background; all show different scenes from the deceased headman's life, offering an unparalleled glimpse of Sogdian life in China. Cultural Relics Publishing House.

PLATE 15. ZOROASTRIAN ART FROM THE AN JIA TOMB
The Sogdians formed the largest non-Chinese community in China between 500 and 800 CE.
This is the tomb of a Sogdian with a typical Chinese stone tomb entranceway modeled after
Chinese homes, but with Zoroastrian art above the doorway. The painting depicts two priests
flanking a Zoroastrian fire altar. Curiously the bones of the deceased were placed outside
the door, not inside the tomb on a funerary couch as was customary for Chinese at the time.
Cultural Relics Publishing House.

PLATE 16A. THE TOMB OF XINJIANG'S FIRST ISLAMIC RULER

This tomb-shrine of the first Karakhanid king to convert to Islam, Sultan Sutuq Bugrakhan, is in the city of Atush, some 28 miles, or 45 km, northeast of Kashgar, in western Xinjiang close to the Kyrgyzstan border. This mazar tomb is among the most venerated sites in Xinjiang, but attendance has declined since a Beijing-based tourism company renovated the site and started charging each visitor an admission fee. Courtesy of Mathew Andrews.

PLATE 16B. WOMAN PRAYING AT THE TOMB OF IMAM MUSAKAZIM

Here a woman kneels in prayer before the tomb of the imam at the Musakazim Mazar, outside Khotan. Offerings on the tomb include sheep skins and multicolored flags with quotations from the Quran. In Khotan, where the armies of the Muslim Karakhanids defeated the king's armies in 1006—beginning the Islamification of Xinjiang—visitors frequently hang animal carcasses stuffed with straw or a flag on a pole above the grave of the deceased. Courtesy of Mathew Andrews.

THE CHINESE TOMB OF A SOGDIAN HEADMAN

The lintel above the doorway to An Jia's tomb skillfully integrates Chinese and Sogdian motifs. A priest-bird with a man's head and torso but a bird's legs and distinct claws stands upright. Wearing a padam face mask, he tends the table bearing bowls and vases with flowers. He represents the Zoroastrian god Srosh, associated with the rooster, who helps the soul cross the bridge from this world to the next and who also serves as a judge in the next world. Above the priest-bird floats a Chinese-style musician surrounded by clouds. The figure on the lower right, who wears a white cap and has a pronounced mustache, is the deceased sabao, An Jia, himself. Cultural Relics Publishing House.

men and women at parties. An Jia's funeral bed depicts the dance three times (see color plate 14).

The panels from An Jia's tomb show little, if any, mercantile activity. Camels bearing goods appear on one of the panels at the back, but the context seems more diplomatic than mercantile. On the same panel, An Jia appears to be conversing with a Turkish leader in his tent.[14] If the camels are indeed carrying trade goods, then these are gifts to be exchanged following the completion of negotiations, a practice that accords with the envoy-dominated trade described in earlier chapters, most notably in the portrayal of emissaries and the gifts they bear in the Afrasiab palace of Samarkand.

A second Sogdian tomb, found 1.4 miles (2.2 km) east of An Jia's tomb in 2003, offers fascinating parallels.[15] The deceased was named Wirkak, a Sogdian name derived from the word for "wolf," and his Chinese family name was Shi; the space for his Chinese given name was left blank, so it is unknown. Like An Jia's tomb, Wirkak's tomb had a Chinese-style sloping walkway leading to the tomb chamber. Whereas An Jia had a stone bed, Wirkak had a stone house 8 feet

(2.46 m) long, 5.1 feet (1.55 m) wide, and 5.18 feet (1.58 m) high with different scenes on the outside walls. Sand had filled the tomb, and archeologists found only this stone house, with a broken roof, inside. There were no other grave goods.

Shi Wirkak's epitaph was in an unusual position above the door of the stone house. Even more unusual, his epitaph had two versions: one in Sogdian on the right, and one in Chinese on the left.[16] The two texts overlap in their account of the facts of Shi Wirkak's life but are not translations of the same text. The scribe(s) who wrote the texts had a weak command of both languages. The two texts concur that Wirkak died in 579, the same year as his wife; had three sons; and served as a sabao in Wuwei, Gansu, where An Jia had also been a sabao. The Sogdian text concludes: "This tomb [i.e. god-house] made of stone was constructed by Vreshmanvandak, Zhematvandak, and Protvantak [or Parotvandak] for the sake of their father and mother in the suitable place," an indication that the term "god-house" must have referred to the house-shaped sarcophagus placed in the tomb.[17]

The stone house had a roof and a base, and the front had two doors and two windows. Bird-priests, similar to those above the door of An Jia's tomb, tend fires beneath the windows, and many elements on the stone house deeply resemble motifs from the An Jia tomb: a banquet, hunting scenes, the deceased inside a tent talking with someone of a different ethnicity. Some of the images are downright puzzling: who, for example, is the ascetic in the cave on the left edge of the northern side? Laozi? A Brahman? Given the openness of the Sogdians to deities from other religious systems, they may never be identified.

The eastern side of the stone house portrays the progress of the soul of the deceased over the Chinwad Bridge. This arresting scene is much more detailed than any portrayal of Zoroastrian beliefs about the fate of the dead from either Sogdiana or the heartland of Zoroastrianism in Iran.

Every motif—the winged, crowned horses, the winged musicians, the crowned human figures with streamers flying behind (a time-honored way of portraying monarchs in Iranian art)—suggests that Wirkak and his wife are about to enter paradise. The identification of the different elements in this scene rests on parallels between the carvings on the stone sarcophagus and Zoroastrian texts, preserved in their ninth-century versions, indicating close familiarity with these religious texts among Sogdians resident in China in the late sixth century—an important finding, since no Zoroastrian texts have surfaced in China to date.[18]

Both An Jia and Shi Wirkak died in 579, in the closing years of the Northern Zhou dynasty, a time of rapid political change. The ruler of the Northern Zhou arranged for his heir to marry the daughter of one of his generals in 578. That

THE PERILOUS CROSSING TO THE NEXT WORLD
This scene comes from a stone house buried in the tomb of Shi Wirkak. On the lower right, two human Zoroastrian priests wearing *padam* face masks stand facing a bridge. There they conduct the ceremony that sends the souls of the dead off to the next world. On the left, Wirkak and his wife lead a procession including two children (did they predecease their parents?), animals, two horses, and a camel bearing goods across the bridge. Significantly, Wirkak and his wife have made it safely past the monster with ominously bared teeth waiting in the water below. According to Zoroastrian teachings, only those who have told the truth and behaved righteously can cross to the other side of the bridge unharmed; those who have not plunge to their death below as the bridge narrows to razor-width. Courtesy of Yang Junkai.

heir succeeded to the throne in 581 but died soon after, leaving a boy on the throne. At first, the boy's maternal grandfather assumed the position of regent, but in the same year he seized power and founded the Sui dynasty. For the next eight years his armies campaigned all over China, gradually gaining territory, until in 589 he reunified the empire.

The original capital of the Sui dynasty lay in Yangzhou, near the coast of central China, but in 582 the Sui founder relocated his capital to Chang'an, the capital of many earlier and powerful dynasties. He built an entirely new and formally planned city on a site south and east of the city's capital during the Northern Zhou (which was located on the same site as the Han-dynasty capital). The Sui founder ruled for nearly thirty years before dying a natural death in 604. His son succeeded him and led his armies on a series of military campaigns in Korea, which he never succeeded in conquering. The Chinese suffered massive losses, prompting a general to overthrow the emperor and establish the Tang dynasty in 618.[19] Under the Tang, the capital remained at Chang'an except for brief intervals.

When the new city was completed, its 5 yard (4.6 m) high walls ran 5.92 miles (9.5 km) east to west and 5.27 miles (8.4 km) north to south, enclosing a rectangular area of some 31 square miles (80 sq km). Broad main avenues divided the city; the widest was 500 feet (155 m) across, the equivalent of a forty-five-lane highway.[20] The city had 109 districts, called quarters (*fang*). Each quarter had a wall around it; city officials closed the gates every night to enforce a strict curfew. To the north of the city, outside the rectangle, were the palace and various government offices, both civil and military. Only officials and members of the royal family could enter that district. Officials and courtiers tended to live in the eastern half of the city. Because they could afford more spacious houses with gardens, the eastern half of the city was less densely populated. Most ordinary people lived in the western half.

Two markets, known as the Eastern and Western Markets, each occupied an area about 0.4 square miles (1 sq km).[21] A road 400 feet (120 m) wide ran along the outside edge of the market to allow passage of people and vehicles; inside the market were more streets. Both markets, like the quarters of the city, were walled, and the gates were carefully guarded. No officials above the fifth rank (out of a total of nine) were allowed to enter, because the officials who served under Emperor Taizong (reigned 627–49) and who compiled the Tang Code, viewed commerce as polluting. The Tang Code made an exception for market officials, whom it charged with checking weights and setting prices every ten days.[22] Market supervisors issued certificates of ownership to the purchasers of livestock and slaves, who had to present these each time they crossed the border. These officials made sure that the markets opened only at noon and closed two hours before sundown.[23]

The Eastern Market tended to specialize in domestic goods, while the Western Market offered more foreign goods, many delivered by camel trains. Shops selling the same goods clustered together on narrow roads called *hang*. (Even today the Chinese word for expert is *neihang*, "inside the row," and for a layman *waihang*, "outside the row.") The Eastern Market had 220 different groups of shops selling different wares including Chinese brushes, iron goods, cloth, meat, wine, and printed materials. The Western Market offered foodstuffs as well as leather goods, like bridles and saddles, and jewelry and precious stones from all over Eurasia. The markets were packed with goods; a fire in 843 destroyed four thousand dwellings in twelve different rows of the Eastern Market.[24]

Visitors to the markets enjoyed restaurants, wine shops, food stands, and brothels, and traveling merchants could store their goods in warehouses, deposit their money in bank-like institutions, and stay at inns, some with as many as twenty rooms. The dispute between the Sogdian merchant Cao Rokhshan and the Chinese merchant Li Shaojin, discussed in chapter 3, illustrates how the Chinese courts handled a dispute between Chinese and non-Chinese; they applied Chinese law. Tang-dynasty law stipulated that if foreigners from the same country committed a crime against each other, the law of their homeland would apply, but if foreigners of different nationalities were involved, then Chinese law would apply.[25] Recall that both men lived in the capital and traveled to the northwest on business.

Many travelers came to visit the Tang capital of Chang'an, home to some 960,000 people living in 300,000 households, according to the official history of the Tang.[26] In a population of one million people, the majority of the residents were Chinese, but a sizable foreign community lived in the city as well, concentrated around the Western Market.[27] Some foreigners settled in China as the result of treaties. In 631, after the Eastern Turks surrendered to the Tang, nearly ten thousand households were ordered to move to Chang'an, and many of these households were Sogdians in the service of the Turks.[28] When the Tang forces conquered different Central Asian kingdoms, they required their former rulers to send their sons to Chang'an as hostages, further swelling the numbers of foreigners in the city. Perhaps the most famous refugees were the descendants of the Sasanian emperors who fled Iran after the fall of their capital at Ctesiphon to Muslim forces in 651. The last Sasanian emperor, Yazdegerd III, died while in flight, but his son Peroz and grandson Narseh both moved permanently to the city.[29]

These immigrants brought their religious practices with them. At least five, maybe six, Zoroastrian temples stood in the city, four around the Western Market.[30] A single Christian church, affiliated with the Church of the East, was located just north of the Western Market. In modern Xi'an, the Forest of Steles (Beilin) Museum houses hundreds of stone tablets found all over China, the most famous of which, often referred to as the Nestorian stele, provides a history of Christianity under the Tang dynasty.[31]

According to this tablet, the first Christian to arrive in Chang'an was a man named Aluohan; dispatched by the patriarchate in Seleucia-Ctesiphon (in modern-day Iraq) in 635, he established the earliest outpost of the Church of the East in China.[32] The founding of this church coincided with a mass migration of Persians from their homeland in Iran, then under siege by Muslim armies, to China and other points east. Seventy names, in Syriac script with Chinese transcriptions, along with these individuals' positions in the church hierarchy, follow the main inscription. Some of the names, like Hope of Jesus, are unmistakably Christian, while others, such as Given by the Moon God Mah, are originally derived from Zoroastrianism but had become common names used throughout Mesopotamia. Each of the names has a Chinese transcription. It seems likely that most of the seventy signatories were foreign, not Chinese.

VESTIGES OF CHRISTIANITY IN THE TANG CAPITAL
Headed by a cross with four even sections, which was commonly used by the Church of the East, this text was carved onto a stone stele in 781. Discovered in 1625, the rubbing was shown by a Chinese official to Jesuit missionaries, who were overjoyed to learn that they were not the first Christian missionaries in China. They sent the rubbing to Europe, and by the 1670s both the Chinese and Syriac-language portions of the text had been translated. Cultural Relics Publishing House.

The Church of the East established churches in a few major Chinese cities: Chang'an, Luoyang, Guangzhou (Canton), and possibly in a few other places. Members of the Church of the East, largely Iranians and Sogdians, received the support of the Tang dynasty throughout the seventh and eighth centuries, but in 845 the Tang emperor issued a ban whose primary target was Buddhism but included Christianity as well. Buddhism survived, but the Church of the East did not.

No traces of this or any other religious institutions survive in today's Xi'an. In fact, the aboveground city of Xi'an contains remarkably few structures from Chang'an at its peak during the Tang. The visitor will look in vain for remnants of the glorious wide avenues. The wall one sees today is very large—so large that one can ride a bicycle or drive a golf cart on top of it—but it dates to the Ming dynasty (1368–1644), not the Tang. The only Tang-dynasty structures still standing are two brick towers: the Big Goose Pagoda and the Small Goose Pagoda. Emperor Taizong built the Big Goose Pagoda to house the books Xuanzang brought back from India; Xuanzang supervised a team of translators there.

Only below ground, in tombs, can one hope to find a taste of the city's past glory. Unlike other sites on the Silk Road, Xi'an's climate is moister than that of the Taklamakan, so that buried paper eventually disintegrates. Still, thanks to the reuse of waste paper, a fascinating set of receipts from a pawnshop in Chang'an has survived in the arms of a figurine excavated in the Astana grave-yard at Turfan. The documents mention several place-names unique to the Tang capital and so are almost certainly from Chang'an.

Craftsmen based in the Tang capital used discarded pawn slips to make the figurines that were subsequently placed in the joint grave of a man and his wife buried at Astana.[33] The husband died in 633, before the Chinese conquest of 640, and the wife more than fifty years later in 689. The figurine's fine brocade clothing and carefully worked head, pictured in color plate 8, also look as though they were produced in a workshop in the capital. The place-names mentioned in the documents have dated the pawnshop tickets to between 662, when the Guanyin Monastery changed its name, and 689, when the wife was buried in the joint tomb.

The discarded pawn tickets show how the ordinary inhabitants of Chang'an made ends meet during the seventh century. Each ticket follows the same format: item pawned, name of borrower, date (month and day, not year), the amount of money loaned, the amount of money paid back, the address and (sometimes) the age of the borrower. The slips list twenty-nine people by name yet give the occu-pations of only two individuals: one was a dyer and another made hairpins. When the pawned item was returned, the pawnshop employees cancelled the transac-tion by drawing a line (in the shape of a 7) across the ticket. Fifteen sheets of paper record fifty-four transactions (the last sixteen are incomplete), which are the ear-liest surviving pawnshop records found in China to date. In almost all of the transactions the borrower deposited an item of clothing (sometimes silk, some-times simply cloth) or a piece of cloth (also used as a form of currency during the Tang) and received a certain number of coins, usually around a hundred, in exchange. Only two transactions involved goods besides clothing or cloth; one borrower put up a bronze mirror against a loan of seventy coins, while another presented four strings of pearls for 150 coins. The borrowers paid interest at a rate of 5 percent each month, which was within the limits set by Tang law (and far lower than the rates paid by borrowers in Turfan during the same period).

A second set of records, also preserved as part of a figurine, suggests that those frequenting the pawnshop near the Guanyin Monastery were relatively well off. These list a total of 608 transactions, even small loans, made by Chang'an shops to city dwellers who paid with "medicine, cloth, beans, and wheat bran." One-fourth of these transactions were made by women, evidence that the female residents of the capital did leave their homes, even if Confucian ideals portrayed virtuous women as always staying inside.[34]

Another surprise find, this time from the capital itself, offers insight into those at the opposite end of the social spectrum, the wealthiest of the city's dwellers.[35] In 1970, during the Cultural Revolution, Xi'an archeologists uncovered two clay pots (25 inches, or 64 cm high) and one silver pot (10 inches, or 25 cm high) in Hejiacun, or Hejia Village, then in the southern suburbs. They were buried about 1 yard (.9 m) under the ground and 1 yard (.9 m) apart from each other. At the time, the authorities were building a detention center; a hostel for government officials now occupies the unmarked site. The three pots held over one thousand different items including gold and silver artifacts, precious gems and minerals, medicines, and an extraordinary coin collection. If the collection originally included more fragile items, like textiles or books, they have not survived. One of the largest hoards of buried treasure ever found in China, the Hejia Village collection certainly contains the most valuable and the most beautifully worked Silk Road artifacts.

No definitive evidence of the owner's identity survives. Almost everyone assumes that the hoard's owner intended to come back after some kind of disturbance—a rebellion? bandit attacks? a natural disaster?—but never did. The hoard was buried in a quarter approximately 0.6 miles (1 km) east of the Western Market and 2 miles (3 km) west of the Eastern Market. The best clue to the hoard's date is several silver biscuits with labels identifying them as tax payments. Before 780 the Tang dynasty required that its subjects pay three different types of taxes: *zu* (rent in grain), *yong* (corvée labor), and *diao* (cloth), but districts were allowed to substitute other goods. Four round silver biscuits, about 4 inches (10 cm) in diameter and weighing over 14 ounces (400 grams), are incised with crude characters that identify them as tax payments from two subprefectures in Guangdong Province. One is dated 722; three are dated 731. Inscriptions on these biscuits give their exact weights as well as the names of the officials who weighed them.

After the authorities received such biscuits, they melted them down into larger lumps, the largest weighing over 17 pounds (8 kg), which were labeled in black ink with the name of the storehouse where they were held—the Eastern Market Storehouse—and their weight and the official who weighed them.[36] Because central government officials melted down the biscuits they received from localities to make these larger lumps, it seems most likely that the hoard was buried not long after 731, the latest date on the biscuits. Many of the intricately worked gold and silver bowls in the collection bear similar labels, always

TABLE 5.1 HEJIACUN VILLAGE FIND CHART

Gold		Silver		Coins	
3	eating vessels	55	bowls	1	knife of 'Jimo' from the kingdom of Qi
5	drinking cups	53	plates	1	shovel-shaped coin of Spring and Autumn Period
3	medicine containers	6	platters	4	early Han dynasty coins
2	washing basins	12	drinking cups	11	coins from the region of Wang Mang
10	hair pins	46	medicine containers	2	Six Dynasties coins
2	armlets	12	washing basins	1	'Gaochang jili' coin from Turfan (5th/6th century)
12	miniature dragons	1	lamp head (?)	1	Byzantine solidus of Heraclius (r. 610–640)
1	comb base	4	jugs	1	Sassanian drachm of Khusrau II (r. 590–628)
4388	grams gold foil	1	incense burner	5	Japanese silver coins with the legend 'Wado kaichin' (708–15)
126	grams of gold dust	1	spherical censer	421	silver (including some bronze?) Tang dynasty coins with the legend 'Kaiyuan tongbao'
		1	box		
		23	fasteners	30	gold 'Kaiyuan tongbao' coins
		1	vessel with a spout		

Minerals and Glass				Medicines	
1	agate cup with gold bull head	55	white agate horse harnesses	1	block of yellow lead (litharge)
1	agate wine cup	53	white jade belt decorations	15	types of mineral powder, all in inscribed containers, including stalactite and gold
1	agate mortar	6	sapphires		
1	jade pestle	12	rubies		
1	white jade wine cup	46	green agates		
1	block of jade	12	topaz		

(continued)

TABLE 5.1 (CONTINUED)			
Minerals and Glass			Medicines
1	crystal cup	1	white jade bracelet with gold decorations	
1	glass bowl	4	pieces of coral	
9	ceremonial hip belts	1	piece of amber	

Source: Preliminary site report published as 'Xi'an nanjiao Hejiacun faxian Tangdai jiaozang wenwu', *Wenwu* 1972:1, pp. 30–42. Reprinted with permission from *Orientations*, February 2003 issue, p. 15.

in black ink, giving their weight, an indication that they, too, were held in a government storehouse. Government officials apparently stored tax silver at three different stages in its life cycle: when it was first mined and submitted by various localities, after it had been melted into large lumps, and finally after it had been worked into gold and silver vessels.

Forty-six different silver vessels served as medicine containers that were labeled with both the weight and the grade of their contents: "stalactite of upper-upper grade" or "stalactite of medium-upper grade." Over 4.4 lbs (2 kg) of stalactite powder of different grades was buried in the hoard; Tang medical guides suggest daily doses of around 1.4 ounces, or 40 grams, for one or two hundred days to either calm the nerves or increase one's energy. The 4.4 ounces (126 grams) of gold dust probably had medicinal uses, as did a block of litharge, a lead oxide added to skin ointments to cure cuts and blemishes.[37]

Museum exhibits about the Silk Road or Tang-dynasty Chang'an often feature the Hejiacun gold and silver vessels, because they combine different elements of Iranian and Chinese art in extraordinarily pleasing ways.[38] In surviving paintings from the Sogdian city of Panjikent and Sogdian tomb panels found in China, Sogdian artists frequently mixed scenes showing Sogdian life, such as hunting or banquets with pictures of activities pursued by peoples, often Chinese, from other societies.

No one can tell by looking at a metal cup or container where it was made or who made it. Historians of technology tend to assume, though, that classic Sogdian shapes without Chinese motifs were made in Sogdiana and imported to China (if they were found in China), while any vessel whose shape departs from Sogdian prototypes was probably made in Chang'an, by Sogdian or Chinese craftsmen. By this measure, few of the Hejia Village vessels appear to be distinctly Sogdian: many more vessels have Chinese-style shapes.

A CUP FROM THE HEJIACUN VILLAGE HOARD
This gilt silver cup, measuring 2 inches (5.1 cm) tall, with a mouth 3.6 inches (9.1 cm) across, has several identifiable Sogdian characteristics: eight lobes, a thumb ring attached to a triangular medallion holding a deer, and a pearl border trim at its base. The exterior of the cup, like the murals on the northern wall of the Afrasiab house at Samarkand, alternates active scenes of men hunting, squarely in the tradition of Iranian royal art, with portraits of delicate women in Chinese gowns engaged in daily activities, like getting dressed or playing an instrument. Cultural Relics Publishing House.

The owner of the treasure separated the imported items from the other treasures and buried them in the silver jar with the handle; on the lid of the jar, he listed these goods.[39] A miniature rock-crystal bowl, only 1 inch (2.5 cm) tall and 3.8 inches (9.6 cm) across, has eight lobes, an identifying characteristic of Sogdian manufacture. Rock crystal occurs naturally but looks like glass when it is free of imperfections. The main constituent of both glass and rock crystal is silica, and one can make glass by melting rock crystal, but only at high temperatures—above 3,000 degrees Fahrenheit (1,700 degrees Centigrade), temperatures far too hot for any premodern workshop to achieve. In addition to the rock-crystal bowl, the hoard contained a glass vessel that must have been imported from the west, since Chinese craftsmen learned how to make opaque glass in ancient times but translucent glass only much later.[40] Historically, most glass was made from sand, limestone, and sodium carbonate.

Other imported items in the silver vase included gems not mined anywhere within the Tang empire: seven sapphires, two rubies, one topaz, and six agates. The largest, the topaz, weighed 119 grams (596 carats); the smallest (one of the rubies) was just 2.5 grams (12.5 carats). Rubies and sapphires originated in Burma, Sri Lanka, Thailand, and Kashmir, India; topazes came as well from Burma and Sri Lanka as well as Japan and the Russian Urals. The unusual moss green color of the agates found at Hejia Village suggests an Indian source.[41] A beautiful rhyton drinking vessel crafted from carnelian, a brownish-red agate, was probably made in Gandhara or the Tocharistan region of Afghanistan.[42]

This composition of the hoard, with a few imported items and many more locally made vessels, fits the overall pattern of Silk Road trade. Relatively few goods traveled long distances overland; those that did were often precious gemstones that were small, light, and easy to carry. As Muslim armies conquered more territory, increasing numbers of migrants, including many skilled metal craftsmen, came to China and chose to settle in Chang'an, where many non-Chinese lived already. After Sogdian metalsmiths had migrated to China, they settled down and began to make vessels similar—but not identical—to those they had made in their homeland. As they learned more Chinese motifs and adjusted to a new clientele, they produced more hybrid items like the cup with its mixture of Chinese and Iranian elements.

A list of gifts that the emperor exchanged with An Lushan, before the Turco-Sogdian general rebelled, includes many items corresponding to objects in the Hejiacun hoard: Iranian-style silver ewers, parcel-gilt silver bowls, agate dishes, jade belts, coral, pearls, incense, and medicine in gold and silver boxes. In return the general gave Iranian-style bottles and plates made from silver and gold.[43] This list of gifts confirms that the vessels in the Hejiacun hoard came from the highest level of Chang'an society, the emperor and his top-ranking courtiers.

Of all the items buried at Hejia Village, the most difficult to explain is the collection of 478 coins. Six were definitely made outside of China: one silver coin minted during the reign of the Sasanian emperor Khusrau II (reigned 590–628) and five silver coins from Japan, dating to 708–15. There was a seventh coin, apparently a gold coin minted by the Byzantine emperor Heraclius (reigned 610–40), but, like so many of the Byzantine coins found in China, it is an imitation made in China, not a genuine Byzantine coin. Equally unusual was a selection of twenty historic Chinese coins. The earliest, dating to about 500 BCE, were examples of China's first currency, shaped like a shovel and a knife. Also included were coins from the Han dynasty (206 BCE–220 CE) and the centuries of disunity before the Tang unification. The final group of coins was the largest: 451 stamped with the Kaiyuan reign period (713–41). The Kaiyuan coins included bronze examples, which circulated widely at the time, as well as silver and gold coins, apparently specially made for the emperor to give out at parties (one such party occurred in 713, according to the official histories).[44] The composition of the coin collection, including foreign-made, historic, and contemporary examples, has prompted some to wonder if it belonged to a private collector.[45]

How can we best explain the varied composition of the Hejia Village hoard? Although some items, like the medicinal powder and the coin collection, may seem as though they belonged to an individual, more of the collection—particularly the tax biscuits—looks as though it came from a government storehouse. All the items labeled with their weight and the name of the weighing official also point to an official storeroom. The coins may have belonged to a private coin collector, but no other collections from the Tang have been found; they could also have been kept by the section of the government that minted coins as a kind of reference collection. In premodern China, the line between individual and government property was not as sharp as in modern societies. Perhaps an official who worked in the mint added a few of his own possessions to the government property at the time of burial.

When would someone in Chang'an have been most likely to bury such an extraordinary collection of treasures? The first great rebellion that shattered the steady peace of the first century and a half of Tang rule occurred in 755, when An Lushan (or An Rokhshan) led a military uprising against the Tang emperor Xuanzong. After conquering Luoyang, An Lushan and the rebels took Chang'an in 755, forcing the emperor to flee the capital with his beautiful consort Yang Guifei. En route to Sichuan, the imperial guard threatened to mutiny unless the emperor killed Yang Guifei, and the emperor gave the order to strangle her. He then relinquished the throne in favor of his son.

The new emperor did not have enough troops to defeat the rebels and was forced to cede the power to tax to regional governors, who provided him with the troops he needed. For the next seven years, the war between the rebels and the Tang forces continued. Even though An Lushan was assassinated in 757 and his second-in-command was also assassinated in 761, the rebels maintained a strong presence until the Tang emperor asked the help of the Uighur kaghan, whose troops defeated the rebel army in 763.[46] The Uighurs were allowed to sack the Tang capital as a reward for their services, and they devastated the city.

When the Tang forces finally regained control of the empire, they took measures against the Sogdians, whom they blamed for the rebellion. They replaced the character "An," meaning "peace," in all the names of gates and streets in the capital; many people, both Sogdian and not, whose family name was An, adopted new surnames.[47] One account of the rebellion recounts that the general Gao Juren, himself ethnically Korean, who wrested control of Beijing from the rebels "ordered that those who killed *hu* [Iranians, most likely Sogdians] would be richly rewarded. As a result, the *jiehu* [a sub-set of the *hu* that An Lushan belonged to, possibly those living in north China] were completely exterminated. Small children were tossed in the air and caught on lances. Those who had big noses like the Sogdians and those who were killed by mistake for this reason were extremely numerous."[48]

The targeting of Sogdians marked a new and ugly chapter in the history of the Silk Road. Previous dynasties had sometimes ordered the closing of monasteries and the forced laicization of monks and nuns, but no earlier ruler had ever targeted a minority group within the larger Chinese population in this way. Pogrom-like attacks on Sogdians did not occur everywhere Sogdians lived, but in Chang'an a new climate of intolerance seems to have set in. Even so, many foreigners living in Chang'an decided to stay within China, with many relocating to the area south of Beijing in modern Hebei Province, rather than risk returning to Islamified areas of Sogdiana and Central Asia.

The final defeat of the rebels did not bring peace to the beleaguered capital. In late 763 an army from the newly united Tibetan Empire attacked Chang'an and pillaged the city for two weeks before retreating. They continued to do so for the next twenty years. The Tang armies were powerless against the forces of the Tibetans, who, along with the Uighurs, succeeded the Tang as Asia's leading military power for more than a century.

When the Tibetans gained control of Gansu in the 780s and Kucha in the 790s, the Tang saw its revenues decline even further. In 787, in response to the fall of Gansu Province, the prime minister Li Mi proposed a budget-cutting measure: slashing the subsidies for all foreign envoys resident in the capital. He was "aware that many of the Central Asians were long-term residents, some having been in the capital for more than forty years, that they had all married, purchased land and housing and made other investments on which they earned interest, and that they had no intention of ever returning to their homelands."[49] The minister put the number of foreign envoys, most of them Sogdian, at four thousand, a surprisingly high figure given that many foreigners would have fled or concealed their identity after the An Lushan rebellion.

Fictional tales document the lives of these Sogdians, particularly rich merchants, who remained in Chang'an after 763. A new genre of short story, the "wonder tale," peaked in popularity in the early ninth century.[50] Different authors describe the Sogdians as possessing the same traits: excessive generosity coupled with an uncanny ability to judge goods, especially jewels. In exile from their homeland, many were born to noble families but forced, in these narratives, to take menial jobs so that they could survive in China.

In one story set in Chang'an in the years after the An Lushan rebellion,[51] a young man from a wealthy Chinese family finds an unusual rock, "half ocean-colored, half red, with deep stripes," on the beach. He chances upon the annual gathering of some thirty foreign merchants: "The person with the most valuable treasures wears a hat and sits in the place of honor; the others sit in ranks below him." The youth watches as they compare their riches—one merchant has four beautiful pearls, one more than an inch across. Others present their wares, mostly pearls, and then the youth displays his stone to the assembled merchants, who promptly stand up and escort him to the place of honor. When he asks for one million strings, they retort, "Why are you insulting this treasure of ours?" and insist on paying ten million. It turns out that the jewel is a national treasure that has been lost for over thirty years; they call it the "treasure mother," because their king places it on the shore, prays to it in the evening, and when he returns the next morning, he finds the precious stones that have surrounded it of their own accord. The jewel's magic powers fulfill the genre's promise of marvels, but the setting is realistic: it is entirely plausible that thirty or so Sogdian merchants would gather annually in the Tang capital.

Stereotypically wealthy Iranian merchants also appear in a different literary genre, model legal decisions. During the Tang dynasty, and particularly after 755, increasing numbers of young men sat the civil service examinations, and they proved ready consumers for this type of literature. Not based on actual legal cases, these model decisions treated hypothetical situations that allowed authors to display their reasoning skills.

One model decision tells of two Sogdian brothers who live in Chang'an.[52] One is so wealthy that his garden, pond, house, furniture, and male and female servants "rival those of marquises and princes." His brother, on the other hand, is so poor that he is unable to repay the loan of a garment from another wealthy Sogdian merchant. That merchant takes the wealthy brother to court for refusing to pay the poor brother's loan, and the prefect rules that the wealthy brother must give some livestock to the younger brother so that he does not die of starvation.

The marvel tales and the model cases document the existence of a powerful stereotype: Tang-dynasty authors viewed Sogdian merchants as tremendously wealthy because of the jewel trade. Sogdian merchants did indeed deal in jewels and gemstones, which had the twin advantages of being both valuable and light. But the existence of a stereotype does not make it true: we cannot conclude that the Silk Road trade was so prosperous that it enriched thousands of Sogdians living in Chang'an. Of the thousands of Sogdians who settled in the cities of Tang-dynasty China, merchants constituted only a minority.[53] Emissaries, military dependents, refugees, farmers, metalsmiths, and soldiers also came in large numbers.

In 843 the emperor gave voice to the persisting anti-foreign sentiment in the capital when he banned Manichaeism, and two years later in 845 forbade the practice of Buddhism, Zoroastrianism, and Christianity. His stated goal was to increase the amount of money available for minting coins, so he ordered that statues and bells be melted down. In addition, the authorities confiscated the property of all but a handful of Buddhist monasteries in Chang'an and Luoyang. When the emperor died in 847 his successor lifted the ban on Buddhism but not on the other religions.

These measures came at a time when the dynasty was ceding large chunks of territory in the northwest to newly powerful regional leaders, often former military commanders who controlled their own armies and who gradually refused to pay taxes to the ruling dynasty. After the withdrawal of Chinese troops from the Taklamakan oasis towns in the 750s, the land routes gradually declined, while sea travel gained primacy.[54] Though perilous, sea travel had occurred in earlier centuries, and many of those traveling by boat began their journeys at Chang'an.

Since ancient times the residents of Southeast Asia had voyaged by boat in the South China Sea and the western Pacific, and over time they linked different coastal routes together to form longer routes. By at least the first century of the Common Era sailors had learned both how to harness the monsoon winds and how to navigate the straits of Malacca so that they could sail all the way from China to India, but they had to stop for several months in Srivijaya (modern-day Palembang, on the island of Sumatra in Indonesia) to wait for the winds to shift.[55]

The monk Faxian (active 350–414) wrote vividly about the difficulties of sea travel between India and China. Living more than two centuries before Xuanzang, he had the same motivation for going to India: to study texts in the original that were not available in China. On the outward leg, he proceeded overland from Chang'an through Khotan and then to India. After studying for more than six years in the major Buddhist centers on the Ganges River, he caught a boat to Sri Lanka at the port of Tamluk, on the mouth of Hoogly River, south of Calcutta in West Bengal.[56]

The two-week voyage to Sri Lanka turned out to be the only uneventful leg of his long sea voyage. In Sri Lanka Faxian visited an image of the Buddha made from jade and other precious substances that stood over 22 feet (6.6 meters) tall. While he was in the temple, a merchant, probably Chinese, presented a white silk fan as a donation. Suddenly, in a rare personal note, Faxian admits to being overcome with homesickness and weeping.[57] Faxian stayed for two more years in Sri Lanka, where he noted the presence of "many scholars, venerable monks, sabao and merchants."[58] As in Sogdian Ancient Letter 5, Sogdians used the term sabao to indicate the leaders of their communities, and here Faxian contrasts the Sogdian sabao with Chinese merchants.

Faxian does not give the reasons for his decision to take the sea, and not the overland, route to China, but for those departing from either Tamluk or

Sri Lanka, the sea route was faster and cheaper. In Sumatra he found passage on a "large merchant boat" carrying two hundred people, which was tied to a smaller boat intended for use as a lifeboat.[59] After three days, a great wind— perhaps a typhoon—rose up and did not subside for thirteen days. Those in the smaller boat cut the line connecting them to the larger boat. The merchants, desperate to save their lives in the leaking larger boat, pitched much of their cargo overboard, but Faxian refused to part with the Buddhist texts he had so painstakingly collected. He prayed to the bodhisattva Guanyin, the Buddhist goddess of mercy, for protection, and his account reports that she answered his prayer. When the storm subsided, the larger boat landed on an island where the crew was able to patch the leak and proceed to Sumatra.

Faxian stayed in Sumatra for five months before taking a different ship, about as big as the first, which could carry two hundred people on their way to Guangzhou, along with fifty days' worth of provisions. This leg of the journey proved to be even more perilous than the trip from Sri Lanka to Sumatra. After more than a month on the water, a "black wind and torrential rain" rose up. Faxian again prayed to Guanyin. The Indian passengers had a different response: blaming the Chinese monk for the storm, they decided to leave him alone on an island and continue on without him. Faxian calls these Indian passengers "Brahmans," the general Chinese term for all Indians. The person who paid for his passage interceded on the monk's behalf and threatened that the Chinese ruler, himself a Buddhist, would punish the passengers if they abandoned the monk. Hesitating, the Indians could not bring themselves to abandon Faxian and so permitted him to continue his journey.

The persistently cloudy skies prevented the ship's navigators from determining the right course. Since they did not use a compass, they could only set their course by examining the position of the sun, moon, and stars. When it rained or was cloudy, they had no way to determine their location. They knew that the trip to China should take fifty days, but they simply could not get their bearings. The boat continued to sail in the ocean, its food and water supplies fast dwindling. After seventy days at sea—twenty more than planned—the crew distributed two Chinese pints of water to each passenger and began to cook with seawater. The ship shifted its course northwest in search of land. After eleven more days, it made landfall.

On the basis of the plants they saw on shore, the passengers concluded that they were somewhere in China and sent Faxian to ask where. When he returned to the ship, he informed them that they had arrived at the southern shore of the Shandong Peninsula, about one thousand miles (1,600 km) north of their original destination of Guangzhou. Faxian's trip vividly illustrates the perils of sea

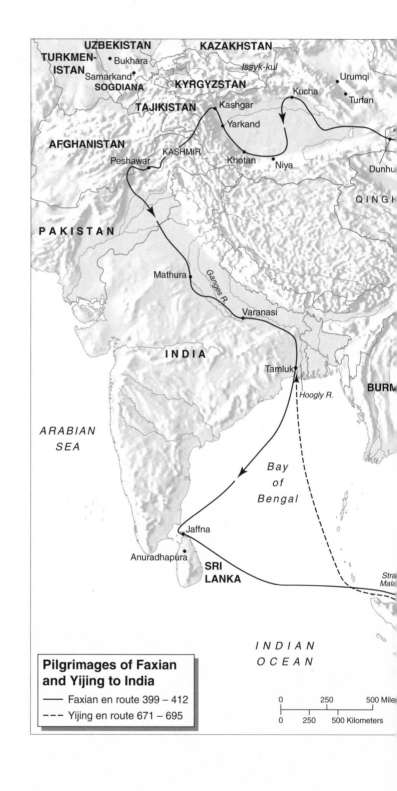

Pilgrimages of Faxian and Yijing to India

— Faxian en route 399 – 412

--- Yijing en route 671 – 695

travel before 1000, approximately the time the Chinese began to use compasses while on shipboard. (They had been using them on land for more than a thousand years.)[60] Even with all its perils, Faxian's sea journey was three years shorter than the outbound overland leg, which had taken him six years.

In the late seventh century, when the Buddhist monk Yijing (635–713) traveled to India to seek original Buddhist texts, he also sailed there and back by ship. Like Faxian, he started his trip in Chang'an. He then traveled to the port city of Yangzhou in modern-day Jiangsu. There he met an imperial envoy who paid for his passage to Guangzhou. In Guangzhou he arranged with the captain of a "Persian ship" to travel to Palembang on the island of Sumatra. (The ship may have had a Persian crew or captain, or it may simply have been Persian in style.)

Departing in late 671, the two men arrived in Palembang after less than twenty days. Yijing describes constellations in the sky, a clue that Chinese sailors were still navigating by the stars and did not use the compass. After six months of studying Sanskrit in Palembang, Yijing then made his way by boat along the northern edge of the island of Sumatra, crossed the Indian Ocean without stopping at Sri Lanka, and arrived at the port of Tamluk, near modern Calcutta, early in 673, slightly more than a year after his departure from China.

Yijing took the same route back to Palembang, where he planned to stay to record more texts. In 689 he wrote a letter to supporters in China asking for paper, ink, and money to pay scribes to write these texts. He boarded a ship in port so that he could mail the letter, but "just at that time the merchant found the wind favorable, and raised the sails high," carrying the reluctant Yijing all the way back to Guangzhou.[61] The suddenness of his trip testifies to its frequency. Yijing said that he went to Guangzhou simply because of the workings of karma, but his experience shows how developed sea travel had become since 400 when Faxian traveled. The express boats that sailed from Palembang to Guangzhou stopped for no one—not even someone who had boarded the ship in error.

On his arrival in Guangzhou, Yijing announced his intent to return to Palembang. His friends introduced him to another monk who wanted to study in India, and, in the same year that he arrived, after the monsoon winds had shifted, the two men went back to the island to retrieve the books Yijing had left behind. Yijing stayed there until 695, when he finally came home to China, again by boat.

The trip between Palembang and Guangzhou had become so routine that Yijing managed it three times in his lifetime, and others plied the route too. After Yijing returned to China he wrote a collective biography of fifty-six monks who had traveled to India. Forty-seven were Chinese, one was Sogdian, and eight were from the Korean kingdom of Silla. Of the fifty-six, twenty-one traveled overland and thirty traveled by sea. Yijing's sample may exaggerate the size of the sea trade, since he recorded the names of monks that he learned about during his travels on the sea route and during the months he stayed at Palembang, but even so his survey suggests the popularity of sea travel in the late 600s.

The sea routes continued to grow in importance. Many of those sailing to Chinese ports in the ninth century were Arabs who came from the ports of Iraq, particularly Basra; the trip took around five months.[62] One early description of China written in Arabic dates to 851; the anonymous author gathered testimony from people who had personally visited China.[63] He reports that the Chinese authorities at the port of Guangzhou, the main port of entry for those coming from Iraq, seized the cargo of any foreign merchant, collected a 30 percent tax, and then returned the goods after six months. The Chinese merchants bought ivory, frankincense, cast copper, and tortoise shells, and they paid in bronze coins; in exchange they offered "gold, silver, pearls, silk, and rich stuffs in great abundance," as well as "an excellent kind of cohesive green clay with which they make cups as fine as phials in which the light of water is seen," that is, porcelain.[64] Since the authorities required the same travel passes that they did of those entering China overland, all merchants had to report their exact itineraries before they could enter China. The author is remarkably positive about China. He portrays the Chinese legal system as fair, even to foreigners, and he describes the bankruptcy law of the Chinese in great detail.

In 916 a geographer named Abu Zayd copied this account in full and then wrote a sequel to it. Overall, he finds the earlier account accurate, and he mentions a "man of undoubted credit" who helped him make corrections. This informant, he writes, "told us also that since those days [the years before 851] the affairs of China had put on quite another face; and since much is related, to show the reason why the voyages to China are interrupted, and how the country has been ruined, many customs abolished, and the empire divided." He elaborates: an 877 uprising in Guangzhou, led by a former examination candidate named Huang Chao, led to the deaths "in addition to the Chinese [of] one hundred and twenty thousand people, Muslims, Christians, Jews and Zoroastrians who had sought refuge in the city."[65] Many doubt the accuracy of this figure: another Arabic source reports that 200,000 perished in Guangzhou, while Chinese sources give no specifics at all.[66] Whatever the exact death toll, the Huang Chao rebels dealt a severe blow to both Guangzhou and the sea trade.

After looting Guangzhou, the rebels arrived in Chang'an early in 881, burned down the Western Market, seized the palace, and sacked the city. Government armies succeeded in driving the rebels out of the city, which they then proceeded to loot themselves. The emperor was reduced to a mere figurehead. The poet Wei Zhuang described the city after the rebels had left:

> Chang'an lies in mournful stillness: what does it now contain?
> —Ruined markets and desolate streets, in which ears of wheat are
>   sprouting.
> Fuel-gatherers have hacked down every flowering plant in the Apricot
>   Gardens,
> Builders of barricades have destroyed the willows along the Imperial
>   Canal.
> All the gaily-colored chariots with their ornamented wheels are scattered
>   and gone.
> Of the stately mansions with their vermilion gates less than half remain.
> The Hanyuan Hall is the haunt of foxes and hares.
> The approach to the Flower-calyx Belvedere is a mass of brambles and
>   thorns.
> All the pomp and magnificence of the older days are buried and passed
>   away;
> Only a dreary waste meets the eye; the old familiar objects are no more.
> The Inner Treasury is burnt down, its tapestries and embroideries a
>   heap of ashes;
> All along the Street of Heaven one treads on the bones of State officials.[67]

Chang'an remained the capital for twenty more years, but then in 904 the general who ruled behind the fiction of the Tang dynasty ordered the emperor's servants killed and the imperial palace dismantled and floated down the Wei River to Luoyang. In 907 he killed the last Tang emperor, seized power outright, and founded a new dynasty. The once-glorious Tang capital lay in ruins, never to recover. The severing of the trade routes to the capital isolated the oases of the northwest, and the Silk Road trade entered a new, quieter era.

CHAPTER 6

The Time Capsule of Silk Road History
The Dunhuang Caves

If you are going to visit only one Silk Road site, make it Dunhuang. The physical setting is spectacular. Deep-green poplar and willow trees line the lush oasis. Framed by rocky cliffs, some five hundred caves contain strikingly beautiful Buddhist wall paintings blending motifs from India, Iran, China, and Central Asia. The more than forty thousand scrolls found in the library cave, shown on the next page, form the largest deposit of documents and artifacts discovered anywhere along the Silk Road.[1] The texts of different religions placed in the library cave—Buddhism, Manichaeism, Zoroastrianism, Judaism, and the Christian Church of the East—show just how cosmopolitan this community was. Throughout the first millennium, Dunhuang was an important garrison town, Buddhist pilgrimage center, and trade depot. After the year 1000, though, the city gradually declined into a backwater. In 1907, when Aurel Stein made it the destination of his Second Central Asian Expedition, only a handful of Europeans had visited. His discoveries there secured him both a knighthood in Britain and lasting infamy in China.

On his Second Expedition, Stein drew on his earlier experiences of leading a team through the Taklamakan Desert, excavating documents and artifacts, and publishing them responsibly and promptly. In the six years since the First Expedition to Khotan and Niya, Britain's rivalry with other nations had intensified; the Russians, Germans, Japanese, and French all had teams exploring and removing antiquities from Xinjiang.[2] Stein applied for funds so that he could be away for two full years. His goal was to retrace his route from Kashmir to Khotan and then travel through the desert all the way to Dunhuang, on the western edge of Gansu Province, which lay 800 miles (1,325 km) away as the crow flies, 950 miles (1,523 km) by road.

Stein first learned about the Dunhuang caves in 1902, when the Hungarian geologist Lajos Lóczy gave a paper at a congress of Orientalists in Hamburg, Germany. Lóczy had been one of the first Europeans to visit the site in 1879; at the time only two monks lived year-round at the near-deserted site. Although an

STEIN'S DOCTORED PHOTOGRAPH OF THE LIBRARY CAVE AT DUNHUANG
This photograph shows cave 16, with an image of the Buddha on the central platform, and, on the far right, a small, high doorway to the secret library cave that was sealed sometime after 1000 CE. Discovered around 1900, the library cave held some forty thousand documents in Chinese, Tibetan, and other lesser-known Silk Road languages, the largest single cache of original documents ever found on the Silk Road. By overlaying two different negatives, Stein later added the two piles of manuscripts to the original photograph of the cave.

expert in soil and rocks, Lóczy identified the importance of the Buddhist murals in the caves, which Chinese scholars tended to ignore in favor of scroll paintings.[3] The earliest wall paintings at Dunhuang dated to the fifth century CE, much earlier than any surviving painting on silk.

The staff of the Second Expedition, like the First, included men to tend the camels and horses, surveyors who could also take photographs, personal servants, and cooks. Also joining the group was a messenger capable of traversing hundreds of miles through the desert without getting lost; his task was to visit nearby towns so that he could retrieve and deliver Stein's mail and his funding, which the Government of India paid in silver ingots.

Stein's command of spoken Uighur (the language he called Turki) was useful for work in Xinjiang, but not in Gansu, where Chinese was the dominant language. Dunhuang first came under Chinese rule in 111 BCE, when the Han dynasty established a garrison at Dunhuang after a successful military campaign. (The Xuanquan post station was part of Dunhuang.) The Chinese controlled the region off and on until 589 CE, when the Sui dynasty reunified China. From that point on Dunhuang was continuously under Chinese rule.[4] At this regional center of learning, the local people studied Chinese characters in school and wrote in Chinese.[5] On the recommendation of the British consul at Kashgar, Stein hired a Chinese secretary, Jiang Xiaowan. Jiang could not speak Uighur, and communication was initially difficult. Stein never learned to read Chinese, but, after the two men had traveled together for a few weeks, Stein picked up enough spoken Chinese to make himself understood.

As Stein made his way toward Dunhuang in the spring of 1907 he heard a rumor, first from a Muslim trader on the run from creditors, that the caves held much more than wall paintings. The trader told him about the discoveries of a former soldier named Wang Yuanlu, who had come to Dunhuang in 1899 or 1900 after leaving the Qing army. Like many soldiers, he had been converted to Daoism by a wandering teacher, and so Stein called him "Daoist Wang." He was barely literate. Soon after Daoist Wang's arrival at the site, he knocked on a cave wall, heard that it was hollow, and discovered the library cave (cave 17) behind it.[6] After dismantling the wall, Daoist Wang presented a few individual scrolls to local and provincial officials, and at least one of these officials, a scholar of ancient Chinese script named Ye Changchi, grasped their importance. Yet, severely pressed for funds in the years after the Boxer Rebellion, the authorities decided not to remove the documents, ordering that they remain in the cave under Daoist Wang's care.

When Stein and his secretary Jiang first visited the site in March, 1907, Daoist Wang was away "on a begging tour with his acolytes." They took the opportunity to wander around the cliffside caves, which were open to the elements and entirely unguarded. Stein noted the accuracy of a tenth-century description:

> In this valley there is a vast number of old Buddhist temples and priests' quarters; there are also some huge bells. At both ends of the valley north and south, stand temples to the Rulers of the Heavens, and a number of shrines to other gods; the walls are painted with pictures of the Tibetan kings and their retinues. The whole of the western face of the cliff for a distance of two *li* [two-thirds of a mile, or one km], north and south, has been hewn and chiselled out into a number of lofty and spacious sand caves containing images and paintings of Buddha. Reckoning cave by cave, the amount of money lavished on them must have been enormous. In front of them pavilions have been erected in several tiers, one above another. Some of the temples contain colossal images rising to a height of 160 feet [49 m], and the number of smaller shrines is past counting. All are connected with one another by galleries, convenient for the purpose of ceremonial rounds as well as casual sightseeing.[7]

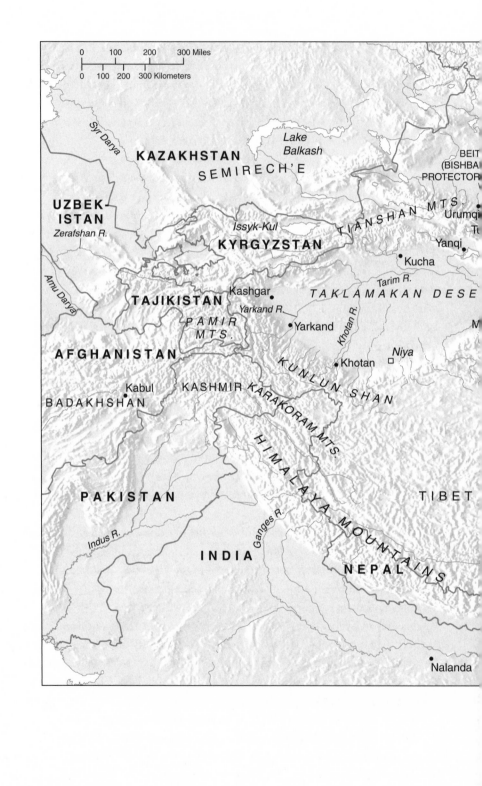

The Dunhuang Region

□ Ancient site

ÖTÜKÄN

Orkhon R.

MONGOLIA

Hami

GOBI DESERT

Yellow R.

Mt. Wutai

Liuyuan

ulan Xuanquan Guazhou(Anxi) Changle Village

Dunhuang Yumen

p Nor Suzhou (Jiuquan)

N SHAN MTS. Peddler's Ganzhou
route

Yellow R.

Liangzhou
(Wuwei)

houchang Thousand Lanzhou
Buddha
Caves Yellow R.
(Qianfodong) Luoyang
and Three Realms
(Sanjie) Monastery Chang'an
(Xi'an)

Yangzi R.

Yellow R.

Yangzi R.

CHINA

maputra R.

Yangzi R.

Pearl R.

Pearl
River
Valley

THE DUNHUANG CAVES AS STEIN FIRST SAW THEM
In 1907, when Aurel Stein first arrived at Dunhuang, the caves had no doors and were completely exposed to the elements. Visitors had to climb up the walls and through holes connecting the caves. Now under the management of the Dunhuang Research Institute, the caves all have walls and locked entrances, and a system of concrete walkways and stairways connects the 492 caves at the site. Courtesy of the Board of the British Library.

Although most of the pavilions in front of the caves had since collapsed, Stein noted, many images and paintings remained intact.[8]

According to an inscription in one of the caves, a monk had visited the site in 366 CE, the date that the first cave was dug. Of the 492 caves at the Thousand Buddha (Qianfodong) site, the Dunhuang Research Institute dates the site's earliest caves to the Northern Liang dynasty (422–39) and the latest to the thirteenth or fourteenth centuries.[9] The earlier caves, like those at Niya or Kucha, show individual buddhas or scenes from the historic Buddha's earlier lives; those built after 600 often depict narrative scenes from Buddhist texts. The caves were dug from extremely friable and soft gravel conglomerate, and several collapses occurred in the sixth and seventh centuries. The constant streams of visitors in recent years have damaged the caves further still, and the Dunhuang Institute has built facsimile caves in the hope of reducing the tourist traffic and the resulting damage to the paintings. They grant access to only a few, often charging high fees to enter the most famous of the caves (several hundred dollars per head is not unusual).

In 1907, after Stein and Jiang had finished their initial exploration of the site, they encountered a young Tibetan monk. When Jiang later met with him one on one, the monk showed him a single manuscript written in Chinese characters. While Jiang realized that the Chinese term for "bodhisattva" appeared multiple times, Stein's secretary could not make sense of the text because he had no experience reading Buddhist materials. Stein wanted to reward the monk for showing them the scroll, but Jiang "advised moderation. A present too generous might arouse speculations about possible ulterior motives." Stein and Jiang compromised on a price, and Stein gave a "piece of hacked silver, equal to about three rupees or four shillings." As Stein explained in his first publication about the discovery, *Ruins of Desert Cathay*, "In secret council Jiang and myself had discussed long before how best to get access to the find, and how to break down if necessary any priestly obstruction."

Understanding the sensitivity of the task, Stein and Jiang kept their discussions secret. Unlike the other sites that Stein had excavated, Dunhuang was a place of "actual worship," and Stein wondered what "difficulties" he would meet. "Would the resident priests be sufficiently good-natured—and mindful of material interests—to close their eyes to the removal of any sacred objects? And, if so, could we rely on their spiritual influence to allay the scruples which might arise among the still more superstitious laity patronizing their pilgrimage place?" Even before meeting Daoist Wang, Stein resolved to restrict his activities to photographing and sketching, since devotees were bound to object to the removal of any statues or paintings.

Since Daoist Wang was away, Stein decided to investigate a line of watchtowers extending west from Dunhuang, and he found the Sogdian Ancient Letters at this time. When he returned to the caves on May 15, 1907, he witnessed an annual religious festival attended by "fully ten thousand" people. While Stein kept his distance, Jiang persuaded Daoist Wang to meet with Stein. Apprehensive, Daoist Wang walled up the only opening to the library cave. When the two men finally met, Stein recorded his initial impressions of Daoist Wang: "He looked a very queer person, extremely shy and nervous, with an occasional expression of cunning which was far from encouraging. It was clear from the first that he would be a difficult person to handle."

In narrating his experience at Dunhuang, Stein continuously alludes to the difficulties he and Georg Bühler, his advisor at University of Vienna, had in obtaining Sanskrit manuscripts in India. At one point, in 1875, Bühler actually glimpsed the manuscript that he had come to India to study, but then the owner hid it away, and Bühler died without ever seeing it again. One of Stein's greatest scholarly triumphs while in India was purchasing that very manuscript fourteen years later.[10]

Stein understood that the Dunhuang library cave posed challenges far different from getting lost in the desert or excavating abandoned ruins as at Niya: he had to draw on his ability, acquired in India, to wrest manuscripts from their human guardians. After meeting Daoist Wang for the first time, Stein prepared himself "for a long and arduous siege."

On Jiang's advice, Stein made a conscious decision not to discuss scholarship or archeology with Daoist Wang. Instead he invoked the memory of the Buddhist pilgrim Xuanzang, his "Chinese patron saint." Stein recounted what he had told Daoist Wang in his halting Chinese: "my devotion to Xuanzang: how I had followed his footsteps from India across inhospitable mountains and deserts; how I had traced the ruined sites of many sanctuaries he had visited and described; and so on." Stein sustained the pretense that he was a devotee of Xuanzang's; before his departure on June 13, he even paid for a new "clay image" of Xuanzang. Telling Daoist Wang that the scrolls were intended for a "temple of learning" in India, Jiang and Stein misled Daoist Wang so that he would think that Stein, like Xuanzang centuries earlier, was collecting Buddhist manuscripts for a distant monastic library.

After their first meeting, Stein left Jiang to negotiate alone with Daoist Wang. That night, under the cover of darkness, the Daoist brought a single roll to the secretary. When this turned out to be a Buddhist text translated by Xuanzang, Jiang immediately reported this auspicious sign to the Daoist. Daoist Wang removed the temporary wall blocking access to the cave that he had put up.

Negotiations then proceeded more smoothly. The three men agreed on the need for absolute secrecy. In Stein's telling, Daoist Wang stipulated: "that nobody but us three was to learn what was being transacted, and that as long as I [Stein] was on Chinese soil the origin of these 'finds' was to be kept entirely secret." For the next three weeks Daoist Wang brought Jiang different scrolls, and he and Stein set aside the most important. Near the end of their stay, Daoist Wang panicked and returned everything to the cave, but again Jiang intervened. After Jiang and Stein had made their final selection, two of Stein's most trusted men sewed the scrolls in sacks so that no one could tell what they were.

Each step of the way, Stein reports the different conversations over price. After he and Jiang set a target, Jiang negotiated directly with Daoist Wang. Here Stein followed a practice common at the time: foreign residents all over Asia frequently entrusted their employees and servants to purchase groceries and other goods on their behalf. When Jiang and Wang reached a price of 130 British pounds for seven packing cases of manuscripts and five of paintings and other objects, Stein rejoiced in a letter to his close friend Percy Stafford Allen: "The single Sanskrit Ms. [manuscript] on palm leaf with a few other 'old things' are worth this."[11]

After Stein's departure in the summer of 1907, Daoist Wang continued to sell off the documents in the library cave to finance repairs to the cave complex. Jiang returned to Dunhuang in the fall of that year and bought another 230 bundles of material, which he sent on to Stein. Stein's haul totaled some eleven thousand documents. In 1908 Paul Pelliot, the gifted French Sinologist, bought seven thousand documents and shipped them to Paris.[12] In 1910 the Chinese government ordered that the remaining ten thousand documents in Chinese (not those in Tibetan) be transferred to Beijing, but Daoist Wang kept some, and others were stolen en route to Beijing.[13] In 1912 the Russian S. F. Ol'denburg purchased roughly ten thousand documents, and in 1914 Stein returned to Dunhuang one final time and bought six hundred more scrolls.[14]

Stein triumphantly recounted his experiences at Dunhuang to a live audience in a series of lectures he gave at Harvard in 1929. When Stein returned to the site in 1914, Daoist Wang greeted him warmly and showed him the detailed accounts of how he had spent the money to refurbish the caves. "In view of the official treatment his cherished store of Chinese rolls had suffered, he expressed bitter regret at not having previously had the courage and the wisdom to accept the big offer I had made through Jiang Siye [Jiang Xiaowan] for the whole collection en bloc."[15] Since he had paid Daoist Wang more money than anyone else (the Chinese government had paid nothing), Stein reasoned that he should have been able to buy the whole collection and ship it out of China. Even in 1929, when so many European and Chinese scholars concurred that Chinese antiquities should remain in China, Stein saw nothing wrong with taking documents and objects from China.

In thinking about the removal of the Dunhuang documents to other countries, we should resist the urge to judge Stein by modern standards rather than by those of his own time. Today many observers support the return of the Elgin Marbles to Greece. Consider, though, that Stein and the other explorers were operating at the height of imperialism before World War I. The European powers and Japan all sent teams to Xinjiang to excavate, and few contemporary observers voiced scruples. Among the few who did were Albert Grünwedel of Germany and the Russian scholar S. F. Ol'denburg, who both criticized Le Coq and others for removing wall paintings from their original sites.[16]

Foreign visitors had legitimate grounds for concluding that library cave materials were safer if taken away from Dunhuang. The caves at Dunhuang had suffered damage during the Muslim uprisings of 1862–77, and Stein was acutely aware of how restive the local population was.[17] Only one month after Stein left, in June 1907, the town exploded in a riot over grain prices.

Chinese views of Stein's conduct have softened over the years. During the Cultural Revolution, he was a thief, pure and simple. Even in the mid-1980s, when I was in graduate school, a Chinese classmate bristled with rage when our professor said that, if he were a Dunhuang document, he would prefer to have been taken to either Paris or London, because the conditions of preservation were so much better than those in Beijing. In 1998 the full Chinese translation of *Serindia*, including Stein's detailed account of the negotiations at Dunhuang, appeared with a thoughtful preface by a prominent Chinese archeologist, Meng Fanren. *Serindia*, with its team of authors who translated the different materials Stein found, represented "the very highest level of research in this field before the 1920s," yet Stein's individual actions, Meng concluded, constituted "plundering behavior which deserves severe and justified criticism."[18]

Advances in publishing have made the Dunhuang documents held in foreign countries increasingly available to Chinese scholars: first came the distribution of microfilm in the late 1970s, then the publication of multivolume sets with clearly legible photographs in the 1990s, and now the ongoing loading of photographs onto the website of the International Dunhuang Project based in London.[19] In 2005 Professor Rong Xinjiang of Peking University, one of China's leading historians of the Tang dynasty, published an article in China's leading academic history journal, *Lishi Yanjiu* (Historical research), in which he contrasted the actions of Stein, who did not tell Chinese scholars of his finds, with those of Pelliot, who gave Chinese colleagues photographs of the materials he had purchased and shipped to Paris. Professor Rong reminded his readers of one indisputable fact: for all their calls to protect the Dunhuang documents, no early twentieth-century Chinese scholar ever left the comfort of his own home. Not one followed Stein and Pelliot's example and personally visited the site of Dunhuang. The wholesale removal of the Dunhuang documents was the result.[20]

Still, even by the standards of his own day, Stein's actions still seem deceitful. He claimed to be a devotee of Xuanzang. He knowingly paid a fraction of the market price for the scrolls and paintings. He took extreme measures to maintain secrecy, doing everything at night, and telling a minimal number of people what he was doing. One cannot help wondering why Stein writes so openly about being so clandestine.

Although Stein does not specifically mention William Matthew Flinders Petrie in his discussion of Dunhuang, his other writings frequently acknowledge his influence.[21] Petrie, the leading British archeological excavator in Egypt, came to visit Stein in 1902 after Stein had returned from the First Expedition. In the preface to *Ancient Khotan*, Stein called Petrie an "archeological explorer of unequalled experience."[22] In 1904 Petrie published *Methods & Aims in Archaeology*, a step-by-step guide through all stages of an excavation: equipping an expedition, digging in the field, and the publication of results. Having excavated in Egypt, Petrie instructs archeologists how to work in poorer countries, explaining how to use small amounts of money to ensure that workmen submit their small portable finds to the excavator rather than sell them on their own: "Nothing can ensure better care than paying for it," he concludes. Petrie also advised his readers to publish their results in two volumes, a cheaper version with fewer plates for "students and the general public" and "a magnificent edition for libraries, book-collectors, and rich amateurs." Stein closely followed his advice; even the layout and typeface of his books replicated those of Petrie.[23]

In a prescient chapter entitled "Ethics of Archaeology," Petrie explains that once archeologists have finished digging at a site, nothing remains for future generations to find. The archeologist can place objects in museums, but these are bound to fold, ultimately leaving published books as the only record. "The only test of right is the procuring of the greatest amount of knowledge now and in future," he concludes. Petrie disparages the governments that frequently pass regulations that keep foreign archeologists from digging but allow the "ignorant peasant" to "dig and destroy" as he pleases. Stein's preface to *Ancient Khotan* quotes Petrie's injunction that investigators had to "work with the fullest care and detail in recording, to publish everything fully."[24] Stein's frankness about evading Chinese government regulations and negotiating with Daoist Wang perfectly embodies the pragmatic spirit of Petrie's manual: like his mentor, Stein sought to procure "the greatest amount of knowledge now and in future" and had no scruples about shipping documents and artifacts out of China.

In line with Petrie's instructions, Stein tried to reconstruct the original context of cave 17 as best as he could. The layer-by-layer arrangement of materials in the library cave indicated that it was not a randomly preserved collection of documents and paintings. Clearly an individual or a group had deliberately placed this particular collection of materials in the cave. But why? The presence of scraps of paper prompted Stein to assume that the cave was a repository for wastepaper.

Professor Rong has carefully cross-checked Stein's account against both Chinese sources and Paul Pelliot's account. Even though Stein did not have the opportunity to examine the library cave carefully, his writings remain the most detailed description of the cave, whose original arrangement was irretrievably destroyed when Daoist Wang opened the cave first for Stein and the following year for Pelliot. Challenging the wastepaper hypothesis, Professor Rong proposes a different explanation for the placement of the documents in the library cave.[25]

In many ways, the term "library cave" that Stein used is misleading. The library cave is not a separate cave; it is a small storeroom, measuring just under 10 feet (2.90 m) square and under 9 feet (2.66 m) high. It was originally hidden from view, but Daoist Wang discovered it when he tapped on the wall of cave 16 and realized that an empty space lay behind it. Daoist Wang broke through the wall and found a storeroom.

The library cave originated as a memorial to the powerful monk Hongbian, who was appointed controller-in-chief of Buddhist monks by the Tang emperor in 851. After he died in 862 his disciples placed items associated with him in the cave and came to visit the cave to pay their respects.[26] Then sometime early in

THE NORTHERN WALL OF THE LIBRARY CAVE
The walls of the hidden library cave were all blank except for the northern wall, which shows two acolytes and two trees framing the monk Hongbian's statue on the center platform. To the right stands a nun holding a round fan decorated with phoenixes; to the left, a lay woman in a man's robe clasps a walking stick. This painting dates to the period when the small cave was used as a funerary cave for the monk Hongbian.

the tenth century, the monks began to use the cave as a storeroom for manuscripts.[27] When he cleared out the storeroom sometime around 1900, Daoist Wang removed the statue. Subsequently, the Dunhuang Research Institute returned it to its original position, where it is today.

Many of the texts in the library cave have labels giving the names of the monasteries that owned them. During the tenth century Dunhuang was a Buddhist center with some fifteen monasteries, and the Three Realms (Sanjie) Monastery was one of the smaller ones there.[28] Because its name appears more frequently on the texts found in the library, the Three Realms Monastery likely used the cave to store its manuscripts.

An important clue to the purpose of the library cave comes in a preface to a Buddhist text written by a monk named Daozhen (active 934–87). He explained why he collected materials for the monastery library: "Having seen that among the contents of the storehouse of his temple the sets of scriptures and commentaries were incomplete, thereupon bowed his forehead to the ground and, with devout sincerity, took an oath and made prayers: I [Daozhen] will go carefully through the cartons and storehouses of all the families, seeking after old and decayed scriptural texts. I will gather them in the monastery, repair and patch them from beginning to end, and pass them down to other ages."[29] Sometime after 987, when Daozhen died, other monk-librarians continued to collect manuscripts for the Three Realms Monastery collection.

The Dunhuang monasteries all maintained lists of the texts they hoped to acquire, an indication that they were still collecting texts and paintings in the years before the closing of the cave. The earliest text in the cave, a Buddhist text, is dated 405, the latest to 1002.[30] The scrolls in the library cave included far more than simply Buddhist texts.[31]

Because paper was expensive at Dunhuang, students at monastery schools practiced writing characters in the unused margins or on the reverse side of Buddhist texts that had been discarded. The monastic schools trained students to read and write; some became monks, some did not.[32] These students began just as students of Chinese today do, by copying out individual characters over and over, gradually progressing to study more difficult texts. The Dunhuang manuscripts contain many errors, since the students were not all advanced; often teachers crossed out a student's mistaken character and inserted the correct one next to it. Students copied all kinds of materials in their quest for literacy: Buddhist texts, of course, but also contracts, model letters, literary exercises (such as a dialogue between Water and Tea), and long narratives called "transformation texts."[33]

The most famous text from the library cave is the Diamond Sutra, which was not copied by hand but printed with woodblocks. The Chinese first developed this method in the early eighth century when they realized that they could take a sheet of paper with characters on it, glue it face-down on a block of soft wood, cut out the wood around the characters to form a reverse image, and then print the positive image using that block. The Diamond Sutra from Dunhuang consists of seven woodblock-printed sheets that have been glued together (shown on page 236).

The dedication explains that a Buddhist devotee, on behalf of his parents, commissioned the text for the benefit of all. Such an action generated merit for his parents and for himself. The Diamond Sutra bears the date of the fifteenth day of the fourth month in 868. Cave 17 contained fragments of books printed on woodblocks before 868, including an almanac from 834, but the Diamond Sutra is the earliest complete printed book in the world.[34] Scholars recognize that Dunhuang, unlike Sichuan, was not a printing center; the vast majority of the texts in the cave were manuscripts copied by hand.

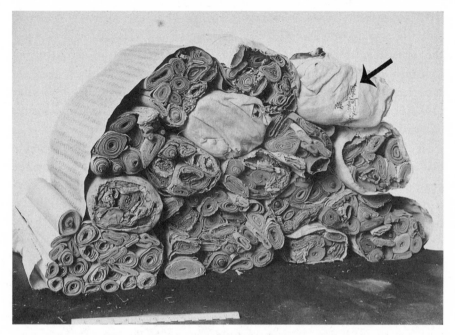

CALL NUMBERS FOR A BUDDHIST LIBRARY
The Chinese scrolls in cave 17 were divided into bundles of a dozen or so and then each covered with a separate wrapper. Unusually, one label on the upper right is still visible; it gives the name of the Buddhist text along with its number from the *Thousand-Character Classic*, which served as the equivalent of a modern library call number. Courtesy of the Board of the British Library.

The monk-librarians at Dunhuang used a sophisticated method to catalog Buddhist texts. They consulted catalogs of large Buddhist monastic libraries in the Tang capital of Chang'an that divided all Buddhist texts into categories such as sermons, regulations, or histories.[35] A primer called *The Thousand-Character Classic* consists of one thousand characters with no repetitions, making it a kind of Chinese alphabet. The Buddhist librarians assigned a single character to each Buddhist text and then grouped many of the Chinese-language scrolls into what Stein called "regular library bundles."

One thousand and fifty of these bundles contained twelve or so scrolls in Chinese; in addition, there were eighty packets and eleven large texts written on leaf-shaped pages called *pothi* in Tibetan, the language introduced in 786.[36] In that year, the Tibetans helped the Tang dynasty to suppress a rebellion, but, when the Tang failed to make the promised payment, the Tibetans conquered Dunhuang. The bundles all originally had outside wrappers, but because none of the people who first saw them—Daoist Wang, Jiang Xiaowan, Stein, or Pelliot—grasped their significance, only a few survive.

In addition to the regular bundles of Chinese- and Tibetan-language materials, the custodians of the library cave also included another type of bundle that Stein called either "miscellaneous" or "mixed" bundles.[37] These comprised Buddhist texts written on palm-leaf-shaped pothi slips or scrolls in Sanskrit, Khotanese, Tibetan, Uighur, and Sogdian. Some of these were complete copies of Buddhist texts; others were fragmentary. They also placed paintings (almost always of Buddhist deities), scraps of paintings, damaged ends of sutra rolls, and individual sheets of paper in the cave. In addition, they saved scraps of material that might be of use in future repairs to Buddhist manuscripts. While those in charge of larger monastic libraries might have discarded these scraps, the small size of the Three Realms Monastery collection made the custodians more cautious. Since any unknown materials might come in handy in the future, everything with writing on it was worth saving. For these reasons, cave 17 contains a huge variety of material. Unlike the recycled shoe soles from Turfan, this is not a random collection of documents; everything in cave 17 had some kind of connection to Buddhism, either because it was copied on the back of a Buddhist text or because students in monastic schools wrote it.

Sanskrit, Sogdian, Tibetan, Uighur, Khotanese: the various languages of the materials in the cave fully justify Stein's label, "The Polyglot Library."[38] In some cases, a single sheet of paper reveals the existence of a religious community, or perhaps a lone traveler, about which nothing else is known. One sheet of paper from cave 17 is an eighteen-line prayer written in Hebrew; each line starts with a letter in the Hebrew alphabet followed by a selection from Psalms, shown in color plate 12. Folded over several times, it served as a protective talisman, which was sewn into a small pouch and worn by the bearer, most likely around the neck.[39] Perhaps a Jewish traveler came to Dunhuang; equally likely, someone purchased the talisman (the shape of the letters suggests it was made in Babylon) and brought it to Dunhuang. Similarly, only two sheets of paper from the cave document the existence of a Sogdian-speaking Zoroastrian community. One sheet bears lines from the Avesta, the earliest Zoroastrian text; another shows two different Zoroastrian female deities facing each other.[40]

The Iranian religion of Zoroastrianism is one of the "three different teachings," a term Chinese scholars use to denote the two Iranian religions of Zoroastrianism and Manichaeism as well as the teachings of the Church of the East, based in Syria. All originated outside of China, entered the empire during the Tang dynasty, and did not survive the religious bans of 845. The librarians' eclecticism makes cave 17 the single most informative repository of primary sources about the different religions of the Silk Road.

The religious texts in the library cave indicate that people living at Dunhuang tolerated each other's beliefs to an extraordinary extent. The monks putting aside these texts did not necessarily know the languages in which they were written and probably could not read them. But their willingness to preserve texts written in other languages underlines the cosmopolitanism characteristic of the Silk Road. Even though they lived in a small community of some 30,000 people, they respected other people's languages, writings, and probably even their right to worship as they liked.[41]

The sources from the library cave, like those from Turfan and the Christian monument in Xi'an, are particularly important because they offer the view of the devotees, not that of high-ranking clergy or the Chinese authorities, whose views so often shape the historical record about religion. As instructive as they are, the Dunhuang texts do not describe the congregations of these different religions, with the result that we know little of their size. If all the surviving texts from a given religion are in a foreign language, we can surmise that the church did not attract many Chinese converts; on the other hand, Chinese-language translations point to the presence of local converts.

The survival at Turfan of Manichaean texts in multiple Iranian languages—Parthian, Middle Persian, and Sogdian—and old Turkic, and at Dunhuang in Chinese, have made it possible for scholars to study the teachings of a world religion otherwise known largely through the writings of Saint Augustine, who wrote in his *Confessions* about being a Manichaean before converting to Christianity.[42] The library cave holds a total of three Manichaean texts written in Chinese characters.

Even though some of the texts are written in Chinese characters, they suggest that most Manichaean believers spoke an Iranian language. The longest of the three, a hymn scroll, uses Chinese characters to phonetically record twenty different Sogdian-language hymns and prayers. Because the text does not translate these hymns, they remain incomprehensible to a native speaker of Chinese. Someone who knew how to speak Sogdian but couldn't read it—the child of Sogdian migrants to Dunhuang, say—could use these pronunciation guides to sing along with the congregation.[43] One hymn in the hymn scroll, "Praise of the World of Light," appears to be a direct translation of a Parthian text found at Turfan. But the Chinese version equates the World of Light with the Amitabha Buddha's Western Paradise. The Light World is a "world of perfect bliss," where "everything is light, and no place is dark; where all buddhas and envoys of Light live" and "everything is clean and pure, eternally happy, calm and quiet, undisturbed and unhindered; one receives happiness and has no worry or affliction."[44] Mani urged his followers to use the terminology of existing religions in seeking converts. This text beautifully illustrates this chameleon strategy by naming Mani as one of the three most important teachers in China along with Buddha and Laozi; in this telling Mani has assumed Confucius's position.

Another Manichaean text even more closely mimics a Chinese text. The prologue of the small scroll sounds exactly like the prologue to the famed Buddhist text of the Diamond Sutra. Yet in this version, Mani—not the Buddha—addresses a disciple: "Good indeed! Good indeed! In order to benefit the innumerable crowds of living beings, you have addressed to me this query, profound and mysterious. You thus show yourself as a good friend to all those living beings of the world who have blindly gone astray, and I will now explain the matter to you in detail, so that the net of doubt in which you are ensnared may be broken forever without recall."[45] Even the title misleads: the text is called *The Compendium of the Teachings of Mani the Buddha of Light.* The text so closely resembled a Buddhist text that it fooled even an expert like Pelliot, who chose not to take it to Paris, and today it is one of the most important texts in the Beijing Library Collection. Sogdian missionaries prepared this translation in response to an imperial order issued in 731; they hoped to convert the Chinese emperor himself.

The missionaries of each church took different approaches to translation. Whereas the Manichaeans freely adopted Buddhist terms, the Christians from the Church of the East insisted on strict accuracy in translation, no matter how confusing the result might be.[46] What was the best way to render "God the Father, the Son, and the Holy Ghost," into Chinese? The translator of the hymn "Gloria in Excelsis Deo" chose the most literal solution: "Merciful father, Light son, King of the pure wind." Of the three terms, only "merciful father" would have made sense to a Chinese convert. On the same sheet of paper is a list of holy books entitled "The Book of Honor." It states that the three bodies of the "father emperor," the "son emperor," and the "witness" all form a single body—i.e., the Holy Trinity—another teaching that would certainly have puzzled a Chinese audience.[47] A note at the end of this list refers to Jingjing (or Adam), the author of the Christian stele of Ch'ang-an, indicating that it, like the stele, was composed sometime in the late eighth century, a period when the Church of the East was active in China.

The nature of the materials in the cave changed quite noticeably in the mid-eighth century. Before the An Lushan rebellion, almost all of the texts in the cave came from central China and consisted of Buddhist texts. The latest text in the cave from Chang'an is dated 753; after that date, all the texts were locally produced.[48] At this time, lay students began to copy a much larger variety of material, including—in addition to Buddhist texts—contracts, charters for lay associations, and literary texts. They even doodled in the margins of texts.[49] One hand copy of a market certificate, written sometime between 742 and 758, records the purchase of a thirteen-year-old non-Chinese slave boy for twenty-one bolts of raw silk. Adhering exactly to the detailed regulations of the Tang Code, it lists the names and ages of the seller, slave, and five guarantors, confirming that the Tang enforced the code throughout its realm.[50]

In 745 the Tang central government sent a payment of fifteen thousand bolts of silk in two installments to a garrison near Dunhuang.[51] A bureaucratic document about someone's salary allows us to see exactly how the Tang state made such payments. The central government deposited two shipments of silk in a commandery in Liangzhou (modern Wuwei, Gansu), about 435 miles (700 km) east of Dunhuang, the location of the regional military headquarters. From there, the silk was shipped to the Dunhuang garrison. As the French scholar Éric Trombert astutely remarks, "One has here a concrete example of two military convoys, each carrying more than 7,000 bolts of silk, that has nothing in common with the images of caravans of private merchants to which we are accustomed."[52] These individual payments of seven thousand bolts of silk are much higher than all the individual transactions recorded in the Turfan documents, which involved at most a few hundred bolts of silk. This document shows just how important the central government's payments to the military were.

The Tang government had a complex monetary system in which three different currencies—textiles (both hemp and silk), grain, and coins—circulated alongside one another. Confusingly, the central government used a single aggregated unit to represent all three goods. The payment to the Dunhuang garrison included six different types of woven silk and silk floss. Because different localities paid their taxes using locally produced cloth, the Tang authorities simply transferred those textiles to the Dunhuang garrison. Garrison officials converted the tax cloth first into coins and then into grain, some used to feed the soldiers in the garrison, some paid directly to local merchants. This record affords a rare glimpse of payments sent to the military before the An Lushan rebellion: the Tang government injected massive amounts of money—in the form of woven cloth—straight into the Dunhuang economy.

As earlier chapters have recounted, in 755 the central government lost control of the northwest. In an attempt to defeat the rebels, the Tang emperor turned to the rulers of the Tibetan Empire for help. The Yarlung dynasty of Tibet was a relative newcomer to Central Asian politics. Before 617, the Tibetan plateau, some 13,000 to 15,000 feet (4,000–5,000 m) above sea level, was home in the north to herders who raised horses in the grasslands and, in the south, to farmers who planted barley in the river valleys.[53] With no indigenous writing system, they knotted cords and marked tallies as their means of record keeping. Around 617 the rulers of the Yarlung dynasty, who took their name from the river valley to the southeast of Lhasa, unified Tibet for the first time. They modified the Sanskrit alphabet to form their own writing system, and, at the same time, adopted elements of the Tang legal system.

In 755, after An Lushan rebelled, the Tang emperor wrote to the Tibetans, promising large payments in exchange for their help in suppressing the rebels. The Tibetans were fine horsemen, and the Chinese admired their military equipment. As the official history of the Tang explains, "Their armor is excellent. They clothe their entire body in it, except for their two eyes. Even powerful bows and sharp knives cannot harm them very much."[54] Although ostensibly in the service of the Tang, Tibetan soldiers raided the capital of Chang'an for two weeks in the fall of 763 before retreating. Each autumn until 777 the horsemen returned to plunder Chang'an, and the weakened Tang armies could not keep them out.

During the 760s and 770s, when they were at peak strength, the Tibetans gradually increased the territory under their control and expanded into Gansu. In 781 they conquered the town of Shouchang, south of Dunhuang, and in 786, when the Tang government failed to pay the stipulated amount for their assistance in putting down a rebellion, they seized the prefectural center of Dunhuang. Governing eight former Tang-dynasty prefectures in the Gansu corridor, the Tibetans appointed a council of generals to rule the military districts. The Tibetans immediately established a dual administration headed by a Tibetan military governor and the highest civil official, in Dunhuang, who was often Chinese. Each district was further subdivided into units of one thousand, and these into twenty units of fifty households. The head of the smaller fifty-household units assigned each household tasks so that they could fulfill their labor obligation to the state.[55]

Some male residents in the Tibetan-occupied territory were conscripted into the army, while others labored in military colonies. In addition to serving as guards, those in the colonies cultivated crops and paid agricultural taxes in grain, which they had to carry to collection points, sometimes several days' travel away. The Tibetans staffed their army using corvée labor; they did not pay their soldiers with bolts of cloth, grain, and coins as the Tang dynasty had.

The imposition of Tibetan rule in Dunhuang had an immediate effect on the local economy, as contracts written in both Tibetan and Chinese show.[56] In 788–790, a few years after the Tibetans took Dunhuang, the financial records of a storehouse mentioned coins; this is the latest known Chinese-language reference to coins.[57] It is possible that some Chinese coins, perhaps those minted before 755, circulated in the ninth and tenth centuries, but under Tibetan rule coins largely dropped from use. During the Tibetan period, prices are given in either measures of grain or bolts of cloth.[58] A representative contract, dated 803, documents the sale of a cow for a price of twelve piculs of wheat (20–30 bushels, or 720–1080 L) and two of millet (3.5–5 bushels, or 120–180 L). The penalty for breach of contract is also denominated in grain: three piculs of wheat (5–8 bushels, or 180–270 L).[59] With only a few mentions of *dmar* (the Tibetan word for "copper," which probably indicates bronze coins), the contracts record exchanges almost entirely in grain.[60] Sometimes people borrow cloth or paper, but they always pay back their debts using grain.

Earlier analysts saw the Tibetan occupation from 786 to 848 as a brief interlude in Dunhuang's history, with few lasting repercussions. Sixty years, however, was sufficiently long that the residents of Dunhuang adopted some Tibetan customs. In the early years of Tibetan rule, most Chinese followed Chinese practice and used a family name followed by a given name. But over time the Chinese residents of Dunhuang adopted more and more Tibetan-sounding names. By the second or third generation of Tibetan rule, some even gave up their use of Chinese family names and used only a first name, just as the Tibetans did.

Some Chinese living under Tibetan rule made an even bigger change: they stopped writing in Chinese and adopted the Tibetan alphabet. Immediately following the Tibetan conquest, local scribes learned the language in order to draft government documents for officials or contracts for Tibetan speakers. Between 815 and 841 the Tibetan military governor launched a large-scale initiative to copy Buddhist texts. The project employed over one thousand scribes, many of them Chinese.[61] As they copied texts, these scribes grew more proficient in writing Tibetan. They realized that it was easier to use a phonetic alphabet than to memorize thousands of Chinese characters.

As the rulers sponsored the mass copying of Buddhist sutras in the hope of generating merit, so too did they finance the construction of new caves. The sixty-six caves built in the Tibetan period have several distinguishing characteristics: they often feature mandalas, or diagrams of the cosmos, among other elements from esoteric Buddhism. Cave paintings from this period also grant greater prominence to the donors, especially the Tibetan emperor.[62]

During the Tibetan period, Dunhuang artists painted Mount Wutai, and they continued to do so in the tenth century, when Dunhuang came under Cao-family rule. One of the most magnificent caves at Dunhuang, cave 61, dates to just around 950.[63] The upper section of the entire western wall of the cave, a section measuring 11.5 feet (3.5 m) tall by 51 feet (15.5 m) wide, shows the Mount Wutai pilgrimage site in Shanxi Province. The top of the painting shows a heavenly assembly, while the middle shows ninety different buildings at Mount Wutai, each bearing a label, and the bottom shows travelers on their way to the mountain. The painting is not an accurate map of the pilgrimage site; it probably was intended as a guide for viewers unable to visit the site themselves. The cave's patrons included Cao Yuanzhong, the ruler of Dunhuang from 944 to 974, and his wives, one of whom was from Khotan.

Despite occasional outbreaks of armed conflict, the rulers of Dunhuang maintained contact with both the Tang and India during the Tibetan period.

Monks and envoys, dispatched by the rulers of Tibet, China, and India, traveled between Tibet and China, and they often stopped at Dunhuang during their travels. The lack of circulating currency did not prevent envoys and monks from proceeding from one oasis to the next; much as they had in earlier periods, rulers provided emissaries with escorts, transport, and food.

In 848 a Chinese regime reestablished control at Dunhuang, but the use of Tibetan persisted. Earlier generations of scholars assumed that the Tibetan-language materials in cave 17 must have been written before 848; more recently scholars have come to realize that Tibetan remained in use as a lingua franca even after 848.[64] Under Tibetan rule, the pilgrimage route from Tibet to Mount Wutai, which passed through Dunhuang, saw an increase in traffic. Also from the library cave are copies of five letters of introduction, in Tibetan, for a Chinese monk traveling to Tibet; they, too, date to the period after 848, when Chinese armies expelled the Tibetans from Dunhuang.[65] The letters explain that the monk is going to India to study at the great Buddhist center at Nalanda and to obtain relics. Beginning his journey at Mount Wutai, the monk visited several towns on the way to Dunhuang, where he left the letters behind, presumably because he did not need them in Tibet.

Another Tibetan-language manuscript was dictated by an Indian monk to a Tibetan disciple who could understand some Sanskrit but made many spelling mistakes. The document explains that in 977 (or possibly 965), the Indian monk Devaputra traveled from India to Tibet and then to Mount Wutai; on his way back, near Dunhuang, he bestowed his teaching on a disciple. The text gives many technical terms in Tibetan, followed by the approximate Sanskrit spelling.[66] Tibetan monks encouraged the study of Sanskrit, possibly because their own alphabet was modeled on Sanskrit, making it more accessible.[67] At least some monks must have spoken Sanskrit to communicate, most likely with other learned monks, in monasteries just as Xuanzang did on his way to India.

In 842, when the confederation of peoples who had supported the rulers suddenly broke apart, the Yarlung dynasty collapsed, and Tibetan control over Dunhuang weakened. In 848 the Chinese general Zhang Yichao organized an army that expelled the remaining Tibetans.[68] The Tang dynasty was much weaker than it had been before the An Lushan rebellion. Even within central China (the area often called "China proper," which includes the Yangzi, Yellow, and Pearl River valleys), the Tang had ceded political control to military commanders who collected taxes and financed their own armies, sometimes sending some revenues to the center. Like these commanders, Zhang Yichao received the title of military governor from the Tang court in 851. Zhang pledged allegiance to the Tang dynasty but in fact governed Dunhuang as an independent kingdom. Under Zhang family rule, Dunhuang sent envoys to the Tang capital at Chang'an to present tribute to the Tang emperor, much as other independent Central Asian rulers did.

Zhang did not gain complete control in 848; his armies fought those of the Tibetans again in 856, as a literary text entitled "Zhang Yichao Transformation Text" relates. Of all the literary genres represented in cave 17, transformation texts, which alternate passages of prose with poetry, are the most distinctive. Transformation texts combine stretches of sung poetry and recited prose (this literary genre existed in Kuchean, too). The library cave preserved thirty or so examples of Chinese-language transformation texts; they survive nowhere else.[69] Most broadly, the term "transformation" refers to the different transformations of creation; monk storytellers performed these tales to help their audience members escape from the cycle of life, death, and rebirth from which all Buddhist teachings offered escape. Transformation texts contain a tell-tale formula: "Please look at the place where [a specific event] happens; how does it go?"[70] As they narrated these tales, storytellers pointed to scenes in scroll paintings so that the audience could picture the events they described.

The Zhang Yichao transformation text, which describes several battles in 856 between Zhang's army and the tribes fighting on the Tibetan side, sets the scene using words:

> The bandits [the Tibetan coalition] had not expected that the Chinese troops would arrive so suddenly and were totally unprepared. Our armies proceeded to line up in a "black-cloud formation," swiftly striking from all four sides. The barbarian bandits were panic-stricken. Like stars they splintered, north and south. The Chinese armies having gained the advantage, they pursued them, pressing close at their backs. Within fifteen miles, they caught up with them.

Then, just as the narrator points to a scene showing the army, he says, "This is the place where their slain corpses were strewn everywhere across the plain."[71] None of these scroll paintings survive, but a cave painting done in 861 does show Zhang's army on parade.[72]

This cave was completed in 865. Four years earlier, General Zhang Huaishen, the nephew of the Chinese ruler Zhang Yichao, began work on the cave, the first to be financed by a member of the ruling Zhang family. The inscription explains that Zhang Huaishen

> had a strong desire to carve a cave. He looked around the whole area, but there was no place at all, except for a single cliff, where cutting was

ZHANG YICHAO'S ARMY

Zhang Yichao's troops carry fluttering banners. Some figures wear plain robes favored by the Chinese, while others are dressed in brightly patterned fabrics often worn by Uighurs and other non-Chinese peoples. The painting offers a glimpse of the diverse peoples who supported Zhang-family rule. Drawing by Amelia Sargent.

possible. Undaunted by the enormity of the work to be accomplished, his spirit was concentrated to the point where it could pierce stone, his purpose strong enough to move the mountain.

Then he prayed to the heavenly spirits above, gave thanks to the earth spirits below, divined to find an auspicious time, and calculated the day for the work to start. The cutting and chiseling had hardly begun, when the mountain split of its own accord; not many days had elapsed, when the cracks opened to a hole. With further prayers and incense, the sands began to fly, and early in the night, suddenly and furiously, with a fearful rush, there was the sound of thunder, splitting the rock wall, and the cliff was cut away.[73]

The author offers a step-by-step account of how to make a cave: workmen started by digging a crack, which they gradually expanded until it could hold wall paintings and statues. The process of digging a cave was labor-intensive but did not require the use of expensive materials. Local artists lived on site, in the northern cave complex, where archeologists have found numerous artists' workshops, some complete with pots of paint.[74] In the ninth century most artists belonged to

TABLE 6.1 THE RULERS OF INDEPENDENT DUNHUANG, 851–1002

Ruler	Reign
Zhang Yichao	851–867
Zhang Huaishen	867–890
Zhang Huaiding	890–892
Suo Xun	892–894
Zhang Chengfeng	894–910
Cao Yijin	914–935
Cao Yuande	935–939
Cao Yuanshen	939–944
Cao Yuanzhong	944–974
Can Yangong	974–976
Cao Yanlu	976–1002

local workshops, and by the mid-tenth century the local government had established a painting academy staffed by artist-officials.[75]

Like the Tibetan rulers before him, Zhang Huaishen and his successors sponsored the construction of many new caves. Building a cave was an intensely religious act: when one ruler decided to dig a cave, he and his wife ate vegetarian food for an entire month and then lit lamps, burned incense, and paid monks to pray and copy sutras, all in the hope of generating Buddhist merit. Only then did they begin construction of the cave.[76]

Some of the caves at Dunhuang contain portraits of Zhang Yichao and the rulers who succeeded him: around 925 Cao Yijin, who had taken over from the Zhang family in 914, commissioned a series of portraits of his predecessors in cave 98. On viewing these portraits, any visitor might imagine, as the Cao-family donors surely desired, that the order of succession had been smooth. In fact it was anything but. Zhang Yichao's nephew Zhang Huaishen succeeded him on his death in 867 and ruled until 890, when his cousin, a son of Zhang Yichao, killed him, his wife, and six children. The new ruler, Zhang Huaiding, ruled for a year before dying a natural death; the next ruler came to the throne as a minor and was overthrown by his guardian Suo Xun. In 894 the former ruler regained power and stayed on the throne until 910. The last years of Zhang-family rule coincided with the closing years of the Tang dynasty, a time of great political uncertainty, when the emperors were first held prisoner and then overthrown in 907.[77]

In 915 Cao Yijin, the son-in-law of the last Zhang-family ruler, took the throne, and his family ruled until 1002. After that year records do not refer to any Cao by name, suggesting that the Uighur Kaghanate based in Ganzhou (now Zhangye, Gansu Province), had gained control of Dunhuang. In the eighth century the Uighurs had originally been united, but broke apart in 840 following the Kirghiz destruction of the unified Uighur Kaghanate, which prompted Uighurs to flee to both Turfan (the Western Uighur Kaghanate included Beiting, Gaochang, Yanqi, and Kucha) and Ganzhou, the site of a second, smaller kaghanate.[78] In 1028 the Uighur Kaghanate at Ganzhou fell to the Tanguts, and in the 1030s Dunhuang followed, both becoming part of the Xi Xia realm, which included part of northwest China. We know little about the power struggles after 1000, simply because no materials from cave 17 or any other excavated documents describe these events in detail.

Between 848 and 1002, just as during the preceding period of Tibetan rule, the travelers who appear most often in the documentary record are envoys and monks. The Zhang and Cao families maintained diplomatic relations with all of their neighbors; they sent and received gift-bearing missions from the Tang capital at Chang'an and from other closer rulers as well, most notably the rulers of Khotan and the Uighur Kaghanates.[79] Although many documents record the coming and going of emissaries, few detail what gifts they presented and what they received in return. For that reason one inventory of gifts given and received by a delegation that traveled to Chang'an in 877 is particularly important.

In 877 Zhang Huaishen, Zhang Yichao's nephew, had been ruling Dunhuang for ten years, but the Tang emperor had not yet recognized him as a legitimate successor. He sent the delegation with a request for a formal banner that would acknowledge him as the military governor of Dunhuang, the title that his uncle had held before him. The 877 delegation presented one ball of jade (weight not specified), one yak tail, one antelope horn (presumably for medicinal use), and one letter to the Tang emperor.[80]

Hosting the delegation for nearly four months (they arrived on the twenty-seventh day of the twelfth month and left on the eleventh day of the fourth month), the Chinese divided the group into three levels (the top three officials, thirteen lower-level officials, and thirteen carriers), and gave different gifts to each group. For example, the three men in the highest rank received fifteen bolts of cloth (the documents do not specify what kind), one silver bowl, and one suit of brocade. Those in the second and third ranks received correspondingly less: the thirteen men in the second tier were given ten bolts of cloth (not fifteen), a silver cup (not a bowl), and a suit, while the thirteen men in the bottom tier received eight bolts of cloth, a suit, and no silver. Combining these with the gifts from other branches of the government, the group collectively was given a total of 561 bolts of cloth, five silver bowls, fourteen silver cups, and fifty suits. In addition, each member of the group received forty-three bolts of cloth to cover travel expenses—literally, "the cost of camels and horses," a total of 1,247 bolts, more than twice the amount of cloth that the delegation received. Once they had gathered all the gifts together, they drew up an inventory, placed everything in leather bags with wooden tags, and then stamped the tags, sealing them shut. The gifts were opened only on arrival in Dunhuang. In 878 the delegation returned without the banner; only in 888 did the Tang court grant the desired honor.[81]

Although the Tang emperor did not grant the desired banner, he bore all the expense of hosting the delegation and the cost of the many gifts it bestowed on the members of the delegation. For the entire history of the Silk Road—going back to Sogdian delegations recorded at Xuanquan—members of tribute delegations had, in addition to the presentation of the formal gifts that was their duty, engaged in private trade on the side. We do not know how much the individual members of the trade delegation benefited from any dealings they were able to conduct—they did not record such transactions—but the amount of silk clothing given to each constituted a major gift.

Many envoys traveled to Dunhuang in the period of Cao-family rule, we learn from accounts detailing the beer and provisions provided to them.[82] One register, probably from 964, records the beer consumption of fifty different visiting diplomats in just under seven lunar months: one from the Song dynasty, fourteen from Tibet, eleven from Khotan, one from the Turfan Uighur Kaghanate, seven from the Yizhou Uighur Kaghanate, and seventeen from the Ganzhou Uighur Kaghanate.[83] Most of the visitors stayed a few days, but one group stayed 203 days, which must have been a burden for their hosts, who provided flour for the morning and evening meals and a round, flat wheat cake at lunch.

As these registers show, Dunhuang officials hosted people of all social ranks during this period: the crown prince of Khotan, envoys, monks, workmen, scribes, artists, and even a single "walking non-Chinese," a term that most likely denoted an itinerant trader of some type. A similar register mentions a "Persian monk" and a "Brahman," both again apparently traveling on their own.[84] Because of the detailed registers, we know about these particular individuals, but not the many other travelers to and from Dunhuang who have left no traces in the historical record.

Other groups, including refugees and robbers, were traveling, too. Thieves are perhaps the least documented group of all. The pilgrim Xuanzang was once robbed of everything, including his clothing. Travelers frequently allude to the risk of crime and often traveled in groups to avoid being robbed.

Members of these official delegations were so sure that they would profit from participating in a tribute mission that they took loans out to rent camels for their journeys. Cave 17 preserved five such loan contracts.[85] The contracts anticipate various reasons why the borrower might not return the camel: the animal might fall sick or die en route, might get lost or be stolen, or might be stolen by the envoy himself.[86] All follow the same format: they explain that the person taking the camel was participating in a tribute mission, give the rental price of the camel—always in bolts of cloth—to be paid on the borrower's return, and then specify a penalty should the borrower not return. Gone are the standard bolts of silk used by the Tang dynasty; these contracts specify the length and width of each bolt of silk that is borrowed, further confirmation that the Dunhuang

A ROBBERY ON THE SILK ROAD
Here a brigand holding an enormous blade menaces a group of merchants, who cower before him with their unloaded goods laid out on the ground as their donkeys look on. A rare depiction of robbers on the Silk Road, this depicts a miracle performed by the Buddhist deity Guanyin, who drove away the thieves in response to prayers by her devotees. Drawing by Amelia Sargent.

economy of the ninth and tenth centuries operated differently from when the Tang was at the peak of its power before 755. It is not simply that no coins circulated; even the standard-sized bolt of silk fell from use as the Silk Road economy reverted to a subsistence economy.

While some people, like envoys and monks, traveled to towns beyond Dunhuang, many more remained enmeshed in the local economy. Many of Dunhuang's residents joined mutual aid societies. The charters they signed shed much light on their concerns. Small groups of local people, usually between fifteen and twenty individuals, joined these societies so that they could pool their resources. Some of the groups were largely social, meeting once a month, and had charters that required each member to bring a small contribution—a measure of grain or of beer—to the meeting. Other groups helped each other survive unexpected expenses. If one member of the group had to pay for the wedding or the funeral of a relative, he or she had use of that month's revenues. People with roughly equal incomes formed groups because they could afford similar contributions.[87] The wealthiest people in Dunhuang joined lay associations that sponsored the construction of new caves.[88]

The monasteries were the richest institutions in local society. They had sufficient surplus grain that they could make loans to the poor, and many of these contracts survive. Local people borrowed grain so that they could get enough seed to plant in the spring. Their very survival depended on these loans. The poor lived on the edge: parents were often forced to sell their children or put them up for adoption.[89]

The monasteries kept track of these loans and also maintained detailed inventories of all their property.[90] These inventories document the holdings of the richest local institutions. Since the wealthy frequently made contributions to the monasteries to gain merit, the Buddhist monasteries—like their counterparts in Europe—had large collections of valuable goods. Yet because archeologists have not yet uncovered any monastic treasuries, we must rely on written inventories documenting monastic holdings. Many items are preceded by the word *fan*, meaning "foreign," and some scholars have concluded that these items must indeed be of foreign manufacture. But this is not necessarily the case. French fries are not made in France; they are simply French in inspiration.[91] Similarly, in the case of the items listed on the monastic inventories, without a given item in hand it is impossible to know if it was truly foreign made or just foreign in style.

The goods listed in the monastic inventories fall into four categories: textiles, metalware, incense and fragrance, and precious stones. Where some of the textiles are clearly of local manufacture (Khotanese felt, for example), others, such as "Iranian brocade" or "Merv silk," appear to be imported. It is possible, though, that these textiles were not made outside of China but simply copied foreign silks. The same is true of the thirty-seven listed metal goods. A "silver censer with silver lions" is plausibly from the Iranian world, but an "Iranian-style lock" was too heavy and too utilitarian to transport overland over long distances. These locks were probably made by local metalsmiths. "Hufen," often translated as "Iranian powder" occurs frequently on the list of fragrances; this is the name for ceruse, a white-colored, lead-based makeup powder, which also appears in the Sogdian Ancient Letters. The adjective "hu" often means "Iranian" or "Iranian-style" in Dunhuang documents, but in this instance it means "paste," because one had to mix ceruse with water before applying it to one's skin.[92]

Only one category in the monastic inventories is definitely of foreign origin: precious stones, including lapis lazuli (from Badakhshan in the northeast corner of Afghanistan), agate (from India), amber (from northeastern Europe), coral (from the ocean, most likely via Tibet), and pearls (usually from Sri Lanka). The foreign merchants in Tang tales almost always deal in precious stones, and precious stones were the one commodity that was sufficiently light that an individual merchant could carry a small bag on his person over long distances.

Other materials from Dunhuang confirm our impression of an economy in which largely locally made goods circulated. These goods included silks of all different varieties, cotton, fur, tea, ceramics, medicine, fragrances, Khotanese jade, and draft animals.

Who brought these goods to Dunhuang? Many of the emissaries going back and forth conducted trade on the side, and they are the most likely agents of transmission. Dunhuang served as a center for envoys from surrounding towns, and delegations often presented goods, such as cotton textiles woven in Turfan or jade from Khotan, that they had purchased in the course of their travels.[93] Envoys were one group whose movements are well-documented in the materials from cave 17, which rarely mention merchants. Interestingly, those that do are in non-Chinese languages, specifically Sogdian, Uighur Turkish, or "Turco-Sogdian," a mixed language combining elements of both. These shed considerable light on the comings and goings of caravaneers.

Around the year 1000 Sogdian began to gradually die out. Sogdian ceased to be used as a written language, and many (but not all) former Sogdian-speakers turned instead to Turkish. A small group of documents from cave 17 offer a glimpse of this linguistic shift just as it was occurring. They are in Turco-Sogdian, which is basically Sogdian but with a strong Uighur influence, in the form of Turkic loanwords and, more importantly, Turkic constructions unknown in earlier Sogdian.[94] This small group includes an account written by a low-level merchant who reports to his employer which different commodities he obtained from producers. The author, possibly a member of the Church of the East, moves from village to village, picking up pieces of woven cloth from different weaving households, most likely individual families, who produce the cloth. He records just how far he travels on this trip: 60 miles (100 km) to the village of Changle, which is 60 miles (100 km) northeast of Dunhuang and 30 miles (50 km) west of Guazhou, also in Gansu Province. This account accords with the dearth of coins reported in Chinese and Tibetan documents from cave 17.

One letter begins by giving the total amount of cloth the agent is carrying: one hundred pieces of "white" and nineteen pieces of "red" *raghzi* cloth, which is used to make warm winter clothing.[95] (*Raghzi* is a Sogdian word, meaning either wool or some other type of cloth made from fur.) The pieces dyed red are worth more than undyed pieces; the agent usually trades three pieces of undyed cloth for two of dyed, and four dyed pieces of cloth are worth a single sheep. On his next transaction, he picks up four dyed pieces and twenty-one undyed. He records each transaction carefully, and they are all similarly small. This is a classic peddler's itinerary: covering a limited terrain, dealing in locally produced goods, and consisting largely of trading one item for another.

The author of this letter, which dates to the late ninth century, was equally comfortable writing in both Sogdian and Uighur. Writing in the mid-eleventh century, the lexicographer Mahmud of Kashgar described the Sogdian residents of Semirech'e, in what is now Kazakhstan, as speaking both Sogdian and Uighur, but within two hundred years the Sogdian language had died out.[96]

Another group of documents, in Uighur, complements this picture of the peddler trade in the Turco-Sogdian documents. Uighur was the language of the Uighur kaghanates. Few documents in cave 17 are in Uighur—some forty or so.[97] These include religious texts, lists of merchandise, letters, and legal decisions, which mention various locally made goods: cloth (including silk, wool, and cotton), slaves, sheep, dye, camels, lacquer cups, combs, casseroles, steel small knives, pickaxes, handkerchiefs, embroidery, whey, and dried fruits. A few goods, such as silver bowls or silver quivers, may have been of foreign manufacture, yet only musk and pearls are definitely foreign (one letter mentions 117 pearls, the most valuable single item).[98] The authors of these materials describe a world bounded to the east by Suzhou, modern Jiuquan in Gansu Province; to the north by Hami, Xinjiang, and Ötükän on the upper reaches of the Orkhon River; to the west by Miran, near the Tibetan border; and to the southwest by Khotan. The Uighur materials portray a commercial world exactly like that of the Turco-Sogdian materials: local peddlers traveling within a circumscribed area and trading one locally manufactured good for another.

Other scholars have seen these Turco-Sogdian and Uighur documents as evidence of a thriving Silk Road trade.[99] The mere mention of trade confirms their expectations. Although the documents refer only to small-scale transactions involving largely local goods, those predisposed to see a large-scale Silk Road trade see this as sufficient evidence. But all the documents this book has examined—with the exception of the government documents listing massive payments to troops stationed in the northwest—point to a small-scale, local trade, rather than a thriving long-distance trade.

When Aurel Stein first arrived in Dunhuang on March 23, 1907, he encountered a merchant named Sher Ali Khan from Kabul, Afghanistan. His caravan of forty camels traveled from Afghanistan to Khotan and then on to central Gansu; on his way home, he took the Southern Silk Road route as well. His business model was simple. He sold British textiles purchased in Kashmir and Yarkand to the Chinese and bought Chinese silk and tea to sell on his return to Kabul. Sher Ali Khan offered to carry Stein's mail to Kashgar, and Stein, always glad of a chance to correspond with his friends, immediately began drafting letters and finished writing only at 3 in the morning. Stein then set off to explore the watchtowers of Dunhuang, where he found the Sogdian Ancient Letters. To Stein's dismay, one evening, as he returned to his camp, he glimpsed Sher Ali Khan's caravan, which had covered "in eleven days less than eighty miles." It turned out that the caravan had hired an inexperienced guide who had lost his way in the desert. The disappearance of two valuable ponies delayed the caravan further still. Stein said goodbye to Sher Ali Khan a second time, and, to his surprise, the letters actually arrived in England. His friends received them in the end of September, about six months after he had written them.[100]

In the early twentieth century Sher Ali Khan's caravan carried mostly local merchandise—with the exception of the English woven goods that were newly available in Kashmir and Yarkand. His particular caravan covered a lot of ground, but most of the traders whom Stein and Hedin encountered moved along shorter routes. The documents in cave 17 suggest that the caravans traveling one thousand years earlier were basically the same.

In the Dunhuang economy of the ninth and tenth centuries, locally produced goods circulated in small quantities. Traffic to distant places was limited, commodities of foreign origin rare. The trade had little impact on local residents, who continued to live in a subsistence economy. State-sponsored delegations played a key role in the movement of goods; envoys, including monks, are the one group that was certainly moving from one place to another. This picture of the Silk Road trade matches that given by the excavated materials from the other sites. Rather than trying to explain why the Dunhuang documents do not mention long-distance trade with Rome and other distant points, we should appreciate just how accurate their detailed picture of the Silk Road trade is.

A ROYAL ORDER IN KHOTANESE

In 970 the king of Khotan sent this royal edict to the ruler of Dunhuang, who was his uncle. The use of the Chinese character *chi*, or "edict," shows how great the influence of Chinese culture was on the royal family. Preserved in the Dunhuang library cave, this is one of the few surviving tenth-century Khotanese documents that was written in the town of Khotan itself and not outside it. Courtesy of Bibliothèque Nationale de France.

CHAPTER 7

Entryway into Xinjiang for Buddhism and Islam

Khotan

Khotan, like nearby Kashgar, is famous for its Sunday market, where tourists can buy locally made crafts, naan bread, and grilled mutton on skewers. As visitors watch farmers fiercely bargaining over the price of a donkey, it's easy to imagine that Khotan has always been this way—but this is an illusion. The predominantly non-Chinese crowd prompts a similar reaction: surely these are the direct descendants of the earliest Silk Road settlers. In fact, though, a major historic break divides today's Khotan from its Silk Road past. The Islamic conquest of the Buddhist kingdom in 1006 brought a dramatic realignment to the region. Eventually Khotan's inhabitants converted to Islam, as did those of the surrounding oasis towns, making Islam the principal religion in the region today.[1] They also gradually gave up speaking Khotanese, the language shown on the facing page, for Uighur, the language one hears most often in the city today.

Almost all the materials about pre-Islamic Khotan come from outside the city. Because the oasis sits at the confluence of two major rivers, the environment is relatively well-watered. Extensive irrigation and occasional floods have created a damp environment in which paper and wood cannot survive. Documents about and artifacts from Khotan were preserved in neighboring—and far dryer—desert regions. There are nine major sites: Shanpula, Niya, Rawak, Endere, Melikawat, Yotkan, Dandan Uiliq, Domoko, and, finally, Dunhuang. The earliest finds, dating to the third century BCE, are from Shanpula, while the latest, from just before the Islamic conquest, come from the library cave at Dunhuang. Some of these sites are located within the city itself; Dunhuang, in contrast, lies 800 miles (1,325 km) to the east. The materials excavated from these multiple sites make it possible to reconstruct Khotan's remarkable history.

Khotan was the largest settlement in southwestern Xinjiang and thus the ideal portal for religions entering the Western Regions from neighboring lands. The first Buddhists came from India sometime around 200 CE, and for eight hundred years, as Buddhism moved east and became the most important

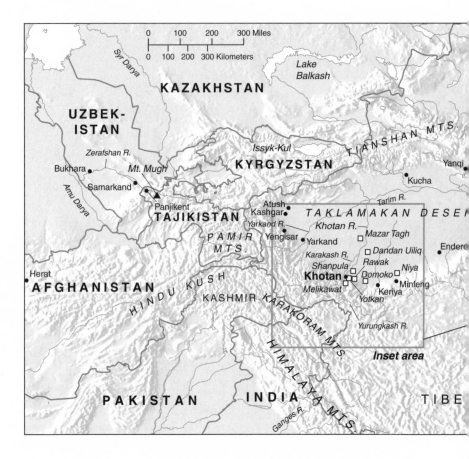

religion in central China, Khotan served as a major center for the study and translation of Buddhist texts.

In 644, when the Chinese monk-pilgrim Xuanzang passed through Khotan, the inhabitants related this legend of the kingdom's founding: after a son of the great Buddhist ruler Ashoka (reigned 268–32 BCE) was banished from the Mauryan Kingdom in India, he crossed the Pamirs into Khotan and became a shepherd, leading his flocks through the barren desert in search of grass. Childless, he stopped to pray at a temple to the Buddhist guardian of the north. A male child then appeared at the deity's forehead, while the earth in front of the temple produced a liquid "with a strange taste, sweet and fragrant as breast milk" for the infant.[2] Later versions of this myth have different protagonists—sometimes the prince's ministers—who come to Khotan, and some describe a dirt breast emerging from the earth, but they agree that migrants from India founded the settlement.

These early versions of the kingdom's founding do not mesh with the archeological record, which indicates that the site's earliest residents were nomads

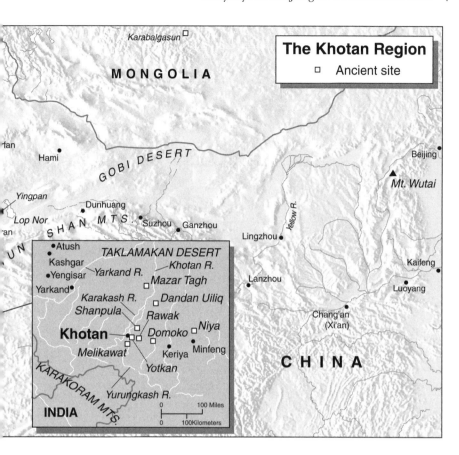

The Khotan Region
□ Ancient site

from the Eurasian steppe, not migrants from India. The Shanpula (Sampul in Uighur) cemetery, lying 20 miles (30 km) east of Khotan, contains materials dating from the third century BCE, the time of the kingdom's purported founding, to the fourth century CE.[3] This ancient burial site is worth a visit. Abandoned skulls, wooden tools, and bright red scraps of wool, some two thousand years old, poke out above the ground's surface. Ancient graves lie next to a modern Muslim burial ground, whose caretakers have joined forces with archeological authorities to protect the much-disturbed site from further plundering.

In the early twentieth century, scavengers sold Aurel Stein some scraps of paper and small wooden items from Shanpula, but Stein never visited the site himself.[4] No one excavated the site systematically until the early 1980s, when heavy rains exposed many burials. Between 1983 and 1995, local archeologists excavated sixty-nine human graves and two pits for horses in an area of 2 square miles (6 sq km). Like many steppe peoples, the inhabitants of Shanpula gave their horses elaborate burials, interring one with a beautifully woven saddle blanket.

The Shanpula graveyard also contained mass graves with up to two hundred people placed in a single pit. The women were buried wearing voluminous woolen skirts, whose many stains and multiple signs of mending indicate previous use by the living. The funerary skirts bear decorative bands of woven tapestry 6.3 inches (16 cm) tall, which were made separately on a small loom; for every color change, the weaver cut off the warp threads and replaced them with a new color.[5]

The Shanpula site produced vivid evidence of exchanges with peoples living to the west, none more telling than the leg of a man's trousers cut from a piece of tapestry, shown in color plate 13 and on the jacket of this book. (All the other trousers found at the site were undecorated.) A centaur occupies the top panel, while a soldier with Western-looking facial features stands below. Although Rome, where images of centaurs were common, is a possible source, certain motifs—particularly the animal heads on the soldier's dagger—indicate that the kingdom of Parthia in northern Iran, nearer to Khotan, was the more likely place of origin.[6]

Goods from other societies were buried in the Shanpula graves as well. Four mirrors were of Chinese manufacture and date to when the Chinese first stationed garrisons in Khotan at the end of the first century CE. The dynastic history of the Han records the oasis's population as 19,300 people living in 3,300 households.[7] The mirrors, like those found at Niya, were most likely gifts presented by Chinese envoys to local rulers.

By the year 300 CE, the mass burials die out, an important indicator of cultural change. The later graves at Shanpula, which contain single individuals buried in rectangular pits, closely resemble those at Niya and Yingpan, suggesting that a related population had moved to Khotan by the third and fourth centuries CE and displaced the earlier residents.

This was the time of the Kharoshthi documents from Niya, which frequently mention Khotan, some 150 miles (250 km) to the west of Niya. The Niya officials welcomed refugees from Khotan even as they bemoaned the cavalry attacks and raids by the Khotanese.

Distinctive Sino-Kharoshthi coins, with Chinese characters on one face and Kharoshthi script on the other, testify to the extensive contacts the people of Khotan had with their neighbors. The Khotanese kings created their own hybrid coinage that combined elements of Kushan and Chinese coinage. Numismatic scholars have been unable to match the names of the kings on these coins with the kings mentioned in Chinese sources, making it difficult to date the coins absolutely, but they were probably minted sometime around the third century CE.[8]

With the weakening of the Kushan Empire in the second or third centuries CE, Indian migrants who crossed the Pamirs introduced Buddhist teachings to Khotan as they did at Niya. A prominent Chinese translator traveled from Luoyang to

DECORATIVE SKIRT BAND FROM SHANPULA
This skirt band shows a stag, its head weighed down by exaggerated antlers that fill the entire vertical frame. Colored pink, red, and blue, his four legs and tail stand out from the navy background. A creature—perhaps a bird with its head facing upward—rides on its back. Deer with giant antlers often occur in the art of neighboring Central Asian nomadic peoples.
© Abegg-Stiftung, CH-3132 Riggisberg, 2001. Photo: Christoph von Viràg.

Khotan in 260 in search of the original version of an important Sanskrit text. After working for twenty-two years, he sent the written Sanskrit sutra to Luoyang but chose to remain in Khotan, where he died.[9] This account, preserved in an early sixth-century Chinese catalog of Buddhist texts, is the first written mention of Buddhism in Khotan.

Khotan's most imposing Buddhist ruin, Rawak, dates to this period as well. The site lies 39 miles (63 km) north of Khotan in the desert, east of the Yurungkash River. Visitors today take a car or bus to a location a few miles from the site, and then either walk (if it is not too warm) or ride a camel. The desert is blistering hot, and extraordinarily fine sand gets into everything, yet it teems with life: small plants, lizards, and rabbits thrive under foot, while hawks and larks fly overhead. Eventually visitors reach a guardhouse, where an incongruous chain stretches across the road and a sign identifies the archeological site. A central monument surrounded by sections of a wall is visible. Sand covers much of the ruin, and one can easily imagine the shifting dunes obscuring the whole edifice in a few years' time.

Rawak profoundly impressed Aurel Stein on his arrival in April 1901. Realizing that he needed to remove massive amounts of sand before he could map the site, he sent for additional laborers to help the dozen workers in his crew. Spring windstorms blew sand into everyone's eyes and mouths, making all physical labor trying. Working section by section, the crew eventually uncovered the central stupa, the monument designed to hold relics of the Buddha. It stood an imposing 22.5 feet (6.86 m) tall and formed the shape of a cross, with stairways on each of the four sides.[10] As the workmen shoveled away the sand, they uncovered a huge, rectangular interior wall. In addition, they unearthed the southwestern corner of an exterior wall, which originally extended all the way around the interior wall.

As worshippers walked around the monument, they proceeded through an impressive walkway, viewing the statues on both sides. Stein supposed that a wooden roof must have covered the walkway between the interior and exterior walls simply because the statues were so breakable. Some oversize statues, standing 12 or 13 feet (around 4 m) tall, depict buddhas; the smaller figures, their attendants.

The absence of wood makes carbon 14 testing impossible; one can only date the statues by rigorous stylistic comparison to other Buddhist statuary.

SKIRT FOR THE DEAD, SHANPULA

This, one of the largest skirts from Shanpula, measured 6 feet 2 inches (1.88 m) at the top edge, which was gathered around the deceased's waist. The lower edge of the skirt extended a full 16 feet 6 inches (5.03 m) in length. Too unwieldy to be worn in daily life, this skirt was made specifically for the use of the dead. © Abegg-Stiftung, CH-3132 Riggisberg, 2001. Photo: Christoph von Viràg.

THE WALLS OF RAWAK MONASTERY OUTSIDE KHOTAN

This photograph by Stein's crew shows the square central stupa at Rawak and the interior wall, over 3 feet (1 meter) tall. This wall, measuring 163 feet by 141 feet (50 m by 43 m), encircled the stupa, enclosing an area just under half an American football field. This wall formed a corridor that devotees used to circumambulate the stupa.

Since the Rawak figures closely resemble the earliest Buddhist statues from Gandhara and Mathura, India, the first phase of construction at the site probably occurred in the third and fourth centuries CE, and a second phase followed in the late fourth and early fifth centuries, roughly the same time as the Miran site.[11]

Rawak is much larger and more magnificent than any of the other stupas along the southern route (including the square stupa at Niya found by the Sino-Japanese expedition). Its size testifies to the wealth of the oasis. The Chinese monk Faxian who passed through Khotan on his way to India in 401 also remarked on the oasis's prosperity and the extent of support for Buddhists among the populace, who, he reported, each built a small stupa in front of their doors.

Khotan had fourteen large monasteries as well as many smaller ones, and Faxian and his companions stayed in one of the large monasteries. Each year, this monastery sponsored a four-wheeled cart in a lavish Buddhist procession. Standing over 24 feet (7 m) tall, and decorated with jewels and banners, the float housed images of the Buddha and two attendants made of gold and

THE FRAGILE STUCCO STATUES AT RAWAK

After cleaning the sand off, Stein examined the stucco statues and concluded that they must have originally had wooden frames inside. Since the interior frames had disintegrated, the statues were too fragile to transport. Stein opted to photograph the statues and ordered his men to use ropes to prop up their heads, but the delicate heads snapped off anyway.

silver. Faxian also described a new monastery built to the west of the oasis, which had just been completed after eighty years. The complex had a great hall, living quarters for monks, and a stupa standing some 66 yards (60 m) high.[12]

Faxian sometimes exaggerates the number of Buddhists or the depth of their devotion, but he does not distort the basic facts. The monasteries of Khotan were indeed wealthy. The monks of Khotan lived very differently from the Buddhists of Niya, who resided with their families and participated only occasionally in Buddhist rituals. Amply supported by donations from the king and other wealthy patrons, the Khotanese Buddhists could devote themselves full-time to study and the performance of rituals.

In subsequent centuries, with the enthusiastic support of local kings, Khotan continued to thrive as a center of Buddhist learning. Visiting in 630, the Buddhist monk Xuanzang listed the main local products: rugs, fine felt, textiles, and jade. Khotan was famous for its jade (technically nephrite), large chunks of which the inhabitants found in the riverbeds around the oasis. Khotan's two largest rivers are named the Yurungkash ("White Jade" in Uighur) and the Karakash ("Black Jade"), and they merge north of the city to form the Khotan River. The jade found in the two rivers differs in color, and implements made from the lighter-colored Khotanese jade have been found in a royal tomb, dating to 1200 BCE, in the central Chinese city of Anyang.

In 1900, when Aurel Stein first came to Khotan, the inhabitants were still prospecting for jade in the riverbeds. In addition, they had expanded their search to include gold and also antiquities. As he noted wryly, "'Treasure-seeking,' *i.e.*, the search for chance finds of precious metal within the areas of abandoned settlements, has indeed been a time-honored occupation in the whole of the Khotan oasis, offering like gold-washing and jade-digging the fascinations of a kind of lottery to those low down in luck and averse to any constant exertion."[13] These were the very men on whom Stein depended so heavily in his own excavations and explorations.

In Khotan itself, Stein purchased surface finds at Yotkan, the site of the ancient capital, but, to his frustration, no ruins survived. He did not excavate, which is puzzling, because today the visitor sees tantalizing evidence of fallen walls and buildings spread over a large area. Stein did find small clay figurines of monkeys everywhere.[14]

Modern visitors can go to Yotkan, but it is more interesting to go to Melikawat, a ruin on the Yurungkash River, 22 miles (35 km) south of the city. There, multiple sand dunes sit on a barren, but evocative, moonscape occupying several square miles (10 sq km) of an ancient city lost in the dunes. One can hire a donkey cart and wander in the hills of sand—or proceed on foot. Local children offer various scavenged items for sale; tourists scan their trays of obviously manufactured fakes, hoping to spot a genuine item.

In 1901, after leaving Niya and going west for eight days, Aurel Stein found a wooden slip with the earliest evidence of the indigenous language of Khotan in Endere (modern Ruoqiang), an oasis 220 miles (350 km) to the east of Khotan. The wooden slip surfaced in the ruins of a house near a Buddhist stupa. Like the Niya documents, this slip, too, is written in Kharoshthi script, but the handwriting and the spelling are not exactly the same as those at Niya. Because of the many similarities, most scholars assume that the slip dates to the third or fourth centuries CE.[15]

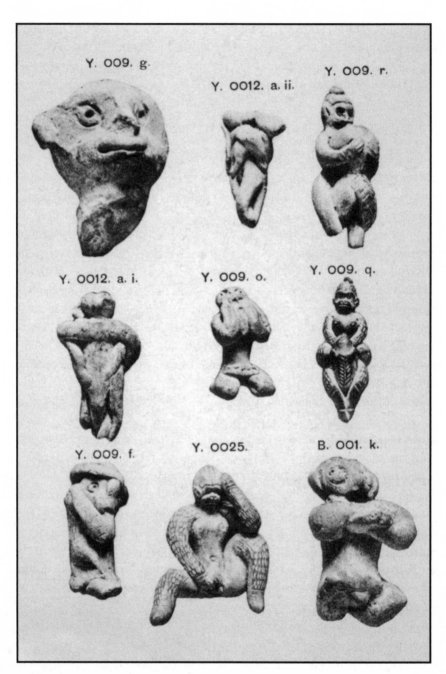

Y. 009. g.

Y. 0012. a. ii.

Y. 009. r.

Y. 0012. a. i.

Y. 009. o.

Y. 009. q.

Y. 009. f.

Y. 0025.

B. 001. k.

CLAY MONKEYS FROM YOTKAN
As was his usual practice, Stein carefully numbered and arrayed the different clay monkeys he found at Yotkan on a tray so that they could be photographed. Their sexually explicit positions suggest their use as talismans to enhance fertility.

Since the document is so important for the study of Khotan, let us consider the full text:

> On the 18th day of the 10th month of the 3rd year, at this time in the reign of the king of Khotan, the king of kings, Hinaza Deva Vijitasimha, at that time there is a man of the city called Khvarnarse. He speaks thus: There is a camel belonging to me. That camel carries a distinguishing mark, a mark branded on it, like this—VA SO. Now I am selling this camel for a price of 8,000 masha [most likely Chinese coins] to the suliga Vagiti Vadhaga. On behalf of that camel Vagiti Vadhaga paid the whole price in masha, and Khvarnarse received it. The matter has been settled. From now on this camel has become the property of Vagiti Vadhaga, to do as he likes with it, to do everything he likes. Whoever at a future time complains, informs, or raises a dispute about this camel, for that he shall so pay the penalty as the law of the kingdom demands. By me Bahudhiva this document (?) was written at the request of Khvarnarse.

This document records the sale of a camel for 8,000 Chinese coins by a Khotanese man to a Sogdian named Vagiti Vadhaga. (The word *suliga*, used to describe Vagiti Vadhaga, originally meant "Sogdian" but later took on the broader meaning of "merchant.")

The use of the Khotanese king's reign year to date the contract suggests that it was drawn up in Khotan and carried to Endere. Scholars of the Khotanese language observe that all the names in the contract—the king's, the seller's, the purchaser's, the scribe's—all take Iranian forms. "King of kings" is the standard Iranian term for ruler, and "hinaza" is an Iranian word meaning "general." Thus, a single wooden slip—another of Stein's chance finds—documents the use of an Iranian language in Khotan in the third or fourth centuries, at the same time that the residents of neighboring Niya were speaking the Indic language of Gandhari.

The first documents in the Khotanese language surfaced on the antiquities market in 1895. A British captain named S. H. Godfrey bought them from some local merchants, who claimed that they had been found in Kucha, and sent them to Augustus Frederick Rudolf Hoernle, the secretary of the Royal Asiatic Society of Bengal, who had deciphered the Bower Manuscript, the first major manuscript find in Xinjiang. In the following years, the British consul based in Kashgar, George Macartney, bought more documents and asked Hoernle to decipher them as well.[16] In 1899 Hoernle left India and retired to Oxford; continuing the practice of his predecessors, Stein sent him all manuscripts written in Brahmi script, which replaced Kharoshthi after it fell from use about 400 CE.[17]

As early as 1901 Hoernle realized that some of the manuscripts, though written in Brahmi script, were in a language distinct from Sanskrit: "Only a few of the words or phrases have, as yet, been determined, but these seem to prove clearly that the language of the documents is an Indo-Iranian dialect, having affinities both with Persian and the Indian vernaculars, in addition to peculiarities of its own which connect it with the dialects of the Western Highlands of Central Asia."[18] Initially Hoernle did not know if Khotanese was an Iranian language that borrowed a huge vocabulary from Sanskrit or a Sanskritic language with many Iranian words. A linguist encountering English would confront a similar problem: English might appear to be a Romance language with a large Germanic vocabulary, but it is actually a Germanic language that, after the Norman Conquest of 1066, absorbed many French words. By 1920 a scholarly consensus had formed: Khotanese was an Iranian language, contemporary with Middle Persian and Sogdian, with an extensive vocabulary borrowed from Sanskrit.

Because the script, spellings, and grammar of the different phases of Khotanese vary, Prods Oktor Skjærvø, the Aga Khan Professor of Iranian at Harvard, sees three distinct phases in the history of the language: Old Khotanese (fifth to sixth centuries), Middle Khotanese (seventh to eighth centuries), and Late Khotanese (ninth to tenth centuries). Each phase is associated with a specific group of manuscript finds: examples of Old Khotanese are almost exclusively translations of Buddhist texts of unknown provenance; the Middle Khotanese texts surfaced at Dandan Uiliq; and the Late Khotanese texts came from cave 17 at Dunhuang.[19]

Only one manuscript in Old Khotanese is not a translation of a Buddhist text from Sanskrit: *The Book of Zambasta*.[20] The text is named for the official who commissioned it: at several places, the text states, "The official Ysambasta with his son Ysarkula ordered this to be written." (The English letter *z* best approximates the sound of the combined *y* and *s*.) This, the most important work of literature in Khotanese, is an anthology of Buddhist writings. The text's author is modest: as he explains, "Since I have translated this into Khotanese, however extremely small and poor my knowledge, I seek pardon from all the *deva* [divine] buddhas for whatever meaning I have distorted here. But whatever merits I may have obtained here, may I surely through these merits realize *bodhi* together with all beings also." *Bodhi*, the knowledge and understanding of Buddhist teachings that comes with enlightenment, is a key teaching of the text, as is emptiness.

The Book of Zambasta covers familiar ground for all students of Buddhism. One chapter on the topic of women's wiles and how the listener can best withstand them stands out, since few Buddhist anthologies include such a discussion.[21]

The chapter warns, "Those women's cunning arts they learn without a teacher," and concludes, "The official Ysambasta with all his sons [and] daughters,"— this is the only mention of Zambasta's daughters—"ordered [me] to write [this]. May I surely become a Buddha." The author adds a final comment: "The Acarya ["teacher," a term of address for monks] Siddhabhadra read this section on women many times for the restraining of his mind: 'Thus indeed I remained as agitated as the ocean when I had read this sutra. Then in fact there was no lying quiet for me, like the eyelashes, the hairs between the eyebrows, the hairs on the cheeks.'" This confession comes as a rare human note in what is often a dry anthology.

Proceeding chapter by chapter, *The Book of Zambasta* paraphrases certain Buddhist narratives, many associated with Mahayana teachings. It relates the tale of how the Buddha outsmarted the heretic magician Bhadra, who used his magic to transform a cemetery into a "palace of the gods." One chapter recounts the Buddha's biography and his enlightenment, while another narrates the Buddha's departure and his entrusting of this world to the Maitreya Buddha. The chapter about the Maitreya has the same content as the text that was translated from "twghry" into Uighur, which underpinned Sieg and Siegling's identification of the Tocharian language. *The Book of Zambasta* beautifully illustrates Khotan's place as a central node for monks traveling among all the countries of the region, because it anthologizes and paraphrases texts from Sanskrit, Chinese, Tibetan, and Uighur, among other languages.[22]

The Book of Zambasta does not survive in its entirety. Two hundred and seven leaves of an original 298 are held in libraries in Calcutta, St. Petersburg, London, New Haven, Munich, and Kyoto. The Russian consul Nikolai Petrovsky purchased 192 leaves from locals in Kashgar, so no one knows the book's original findspot.[23] Scholars have identified five different manuscripts from which these leaves were drawn, the earliest dating to between 450 and 500.[24]

At the time that *The Book of Zambasta* was written, Khotan was an independent kingdom. In the early 600s it became a vassal of the Western Turks, and it was still part of their confederation when Xuanzang visited on his way to India in 630. In the following two decades, the Tang emperor Taizong (reigned 626–49) wrested control of Central Asia from the Western Turks; Tang forces took Turfan in 640 and Kucha in 648. In that year, the king of Khotan shifted allegiance. He sent one son and three hundred camels to aid the Tang army, visited the capital, and left his sons in the Tang capital as hostages. (It was common practice for future rulers to be raised in the capitals of their country's allies so that they could learn their customs.) Khotan became one of the Four Garrisons where the Tang stationed troops in the far west; the other three were Kucha, Kashgar, and Yanqi (between 679 and 719 Tokmak took Yanqi's place).

After 648 Khotan's history was entwined with Kucha's: the Tibetans conquered both oases and ruled them from 670 to 692, when the Chinese regained control, which they retained until 755. Then the An Lushan rebellion prompted them to withdraw their forces from Central Asia.[25] The height of Silk Road contact for Khotan, like Turfan and Kucha, occurred during the seventh and eighth centuries, when the Tang military presence was strongest.

The largest cache of Khotanese-language documents comes from the site of Dandan Uiliq, 80 miles (130 km) northeast of Khotan. Hedin had visited the site in January 1896 on his second trip into the Taklamakan (on the disastrous first foray two of his men had died); a newspaper clipping about the lost city in the desert inspired Stein to apply to the Government of India for funding.[26] Before setting off into the desert in 1900, Stein enlisted the help of Macartney, the British consul in Kashgar, and Petrovsky, the Russian consul, to question the men who had sold them small artifacts and excavated manuscripts. Two of the vendors recommended that Stein contact a Uighur named Turdi, who, as Stein explained, "found his bearings even where the dead uniformity of the sand dunes would to ordinary eyes seem to offer no possible landmark."[27] When the hired guides could not locate Dandan Uiliq, Turdi led Stein's party to the ruins.

At Dandan Uiliq, Stein mapped fifteen structures in small clusters in the desert. The smallest structure measured 5 feet (1.5 m) square, the largest, 23 feet (7 m) by 20 feet (6 m). Some of the structures appeared to be dwellings, and documents found inside indicated that they were the residences of officials, who kept records in both Chinese and Khotanese.

One ruin held multiple leaves from Buddhist texts, evidence of a library at the site. Other structures were clearly religious; housing stucco sculptures, they had frescoes on their walls, many of which depicted deities. Some buildings also contained wooden panels buried in the ground.

Dandan Uiliq was sufficiently remote that most of the finds that were sold at the market must have been, Stein concluded, the product of short trips by a few individuals working alone or in small groups.[28] Stein was wrong about the inaccessibility of Dandan Uiliq. Yes, the site was in the middle of the Taklamakan Desert and not easy to find, but those with sufficient determination could get there. The American geographer Ellsworth Huntington came in 1905, and the German traveler Emil Trinkler and his Swiss companion Walter Bosshard followed in the 1920s. In 1998 Christoph Baumer, a Swiss traveler, journeyed by camel train to the site, where—to the dismay of the archeological authorities—he uncovered several new paintings in an unauthorized dig.[29] Modern technology, in the form of the Global Positioning System and off-road vehicles, has made it even easier for looters to reach Dandan Uiliq in recent years.

HOW THE SECRET OF SILKMAKING LEFT CHINA
Stein's most famous find from Dandan Uiliq was this painted wooden panel measuring 18 inches (46 cm) long by 4 5/8 inches (12 cm) high, which a devotee left as an offering to the Buddha. A woman points to the crown of a princess who, according to legend, smuggled a silkworm cocoon out of China, thus revealing the secret of silkmaking to the peoples living in the Western Regions. In truth, the know-how for raising silkworms and spinning silk left China the same way that papermaking did, carried by people migrating along the Silk Road.

Since 1998 many Khotanese-language documents and objects with no clear provenance—but most likely from Dandan Uiliq or nearby—have surfaced on the antiquities market. Modern Chinese museums and universities face exactly the same thorny dilemma that curators of Western museums do: should they purchase the looted goods and preserve them for scholars to analyze? Or should they refuse to buy them in the hope that doing so will persuade looters to stop raiding ancient sites? If they do not buy them, the manuscripts will be lost; if they do, the unauthorized excavations will continue and quite possibly escalate.

In 2004, the National Library of China in Beijing decided to purchase some documents from Dandan Uiliq. Experts in Khotanese have worked intensively to date these documents, to decipher and translate them, to provide them with a provenance (sometimes possible because they mention some of the same individuals who appear in documents whose findspot is known), and—most important of all—to explain their significance. These new finds have changed our understanding of key developments in Silk Road history.

The earliest documents from the Dandan Uiliq region date to 722.[30] Found at a small settlement south of Dandan Uiliq called Domoko (Damagou in Chinese), these wooden tallies measure an inch (2.5 cm) or less across and range from 7.5 inches (19 cm) to 18 inches (46 cm) long. With a round hole at one end where they were attached to a container holding grain, they have evenly spaced notches that officials marked with ink each time they received a payment of tax grain. Here is a typical example:

> [Chinese text]: Boluodaocai of Bajia delivered 7 *shuo*s [roughly 1.2 bushels, or 42 L] of wheat on the 5th day of the 8th month of the 10th year of Kaiyuan [722]. Clerk: He Xian. Officials: Zhang Bing, Xiang Hui.
> [Khotanese text]: Bradaysaa of Birgamdara delivered 7 *kusa*s of wheat in the year of the shau Marsha.[31]

Both the Chinese and the Khotanese give the name of the taxpayer, the amount of grain paid, and the year of payment (722). The Chinese text gives more information, including the exact day and month of the tax payment as well as the name of the receiving clerk and his superiors. The tallies mention three types of tax grain: barley, wheat, and millet.[32] All the tallies (there are thirty-five in the set bought by the National Library of China; others are in private hands) follow this same format.

These tallies afford a clear glimpse of how Tang-dynasty tax collection system functioned in Khotan. These documents are all bilingual. Living in the modern era, we have grown accustomed to multilingual documents of the European Community and other international organizations. There is something extraordinary, though, in seeing these bilingual grain tallies. In the eighth century, the reach of the Chinese state extended down to the lowest level; even the smallest payment of grain was recorded in Khotanese, the language of the local people, and in Chinese, the language of the rulers. Similarly, all the officials in the government had both Chinese and Khotanese titles. The Khotanese bureaucracy employed clerks who could translate Khotanese documents into Chinese; some Chinese-language documents refer to petitions in Khotanese from the local people that were translated so that Chinese officials could understand them.[33]

A different group of wooden documents, only in Khotanese and most likely contemporary with the grain tallies, reveals more about local society. Shaped like a box and made from two pieces of wood, an undertablet holds a cover tablet that, like a drawer, can be pulled in and out with a knob. Writing covers almost every surface, including the interior, sides, and exterior of the two pieces of the box. These pieces record contractual agreements among different residents.[34]

These documents refer to an "assembly" that enforces decisions reached by officials, a distinctive feature of Khotanese society. One dispute involved payment for the use of water for irrigation; the officials hearing the case stipulated that one man should temporarily receive the water, which belonged to the village collectively, and that the village should retain the right of future use. The decision ends with the phrase "This case was presented in the judicial assembly before" two officials, whose names are given.[35]

This case shows that, by the early eighth century and quite possibly earlier, the Khotanese had developed a sophisticated legal system in which individuals recorded transactions such as the transfer of irrigation rights, a loan, or the adoption of a child. Witnesses vouched for the details of these transactions, and officials signed the documents—customarily before an assembly—to ensure that they were maintained. Once a decision had been reached, everyone in the community was supposed to abide by it. Whole villages bore some collective tax responsibilities; when a village had paid the required tax, officials issued a receipt—but only for payment in full.

This system was in place in 755, when the An Lushan rebellion erupted in central China. In the following year, the Khotanese king sent five thousand troops, many of them Chinese soldiers garrisoned at Khotan, to help the Tang emperor suppress the rebels. After 755, the Chinese retained only tenuous control of Khotan. Power rested in the hands of the local commissioner, a Chinese official, who often could not get messages to his superiors in the Chinese capital because overland travel was so difficult.

During the decades after 755, as elsewhere in northwest China, the Chinese state stopped paying military units stationed in the northwest; Dunhuang experienced a coin shortage at this time. Even before 755 Chinese coins may not always have been available in Khotan; in one instance, adoptive parents paid five hundred coins for a child and substituted white silk for the remaining two hundred coins they owed, presumably because coins were already in short supply.[36]

Some Chinese-language documents from Dandan Uiliq, which date to the 780s, record loans for over ten thousand coins.[37] We cannot tell if coins were actually paid or were simply used as a unit of record while local people substituted cloth or grain as payment. In one bilingual contract, the Chinese text mentions payment in coins, while the Khotanese version specifies how much cloth was paid as a substitute for coins.[38] By the end of the eighth century, a subsistence economy in which textiles and grain in measured amounts served as money replaced the coin economy of earlier times.

The Chinese forces continued to collect taxes from the Khotanese populace, as shown by a document requisitioning sheepskins for the soldiers' winter clothing. This document, like others found in a single cache at Dandan Uiliq, was addressed to a local official named Sidaka who served as *spata*, the village head in charge of nonmilitary matters. The author of the document, himself also a spata officeholder, explains that, since the people in Sidaka's hamlet own 90 sheep, they owe 28 sheepskins; the tax rate is 2 sheepskins for every 6.5 sheep owned, or 27.69 for the hamlet. Sidaka submitted 27 sheepskins, but his colleague explains that no receipt will be issued until the hamlet pays the full amount due. Such a document presupposes the existence of detailed household registers listing not only the human occupants of the village but also the animals they owned; without such records—some of which have been found—the occupying Chinese government could not have known how many sheepskins to levy from the village.

Yoshida Yutaka, a professor of linguistics at Kyoto University, has painstakingly identified four different places where different Khotanese-language documents were found. Two were at Dandan Uiliq; one contains documents dated between 777 and 788 that mention Sidaka.[39] As this and other documents from the same spot show, Khotan had a Chinese-run government between 777 and 788, the years in which documents with Sidaka's name appear. During these decades, the Tibetans seized on the weakness of the Tang central government and aggressively expanded into Central Asia. After conquering Dunhuang in 786 they fought the Uighurs in Turfan for three years starting in 789 before defeating them in 792, and they conquered Khotan before 796.[40] Historians of the Western Regions have known that the Tibetan Empire collapsed from within during the 840s; during the same decade, the Kirgiz defeated the Uighur Empire based in Karabalgasun, in today's Mongolia, and many Uighurs fled south to modern Xinjiang. The newly discovered documents from Dandan Uiliq make it possible to know which oases fell to the Tibetans or to the Uighurs in precisely which years.

Mazar Tagh was a military fortress on a strategically important route between Kucha and Khotan, which lay 90 miles (150 km) to the south of the fort. It also happened to be in an uninhabited part of the desert; Khotanese cooks and guards served there on fixed rotations.[41] With the conquest of Khotan, the Tibetans gained control of the outpost, which had originally housed Chinese soldiers. One document dated 798 urges the official receiving the document to evacuate the men and cattle in the fortress to a nearby town. The document does not name the enemy, but it is probably the Uighur Kaghanate, which had occupied Kucha around 800.[42]

The Tibetans left much of the previous administration in place; several named individuals continued in office before and after the imposition of Tibetan rule. They issued orders in both Khotanese and Chinese, an indication of how deeply Chinese bureaucratic practices had influenced the Khotanese and then the Tibetans.[43] A few officials continued to use individual Chinese characters as their signatures. Scribes drafted contracts that translated multiple Chinese phrases literally into Tibetan. Those contracts, although never used within Tibet, established models for Tibetan-language contracts at Dun-huang.[44] The Tibetans ruled Khotan indirectly; whenever they needed any-thing, the top official, the commissioner, made a request to his Khotanese counterpart, who then issued the order to the appropriate local officials.[45]

As rich as they are, the tax materials from Dandan Uiliq do not reveal who was traveling along the Silk Road and why. One of the most illuminating docu-ments about cultural contact on the Silk Road surfaced because Stein's men continued to dig on their own even when he did not pay them. After excavating Dandan Uiliq for seventeen days (from December 18, 1900, to January 4, 1901) Stein dismissed some of the crew and took the remaining men to a nearby site, some 7 miles (11 km) away.

When Stein returned to his camp on the first evening, he was startled to see some of the dismissed workers waiting for him. He was even more surprised when they presented him with their finds: near the corner of Dandan Uiliq Structure 13, they had uncovered a crumpled document with Hebrew letters on it. Stein explains why he believed his men had found it where they said they had; the paper was genuinely old (eighth century), and making and planting a forgery would have required a great deal of preparation.[46] Stein was particularly leery of fakes because he had just exposed the fraud of Islam Akhun, the man whose skillfully forged documents tricked Hoernle into thinking that yet another new language had been discovered.[47]

While at Dandan Uiliq, Stein had cleared the sand from Structure 13, where Turdi reported finding multiple silver ingots worth two hundred rupees, or thir-teen pounds British sterling (with a rough value of perhaps one thousand pounds today) in his youth.[48] Even though the structure was big, measuring 60 feet (18 m) on one side, with one room 22 by 18 feet (6.7 by 5.5 m), Stein decided not to excavate when his crew found nothing but a fireplace and a wooden frame.[49] After Stein departed, the dismissed workers dug through a pile of waste, left near the ruin by earlier looters, and recovered the document written in Hebrew letters.

The letter was in New Persian, the language that replaced Middle Persian in Iran during the ninth century. A handful of Jewish-Persian documents have been found at various locations around the world, near Herat, Afghanistan, the Malabar Coast of south India, and Baghdad. The Dandan Uiliq document is not the oldest such example—the oldest dates to the 750s—but it is among oldest Jewish-Persian documents surviving today.[50]

The fragmentary letter is difficult to make out because only the center of the page remains; the words at the beginning and end of each line are gone. The author writes to a business associate, apparently his superior, about different transactions involving sheep, clothing, spikenard (a plant used in medicine and scents), a saddle, stirrups, and straps. Most likely a merchant, he mentions wanting to know his "profit and loss." We do not know why he left Iran, but we can speculate that he (or his ancestors) moved east to escape the Islamic conquest, and he ended up in the Khotan region during a particularly turbulent time.

The letter provides direct testimony that at least one Persian-speaking Jew was in Dandan Uiliq in the late eighth century, but the fragmentary state of the letter makes it difficult to say more. More than a hundred years after the initial find, the utterly unexpected occurred: a second Jewish-Persian letter, almost undamaged, appeared for sale, and the National Library of China purchased it. Zhang Zhan, a graduate student who earned his master's degree at Peking University and who is working on his doctorate at Harvard, published a full transcription and translation into Chinese in 2008; he plans to bring out the English translation in the near future.[51]

The similarities with the old letter are so great that Zhang Zhan is confident that the two letters were written at the same time, in the same place, and by the same person: in the opening years of the ninth century in Khotan. His dating hinges on a sentence in the letter reporting the latest news from Kashgar: "The Tibetans have all been killed."[52] If, as comparison to several Khotanese letters also found at Dandan Uiliq suggests, the letter refers to the Uighur defeat of the Tibetans, then the letter dates to 802, when the Uighurs took Kashgar and expelled the Tibetans.

The new letter opens with eight lines of greetings by the writer "from far away" to the family of his "lord master Nisi Chilag," the recipient of the letter, who was most likely a Jew living in Dandan Uiliq. The new letter then details a dispute about sheep that the writer had with a "landlord": although he gave presents including musk and candy (the meanings of the other commodities he used as gifts are so far unknown), he has not yet received the sheep due to him. Interestingly, he relates a conversation in which the landlord mistook him for a "Sogdian," an understandable error given how many of the merchants along the Silk Road were Sogdian and how few were Jewish.

Jewish merchants have left only a few traces on the Silk Road. Recall that one of the latest inscriptions on the Karakorum Highway was in Hebrew. An Arabic account of a late ninth-century massacre mentioned Jewish merchants living in the southern city of Guangzhou (Canton) alongside Muslims, Christians, and Zoroastrians. And cave 17 contained a folded sheet of paper with an eighteen-line prayer as well as a selection from the Psalms in Hebrew (shown in color plate 12).

In addition to the single Hebrew prayer sheet and tens of thousands of Chinese and Tibetan-language documents, the library cave at Dunhuang contained

A NEWLY DISCOVERED JUDEO-PERSIAN LETTER
In the early ninth century, the author of this letter, most likely a Persian-speaking Jew, used the Hebrew alphabet to write in New Persian to another Jew living in Dandan Uiliq. The author describes a dispute he is having with his landlord, who has not paid the sheep he owes him. Courtesy of National Library of China.

about two thousand Khotanese-language documents, many of them fragments.[53] Like many peoples living in small countries surrounded by powerful neighbors, the Khotanese were adept at learning languages. One Khotanese scribe was so skilled that he copied Tibetan texts; we know that he was Khotanese only because he numbered the pages using Khotanese numerals.[54] How did the Khotanese pick up languages so quickly even though they had no dictionaries?

Several sheets from phrasebooks in Khotanese and Chinese were preserved in the Dunhuang library cave.[55] Dispensing with Chinese characters, these learning aids simply record the sound of the Chinese sentence using Brahmi script and then give the meaning in Khotanese. The extremely skilled philologists who have worked on these texts have reverse-engineered the Khotanese version of tenth-century Chinese pronunciation to reconstruct the original Chinese sentences. Like any good language textbook, the Chinese-Khotanese bilingual list repeats key sentence patterns, all very short, so that the student can practice:

> Bring me vegetables!
> Bring me cucumbers!
> Bring me a gourd!

The phrasebook also includes sentences one can use at a market when buying and selling. Given the many contacts between Khotan and Dunhuang in the tenth century, it seems likely that Khotanese from different walks of life—envoys, monks, merchants—could have benefited from basic instruction in Chinese.

In contrast, the Sanskrit-Khotanese bilingual texts aim at a narrower audience.[56] Sanskrit was easy for Khotanese speakers to learn; because it was written in the same Brahmi script, language-learners could simply copy Sanskrit sentences and commit them to memory. The Khotanese-Sanskrit phrasebook, 194 lines total, begins with a simple conversation:

> How are you?
> Good, thank you!
> And how are you?
> Where do you come from?
> I come from Khotan.

The dialogues mention other places, too: India, China, Tibet, and Ganzhou (the seat of the Uighur Kaghanate in what is now Zhangye, Gansu). The phrasebook teaches how to buy a horse and obtain fodder, how to ask for needle and thread, and how to request that clothes be washed. Some of the dialogues hint at conflict:

> Don't be angry with me.
> I shall not pull out your hair.
> When you speak unpleasantness
> then I shall become angry.

And some even mention sex:

> He loves many women.
> He makes love.

Some of the dialogues make it possible to identify the intended users:

> Do you have any books?
> I do.
> [Which books?]
> Sutras, Abhidharma, Vinaya, Vajrayana.
> Which of them do you have?
> Which of them do you like?
> I like to read Vajrayana.

Only a monk or an advanced student of Buddhism could use such sentences. "Sutras" was a general term for all Buddhist texts, "Abhidharma" referred to the doctrinal texts, "Vinaya" to Buddhist regulations, and "Vajrayana" to Tantric texts. Sanskrit was spoken in monasteries all the way from China to India, as well as Khotan. One conversation reveals more about the target audience:

> I am going to China.
> What business do you have in China?
> I am going to see the bodhisattva Manjushri.

The intended users were monks traveling on the pilgrimage route that became popular in the eighth century. Starting in Tibet or Khotan, they traveled east, stopping at Dunhuang, with their final destination the devotional center for Manjushri at Mount Wutai in Shanxi (about four hours northwest of Beijing by car).

A gap in surviving documents means that we know very little of Khotan's history between 802, when the Dandan Uiliq documents end, and 901, when documents from the library cave record that an official in Dunhuang provided Khotanese envoys with one bundle and eight additional sheets of fine paper.[57] In the tenth century, the Khotanese kings were part of the same international order as the Cao-family rulers of Dunhuang: they sent emissaries to and received emissaries from each other, as well as the Ganzhou and Turfan Uighur Kaghanates and the different dynasties of central China. To travel to central China, Khotanese envoys went first to Dunhuang and then Ganzhou before proceeding to Lingzhou (modern Wuling County, Ningxia), an important stopping point for delegations on their way to the capital. Travel to central China was so uncertain that the Khotanese and the two Uighur Kaghanates frequently sent envoys bearing tribute only as far as Dunhuang, which they sometimes referred to as "China."[58]

The Cao family of Dunhuang and the royal family of Khotan had close ties. The Khotanese king Visa Sambhava, who ruled Khotan from 912 to 966, also used the Chinese name Li Shengtian.[59] Sometime before 936 he married the daughter of Cao Yijin. The Khotanese royal family maintained a residence in Dunhuang where Visa Sambhava's wife often stayed and where the heir to the Khotanese throne lived.[60] The crown prince's residence functioned as a representative office for the Khotanese, and it is very possible that the Khotanese-language documents found in cave 17 were an archive donated by the crown prince's residence to the Three Realms Monastery.[61]

In 938 Visa Sambhava sent envoys from Khotan to Kaifeng, Henan, the capital of the Later Jin. This is one of five instances during his reign when the Khotanese sent delegations to China, which was unified in 960 by the Song dynasty.[62] The Chinese-language records of these exchanges are typically brief: for example, "On the fourth day of the twelfth month [of the second year of the Jianlong reign, or 961] the king of Khotan Li Shengtian sent an emissary to present one jade tablet and one box" to the founder of the Song dynasty.[63] The Chinese would normally record the date, the name of the country sending gifts, the item presented, and sometimes the name of the lead emissary, but little else.

In contrast, a group of some fifteen Khotanese-language documents preserved in cave 17 offer a wealth of detail about one mission, which consisted of seven princes and their entourage who left Khotan, probably in the mid-tenth century near the end of Visa Sambhava's reign.[64] These documents reveal much about the nature of trade on the Silk Road, particularly in the difficult conditions of the tenth century.

The princes and their entourage set off with some 800 pounds (360 kg) of jade.[65] In addition, they carried some leather goods, most likely saddles, harnesses, or other horse tack. Horses and jade were the most common tribute items from Khotan, and other recorded gifts included camels, falcons, yak tails,

THE KHOTANESE KING AND QUEEN AS DONORS IN A DUNHUANG CAVE
This painting from cave 98 at Dunhuang shows the Khotanese king Visa Sambhava (reigned 912–66) and his wife, who was the daughter of the Dunhuang ruler Cao Yijin. Ties between the two families were close, and the Khotanese royal family frequently contributed funds for the construction of caves at Dunhuang. Drawing by Amelia Sargent.

textiles, furs, medicines, minerals, herbs, some types of fragrances, amber, and coral.[66] As was fitting in the subsistence economy of the time, rulers also presented slaves to one another.[67]

Rulers liked these gifts and said so. At one point when the Khotanese and the Uighur Kaghanate of Ganzhou had failed to exchange gifts for ten years, the kaghan wrote to the Khotanese king. (The letter survives only in its Khotanese translation; he probably wrote in either Chinese or Tibetan, the two diplomatic languages of the northwest in the tenth century.) The Uighur kaghan longed for "the many various wonderful things" that the Khotanese delegations had previously brought to him.[68] Most of all, he probably missed the intelligence, particularly about the military strength of rival powers, that only envoys could provide.[69]

Travel from one kingdom to another seemed slow, even to people at the time. As one envoy traveling with the princes from Khotan complained, "I shall go as far as Dunhuang making a difficult journey in forty-five days on foot, which with power to fly in the air I had done in one day."[70] Those who proceeded on horseback took eighteen days to cover 950 miles (1,523 km) by road.[71] No wonder they envied birds the power of flight.

The princes never made it to the Chinese capital; the ruler of Dunhuang felt that travel was too dangerous to go to Ganzhou, where three armies were battling each other in a succession dispute after the Uighur kaghan had died. The Dunhuang ruler insisted that they stay in Dunhuang. The trip ended in total failure, the princes bitterly complained in letters home. Forced to spend the different gifts they carried, the princes ended up utterly destitute, as they wrote:

> All the animals our men had are lost. Our clothes are lost. . . . There is no one with whom we can get out and go to (?) Ganzhou. How can we then come to Shuofang [where the envoys visiting the Chinese capital were first received], since we have neither gift nor letter for the Chinese king? . . . Many men have died. We have no food. How were then an order to come? How can we have to enter a fire from which we can not bring ourselves back?[72]

A letter from their escorts explains how each of the animals was lost.[73]

The ruler who did not allow the princes to continue their journey saw the princes' purpose as quite different from that of the monks traveling with them. Monks sometimes traveled as pilgrims and sometimes as members of official delegations. Rulers received monks because they believed that hosting a powerful monk could bring immediate benefits, whether in the form of miracles or the enhanced prestige accruing to Buddhist patrons. When the princes' delegation fell apart, the monks left the group, took some of the gifts intended for the Chinese, and settled down with wives. This is hardly what we might expect of Buddhists who had taken vows of celibacy, but entirely in keeping with what excavated materials reveal about other Buddhists, whether in Niya or Dunhuang.

The princes could not go on toward Ganzhou because of the unrest; the Dunhuang ruler feared that the Chinese court would hold him personally responsible if the gifts from Khotan did not arrive in the capital.[74] Yet he allowed three monks to proceed—once they had drawn their finger marks on a formal document absolving him of responsibility—because he thought that clerics who did not carry gifts were in less danger.

Two members of the delegation explained how some of the participants reacted to the collapse of the delegation. In each case, the individual in question absconded with the tribute sent by the Khotanese king intended for the Chinese.[75] Of the eight men, only two went to China: one slave who hoped to obtain his freedom and a trader who planned to give "one hundred blankets to the Royal Court."[76] Everyone else returned to Khotan with the pilfered goods.

At various points, the members of the delegation bartered away the gifts to cover their own travel expenses. After delivering a letter to the three monks who had gone on ahead, two men departed from Ganzhou, headed for Dunhuang "to do trade."[77] They were subsequently robbed in Guazhou. During the difficult trip during which so many of the princes' animals died, two of the party "lost their merchandise," and a Sogdian trader could not locate either his pack animals or the "merchandise he had hidden in the mountains."[78] Clearly traders accompanied the unfortunate envoys and encountered some of the same difficulties they did.

The princes engaged in trade as well. One Khotanese prince named Capastaka gave 40 pounds (18 kg) of jade to the Dunhuang authorities in exchange for one hundred fifty bolts of silk, nominally a gift for the Khotanese court, and fifty for his Chinese mother, Lady (Furen) Khi-vyaina. When his brother Wang Pa-kyau wrote to his mother to complain that Capastaka had cheated him, he asked that she send him jade as well: "When the envoys go there do you deign to send a little ira [jade] stone?"[79] It certainly sounds as if he, like his brother, planned to trade jade for silk, which he could use to cover his expenses on the road.

Bolts of silk were the main currency used by travelers, according to a list of expenses incurred by a different group of Khotanese travelers. They spent bolts of silk to buy barley, a camel, and horses, to make payments to a guide, and to give to "forty compatriot merchants." The silk did not always function as money; the travelers also made a garment from one bolt. In addition to paying expenses with silk, the group traded live sheep and antelope skins, an indication that in the Silk Road economy of the tenth century, people accepted goods in kind.[80]

A leading scholar of Khotanese, Professor Hiroshi Kumamoto of Tokyo University, explains why this list of expenditures is unusual: "This is one of the few Khotanese commercial documents found in Dunhuang. They are noteworthy in that the local Chinese documents in the ninth and tenth centuries only mention Khotanese envoys and priests, but hardly ever Khotanese merchants."[81] Kumamoto is absolutely right: few sources from the tenth century mention merchants specifically as a group.

While the Silk Road has long been viewed as a highway for a procession of camels led by a merchant in business for himself, the documentary record challenges this impression. The Khotanese-language documents about the seven princes mention different participants in the delegation: envoys of higher and lower rank, the princes, monks, and lay people.[82] The lines dividing these groups were permeable and became even more so in difficult times. Even the princes resorted to selling jade to obtain silk for travel expenses. In such a situation, anyone and everyone had to engage in trade, but the trade consisted of impromptu exchanges of locally produced and locally obtained goods. If someone needed a particular item, he might pay for it with a bolt of silk, if available, but he might also trade a sheep or even an antelope skin. In such unsettled times few people ventured on the road. Those who did often attached themselves to official delegations, which were entitled to special treatment—even if they did not always receive it.

The Khotanese-language materials from the Dunhuang library cave focus almost entirely on Khotan's relations with its neighbors to the east: Dunhuang, the Uighur kaghanates, the Tang dynasty and its successors in China. Yet the changes taking place to the west transformed Khotan.

The Kirghiz defeat of the Uighurs in 840 prompted the mass migration of the core Uighur populations out of Mongolia south to Turfan and Ganzhou, where they formed smaller successor states called the Uighur Kaghanates. In the aftermath of 840 another tribal confederacy formed: contemporary documents refer to them as "khans" or "kaghans," and modern scholars call them the Karakhanids to distinguish them from other Turkic peoples. Sometime before 955 their leader Satuq Bughra Khan converted to Islam, and his son continued both his military campaigns and the effort to convert the Turkic peoples to Islam. In 960 Muslim chronicles record that "200,000 tents of the Turks" converted to Islam.[83] The chronicles do not specify which Turks they mean or where exactly they were based, but modern scholars assume this passage refers to the Karakhanids, based in Kashgar, 350 miles (500 km) west of Khotan. After the Karakhanid conversion, they ordered their armies to destroy any existing non-Muslim religious structures, including Buddhist temples.

Living on the far eastern edge of the Islamic world, far from the Abbasid capital of Baghdad, the Karakhanid rulers probably converted in order to associate themselves with the great prestige of the Islamic powers. Several contemporary leaders, including those of the Khazars, the Kievan Rus', and the Hungarians, weighed the advantages of each of the medieval world's great religions—Judaism, Christianity, and Islam—and then chose one. The Karakhanid conversion to Islam was similar.[84]

The Khotanese initially defeated the Karakhanid army in 970 and won control of Kashgar. The king of Khotan, Visa Sura (reigned 967–77), the son of Visa Sambhava, sent a royal edict (see page 198) to his uncle, the ruler of Dunhuang, who was the brother of his mother who had married into the Cao family of Dunhuang.

The letter explains why the Khotanese are late in sending tribute to Dunhuang and to the Chinese. The Khotanese king exults in what "wonderful things, wives and sons, elephant and thoroughbred valuable horse and the like" they have obtained in Kashgar—but complains a little, too: "As to what is the work of occupying an alien territory and maintaining the government, that is great and difficult. And as an alien we do not secure control." He amplifies the theme of his government being stretched thin: "The money increases, and the corn, and the transport animals, and men, and troops, but there are many conflicts and men are dying." Although the Khotanese armies have won, the Karakhanid forces lie just outside Kashgar. The victory is not conclusive.

The king's letter closes with a list of gifts for his uncle. From Khotan the king sends the usual items: three lumps of jade (the weight specified for each), a piece of leather armor, some tools and vessels. From the goods captured from the Karakhanids, he has chosen a cup with a silver case and a steel tool, also with a cover.[85] The capture of Kashgar was clearly a major victory for Khotan, and Chinese-language sources record that the Khotanese king wrote to the Chinese asking permission to send them a "dancing elephant" captured from Kashgar, which the Chinese government duly granted.[86]

The Khotanese and the Karakhanids continued to fight after 970, but the sources give no details about the progression of the war. We know only that in 1006 the leader of the Karakhanids, Yusuf Qadir Khan, launched a major military campaign toward the west. Accordingly, scholars assume that he had successfully conquered Khotan before 1006 but not too much before.[87] Mahmud al-Kashgari (d. 1102) wrote a famous poem about the conquest of Khotan:

> We came down on them like a flood,
> We went out among their cities,
> We tore down the idol-temples,
> We shat on the Buddha's head![88]

Waves of panic spread eastward. Cave 17 in Dunhuang does not record the fall of Khotan, possibly because, as Professor Rong Xinjiang of Peking University speculates, the news of the destruction of the Buddhist buildings in Khotan prompted the sealing of the library cave, which included its rich Khotanese-language holdings.[89]

Overnight, Khotan stopped being Buddhist. The historical record is painfully scanty. We know that soon after Khotan's fall the Kitan ruler of the Liao dynasty gave a gift to the Dunhuang ruler of horses and "beautiful jade" that could only have come from the vanquished Khotan.[90] The next mention of Khotan is in Chinese records, which record a tribute mission from the Karakhanid-controlled Khotan in 1009.[91]

The sources, largely chronicles focusing on rulers, reveal very little about the impact of Islam on the new Karakhanid subjects. One exception is some documents in Arabic and Uighur that were "discovered under a tree in a garden outside Yarkand in 1911." Yarkand is about 100 miles (160 km) to the west of Khotan. These materials, like so many other documents found in the region, were sent for safekeeping to the British consul George Macartney. The group includes three contracts in Uighur and twelve in Arabic, five of which are written using the Uighur alphabet. Reflecting the transition from the Uighur to the Arabic alphabet, these materials date to the period between 1080 and 1135, about one hundred years after the Karakhanid conquest.

The contracts all concern the sale of land; the three legal judgments treat the appointment of a guardian, inheritance division, and land rights. The Karakhanid state, at least by 1100 and at least in Yarkand, implemented the rudiments of Islamic law. Legal officials knew enough Arabic to draft simple legal documents in Arabic and then to translate them into Uighur for the parties involved and the witnesses, some of whom signed in Arabic, some in Uighur.[92] Three of the Arabic documents explicitly state that the document was translated into a language known to the participants and read aloud to them. At the minimum, the legal officials of the Karakhanid state were familiar with Islamic law, but the effects of the state's conversion to Islam on ordinary people are still little known.[93]

While the Karakhanids may have converted to Islam, the other oasis kingdoms in the Western Regions did not. The Uighur rulers of Kucha and Turfan supported both Manichaeism and Buddhism in different periods; the Xixia, who controlled Ganzhou, Dunhuang, and the southern Silk Route east of Khotan, were also Buddhist.[94] This three-way division of Xinjiang continued in the twelfth-century, a period when Xinjiang nominally came under the rule of the Western Liao, a successor state to the Liao dynasty (907–1125) of north China. Under them, the Church of the East increased its influence throughout Xinjiang, particularly among the Kereit and Naiman tribes of the Mongols.[95]

Then in 1211 a Naiman leader named Küchlük took over the Western Liao. Originally an adherent of the Church of the East, Küchlük converted to Buddhism and became a ferocious opponent of Islam. He attacked both Kashgar and Khotan, forcing the inhabitants of both cities to renounce Islam and adopt either Christianity or Buddhism. But Küchlük was the last ruler in the region to ban Islam. In 1218 he was defeated by Chinggis Khan (Genghis Khan is the transliteration of the Persian spelling), who had unified the Mongols in 1206 and launched a series of stunning conquests. Chinggis rescinded Küchlük's religious policies.[96]

The Mongol conquests continued after Chinggis's death in 1227; by 1241 the Mongols had conquered much of Eurasia, creating the largest contiguous empire in world history. They pursued a policy of general religious tolerance, giving support to all holy men while privileging their own shamanistic traditions. During the period of Mongol unification, sometimes called Pax Mongolica, it became possible—for the first time in world history—to travel all the way from Europe to China, on the easternmost edge of the Mongol Empire. Many people made the trip, and some left records of their travels. Most travelers began at the Crimean Peninsula and crossed the vast ocean of unbroken grasslands all the way from Eurasia to modern Mongolia. They did not use the traditional Silk Road routes around the Taklamakan.

Curiously, Marco Polo was an exception. He claimed to have taken the southern Silk Road route through Khotan, and no one knows why he did not take the more traveled grasslands route. Marco left Venice in 1271 at the age of seventeen, traveling with two uncles. The Mongol Empire had broken into four sectors only ten years earlier. Each sector was ruled by one of Chinggis's sons. The Chaghatai Khanate stretched all the way from Turfan in the east to Bukhara in the west and included the territory of modern Xinjiang. In the company of his uncles, Polo visited Yarkand and Khotan, both in the Chaghatai Khanate, on his way to China:

> Let us turn next to the province of Yarkand, five days' journey in extent. The inhabitants follow the law of Muhammad, and there are also some Nestorian Christians. They are subject to the Great Khan's nephew, of whom I have already spoken. It is amply stocked with the means of life,

especially cotton. But since there is nothing here worth mentioning in our book, we shall pass on to Khotan, which lies towards the east-north-east.

Khotan is a province eight day's journey in extent, which is subject to the Great Khan. The inhabitants all worship Muhammad. It has cities and towns in plenty, of which the most splendid, and the capital of the kingdom, bears the same name as the province, Khotan. It is amply stocked with the means of life. Cotton grows here in plenty. It has vineyards, estates, and orchards in plenty. The people live by trade and industry; they are not at all war-like.[97]

These descriptions of Yarkand and Khotan typify Polo's narrative. Repetitive, and startlingly short of persuasive detail, they hardly read like an eyewitness account. Polo then describes a place called Pem, not yet identified by scholars. The entry repeats much of the same information as that for Khotan, with one significant addition about jade:

Passing on from here, we come to the province of Pem, five days' journey in extent, towards the east-north-east. Here too the inhabitants worship Muhammad and are subject to the Great Khan. It has villages and towns in plenty. The most splendid city and the capital of the province is called Pem. There are rivers here in which are found stones called jasper and chalcedony in plenty. There is no lack of the means of life. Cotton is plentiful. The inhabitants live by trade and industry.

It certainly seems as though Polo's information is incorrect: the information he gives for Pem all fits Khotan. But his Pem could be Phema, an ancient name for Keriya, the oasis between Khotan and Niya.[98] Polo's description of Pem continues:

The following custom is prevalent among them. When a woman's husband leaves her to go on a journey of more than twenty days, then, as soon as he has left, she takes another husband.

Historians have debated the veracity of Polo's account for centuries; generally speaking, historians of China have more reservations about Polo, perhaps because they have access to so many other sources, than do historians of the Mongols, who heatedly argue for the reliability of Polo's account on the basis of his insider knowledge of Yuan-dynasty court politics.[99] Everyone concurs that medieval travel accounts often contain descriptions of places—like Khotan and

Pem—that their authors never actually visited. Medieval readers did not expect Polo to have direct knowledge of each place he mentioned.

Merchants, like Polo and his uncles, provided a crucial service for the Mongols. Because they were businessmen, they knew how to convert the vast holdings of gold, silver, and other plundered goods taken in battle, and find creative ways to exchange these assets for things the Mongols really wanted, like textiles. The Mongols lent vast sums of silver to groups of merchants with whom they formed partnerships; the merchants used this money to purchase wares. These merchants were predominantly Central Asian Muslims but also included Syrians, Armenians, and Jews. Polo and his uncles may have entered into a similar implicit partnership agreement.[100] These partnerships were new and unlike anything during earlier Chinese dynasties.

In the 1300s the Mongol Empire began to unravel, with the different sectors becoming independent of each other. Although the Yuan-dynasty emperors in China did not convert to Islam, the rulers of the three other sectors, including the Chagatai Khanate, did. In the early 1330s the first Muslim ruler of the Chagatai Khanate took the throne, and he encouraged his soldiers to convert to Islam. His subjects already included some Muslims; these measures increased their numbers.[101] The influence of Islam increased in Central Asia during the reign of Timur the Lame (Tamerlane, reigned 1370–1405), who was also a Muslim. In the late 1300s the descendents of the Chagatai Khanate rulers gained control of much of Xinjiang, while a native Chinese dynasty, the Ming, succeeded in pushing the Mongols out of central China back to their homeland in Mongolia. In the following centuries, the oases of modern Xinjiang continued to send tribute missions to the Ming court at Beijing. As late as 1400 Buddhism was still flourishing in Turfan, according to accounts from envoys.[102]

In 1602 one European, Bento de Goes, a Jesuit born in the Azores, grew a beard and allowed his hair to grow long. Disguised as a Persian merchant, he traveled all the way from India to China.[103] He adopted the name Abdullah Isai. Abdullah means "servant of God" in Arabic, while Isai is a Spanish version of the Arabic name Isa (Jesus). At his first stop, Kabul, he met the mother of the king of Khotan (also the sister of the king of Yarkand) who had been robbed and needed funds. De Goes sold some of his goods so that he could lend her six hundred pieces of gold interest free, and she promised to pay him back with Khotanese jade. The route west over the Pamirs to Yarkand was so fraught with danger that his caravan of five hundred men hired four hundred guards to protect them.

After arriving safely in Yarkand, de Goes proceeded to Khotan, where he was able to collect the jade due to him. Then he had to wait in Yarkand a full year for a caravan to Beijing. Caravans were hard to organize. In this case, the Chinese stipulated that the caravan could have only seventy-two merchants. The ruler of Yarkand sold the position of caravan leader to the highest bidder, who paid two hundred sacks of musk for the position, and the other seventy-one positions in the caravan went for less. When every spot was finally filled, the caravan set off along the northern route around the Taklamakan in the fall of 1604.

De Goes left the main caravan and visited Turfan, Hami, and Jiayuguan with two companions. Given permission to enter China, he arrived at Suzhou (modern Jiuquan in Gansu) on Christmas 1605. There he sent a letter to Matteo Ricci, who had been in Beijing since 1601, who dispatched a Christian convert to visit de Goes. On arrival, he confirmed what de Goes suspected: that the Cathay mentioned by earlier travelers was the same place as China. Eleven days after the disciple reached him, de Goes died in 1607.

De Goes's travel partners divided his property and apparently shredded his diary, leaving only a few sections which fellow Jesuits managed to salvage and send to Ricci. His account of the tribute trade is the most detailed that survives for the modern period. Few caravans traveled from Central Asia to China; those that did maintained the pretense that they were presenting tribute to the Ming emperor. Caravans at this time sought strength in numbers.

As few caravans entered Xinjiang during the 1600 and 1700s, hardly any travelers left the region during these centuries. A handful of Muslims based in Xinjiang and Gansu traveled to the Middle East, often to study with Sufi teachers; some of them performed the hajj and went to Mecca as well. In the 1600s a Sufi teacher from west of the Pamirs crossed into southern Xinjiang and Gansu, where he preached with great success. His son Khoja Afaq, born in Hami, continued his teaching and became extremely well known. In the 1700s his successors traveled to Yemen, where they studied with Naqshabandi teachers. On their return, they were unusually influential. They spoke with great authority, because so few Muslims had the chance to study outside of Xinjiang.[104] In time, the descendants of these Sufis became the Khoja rulers of Khotan and Yarkand, where they implemented Islamic law and their subjects prayed at mosques and abstained from eating pork. Under their influence, Xinjiang became fully Islamicized.

In 1759 the Manchu armies of the Qing dynasty defeated their last rival and gained control of the Western Regions.[105] The Qing government created the province of Xinjiang, which means "new territory." Delegating power to local headmen, Manchu officials used the Arabic alphabet to translate imperial edicts into Uighur. People living in Xinjiang were subject to different laws than those living in central China: while the Manchus required their Chinese subjects to shave their foreheads and tie their hair into queues, Muslims in Xinjiang were permitted to keep their own hairstyles. Only high-ranking Muslims could apply to the government for permission to wear the queue, which they associated with success.[106]

During the period of Qing control the economy improved. As in the Tang, there was a massive infusion of cash and textiles to support the army, trade links were revitalized, and merchants began to risk travel on longer trade routes. But in 1864 the Qing lost control of Xinjiang, when the province revolted, and in 1865 a strongman named Ya'qub Beg gained control of the region. Sensing an opportunity to gain a foothold, both Russia and Britain sent trade missions to Ya'qub Beg's realm, and their reports are remarkably optimistic. Although most of the goods for sale in markets were locally made, the British and Russian agents described a large potential market for foreign goods, particularly textiles and tea (which no longer came in from China). After Ya'qub Beg's death in 1877 the Chinese regained tenuous control.[107]

In the early 1900s, when Aurel Stein and other foreigners entered Xinjiang with travel documents issued by the Qing, they met many Chinese officials, some of whom actively helped them to excavate and remove antiquities from the region. With the revolution of 1911 and the collapse of the Qing dynasty, Xinjiang enjoyed de facto independence while remaining under control of Chinese warlords who paid lip service to Republican China. In the 1920s and 1930s Russia exerted influence over the various strongmen in power, and Northern Xinjiang was in effect a Soviet satellite under Turkic local leadership from 1945 to 1949. Except for rebellions in the early 1930s, southern Xinjiang, the region treated in this book, was under Chinese warlord rule until one leader recognized the rule of the Nationalists in 1944. In 1949 the warlord then in control shifted his allegiance from the Nationalists to the Chinese Communist Party, and Xinjiang joined the People's Republic of China.

Since 1949, Xinjiang's history has in many ways followed that of all of China. The early 1950s were relatively relaxed. The Great Leap Forward campaign of 1958 began a long period of collectivism, with limited freedom to practice religion. In 1976 the Cultural Revolution came to an end. Under Deng Xiaoping, the Communist Party granted more economic and religious freedoms to Chinese citizens, including those living in Xinjiang. After nearly three decades of economic growth there are still tensions between the Uighurs and the Han Chinese population—and occasional outbreaks of violence like those in the summers of 2009 and 2011. All of the interior regions, including Xinjiang, lag behind the booming coastal regions.

Khotan certainly feels less Chinese than other cities in Xinjiang. Few Chinese faces appear in a population that is 98 percent Uighur. Almost all of Khotan's taxi drivers and tour guides are native speakers of Uighur, the Turkic language introduced to the region in the ninth and tenth centuries that completely displaced the Khotanese language.

The memory of the Karakhanid conquest is still alive in today's Xinjiang, where modern Muslims gather at *mazar* shrines. While Islam does not have canonized saints, Muslims early on came to accept that certain individuals have an intimate relationship with God and may intercede with him on behalf of ordinary people.[108] At mazars, pilgrims read the Quran, offer sacrifices, and perform rituals. They also pray for healthy children, recovery from illness, or the well-being of their family members. One of the largest, and most visited, mazars is the tomb of Satuq Bughra Khan, the first Karakhanid ruler to convert to Islam. It is located less than an hour's drive from Kashgar in Atush (see color plate 16A).[109] Another important mazar, some two hours from Yengisar, the Ordam Padishah Mazar, is believed to be the tomb of his grandson.[110] Most likely it was built in the 1500s by a Sufi teacher.[111]

Even today, not everyone who would like to is able to go on the hajj: of the 12,700 pilgrims given permission in 2009 to travel to Mecca from China (out of a population of some twenty million Muslims), six hundred were from Khotan.[112] Those who cannot go on the hajj sometimes visit local mazars in a fixed sequence that takes the better part of a calendar year. The two best-known series are in Khotan and Kashgar, where mazars are dedicated to the lexicographer Mahmud of Kashgar, the Khoja rulers of Xinjiang, and their female relatives. Those participating in these observances sometimes refer to Khotan as the "holy land," a fitting name for the oasis given how early it adopted Islam.

Conclusion
The History of the Overland Routes through Central Asia

The Silk Road was one of the least traveled routes in human history and possibly not worth studying—if tonnage carried, traffic, or the number of travelers at any time were the sole measures of a given route's significance.

Yet the Silk Road changed history, largely because the people who managed to traverse part or all of the Silk Road planted their cultures like seeds of exotic species carried to distant lands. Thriving in their new homes, they mixed with the peoples already there and often assimilated with other groups who followed. Sites of sustained economic activity, these oasis towns were beacons enticing still others to cross over mountains and move through oceans of sand. While not much of a commercial route, the Silk Road was important historically—this network of routes became the planet's most famous cultural artery for the exchange between east and west of religions, art, languages, and new technologies.

Strictly speaking, the Silk Road refers to all the different overland routes leading west out of China through Central Asia to Syria and beyond. Nothing unusual in the landscape would catch the eye of someone flying overhead. The features delineating where the road went were not man-made but entirely natural—mountain passes, valleys, and springs of water in the desert. Not paved, the Silk Road was systematically mapped only in the twentieth century. No one living on these routes between 200 and 1000 CE, the peak period for the Chinese presence, ever said "the Silk Road." Recall that the term "Silk Road" did not exist before 1877, when the Baron Ferdinand von Richthofen first used it on a map (see color plate 2–3).

These routes date back to the very origins of humankind. Anyone who could walk was capable of going overland through Central Asia. In distant prehistoric times, populations migrated along these paths. The earliest surviving evidence of trade goods moving across regions comes around 1200 BCE, when jade traveled from Khotan to Anyang in Henan Province, where the Shang-dynasty

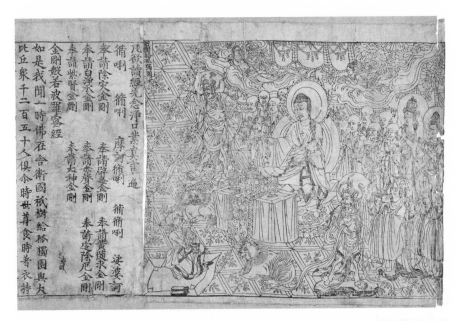

THE WORLD'S EARLIEST KNOWN PRINTED BOOK
Possibly the most famous of all Silk Road documents, the Diamond Sutra is the world's first intact printed book. It is a complete work on seven sheets of paper glued together to form a scroll. Note the gap between the opening illustration of the Buddha preaching and the second sheet of paper, which is all text. The closing dedication gives the date of carving the printing blocks as 868, about 150 years after the first woodblock printed texts appeared in East Asia. The desire to accumulate Buddhist merit was a major motivation for the development of printing. Courtesy of the Board of the British Library.

kings were buried north of the Yellow River. Contact among the different societies bordering central Asia—China, India, Iran—continued through the first millennium BCE.

In the second century BCE the rulers of the Han dynasty sent their first diplomat, a man named Zhang Qian, to the region. The Chinese hoped to negotiate an alliance against their enemy, the Xiongnu people, who lived in what is now Mongolia. The envoy noticed Chinese goods for sale in northern Afghanistan and reported their presence to the emperor on his return. Many books date the beginning of the Silk Road to Zhang Qian's trip. Remember that the emperor sent him for security concerns—not because he valued the trade, which he had not previously known about and which was small in scale. The Han dynasty subsequently dispatched armies to the northwest and stationed garrisons there, always to protect themselves from their enemies to the north. The soldiers in these Chinese garrisons had limited contact with the local populations. The first sustained interactions among the locals, migrants from India, and Chinese soldiers occurred at Niya and Loulan, which is where chapter 1 begins.

In each of the Silk Road communities discussed in this book—Niya, Lou-lan, Kucha, Turfan, Samarkand, Chang'an, Dunhuang, and Khotan—trade existed, but it was limited. In the third and fourth centuries, of nearly one thousand Kharoshthi documents found at Niya, only one mentions "merchants," who would be coming to the village from China when they could assess the price of silk. The few merchants who were traveling were closely monitored. Local officials issued them travel passes that listed each person and animal in the party and specified exactly which towns they could go to in which order. Chinese officials were not the only ones to supervise the trade; officials at Kucha did so as well. Governments played a major role as the purchasers of goods and services.

Markets existed in these different towns, but they offered far more local goods for sale than exotic imports. At one market in Turfan in 743, local officials recorded three prices (high, medium, low) for each of 350 different items, including typical Silk Road goods like ammonium chloride, aromatics, sugar, and brass. Shoppers could buy all kinds of locally grown vegetables and staples as well as animals, some brought over long distances. A wide array of textiles woven in central China and shipped to the northwest were on sale, because the central government used these textiles as money to pay its soldiers, and they in turn used them to obtain goods at the market.

The massive transfer of wealth from central China to the northwest, where many soldiers were stationed, accounted for the flourishing Silk Road trade when the Tang dynasty was at its strongest, before 755. Two shipments of silk in 745 to a garrison in Dunhuang totaled 15,000 bolts, and later encyclopedias report that, in the 730s and 740s, the Tang government sent 900,000 bolts of silk each year to four different headquarters in the frontier areas of the Western Regions—now modern Gansu and Xinjiang. Much larger in quantity than any documented private transaction, these continuing subsidies underpinned the region's prosperity. Almost immediately after the Turco-Sogdian general An Lushan (or Rokhshan, to use his Sogdian name) rose up in 755, when the Tang government cut off payments to the region, the Silk Road economy collapsed.

After 755, the region reverted to a subsistence trade very similar to that in earlier times. One merchant traveled a small circuit roughly 100 square miles (250 km) in area around Dunhuang. This peddler handled only locally produced goods, and his business consisted largely of exchanging one item for another. His report confirms the dearth of coins in the northwest after 800. This kind of low-level trade persisted long after the height of the Silk Road trade. In the early years of the twentieth century both Aurel Stein and Sven Hedin encountered itinerant traders just like this. These exchanges had little impact on the economic life of people living along the Silk Road. Those who worked the land continued to do so, and they did not purchase or produce the luxury goods for which the Silk Road is famous.

This book draws on many documents to show that the Silk Road trade was often local and small in scale. Even the most ardent believer in a high-volume, frequent trade must concede that there is little empirical basis for the much-vaunted Silk Road trade. One might interpret the scraps of evidence differently than this book does, but there is no denying that the debates concern scraps—not massive bodies—of evidence.

Because each site is so distinct and preserves materials in different languages, most scholars work primarily on a single Silk Road site. Individually, they notice that their particular site preserves little direct evidence of the Silk Road trade, and they go to great lengths to explain why. This book demonstrates that this same silence about trade holds true for all the Silk Road sites that have produced documents.

The strongest proponents of trade may believe that more evidence lies still undiscovered under the surface of the ground. This point of view is impossible to refute: which of us can say what discoveries lie in the future? In the meantime, though, this book has taken a close, critical look at the evidence at hand, since that is the only way that understanding of the history and trade of the Silk Road will advance. Excavated evidence has received pride of place in this book because it is genuine and firsthand: generalizations about the trade pale in comparison to actual lists of taxes paid by merchants or travel passes granted to merchants on the road. Yes, the evidence is scant and often missing crucial sections. But it comes from a variety of findspots, making this picture of a local, small-scale trade more plausible.

Despite the limited trade, extensive cultural exchange between east and west—China and first South Asia, and later west Asia, especially Iran—did take place as various groups of people moved along the different land routes through Central Asia. Refugees, artists, craftsmen, missionaries, robbers, and envoys all made their way along these routes. Sometimes they resorted to trade, but that was not their primary purpose in traveling.

The most important and the most influential people moving along the Silk Road were refugees. Waves of immigrants brought technologies with them from their homeland and then practiced those skills in their new homes. The frequent migrations of people fleeing either war or political conflicts in their homelands meant that some technologies moved east, others west. The technologies for manufacturing paper and weaving silk were transported west out of China at the same time that the techniques for making glass entered China. Itinerant artists also moved along these routes, bringing sketchbooks and introducing motifs from their homelands.

The first migrants came from the Gandhara region in what is now Afghanistan and Pakistan to the Western Regions and settled in Niya. These Indian refugees introduced the Kharoshthi script and their writing technology, slotted wooden boards, to the indigenous peoples. They also brought their belief system, Buddhism, with them. Early Buddhist regulations prescribe celibacy for monks, but some of the Niya Buddhists married and had children. Living at home, they only visited monasteries to participate in major ceremonies.

The most prominent migrant community in western China by far was the Sogdians, whose homeland was in Samarkand and the surrounding towns of modern Uzbekistan. They formed settlements in almost every Chinese town, where Sogdian sabao headmen supervised the affairs of the local community. Some Sogdian migrants were merchants; they appear so often in fiction that a stereotype of the rich Sogdian merchant took shape.

One of the most detailed descriptions of the Silk Road trade comes from the eight Sogdian Ancient Letters preserved in an abandoned mailbag outside Dunhuang. The letters, which date to 313 or 314, mention specific commodities: wool and linen, musk, the lead-based cosmetic ceruse, pepper, silver, and possibly silk. The quantities are not large, ranging from 3.3 pounds (1.5 kg) to 88 pounds (40 kg), all consonant with a small-scale trade managed by caravaneers.

Caravans frequently moved along the various overland routes. In the third letter, a Sogdian woman named Miwnay reports that she had five different opportunities to leave Dunhuang, where she was stranded by her errant husband. To make ends meet, she ended up tending sheep alongside her daughter, and other Sogdians proved just as flexible in their choice of occupation after settling in China. They farmed the land, worked as craftsmen, practiced veterinary medicine, or served as soldiers.

The historic capital of Chang'an, now called Xi'an, is famous for its Silk Road art. Perhaps the most concentrated find is the Hejia Village hoard, which contains over a hundred beautiful gold and silver vessels combining Chinese and Western motifs. On close examination, many of these objects turn out to be locally manufactured, either by Sogdians in exile or by Chinese craftsmen who adopted Sogdian motifs. Only the jewels are indisputably imported: light and small, they would have been easy to transport overland.

Like other refugees, the Sogdians brought their religious beliefs with them to China. Some Sogdians gave up their original practices—like exposing the dead and then burying the bones in clay containers called ossuaries—and adopted certain Chinese funerary customs, like burying the dead in tombs with a slanting stairway leading down to an underground chamber. In Xi'an and other Chinese cities, archaeologists have unearthed tombs decorated with scenes of the Zoro-astrian afterlife. One held a bilingual epitaph for the deceased composed in both the Chinese and Sogdian languages.

Each community in the Western Regions hosted multiple migrant communities, many of whom continued the religious practices of their homes. Whereas refugees left their homelands because they had no choice, students of religion traveled to learn more and teachers settled in towns where they could attract students. Some of the most detailed travel accounts come from Chinese monks who traveled to India, both by land and by sea, to study Buddhist teachings. They vividly documented the risks of travel. In the early 400s, Faxian's Indian shipmates almost threw him overboard until they realized that only he could speak Chinese and determine where their ship had landed (hundreds of miles off course, as it turned out).

More than two centuries later, the monk Xuanzang crossed mountain passes where many of his companions perished from the cold, and he survived being robbed of all his possessions, even his clothing. He also encountered brigands so busy dividing up loot that they could not be bothered to steal anything from him. He is the rare traveler to say much about thieves. Police reports from Niya document the losses of a handful of refugees who carried pearls, mirrors, fine clothes of silk or wool, and silver ornaments, but do not identify the culprits. One wall painting at Dunhuang captures the palpable apprehension of merchants held up by an armed bandit—until the bodhisattva Guanyin intercedes to save them.

Buddhist missionaries like Xuanzang were among the most important translators. They worked out a system for transcribing unfamiliar terms in foreign languages, like Sanskrit, into Chinese that still remains in use today. Chinese absorbed some 35,000 new words, some technical Buddhist terms, some common everyday words. People who spoke different languages often encountered each other on the Silk Road. Some, like Kumarajiva, had learned multiple languages since childhood. Others had to learn foreign languages as adults, an even more painful process than it is today given how few language learning aids were available.

Surviving phrase books shed light on the identities of students and their reasons for learning languages. Used in monasteries throughout the first millennium, Sanskrit always attracted students, but so too did Khotanese, Chinese, and Tibetan. After 755, more Buddhist pilgrims traveled from Khotan and Tibet to Dunhuang and then onto Mount Wutai in Shanxi; some went in the opposite direction, going all the way to Nalanda, always an important center of Buddhist learning in India.

Some of these pilgrims traveled on their own, while others served as emissaries sent by one ruler to visit another. Envoys have left a clearer documentary footprint than any other itinerant group. These diplomats carried unusual gifts and letters from one ruler to another; at the same time they brought information about their home societies to their hosts and relayed what they learned on their travels to the rulers who dispatched them. Some were certainly spies.

The Xuanquan wooden slips from Dunhuang document the regular exchange of envoys between the Chinese and rulers to the west at the turn of the Common Era, and diplomats continued to travel in subsequent centuries. At the peak of the Silk Road, all the major powers exchanged emissaries. Chinese envoys traveled to Samarkand, and their Sogdian counterparts went in the opposite direction. The Afrasiab murals at Samarkand give pride of place to envoys, each laden with products from their native lands.

The envoy traffic continued even after the massive contraction of the Silk Road economy after 755. One delegation of seven Khotanese princes was unable to complete their trip because the ruler of Dunhuang would not allow them to leave, as travel had become so dangerous. The delegation's members resorted to impromptu exchanges of locally produced goods to cover their travel expenses, paying with bolts of silk or a sheep or even an antelope skin. Even the Khotanese princes resorted to selling jade to cover their travel expenses.

The documents about the princes' difficulties are among the forty thousand documents in multiple languages preserved in the library cave at Dunhuang, which was sealed sometime after 1002 and serves as a time capsule of Silk Road diversity. The Buddhist librarian-monks who saved the texts collected the teachings of their own religion, of course, but kept all scraps of paper in case they might prove useful in the future. They saved texts written in Sanskrit, Khotanese, Tibetan, Uighur, and Sogdian, and from the religions of Manichaeism, Zoroastrianism, Christianity, Judaism, and Buddhism. The Diamond Sutra is the most famous of all the writings from the library cave, because it is the world's earliest dated printed book, but other texts are arguably more unusual: think of the talisman made from a sheet of folded paper with excerpts in Hebrew from Psalms or the Manichaean hymns sung in Sogdian but written phonetically in Chinese characters. The entire cave embodies the tolerance of different religions that characterized Silk Road communities for nearly one thousand years.

The monks who sealed off the library cave did not record their reasons for doing so, but they knew of the war between the Buddhist allies of the Dunhuang ruler in Khotan and the Muslim Karakhanids. Even if the fall of Khotan in 1006 did not trigger the closing of the cave, it ushered in a new era for the region, which gradually converted to Islam. Over the following centuries each oasis became a self-contained Islamic state, and the very few men who went to Mecca on the hajj exercised great influence on their return. The European travelers who still managed to travel through the region—possibly Marco Polo, certainly

Bento de Goes—described homogenous, isolated communities very different from the cosmopolitan towns of earlier times.

When Sven Hedin made his first foray into the Taklamakan in 1895, he entered a remote world utterly unknown to Europeans. Thanks to the region's dry climate, Hedin, Aurel Stein, and others were able to recover multiple documents and artifacts from before the coming of Islam. Those same conditions of preservation draw visitors today who hope to catch a glimpse of the latest discoveries from this now lost, once tolerant world.

Notes

INTRODUCTION

1. Jonathan M. Bloom, "Silk Road or Paper Road?" *Silk Road* 3, no. 2 (December 2005): 21–26, available online at http://www.silk-road.com/newsletter/vol3num2/5_bloom.php.

2. Jonathan M. Bloom, *Paper before Print: The History and Impact of Paper in the Islamic World* (New Haven, CT: Yale University Press, 2001), 1.

3. Wang Binghua, *Xiyu kaogu lishi lunji* [Collected essays on the archeology and history of the Western Regions] (Beijing: Renmin Daxue Chubanshe, 2008), 1–54.

4. Ferdinand von Richthofen used a red line to draw the main route (based on Ptolemy and Marinus) and blue lines for the information from Chinese geographers. The map appears facing p. 500 in vol. 1 of Richthofen, *China: Ergebnisse eigener Reisen und darauf gegründeter Studien* (Berlin: D. Reimer, 1877).

5. Tamara Chin gave a presentation entitled "The Invention of the Silk Road, 1877" at Yale on February 21, 2008, and plans to publish her findings in the future. See also Daniel C. Waugh, "Richthofen's 'Silk Roads': Toward the Archaeology of a Concept," *Silk Road* 5, no. 1 (Summer 2007): 1–10, available online at http://www.silk-road.com/newsletter/vol5num1/srjournal_v5n1.pdf.

6. *Times of London*, December 24, 30, 1948; Tamara Chin, personal communication, September 6, 2011.

7. Peter C. Perdue, *China Marches West: The Qing Conquest of Central Eurasia* (Cambridge, MA: Belknap Press of Harvard University Press, 2005).

8. Charles Blackmore, *Crossing the Desert of Death: Through the Fearsome Taklamakan* (London: John Murray, 2000), 59, 61, 64, 104, caption to fig. 14.

9. Peter Hopkirk, *Foreign Devils on the Silk Road: The Search for Lost Cities and Treasures of Chinese Central Asia* (Amherst: University of Massachusetts Press, 1984), 45–46; Rudolf Hoernle, "Remarks on Birch Bark MS," *Proceedings of the Asiatic Society of Bengal* (April 1891): 54–65.

10. Sven Hedin, *My Life as an Explorer*, trans. Alfhild Huebsch (New York: Kodansha, 1996), 177.

11. Hedin, *My Life*, 188.

12. Jeannette Mirsky, *Sir Aurel Stein: Archaeological Explorer* (Chicago: University of Chicago Press, 1977), 70 (Ernst's letter with the clipping), 79–83 (Stein's application for funding).

13. Wang Binghua, "'Sichou zhi lu' de kaituo ji fazhan" [The opening and development of the "Silk Road"], in *Sichou zhi lu kaogu yanjiu* [Studies on the archeology of the Silk Road] (Urumqi, China: Xinjiang Renmin Chubanshe, 1993), 2–5; E. E. Kuzmina emphasizes the contacts between Xinjiang and the Semirech'e region of modern-day Kazakhstan in her book *The Prehistory of the Silk Road*, ed. Victor H. Mair (Philadelphia: University of Pennsylvania Press, 2008), 119.

14. J. P. Mallory and Victor H. Mair, *Tarim Mummies: Ancient China and the Mystery of the Earliest Peoples from the West* (New York: Thames & Hudson, 2000), 179–81.

15. J. P. Mallory and D. Q. Adams, *The Oxford Introduction to Proto-Indo-European and the Proto-Indo-European World* (New York: Oxford University Press, 2006), 460–63.

16. Elizabeth Wayland Barber, *Mummies of Ürümchi* (New York: W. W. Norton, 1999).

17. I have written about the Xiaohe site in an earlier publication that contains some errors. Most regrettably, I give the wrong date for the occupation of the site: the correct date is between 2000 and 1800 BCE. "Religious Life in a Silk Road Community: Niya during the Third and Fourth Centuries," in *Religion and Chinese Society*, ed. John Lagerwey (Hong Kong: Chinese University Press, 2004), 1:279–315. Xinjiang Wenwu Kaogu Yanjiusuo, "2000 nian Xiaohe mudi kaogu diaocha yu fajue baogao" [Report on the archeological investigation and excavation at Xiaohe cemetery for the year 2002], *Xinjiang Wenwu* 2003, no. 2: 8–46; Victor H. Mair, "The Rediscovery and Complete Excavation of Ördek's Necropolis," *Journal of Indo-European Studies* 34, nos. 3–4 (2006): 273–318.

18. Sergei I. Rudenko, *Frozen Tombs of Siberia: The Pazyryk Burials of Iron Age Horsemen*, trans. M. W. Thompson (Berkeley: University of California Press, 1970), 115, fig. 55 (bronze mirror); plate 178 (embroidered phoenix on silk).

19. Wang Binghua, "'Sichou zhi lu' de kaituo ji fazhan," 4; site report for Alagou, *Wenwu* 1981, no. 1: 17–22; the silk is shown in Xinjiang Wenwu Ju, ed., *Xinjiang wenwu guji daguan* [A survey of artifacts and ruins in Xinjiang] (Urumqi, China: Xinjiang Renmin Chubanshe, 1999), 165, fig. 0427.

20. The earliest account of Zhang Qian's trip occurs in Sima Qian, *Shiji* [The records of the grand historian] (Beijing: Zhonghua Shuju, 1972), ch. 123; and in Ban Gu, *Han shu* [Official history of the Han dynasty] (Beijing: Zhonghua Shuju, 1962), 61:2687–98. This book cites the punctuated edition of all the official histories published by Zhonghua Shuju in Beijing, which are available online at the Scripta Sinica site maintained by the Academia Sinica of Taiwan: http://hanchi.ihp.sinica.edu.tw/ihp/hanji.htm. A. F. P. Hulsewé explains that the *Shiji* account was probably lost and later reconstructed on the basis of the later *Han shu* account. See his *China in Central Asia: The Early Stage, 125 B.C.–A.D. 23; An Annotated Translation of Chapters 61 and 96 of the History of the Former Han Dynasty* (Leiden: E. J. Brill, 1979), 15–25. He translates the *Han shu* biography of Zhang Qian on pp. 207–38.

21. Helen Wang, *Money on the Silk Road: The Evidence from Eastern Central Asia to c. AD 800* (London: British Museum Press, 2004), 47–56.

22. Discovered in 1987 and excavated in 1990 and 1991, Xuanquan has produced many documents, of which only a small selection have been published to date. See Gansu Sheng Wenwu Kaogu Yanjiusuo, "Gansu Dunhuang Handai Xuanquan zhi yizhi fajue jianbao" [A preliminary excavation report from the ruin of the Han-dynasty office at Xuan-quan, Dunhuang, Gansu], *Wenwu* 2000, no. 5: 4–45, 5 (map of the site's exact location), 11 (the number of bamboo slips).

23. He Shuangquan, *Shuangyu lantang wenji* [Collected papers from the Double Jade Orchid Studio] (Taibei: Lantai Chubanshe, 2001), 30.

24. Joseph Needham, ed., *Science and Civilisation in China*, vol. 5, part 1, *Paper and Printing*, by Tsien Tsuen-hsuin (Cambridge, UK: Cambridge University Press, 1985), 40; *Han shu* 97b: 3991.

25. Nicola Di Cosmo, "Ancient City-States of the Tarim Basin," in *A Comparative Study of Thirty City-State Cultures*, ed. Mogens Herman Hansen (Copenhagen: Kongelige Danske Videnskabernes Selskab, 2000), 393–409.

26. Hu Pingsheng and Zhang Defang, eds., *Dunhuang Xuanquan Hanjian shicui* [Selected explanations of the Han-dynasty bamboo slips found at Xuanquan, Dunhuang] (Shanghai: Shanghai Guji Chubanshe, 2001), 110.

27. Wang Su, "Xuanquan Hanjian suojian Kangju shiliao kaoshi" [An examination of the materials from the Xuanquan Han-dynasty bamboo slips concerning Sogdiana], in *Zhongwai guanxi shi: Xin shiliao yu xin wenti* [A history of China's relations with foreign countries: new materials and new sources], ed. Rong Xinjiang and Li Xiaocong (Beijing : Kexue Chubanshe, 2004), 150, transcribing and explicating Xuanquan document # II90DXT0213 ⑧:6A.

28. Lothar von Falkenhausen, "The E Jun Qi Metal Tallies: Inscribed Texts and Ritual Contexts," in *Text and Ritual in Early China*, ed. Martin Kern (Seattle: University of Washington Press, 2005), 79–123; Cheng Xilin, *Tangdai guosuo yanjiu* [A study of travel pass documents in the Tang dynasty] (Beijing: Zhonghua Shuju, 2002), 2.

29. Hu and Zhang, *Dunhuang Xuanquan*, 77–80, document # I 0112 ⑧: 113–31.

30. Wang Su, "Xuanquan Hanjian suojian Kangju," 155–58.

31. The record appears in Fan Ye, *Hou Han shu* [Official history of the Later Han], (Beijing: Zhonghua Shuju, 1965), 118:2920. Manfred G. Raschke, "New Studies in Roman Commerce with the East," in *Aufstieg und Niedergang der römische Welt: Geschichte und Kultur Roms im Spiegel der neueren Forschung*, vol. 2, part 9.2, ed. Hildegard Temporini (Berlin: Walter de Gruyter, 1978), 853–855nn848–850, discusses the many doubts scholars have about this record.

32. Raschke, "New Studies in Roman Commerce," 604–1361. For his reasons why he believes that Periplus must have been written before 70 CE, see 755n478.

33. Lionel Casson, *The Periplus Maris Erythraei: Text with Introduction, Transla-tion, and Commentary* (Princeton, NJ: Princeton University Press, 1989), 91.

34. Étienne de la Vaissière, "The Triple System of Orography in Ptolemy's Xinjiang," in *Exegisti Monumenta: Festschrift in Honour of Nicholas Sims-Williams*, ed. Werner Sun-dermann, Almut Hintze, and François de Blois (Wiesbaden, Germany: Harrassowitz, 2009), 527–35.

35. I visited the Hangzhou Silk Museum on June 12, 2006, and saw this fragment of silk from Yingyang Qingtai village in Henan province.

36. The most thorough study of Chinese textiles in English is Joseph Needham, ed., *Science and Civilisation in China*, vol. 5, part 9, *Textile Technology: Spinning and Reeling*, by Dieter Kuhn (Cambridge, UK: Cambridge University Press, 1988), 272.

37. Pliny the Elder, *The Natural History of Pliny*, trans. John Bostock and H. T. Riley (London: H. G. Bohn, 1855–57), 6.20 (Seres and Roman women wearing silk and opposition to various imported goods); 6.26 (export of coins to India); 11.26–27 (Coan silk). Available online at http://www.perseus.tufts.edu/hopper/text?doc=Perseus%3atext%3a1999.02.0137

38. I. L. Good, J. M. Kenoyer, and R. H. Meadow, "New Evidence for Early Silk in the Indus Civilization," *Archaeometry* 51, no. 3 (2009): 457–66.

39. Irene Good, "On the Question of Silk in Pre-Han Eurasia," *Antiquity* 69 (1995): 959–68.

40. Lothar von Falkenhausen, "Die Seiden mit Chinesischen Inschriften," in *Die Textilien aus Palmyra: Neue und alte Funde*, ed. Andreas Schmidt-Colinet, Annemarie Stauffer, and Khaled Al-As'ad (Mainz, Germany: Philipp von Zabern, 2000); reviewed by Victor H. Mair, *Bibliotheca Orientalis* 58, nos. 3–4 (2001): 467–70. On the basis of parallels with excavated Chinese textiles, von Falkenhausen dates catalog item no. 521 to between 50 and 150 CE. Catalog item no. 521 was found in a tomb dated to 40 CE, making it one of the earliest dated silks found in the West. Both textiles must have been made before 273, when Palmyra fell to the Sasanians. See also von Falkenhausen's "Inconsequential Incomprehensions: Some Instances of Chinese Writing in Alien Contexts," *Res* 35 (1999): 42–69, esp. 44–52.

41. Anna Maria Muthesius, "The Impact of the Mediterranean Silk Trade on Western Europe Before 1200 A.D.," in *Textiles in Trade: Proceedings of the Textile Society of America Biennial Symposium, September 14–16, 1990, Washington, D.C.* (Los Angeles: Textile Society of America, 1990), 126–35, with the mention of a single Chinese textile from a reliquary in the Basilica of Saint Servatius, Maastricht, the Netherlands, 129; Xinru Liu, *Silk and Religion: An Exploration of Material Life and the Thought of People, AD 600–1200* (Delhi: Oxford University Press, 1996), 8.

42. Pliny, *Natural History*, 6.20.

43. Trevor Murphy, *Pliny the Elder's Natural History: The Empire in the Encyclopedia* (Oxford: Oxford University Press, 2004), 96–99 (luxuries), 108–10 (Seres).

44. Luo Feng, *Hu Han zhi jian—"Sichou zhi lu" yu Xibei lishi kaogu* [Between non-Chinese and Chinese—"The Silk Road" and the archeology and history of the Northwest] (Beijing: Wenwu Chubanshe, 2004), chart of gold coins found in China on pp. 117–20.

45. Vimala Begley, "Arikamedu Reconsidered," *American Journal of Archaeology* 87, no. 4 (1983): 461–81, esp. n82.

46. Raschke doubts that anyone in Rome collected this type of statistic; he believes Pliny is exaggerating on moralistic grounds ("New Studies in Roman Commerce," 634–35): "Thus, both Roman bureaucratic practice and the surviving records from Egypt itself indicate that it would have been impossible for the Elder Pliny to obtain any accurate figures for the annual quantity of the balance of payments deficit in Rome's trade with the East" (p. 636). See also Hsing I-tien's review of Raschke's book in *Hanxue Yanjiu* 3, no. 1 (1985): 331–41, and of its sequel in *Hanxue Yanjiu* 15, no. 1 (1997): 1–31, where Hsing expresses deep skepticism about the extent of Roman-Chinese trade.

47. Qi Dongfang, personal communication, June 2006. One important exception has been studied by Anthony J. Barbieri-Low, "Roman Themes in a Group of Eastern Han Lacquer Vessels," *Orientations* 32, no. 5 (2001): 52–58.

48. Wu Zhen, "'Hu' Non-Chinese as They Appear in the Materials from the Astana Graveyard at Turfan," *Sino-Platonic Papers* 119 (Summer 2002): 1–21.

CHAPTER 1

I have previously published two papers on Niya: "Religious Life in a Silk Road Community: Niya During the Third and Fourth Centuries," in *Religion and Chinese Society*, ed. John Lagerwey (Hong Kong: Chinese University Press, 2004), 1:279–315; "The Place of Coins and Their Alternatives in the Silk Road Trade," in *Sichou zhilu guguo qianbi ji silu wenhua guoji xueshu taolunhui wenji* [Collected papers from the international conference on the Silk Road: Ancient Chinese money and the culture of the Silk Road], ed. Shanghai Bowuguan (Shanghai: Shanghai Shuhua Chubanshe, 2011), 83–113.

1. My discussion of the Stein excavation at Niya throughout this chapter draws on M. Aurel Stein, *Ancient Khotan: Detailed Report of Archaeological Explorations in Chinese Turkestan* (Oxford: Clarendon, 1907), 1:310–15; 2:316–85.

2. Aurel Stein, *On Central-Asian Tracks: Brief Narrative of Three Expeditions in Innermost Asia and North-Western China* (London: Macmillan, 1933), 1–2; Valéria Escauriaza-Lopez, "Aurel Stein's Methods and Aims in Archaeology on the Silk Road," in *Sir Aurel Stein, Colleagues and Collections*, ed. Helen Wang, British Museum Research Publication 184 (London: British Museum, forthcoming).

3. This river is also known as the Konche-daria or Qum-darya.

4. The Sino-Japanese expedition has published two reports: the first, *Zhong Ri Ri Zhong gongtong Niya yiji xueshu diaocha baogao shu* [The report of the Sino-Japanese Japanese-Chinese joint scholarly investigation into the Niya site] (Urumqi, China: Wei-wuer Zhizhiqu Wenwuju, 1996), covers the excavations of 1988–1993, while the years 1994–1997 are covered by the three volumes of second report, with the same title, published in 1999. I am grateful to Lin Meicun for carrying a set of these books to New Haven.

Earlier expeditions to the Lop Nor region include those led by the Russian Prejavalsky in 1876–77, the American geography professor from Yale Ellsworth Huntington in 1906, the Japanese Count Ōtani in 1908–11, Aurel Stein in 1914, Huang Wenbi in 1930 and 1934, the Xinjiang Archaeological Institute in 1959 and again in 1980–81, and the joint Sino-Japanese team who excavated from 1988 to 1997. For a historical survey, see Wang Binghua, "Niya kaogu bainian" [One hundred years of Niya archeology], in *Xiyu kaocha yu yanjiu xubian* [Continuation of investigations and researches about the western regions] (Urumqi, China: Xinjiang Renmin Chubanshe, 1998), 161–86.

5. Jean Bowie Shor, *After You, Marco Polo* (New York: McGraw-Hill, 1955), 172; John R. Shroder, Jr., Rebecca A. Scheppy, and Michael P. Bishop, "Denudation of Small Alpine Basins, Nanga Parbat Himalaya, Pakistan," *Arctic, Antarctic, and Alpine Research* 31, no. 2 (1999): 121–27.

6. Jason Neelis, "*La Vieille Route* Reconsidered: Alternative Paths for Early Transmission of Buddhism Beyond the Borderlands of South Asia," *Bulletin of the Asia Institute* 16 (2002): 143–64.

7. *Antiquities of Northern Pakistan: Reports and Studies*, vol. 1, *Rock Inscriptions in the Indus Valley*, ed. Karl Jettmar (Mainz, Germany: Verlag Philipp von Zabern, 1989).

8. Richard Salomon, *Indian Epigraphy: A Guide to the Study of Inscriptions in Sanskrit, Prakrit, and the Other Indo-Aryan Languages* (New York: Oxford University Press, 1998), 42–56.

9. Richard Salomon, "New Manuscript Sources for the Study of Gandhāran Buddhism," in *Gandhāran Buddhism: Archaeology, Art, and Texts*, ed. Pia Brancaccio and Kurt Behrendt (Vancouver: UBC Press, 2006), 135–47. For more about the early history of

Buddhist schools in this region, see Charles Willemen, Bart Dessein, and Collett Cox, eds., *Sarvāstivāda Buddhist Scholasticism* (Leiden, the Netherlands: Brill, 1998).

10. See charts of formulae in Neelis, "Long-Distance Trade," 323–26.

11. Jettmar, *Antiquities of Northern Pakistan*, 1:407.

12. *Corpus Inscriptionum Iranicarum*, part 2, *Inscriptions of the Seleucid and Parthian Periods and of Eastern Iran and Central Asia*, vol. 3, *Sogdian*, section 2, *Sogdian and Other Iranian Inscriptions of the Upper Indus*, by Nicholas Sims-Williams (London: Corpus Inscriptionum Iranicarum and School of Oriental and African Studies, 1989), 23, Shatial I inscription 254, with parentheses dropped to improve clarity of reading. The original translation of Nicholas Sims-Williams has been changed to reflect Yoshida Yutaka's emendation of the text to mention Tashkurgan. See Étienne de la Vaissière, *Sogdian Traders: A History*, trans. James Ward (Boston: Brill, 2005), 81n42.

13. Karl Jettmar, "Hebrew Inscriptions in the Western Himalayas," in *Orientalia: Iosephi Tucci Memoriae Dicata*, ed. G. Gnoli and L. Lanciotti, vol. 2 (Rome: Istituto Italiano per il Medio ed Estremo Oriente, 1987), 667–70, Plate 1.

14. C. P. Skrine gives a vivid description of his own journey over the pass in 1922. See his *Chinese Central Asia* (London: Methuen, 1926), 4–6.

15. On the basis of the Rabatak inscription in Afghanistan, Joe Cribb and Nicholas Sims-Williams proposed a new chronology for the Kushans in which Kanishka's reign started either in 100 or 120 CE. "A New Bactrian Inscription of Kanishka the Great," *Silk Road Art and Archaeology* 4 (1995–96): 75–142. Analyzing an astronomical manual, Harry Falk proposed the specific date of 127 as the start date for Kanishka's reign: "The Yuga of Sphujiddhvaja and the Era of the Kuṣāṇas," *Silk Road Art and Archaeology* 7 (2001): 121–36. While Falk's dating has not received universal acceptance, many in the field concur that Kanishka's reign probably started between 120 and 125. Osmund Bopearachchi proposes a start date for Kushan rule circa 40 CE in "New Numismatic Evidence on the Chronology of Late Indo-Greeks and Early Kushans," in Shanghai Bowuguan, *Sichou zhilu guguo qianbi*, 259–83.

16. See the chart of the standard histories, their compilers, and dates of compilation or publication in Endymion Wilkinson, *Chinese History: A Manual*, rev. ed. (Cambridge, MA: Harvard University Asia Center, 2000), 503–5.

17. Lin Meicun, "Kharoṣṭhī Bibliography: The Collections from China (1897–1993)," *Central Asiatic Journal* 40 (1996): 189. Prof. Lin translates the biography of Zhi Qian from the *Chu sanzang jiji*, in *Taishōshinshū Daizōkyō* (Tokyo: Taishō Shinshū Daizōkyō Kankōkai, 1962–90), text 2145, 55:97b.

18. Erik Zürcher, "The Yüeh-chih and Kaniṣka in Chinese Sources," in *Papers on the Date of Kaniska*, ed. A .L. Basham (Leiden: E .J. Brill, 1968), 370; Fan, *Hou Han shu*, 47:1580; Yu Taishan, *Liang Han Wei Jin Nanbei chao zhengshi Xiyu zhuan yaozhu* [Annotated selections from the treatise on the Western Regions in the official histories of the Han, Wei, Jin, and Southern and Northern dynasties] (Beijing: Zhonghua Shuju, 2005), 281n221. Because Yu's book provides a valuable supplement to the Zhonghua Shuju edition of the dynastic histories, the notes will often cite it as well.

19. One group, the so-called Greater Yuezhi, moved to northwest India, the official histories in Chinese maintain, while a smaller group, the Lesser Yuezhi, settled in southern Xinjiang, near Niya. Scholars in the field are sharply divided about the reliability and accuracy of this report. As the late John Brough noted,

The story may well be based on real happenings; but there is no independent evidence to enable us to judge how much of it is factual. As in later times, there must have been numerous ethnic groups in Central Asia, many of them nomadic; and it would obviously have been difficult, even a single generation later, to obtain trustworthy information. We should at least be ready to admit that the traditional story may, to a greater or lesser extent, be a theoretical construct, designed to explain the continuing presence of Yuezhi (distinguished as 'Lesser Yuezhi') in regions to the east of the Pamir.

"Comments on Third-Century Shan-shan and the History of Buddhism," *Bulletin of the School of Oriental and African Studies* 28 (1965): 585.

Earlier the Japanese historian Shiratori Kurakichi had noted in his history of the Sogdians: "It has been noticed how the old Chinese authors seem to have been addicted to the practice of tracing the origin of a foreign country to something native to their own country or some name found in their own literature." Shiratori gives several telling examples: the Chinese ascribed Chinese homelands for the Xiongnu, the Japanese, and even the people of the Great Qin, the realm on the western edge of the world, possibly corresponding to Rome. "A Study on Su-t'ê, or Sogdiana," *Memoirs of the Research Department of the Toyo Bunko* 2 (1928): 103.

Others, though, think the authors of the dynastic histories must have had some basis (now lost) for reaching these conclusions. François Thierry, "Yuezhi et Kouchans: Pièges et dangers des sources chinoises," in *Afghanistan: Ancien carrefour entre l'est et l'ouest*, ed. Osmund Bopearachchi and Marie-Françoise Boussac (Turnhout, Belgium: Brepols, 2005), 421–539.

Craig G .R. Benjamin surveys the evidence (the author does not read Chinese but is familiar with the extensive Russian-language literature about archeology) and notes that no archeological evidence indicates a migration out of Xinjiang and then back again. *The Yuezhi: Origin, Migration and the Conquest of Northern Bactria* (Turnhout, Belgium: Brepols, 2007). Anyone interested in this problem should start with Thierry's article and Benjamin's book, both of which survey the extensive secondary literature on this question.

20. For a brief description of Stein's Fourth Expedition, see Mirsky, *Sir Aurel Stein*, 466–69. Professor Wang Jiqing of Lanzhou University has thoroughly studied the photographs Stein took, his correspondence about the confiscated artifacts, and the significance of the artifacts. He has one article in English: "Photographs in the British Library of Documents and Manuscripts from Sir Aurel Stein's Fourth Central Asian Expedition," *British Library Journal* 24, no. 1 (Spring 1998): 23–74. It is a shorter version of his book *Sitanyin di sici Zhongguo kaogu riji kaoshi: Yingguo Niujin daxue cang Sitanyin di sici Zhongya kaocha lüxing riji shougao zhengli yanjiu baogao* [An examination of Stein's archeological diary in China on the Fourth Expedition: A study and reorganization of Stein's handwritten diary on the Fourth Expedition held by Oxford University] (Lanzhou, China: Gansu Jiaoyu Chubanshe, 2004).

21. Mirsky, *Sir Aurel Stein*, 469, citing Stein's letter of February 3, 1931, to Percy Stafford Allen in the Bodleian Library.

22. Enoki Kazuo, "Location of the Capital of Lou-lan and the Date of the Kharoṣṭhī Inscriptions," *Memoirs of the Research Department of the Toyo Bunko* 22 (1963): 129n12; Hulsewé, *China in Central Asia*, 10–11.

23. Ban, *Han shu*, 96A:3875–81; Yu Taishan, *Xiyu zhuan*, 79–93; translated in Hulsewé, *China in Central Asia*, 7–94.

24. The length of the *li* varied over time and space; during the Han dynasty, it was approximately 400 meters. *Cambridge History of China*, vol. 1, *The Ch'in and Han Empires, 221 B.C.–A.D. 220*, ed. Denis Twitchett and Michael Loewe (Cambridge, UK: Cambridge University Press, 1986), xxxviii, gives the length of the *li* as .415 km and notes, "In certain contexts, the term *li* is used rhetorically rather than as a precise indication of distance."

25. Hulsewé, *China in Central Asia*, 29. The characters cannot be read from the photograph in Stein's account. Chinese scholars read the seal as "zhao Shanshan wang"—the edict of the king of Shanshan. Meng Fanren, *Loulan Shanshan jiandu niandaixue yanjiu* [Studies and researches into the dates of bamboo slips and documents from Shanshan and Loulan] (Urumqi, China: Xinjiang Renmin Chubanshe, 1995), 261, no. 625, N.xv.345. Stein also found a seal that read "Shanshan junyin" (the seal of the Shanshan prefecture): *Ancient Khotan*, N.xxiv.iii.74.

26. Aurel Stein, *Serindia: Detailed Report of Explorations in Central Asia and Westernmost China* (Oxford: Clarendon, 1921), 1:219; 1:415 (Rapson's identification of Loulan as Kroraina); 1:217–81, 3: plate 9 (House 14); 1:227 (discovery by Rustam); 1:226 (size of house 24); 1:530 (painting at M5).

27. Brough, "Comments on Third-Century Shan-shan," 591–92.

28. Ban, *Han shu*, 96A:3878–79; Yu Taishan, *Xiyu zhuan*, 84–86; Hulsewé, *China in Central Asia*, 89–91; Brough, "Comments on Third-Century Shan-shan," 601.

29. Helen Wang, *Money on the Silk Road*, 25–26, alerted me to this find; Aurel Stein, *Innermost Asia: Detailed Report of Explorations in Central Asia, Kan-su and Eastern Irān* (Oxford: Clarendon, 1928), 287–92, describes it in detail.

30. Of the original 211 coins, fifty are now in London; they are dated between 86 to 1 BCE, putting the date of the earliest *wuzhu* coins in modern Xinjiang before the beginning of the Common Era. Helen Wang, *Money on the Silk Road*, 295–96.

31. Stein, *Innermost Asia*, 290.

32. Documents excavated from Juyan (Ejina Banner, Inner Mongolia, 90 km northeast of Jinta County, Gansu) and Shule (near Dunhuang and Jiuquan, Gansu) confirm the significant presence of the Chinese military during the Han dynasty. Documents recording large expenditures of over 100,000 coins date to between 140 BCE and 32 CE. Individual soldiers were paid in coin, and they made purchases, often of clothing, using coins advanced to them by the garrison. Helen Wang, *Money on the Silk Road*, 47–56, provides extensive, detailed analysis of these materials.

33. Mariner Ezra Padwa has analyzed each house at Niya: "An Archaic Fabric: Culture and Landscape in an Early Inner Asian Oasis (3rd–4th century C.E. Niya)" (Ph.D. diss., Harvard University, 2007).

34. The jade is called *langgan* and *meigui*. Unfortunately, the tags were not dated, but the characters were written so skillfully in clerical script that the great Sinologist Wang Guowei (1877–1927) believed that they had to date to sometime after 75 CE but before the end of the Han dynasty in 220 CE. *Guantang jilin* [Collected writings from the Guan studio] (Beijing: Zhonghua Shuju, 1959), 833–34.

Édouard Chavannes thought that they were contemporary with other materials from the site and dated them to the third and fourth centuries: *Les documents chinois découverts par Aurel Stein dans les sables de Turkestan oriental* (Oxford: Oxford University Press, 1913), 199–200. The most up-to-date transcription is in Meng Fanren, *Loulan Shanshan jiandu*, 269–71.

35. N.xiv.iii; Meng Fanren, *Loulan Shanshan jiandu*, 269, no. 668.

36. N.xiv.ii.6, N.xiv.ii.19, N.xiv.ii.12.8; discussed in Wang Jiqing, "Sitanyin di sici Zhongya kaocha suohuo Hanwen wenshu" [The Chinese-language documents Stein obtained on the Fourth Central Asia Expedition], *Dunhuang Tulufan Yanjiu 3* (1998): 286.

37. N.xiv.ii.1; discussed in Wang Jiqing, "Hanwen wenshu," 264.

38. Meng Fanren, *Loulan Shanshan jiandu*, 262, no. 627 (N.xv.109), no. 628 (N.xv.353), no. 629 (N.xv.314); 264, no. 639 (N.xv.152); discussed in Cheng Xilin, *Tang-dai guosuo yanjiu* [Research on the *guosuo* travel pass system of the Tang dynasty] (Beijing: Zhonghua Shuju, 2000), 39–44; Wang Binghua, *Jingjue chunqiu: Niya kaogu da faxian* [History of the Jingjue Kingdom: The great archeological discovery at Niya] (Shanghai: Zhejiang Wenyi Chubanshe, 2003), 101.

39. Stein, *Innermost Asia*, 288, 743. J .P. Mallory and Victor H. Mair's *Tarim Mummies* provides the best survey of these finds in English.

40. Xinjiang Weiwuer Zizhiqu Bowuguan Kaogudui, "Xinjiang Minfeng da shamo zhong de gudai yizhi" [Ancient remains in the Taklamakan Desert near Minfeng County [Niya Site], Xinjiang], *Kaogu* 1961, no. 3: 119–22, 126, plates 1–3. At the time, the Xinjiang Museum and Archaeological Institute—now two separate institutions—formed a single unit called the Xinjiang Museum Archaeological Team (Xinjiang Bowuguan Kaogudui).

41. Shown in Ma Chengyuan and Yue Feng, *Xinjiang Weiwuer zizhiqu Silu kaogu zhenpin/Archaeological Treasures of the Silk Road in Xinjiang Uygur Autonomous Region* (Shanghai: Shanghai Yiwen Chubanshe, 1998), 273, figure 62.

42. Éric Trombert, "Une trajectoire d'ouest en est sur la route de la soie: La diffusion du cotton dans l'Asie centrale sinisée," in *La Persia e l'Asia Centrale: Da Alessandro al X secolo* (Rome: Accademia Nazionale dei Lincei, 1996), 212nn25 and n27; Li Fang, ed., *Taiping yulan* [Imperially reviewed encyclopedia of the Taiping Tianguo reign] (Beijing: Zhongghua Shuju, 1960), 820:3652–53, entry for "baidie" (cotton).

43. The textile inscription in Chinese reads: "*yannian yishou yi zisun.*" The mirror reads: "*jun yi gaoguan.*" "1960 Xinjiang Minfeng xian bei da shamo zhong gu yizhi muzang qu Dong Han hezang mu qingli jianbao" [A brief report on the investigation of a joint Eastern Han burial in the burial ground of the ancient site in the middle of the great desert to the north of Minfeng county, Xinjiang], *Wenwu* 1960, no. 6: 9–12, plates 5–6.

44. The Chinese text reads "*wanghou hehun qianqiu wansui yi zisun.*" *Xinjiang wenwu guji daguan* [A survey of artifacts and ruins in Xinjiang] (Urumqi, China: Xinjiang Renmin Chubanshe, 1999), figure 0118. For further analysis of the textiles in tombs M3 and M8, see Wang Binghua, *Jingjue chunqiu*, 111–20.

45. Fan, *Hou Han shu*, 88:2909; Yu Taishan, *Xiyu zhuan*, 233.

46. When Stein excavated the Yingpan site on his Third Expedition, he found some Kharoshthi documents, indicating that the site was occupied in the third and fourth centuries (*Innermost Asia*, 749–61). For a more recent find of additional Kharoshthi materials, see Lin Meicun, "Xinjiang Yinpan gumu chutu de yifeng Quluwen shuxin" [A letter in Kharoṣṭhī unearthed in an ancient tomb at Yingpan in Xinjiang], *Xiyu Yanjiu* 2001, no. 3: 44–45.

47. Zhou Xuejun and Song Weimin, eds., *Silu kaogu zhenpin: Archaeological Treasures of the Silk Road in Xinjiang Uygur Autonomous Region* (Shanghai: Shanghai Yiwen Chubanshe, 1998), 63–74, figure 132 (photo of deceased), figure 133 (detail of face mask), figure 134 (detail of red textile).

48. Wang Binghua, personal communication, fall 2005; Ban, *Han shu*, 96B:3912; Yu Taishan, *Xiyu zhuan*, 201.

49. Hu Pingsheng, *Hu Pingsheng jiandu wenwu lunji* [Collected essays on letters and artifacts by Hu Pingsheng] (Taibei: Lantai Chubanshe, 2000), 190–92.

50. Hou Can and Yang Daixin, *Loulan Hanwen jianzhi wenshu jicheng* [Collected cut paper and documents in Chinese from Loulan] (Chengdu, China: Tiandi Chubanshe, 1999).

51. Itō Toshio, "Gi-Shinki Rōran tonju ni okeru kōeki katsudō o megutte" [A look at trading activities occurring in the military colony at Loulan during the Wei and Jin periods], in *Oda Yoshihisa hakushi kanreki kinen: Tōyōshi ronshū* (Kyoto: Ryūkoku Daigaku Tōyōshigaku Kenkyūkai, 1995), 4, 7.

52. Yü Ying-shih, "Han Foreign Relations," in Twichett and Loewe, *Cambridge History of China*, 1:405–42; Meng Chi, "Cong Xinjiang lishi wenwu kan Handai zai Xiyu de zhengzhi cuoshi he jingji jianshe" [Looking at Han-dynasty political measures and economic policies in the Western Regions on the basis of historical artifacts from Xinjiang], *Wenwu* 1975, no. 5: 27–34.

53. Itō Toshio, "Gi-Shinki Rōran tonju ni okeru suiri kaihatsu to nōgyō katsudō: Gi-Shinki Rōran tonju no kiso teki seiri (III)" [The development of irrigation and agricultural activity in the military colony at Loulan during the Wei and Jin periods: The basic running of the military colony at Loulan during the Wei and Jin periods, part 3], *Rekishi Kenkyū* 28 (1991): 20.

54. Stein, *Serindia*, 373–74, 432, 701 plate XXXVII.

55. Itō, "Gi-Shinki Rōran tonju," presents a careful transcription and study of all these documents.

56. "Sute hu Loulan," literally "Sogdian non-Chinese at Loulan." Chavannes, *Documents chinois*, 886; Hou Can and Yang Daixin, *Loulan Hanwen jianzhi wenshu*, 61–62.

57. The word for the animals is missing, but the measure word is *pi*, suggesting that the transaction involved horses. The word for the person making the payment is missing, and the identity of the people who receive the payment (*zhuren*) is not clear. While Meng Fanren and Duan Qing think it refers to merchants, Itō argues that the *zhuren* are the long-term Chinese residents of the garrison: "Gi-Shinki Rōran tonju," 4–5. The document has been published first by August Conrady in *Die chinesischen Handschriften- und sonstigen Kleinfunde Sven Hedins in Lou-lan* (Stockholm: Generalstabens Litografiska Anstalt, 1920), Document no. 46, 124–25; more recently by Hou and Yang, *Loulan Hanwen jianzhi wenshu*, 99.

58. Vaissière, *Sogdian Traders*, 58; explication of Endere camel purchase, 58.

59. See chart in Meng Fanren, "Loulan jiandu de niandai" [Dates of documents from Loulan], *Xinjiang Wenwu* 1 (1986): 33.

60. Itō, "Gi-Shinki Rōran tonju," 22–23.

61. Brough, "Comments on Third-Century Shan-shan," 596–602.

62. The Sino-Japanese expedition found evidence of a king Tomgraka, who ruled before the five kings previously known, and a king Sulica, who ruled after them, from

336–359. Lin Meicun, "Niya xin faxian de Shanshan wang Tonggeluoqie jinian wenshu kao" [A study of a newly discovered Niya document dated to the reign of King Toṃgraka], in *Xiyu kaocha yu yanjiu xubian* (Urumqi, China: Xinjiang Renmin Chubanshe, 1998), 39. Various scholars have debated the dates proposed by Brough, with some arguing that the award of the *shizhong* title occurred in a different year. Meng Fanren, the leading Xinjiang archeologist at the Institute of Archaeology in the Chinese Academy of Sciences, provides a chart of the five kings' reigns according to four different scholars (Brough, Enoki Kazuo, Nagasawa Kazutoshi, and Ma Yong). The earliest start date for the five reigns is 203; the latest 256. The earliest end date is 290; the latest is 343. Meng prefers 242–332. *Xinjiang kaogu yu shidi lunji* [Treatises on Xinjiang archeology, history, and geography] (Beijing: Kexue Chubanshe, 2000), 115, 117.

63. Thomas Burrow, "Tokharian Elements in Kharoṣṭhī Documents from Chinese Turkestan," *Journal of the Royal Asiatic Society* 1935: 666–75.

64. T. Burrow, *A Translation of the Kharoṣṭhī Documents from Chinese Turkestan* (London: The Royal Asiatic Society, 1940), no. 292, no. 358 (refugees as slaves). Burrow translates the Kharoshthi documents whose meaning he could discern; he omits fragments. Each document, including those not translated by Burrow, is transcribed in A. M. Boyer, E .J. Rapson, and E. Senart, *Kharoṣṭhī Inscriptions Discovered by Sir Aurel Stein in Chinese Turkestan*, 3 vols. (Oxford: Clarendon, 1920–29). Boyer et al. provide both the original identification number assigned by Stein as well as the new sequence numbers (1–764) used by Burrow; they also give the relevant page citation from Stein's site reports for the individual documents.

Boyer et al. also included six documents found by Ellsworth Huntington. Since then, the Sino-Japanese expedition found twenty-three more. They are transcribed and translated into Japanese by Hasuike Toshitaka in *Niya yiji xueshu diaocha* 1:281–338 2:161–76. Many of these documents are fragmentary and await translation into English.

65. Stein, *Central Asian Tracks*, 103–4.

66. Stein describes the discovery in *Serindia*, 1:225–35. The documents from this room are nos. 516–92 in Burrow, *Translation*.

67. Burrow no. 582. Akamatsu Akihiko, " Rōran Niya shutsudo Karoshuti bunsho ni tsuite" [On the Kharoṣṭhī Documents from Loulan and Niya], in *Ryūsa shutsudo no moji shiryō: Rōran-Niya bunsho o chūshin ni*, ed. Tomiya Itaru (Kyoto: Kyōto Daigaku Gakujutsu Shuppankai, 2001), 369–425, especially 391–93.

68. Burrow no. 581.

69. Pictured in Susan Whitfield and Ursula Sims-Williams, eds., *Silk Road: Trade, Travel, War, and Faith* (Chicago: Serindia, 2004), 150.

70. Burrow no. 1.

71. *Cozbo* is also spelled *cojhbo*. Because the Kroraina language does not have a letter for the Iranian "z," the Kharoshthi script uses a "j" with a superscript (transcribed by the Boyer and colleagues as jh) to write the letter. Almost certainly an Iranian word, cozbo is the most common official title appearing in the Niya documents with some forty different people bearing this title. T. Burrow, *The Language of the Kharoṣṭhī Documents from Chinese Turkestan* (Cambridge, UK: Cambridge University Press, 1937), 90–91. Christopher Atwood, "Life in Third-Fourth Century Cadh'ota: A Survey of Information Gathered from the Prakrit Documents Found North of Minfeng (Niya)," *Central Asiatic Journal* 35 (1991): 195–96, provides a very useful list of the cozbo by name and the document numbers

in which they appear. Atwood also points out that the title cozbo has three different mean-ings: "governor of a province," "a specific subordinate officer," and "a very vague sense meaning essentially official."

72. Akamatsu provides a very helpful description of five different types of documents (wedge-shaped [W], rectangular tablet [R], Takhti-shaped tablet [T], oblong tablet [O], document on leather [L], and other), photos of each type, and a persuasive analysis that links the terms used for various orders in the documents with actual surviving documents. He presents a wonderfully clear chart showing the document type for each Kharoshthi document found at Niya and Loulan and its findspot. "Karoshuti bunsho," 410–12.

73. Thomas R. Trautmann, *Kauṭilya and the Arthaśāstra: A Statistical Investigation of the Authorship and Evolution of the Text* (Leiden, the Netherlands: Brill, 1971).

74. Kautilya, *The Arthashastra*, ed. and trans. L .N. Rangarajan (New Delhi: Penguin Books India, 1992), 213–14, 380.

75. Hansen, "Religious Life in a Silk Road Community," 290–91.

76. Burrow no. 39, no. 45, no. 331, no. 415, no. 434, no. 592.

77. Burrow no. 569, and also no. 19, 54, 415, among many others.

78. Burrow no. 207; Atwood, "Life in Third–Fourth Century Cadh'ota," 167–69.

79. As Helen Wang explains, *muli* (from the Sanskrit *mūlya* "price" or "value") meant "price," and one *muli* was the equivalent of one *milima*, a unit of grain. See her detailed discussion of the different types of money used at Niya in *Money on the Silk Road*, 65–74.

80. Helen Wang, *Money on the Silk Road*, 37–38, citing Jiang Qixiang's articles in *Zhoushan Qianbi* 1990, no. 1: 6–11; 1990, no. 2: 3–10; 1990, no. 3: 8–13; 1990, no. 4: 3–11, calculates the world total of Sino-Kharoshthi coins at 352, of which 256 are in the British Museum. François Thierry, "Entre Iran et Chine, la circulation monétaire en Sérinde de Ier au IXe siècle," in *La Serinde, terre d'échanges: Art, religion commerce du Ier au Xe siècle*, ed. Jean-Pierre Drège (Paris: Documentation Française, 2000), 122–25, provides a very helpful overview of documents and coin finds in Khotan and Niya.

81. Burrow nos. 431–32.

82. Burrow no. 133. See also no. 177 and no. 494 for other transactions involving gold but not gold coins.

83. Burrow no. 324. Paul Pelliot accepts the suggestion of F .W. Thomas that the Supiye and Supiya in the Kharoshthi documents were the same people as the Sumpa people mentioned in the Tibetan documents of the seventh and eighth centuries. Pelliot, *Notes on Marco Polo*, vol. 2 (Paris: Imprimerie National, 1963), 712–18; Thomas, trans., *Tibetan Literary Texts and Documents Concerning Chinese* (London: Royal Asiatic Society, 1935), 9–10, 42, 156–59.

84. Burrow no. 494.

85. Burrow no. 255: the speaker hears about the availability of land "from the mouth of this Chinaman." Documents no. 686A and B record the receipt of runaway cows by Chinese.

86. Burrow no. 35.

87. Burrow no. 660.

88. Burrow no. 14. This list of places has fascinated and perplexed scholars of histor-ical geography for over a century, with almost everyone disagreeing about the location of Nina. See Heinrich Lüders, "Zu und aus den Kharoṣṭhī-Urkunden," *Acta Orientalia* 18

(1940): 15–49, discussion of place-names on 36. The authors of the first Sino-Japanese site report identify Nina as Uzun Tati: *Niya yiji xueshu diaocha*, 1:235–36, while Yoshida Yutaka proposes that Nina was the ancient name for the archeological site of Niya: *Kotan shutsudo no sezoku bunsho o megutte* [Notes on the Khotanese documents of the 8th–9th century Khotan] (Kobe, Japan: Kobe City University of Foreign Studies, 2005), 20.

89. See Burrow no. 136, no. 355, no. 358, no. 403, no. 471, no. 629, no. 632, no. 674. Translation emended following Stanley Insler, Edward E. Salisbury Professor Emeritus of Sanskrit and Comparative Philology, Yale University, personal communication, November 14, 2006: "The word in question is 'palayamna-' and is the participle to the verb palāyati 'runs away, flees, escapes.'. . . I see no problem with Burrow's 'fugitive,' although 'escapee,' or 'run-away' might be better."

90. Burrow no. 149. Heinrich Lüders, "Textilien im alten Turkistan," *Abhandlungen des Preussischen Akademie des Wissenschaften, Philosophisch-Historische Klasse 3* (1936): 1–38, discusses the etymology of many of the textile terms appearing in the Kharoshthi documents. Unfortunately, the discussion on 21–24 does not define *somstamni*. The term *māsa* has puzzled analysts, but Helen Wang, curator at the British Museum, makes the intriguing suggestion that it may denote Chinese *wuzhu* coins, which this runaway could have used for his travel expenses. See *Money on the Silk Road*, 68.

91. Burrow no. 566. See also no. 318 for another robbery report that lists different textiles subsequently stolen and recovered.

92. The word in the documents is *vaniye* (from the Sanskrit *vanij*). On August 17, 2008, Stefan Baums very kindly checked the database of the Early Buddhist Manuscripts Project (http://ebmp.org/p_abt.php) and found no other instances of the word.

93. Burrow no. 489.

94. Burrow no. 510, no. 511, no. 512, no. 523. Discussed in Hansen, "Religious Life in a Silk Road Community," 296–300.

95. Jonathan A. Silk, "What, if Anything, is Mahāyāna Buddhism? Problems of Definitions and Classifications," *Numen* 49, no. 4 (2002): 355–405.

96. Richard Salomon, "A Stone Inscription in Central Asian Gandhārī from Endere, Xinjiang," *Bulletin of the Asia Institute* 13 (1999): 1–13.

97. Corinne Debaine-Francfort and Abduressul Idriss, eds., *Kériya, mémoire d'un fleuve: Archéologie et civilisation des oasis du Taklamakan* (Suilly-la-Tour, France: Findakly, 2001).

98. Stein, *Serindia*, 1:485–547.

99. Wang Binghua, *Jingjue chunqiu*, 121.

100. Faxian, *Gaoseng Faxianzhuan*, in *Taishō shinshū Daizōkyō*, 51:857a, text 2085. Compare Samuel Beal, trans., *Si-yu-ki Buddhist Records of the Western World translated from the Chinese of Hiuen Tsiang (A.D. 629)* (1884; repr., Delhi: Motilal Banarsidass, 1981), xxiv. See Marylin Martin Rhie, *Early Buddhist Art of China and Central Asia*, vol. 1, *Later Han, Three Kingdoms, and Western Chin in China and Bactria to Shan-shan in Central Asia* (Leiden, The Netherlands: Brill, 1999), 354, for a discussion of Faxian's route.

101. The Japanese scholar Kuwayama Shōshin has worked extensively on the changes in the route between India and China; see his *Across the Hindukush of the First Millennium: A Collection of the Papers* (Kyoto: Institute for Research in Humanities, Kyoto University 2002); Enoki Kazuo, "Location of the Capital of Lou-lan," 125–71.

CHAPTER 2

Georges-Jean Pinault generously sent detailed comments on this chapter, and his doctoral student, Ching Chao-jung, very kindly critiqued an earlier version of this paper.

1. These are the conventional dates for Kumarajiva's life. In fact, the sources disagree so much that we do not know the year of his birth. See Yang Lu, "Narrative and Historicity in the Buddhist Biographies of Early Medieval China: The Case of Kumārajīva," *Asia Major*, 3rd ser., 17, no. 2 (2004): 1–43, particularly 28–29n64. This helpful article analyzes the major incidents in Kumarajiva's life as his three biographers recount them.

2. Hedin, *My Life as an Explorer*, 250–51. Hedin gives an even more detailed account of his trip in *Central Asia and Tibet: Towards the Holy City of Lassa* (New York: Charles Scribner, 1903), 63–102.

3. Hedin, *My Life as an Explorer*, 253, 261.

4. The Germans counted 235 at the beginning of the twentieth century, but surveys in recent years have uncovered additional caves. Zhao Li, *Qiuci shiku baiwen* [One hundred questions about Kizil Caves] (Urumqi, China: Xinjiang Meishu Sheying Chubanshe, 2003), 12.

5. Albert von Le Coq, *Buried Treasures of Chinese Turkestan* (1928; repr., Hong Kong: Oxford University Press, 1985), 129.

6. Carbon-dated to 320 CE ±80. *Zhongguo shiku: Kezier shiku* [The caves of China: The caves of Kizil] (Beijing: Wenwu Chubanshe, 1997), 1:210. Angela F. Howard provides a very helpful summary of the criteria the Peking University archeologist Su Bai developed to date the caves, which do not have dated inscriptions. See her "In Support of a New Chronology for the Kizil Mural Paintings," *Archives of Asian Art* 44 (1991): 68–83.

7. Xuanzang, *Da Tang Xiyu ji jiaozhu* [An annotated and punctuated edition of Records of the Western Region written during the Great Tang dynasty], ed. Ji Xianlin et al. (Beijing: Zhonghua Shuju, 1985), 61; Beal, *Si-yu-ki*, 21.

8. Le Coq, *Buried Treasures*, 127.

9. Paul Pelliot, the physician and cartographer Louis Vaillant, and the photographer Charles Nouette traveled from Kashgar to Xi'an in 1906–9. Louis Vaillant provides a detailed description of their trip, including the dates they stayed at each site and a map of their itinerary in his "Rapport sur les Travaux Géographiques faits par la Mission Archéologique d'Asie Centrale (Mission Paul Pelliot 1906–1909)," *Bulletin de la Section de Geographie du Comité des Travaux Historiques et Scientifiques* 68 (1955): 77–164.

10. Yu Taishan, *Xiyu zhuan*, 29; Sima, *Shiji* 123:3168–69.

11. Yu Taishan, *Xiyu zhuan*, 187–90; Ban, *Han shu*, 96B:3916–17.

12. Yu Taishan, *Xiyu zhuan*, 180; Ban, *Han shu* 96B:3911.

13. A stele dated 158 CE, found in the mountains near Baicheng, records the name and title of a Chinese general. Éric Trombert, with Ikeda On and Zhang Guangda, *Les manuscrits chinois de Koutcha: Fonds Pelliot de la Bibliothèque Nationale de France* (Paris: Institut des Hautes Études Chinoises du Collège de France, 2000), 10.

14. See the list of monasteries in Mariko Namba Walter, "Tokharian Buddhism in Kucha: Buddhism of Indo-European Centum Speakers in Chinese Turkestan before the 10th Century C.E.," *Sino-Platonic Papers* 85 (October 1998): 5–6. The Buddhist texts in Sanskrit found at Kucha are written in handwriting of the earliest period found in Central Asia and may date from even before the third century. Kuwayama Shōshin, ed., *Echō ō Gotenjikukoku den kenkyū* [Hyecho's "Record of Travels in Five Indic Regions,"

translation and commentary] (Kyoto: Kyōto Daigaku Jinbun Kagaku Kenkyūjo, 1992), 187n207.

15. Buddhist scholars debate the relationship of two Buddhist schools: the Sarvāstivādins and the Mūlasarvāstivādins, with which many fewer texts from Kucha are associated. See Ogihara Hirotoshi, "Researches about Vinaya-texts in Tocharian A and B" (Ph.D. diss., École Pratique des Hautes Études, 2009).

16. *Chu sanzang jiji* [Collected notes on the formation of the Tripiṭaka], text 2145, 79c–80a; Walter, "Tocharian Buddhism in Kucha," 8–9.

17. Silk, "What, if Anything, Is Mahāyāna Buddhism?" 355–405.

18. This was the Korean monk Hyecho, whose Chinese name was Huichao. *Wang Wutianzhu guo zhuan jianshi* [An annotated edition of Record of travels to India] (Beijing: Zhonghua Shuju, 2000), 159.

19. Li Fang, *Taiping yulan*, 125:604, citing *Shiliuguo chunqiu* [The spring and autumn annals of the Sixteen Dynasties]; Trombert, *Les manuscrits chinois de Koutcha*, 11.

20. Yang Lu, "Narrative and Historicity," 23–31.

21. John Kieschnick, *The Eminent Monk: Buddhist Ideals in Medieval Chinese Hagiography* (Honolulu: University of Hawai'i Press, 1997), 19; Bernard Faure, *The Red Thread: Buddhist Approaches to Sexuality* (Princeton, NJ: Princeton University Press, 1998), 26–27.

22. E. Zürcher, "Perspectives in the Study of Chinese Buddhism," *Journal of the Royal Asiatic Society* 2 (1982): 161–76.

23. *The Essential Lotus: Selections from the Lotus Sutra*, trans. Burton Watson (New York: Columbia University Press, 2002).

24. Daniel Boucher, *Bodhisattvas of the Forest and the Formation of the Mahāyāna: A Study and Translation of the Rāṣṭrapālaparipṛchhā-sūtra* (Honolulu: University of Hawai'i Press, 2008).

25. Edwin G. Pulleyblank, *Lexicon of Reconstructed Pronunciation in Early Middle Chinese, Late Middle Chinese and Early Mandarin* (Vancouver: University of British Columbia Press, 1991), 160, 203, 217, 283.

26. Victor H. Mair, "India and China: Observations on Cultural Borrowing," *Journal of the Asiatic Society* (Calcutta) 31, nos. 3–4 (1989): 61–94.

27. Victor H. Mair and Tsu-Lin Mei, "The Sanskrit Origins of Recent Style Prosody," *Harvard Journal of Asiatic Studies* 51, no. 2 (1991): 375–470, especially 392; Victor Mair, personal communication, September 7, 2011.

28. Douglas Q. Adams, *Tocharian Historical Phonology and Morphology* (New Haven, CT: American Oriental Society, 1988), 1.

29. Denis Sinor, "The Uighur Empire of Mongolia," in *Studies in Medieval Inner Asia* (Brookfield, VT: Ashgate, 1997), 1–5.

30. I have used /gh/ in "Twghry" where other scholars have used the Greek letter gamma (γ). Adams, *Tocharian*, 2, quotes the entire passage; Le Coq, *Buried Treasures*, 84, mentions the find. In 1974 forty-four additional leafs from this text were found in Yanqi: Ji Xianlin, trans., *Fragments of the Tocharian A Maitreyasamiti-Nataka of the Xinjiang Museum, China* (New York: Mouton de Gruyter, 1998).

31. Adams, *Tocharian*, 3.

32. Recently, François Thierry has reexamined and retranslated (into French) all the passages about the Yuezhi. After offering several variant readings of the characters for

Dunhuang and Qilian, he raises the possibility that prior to 175 BCE, when the Xiongnu allegedly drove them out, the Yuezhi populated the entire region between the Qilian Mountains and the Tianshan Mountain range (much of Gansu and all of Xinjiang) and not just the Qilian region near Dunhuang as the histories claim. Thierry, "Yuezhi et Kouchans," in *Afghanistan: Ancien carrefour*, 421–539.

33. Christopher I. Beckwith, *Empires of the Silk Road: A History of Central Eurasia from the Bronze Age to the Present* (Princeton, NJ: Princeton University Press, 2009), 380–83.

34. Found at Karabalgasun, the Uighur capital in the Orhkon River valley, the trilingual text was carved on a stele in Sogdian, Chinese, and Uighur.

35. W. B. Henning, "Argi and the 'Tokharians,'" *Bulletin of the School of Oriental Studies* 9, no. 3 (1938): 545–71. Larry Clark discusses several occurrences of the phrase "Four Twghry" and argues that, contrary to Henning's view, the four regions included Kucha. "The Conversion of Bügü Khan to Manichaeism," in *Studia Manichaica: IV. Internationaler Kongress zum Manichäismus, Berlin, 14.–18. Juli, 1997*, ed. Ronald E. Emmerick, Werner Sundermann, and Peter Zieme (Berlin: Akademie Verlag, 2000), 83–84n1.

36. Nicholas Sims-Williams, *New Light on Ancient Afghanistan: The Decipherment of Bactrian; An Inaugural Lecture Delivered on 1 February 1996* (London: School of Oriental and African Studies, University of London, 1997), 1–25.

37. George Sherman Lane, "On the Interrelationship of the Tocharian Dialects," in *Studies in Historical Linguistics in Honor of George Sherman Lane*, ed. Walter W. Arndt et al. (Chapel Hill: University of North Carolina Press, 1967), 129.

38. Stanley Insler, personal communication, April 22, 1999; Lane, "Tocharian Dialects," 129.

39. Douglas Q. Adams, "The Position of Tocharian among the Other Indo-European Languages," *Journal of the American Oriental Society* 104 (July–September 1984): 400.

40. The different people who spoke languages in the Turkic language family did not refer to themselves as Turks; the label came into wider use following contact with Muslim peoples. See P. B. Golden, *Ethnicity and State Formation in Pre-Čingisid Turkic Eurasia* (Bloomington: Department of Central Eurasian Studies, Indiana University, 2001); Golden, *An Introduction to the History of the Turkic Peoples: Ethnogenesis and State-Formation in Medieval and Early Modern Eurasia and the Middle East* (Wiesbaden, Germany: O. Harrassowitz, 1992).

41. Melanie Malzahn, "Tocharian Texts and Where to Find Them," in *Instrumenta Tocharica*, ed. Melanie Malzahn (Heidelberg, Germany: Universitätsverlag Winter, 2007), 79.

42. Georges-Jean Pinault, personal communication, April 3, 2010.

43. Georges-Jean Pinault, "Introduction au tokharien," *LALIES* 7 (1989): 11. See also Pinault's recent publication, *Chrestomathie tokharienne: Textes et grammaire* (Leuven, Belgium: Peeters, 2008).

44. Adams, *Tocharian*, 7n8.

45. Georges-Jean Pinault both analyzes the story and provides a word-by-word and freer translation of excerpts of it. See his "Introduction au tokharien," 163–94. A transcription and translation of the text appears in Pinault's *Chrestomathie tokharienne*, 251–68, with the cited passage on 262.

46. Lane, "Tocharian Dialects," 125, discusses the text, no. 394 in Sieg and Siegling's original inventory of Tocharian A texts.

47. Michaël Peyrot, *Variation and Change in Tocharian B* (Amsterdam: Rodopi, 2008).

48. Pinault, "Introduction au tokharien," 11; Emil Sieg, "Geschäftliche Aufzeichnungen in Tocharisch B aus der Berliner Sammlung," *Miscellanea Academica Berolinensia* 2, no. 2 (1950): 208–23.

49. "The total is now 6,060 numbers, resulting from the addition of the following rough numbers by places where they are kept: 3,480 in Berlin, 1,500 in London, 1,000 in Paris (not counting around 1,000 tiny fragments), 180 in St. Petersburg, 30 in Japan, 50 in China (not counting graffiti and inscriptions)." Pinault, personal communication, April 3, 2010.

50. The name of the site today is Yuqi tu'er, and the French spelling is Douldour-âqour. For a thorough description of the site, see Madeleine Hallade et al., *Douldour-âqour et Soubachi, Mission Paul Pelliot IV* (Paris: Centre de recherché sur l'Asie centrale et la Haute-Asie, Instituts d'Asie, Collège de France, 1982), 31–38.

51. The word kuśiññe means "Kuchean." Pinault, "Introduction au tokharien," 20.

52. Éric Trombert, *Les manuscrits chinois de Koutcha*, 25–27. The Chinese and Kuchean documents Pelliot collected are now held in the collection of the Bibliothèque Nationale. The Ōtani mission from Japan, active in Central Asia in the years before World War I, also purchased documents at Kucha, most likely from the same site. See also Georges-Jean Pinault, "Economic and Administrative Documents in Tocharian B from the Berezovsky and Petrovsky Collections," *Manuscripta Orientalia* 4, no. 4 (1998): 3–20.

53. Édouard Chavannes, *Documents sur les Tou-kiue (Turcs) occidenteaux* (Paris: Adrien-Masonneuve, 1941); Christopher I. Beckwith, *The Tibetan Empire in Central Asia: A History of the Struggle for Great Power among Tibetans, Turks, Arabs, and Chinese during the Early Middle Ages* (Princeton, NJ: Princeton University Press, 1987).

54. Wei Shou, *Wei shu* [History of the Wei dynasty] (Beijing: Zhonghua Shuju, 1974), 102:2266; Yu Taishan, *Xiyu zhuan*, 448, 449n136.

55. Li Yanshou, *Beishi* [History of the Northern dynasties] (Beijing: Zhonghua Shuju, 1974), 97:3217–18; Yu Taishan, *Xiyu zhuan*, 636.

56. François Thierry, "Entre Iran et Chine: La circulation monétaire en Sérinde de 1er au IXe siècle," in Drège, *La Serinde, terre d'échanges*, 121–47, esp. 126. The original passage is: Xuanzang, *Da Tang Xiyu ji jiaozhu*, 54. Variant versions of this passage say gold coins, or simply gold, and do not mention silver and copper coins.

57. Thierry, "La circulation monétaire en Sérinde," 129–35.

58. The Kuchean word for coin, *cāne*, is a loanword derived from the Chinese word for "coin," *qian*. These accounts are translated and discussed in Georges-Jean Pinault, "Aspects de bouddhisme pratiqué au nord de désert du Taklamakan, d'après les documents tokhariens," in *Bouddhisme et cultures locales: Quelques cas de réciproques adaptations; Actes du colloque franco-japonais de septembre 1991*, ed. Fukui Fumimasa and Gérard Fussman (Paris: École Française d'Extrême-Orient, 1994), 85–113; Pinault, "Economic and Administrative Documents." The original documents are held by the Bibliothèque Nationale of France in a collection named Pelliot Kouchéen Bois, série C, 1.

59. Pinault, "Economic and Administrative Documents," 12.

60. Georges-Jean Pinault, "Narration dramatisée et narration en peinture dans la region de Kucha," in Drège, *La Serinde, terre d'échanges*, 149–67; Werner Winter, "Some Aspects of 'Tocharian' Drama: Form and Techniques," *Journal of the American Oriental Society* 75 (1955): 26–35.

61. Klaus T. Schmidt, "Interdisciplinary Research on Central Asia: The Decipherment of the West Tocharian Captions of a Cycle of Mural Paintings of the Life of the Buddha in Cave 110 in Qizil," *Die Sprache* 40, no. 1 (1998): 72–81.

62. Peyrot, *Variation and Change*, 206.

63. Pelliot referred to the pass as Tchalderang; the modern spelling is Shaldïrang. For the most detailed study of these passes, see Georges-Jean Pinault, "Épigraphie koutchéenne: I. Laisser-passer de caravanes; II. Graffites et inscriptions," in Chao Huashan et al., *Sites divers de la région de Koutcha* (Paris: Collège de France, 1987), 59–196, esp. 67n4, citing Pelliot's January 1907 letter to Émile Senart. Ching Chao-jung is currently finishing her dissertation on the secular documents found at Kucha under the direction of Professor Pinault. My discussion is based entirely on Pinault's account: passes buried in snow (67); description of the documents (69–71); formula used in the passes (72–74); use of formal numerals (79); closing formula and date (84–85); table of information (78).

64. No complete examples of the outer case and inner pass survive; see the photos of the extant documents in Pinault, "Laisser-passer de caravans," plates 40–52.

65. Pinault, "Aspects de bouddhisme," 100–101.

66. Linghu Defen, *Zhou shu* [History of the Zhou dynasty] (Beijing: Zhonghua Shuju, 1971), 50:9123.

67. Chen Guocan, "Tang Anxi sizhen zhong 'zhen' de bianhua" [Changes of "zhen" garrison command in the four garrison commands of Anxi during the Tang dynasty], *Xiyu Yanjiu* 2008, no. 4: 16–22.

68. Beckwith, *Tibetan Empire in Central Asia*, 197–202.

69. For a very good summary of the complicated political events, see François Thierry, "On the Tang Coins Collected by Pelliot in Chinese Turkestan (1906–09)," in *Studies in Silk Road Coins and Culture: Papers in Honour of Professor Ikuo Hirayama on His 65th Birthday*, ed. Joe Cribb, Katsumi Tanabe, and Helen Wang (Kamakura, Japan: Institute of Silk Road Studies, 1997), 149–79, esp. 158–59.

70. Moriyasu Takao, "Qui des Ouighours ou des Tibétains ont gagné en 789–92 à Beš-Balïq," *Journal Asiatique* 269 (1981): 193–205; Beckwith, *Tibetan Empire in Central Asia*, 166–68.

71. Éric Trombert, with the assistance of Ikeda On, a Japanese scholar specializing in Chinese documents, and Zhang Guangda, a Chinese historian of the Tang dynasty, has published the definitive edition of these documents. For a list of all dated documents, see Trombert, *Les manuscrits chinois de Koutcha*, 141.

72. Trombert, *Les manuscrits chinois de Koutcha*, nos. 28–30, no. 5.

73. Trombert, *Les manuscrits chinois de Koutcha*, no. 21 (reciting sutras), no. 6 (woman writing letters), no. 19 (size of plots in an agricultural colony), no. 125 (Daoist banners), no. 117 (evaluation of an official's performance).

74. Trombert, *Les manuscrits chinois de Koutcha*, 35.

75. Trombert, *Les manuscrits chinois de Koutcha*, no. 121, no. 131.

76. Trombert, *Les manuscrits chinois de Koutcha*, no. 114 (steel), no. 129 (cloth; the reading of "1,000 feet" is tentative); no. 108 (payments to officials).

77. Trombert, *Les manuscrits chinois de Koutcha*, no. 41. Trombert explains (p. 35) that *xingke* appears to denote those attached to a mobile military unit (*xingke ying*), not the long-distance merchants indicated by the term *yuanxing shangke* in Dunhuang and Turfan documents.

78. Trombert, *Les manuscrits chinois de Koutcha*, no. 121, no. 220, no. 77 (possibly), no. 112.

79. Trombert, *Les manuscrits chinois de Koutcha*, no. 20, no. 93 (exemptions from labor obligations), no. 24 (list of debtors).

80. Helen Wang, *Money on the Silk Road*, 85–87, analyzes these; p. 87 presents a helpful table giving the dates and the amount of coins in each translation. Yamamoto Tatsuro and Ikeda On, *Tun-huang and Turfan Documents Concerning Social and Economic History*, vol. 3, *Contracts* (Tokyo: Toyo Bunko, 1987), 74–76, transcribes the contracts.

81. See Hansen, "Place of Coins and their Alternatives," for a discussion of the scholarly literature on this topic.

82. Thierry, "Tang Coins Collected by Pelliot," 151.

83. Trombert, *Les manuscrits chinois de Koutcha*, 35.

CHAPTER 3

My thanks to all the members of "The Silk Road Project: Reuniting Turfan's Scattered Treasures," which ran from 1995 to 1998, for providing much information and research guidance since then. The findings of that project appeared in *Asia Major* 11, no. 2 (1998), *Orientations* 30, no. 4 (1999), and *Dunhuang Tulufan Yanjiu* 4 (1999). My paper, "The Place of Coins and Their Alternatives in the Silk Road Trade," also discusses Turfan.

1. Yoshida Yutaka, "Appendix: Translation of the Contract for the Purchase of a Slave Girl Found at Turfan and Dated 639," *T'oung Pao* 89 (2003): 159–61.

2. Although historians disagree about the date of Xuanzang's departure—627? 629?—Etienne de la Vaissière makes a convincing case for 629: "Note sur la chronologie du voyage de Xuanzang," *Journal Asiatique* 298, no. 1 (2010): 157–68. See also the most detailed modern biography of Xuanzang by Kuwayama Shōshin and Hakamaya Noriaki, *Genjō* [Xuanzang] (Tokyo: Daizō, 1981), 58–82.

3. Huili composed the first five chapters of the book, which covered the years until 649, when Xuanzang returned to China and was welcomed by the same emperor, Tang Taizong, who had issued the original edict banning foreign travel. Yancong wrote the subsequent five chapters covering the time until Xuanzang's death in 664. See Huili and Yancong, *Da Tang Da Ci'en si Sanzang fashi zhuan* (Beijing: Zhonghua Shuju, 2000), 11. There are two English translations: Beal's, with some archaic phrasings and extensive annotation, and Li's more modern one with no notes. Samuel Beal, trans., *Life of Hiuen-Tsiang, by the Shaman Hwui Li* (London: K. Paul, Trench, Trübner, 1911); Li Rongxi, trans., *A Biography of the Tripiṭaka Master of the Great Ci'en Monastery of the Great Tang Dynasty* (Berkeley, CA: Numata Center for Buddhist Translation and Research, 1995).

Scholars are not certain when either Xuanzang or Huili lived. Alexander Leonhard Mayer has considered the many conflicting sources and, following the account given by Daoxuan in *Xu Gaoseng zhuan* [The lives of eminent monks, continued], concluded that Xuanzang was most likely born in 600 (other possible dates range from 596 to 602). See

Alexander Leonhard Mayer and Klaus Röhrborn, eds., *Xuanzangs Leben und Werk*, vol. 1 (Wiesbaden, Germany: Harrassowitz, 1991), 34 (about Huili), 61 (about Xuanzang). Thanks to Friederike Assandri for providing this reference.

4. Only one brief biography of Xuanzang, in the book *Fodao lunheng* [Balanced discourses on the Buddhist way], specifically says that Xuanzang studied Sanskrit (Kuwayama and Hakamaya, *Genjō*, 43–44).

5. My account of and subsequent quotations from Xuanzang's journey are based on Huili and Yancong, *Sanzang fashi zhuan*, 11–29.

6. Stein calculated the distances as given by Xuanzang using a ratio of 5 *li* to the modern mile, a figure that Stein found Xuanzang used throughout his writings. Xuanzang covered the 218 miles (351 km) from Guazhou to Hami in eleven days of walking ("marches"). Using Xuanzang's account, he drew a map of the route he covered (p. 268). Aurel Stein, "The Desert Crossing of Hsüan-Tsang, 630 A.D.," *Geographical Journal* 54 (1919): 265–77.

7. See the chart by Yoshida Yutaka and Kageyama Etsuko, "Sogdian Names in Chinese Characters," in *Les Sogdiens en Chine*, ed. Étienne de la Vaissière and Éric Trombert (Paris: École Française d'Extrême-Orient, 2005), 305–6.

8. Aurel Stein found the length of the journey credible because Xuanzang's four nights and five days corresponded to the five "marches" travelers took in the early twentieth century. He estimated that Xuanzang had walked 106 miles (171 km) before reaching water. Stein noted, too, that his horses were able to go without water for four days, and he thought it quite possible that they could have gone for longer with no water. ("The Desert Crossing," 276–77.)

9. Kuwayama and Hakamaya, *Genjō*, 48–49.

10. The Gaochang kings and the Western Turk kaghans were related by marriage. During a coup from 614–19, the Gaochang king Qu Boya most likely stayed with the Western Turks. Wu Zhen, "Qushi Gaochang guoshi suoyin" [A gap in the history of the Qu-family Gaochang kingdom], *Wenwu* 1981, no. 1: 38–46.

11. Arakawa Masaharu has recently linked the name of Xuanzang's escort given by Huili with a similar name in an excavated document listing assignments for cart drivers. He suggests that Xuanzang left Turfan in one of these carts in the twelfth month. "Sogdians and the Royal House of Ch'ü in the Kao-ch'ang Kingdom," *Acta Asiatica* 94 (2008): 67–93.

12. Ten kings ruled between 502 and the Chinese invasion of 640. See the chart of Gaochang kings in Valerie Hansen, "Introduction: Turfan as a Silk Road Community," *Asia Major*, 3rd ser., 11, no. 2 (1998): 1–12, chart on 8. For a detailed explanation of the multiple dynasties in power before 502, see Wang Su, *Gaochang shigao, tongzhi bian* [A draft history of the Gaochang kingdom, political section] (Beijing: Wenwu Chubanshe, 1998), 265–307.

13. *Hou Han shu*, 88:2928–29, as translated in Zhang Guangda and Rong Xinjiang, "A Concise History of the Turfan Oasis and Its Exploration," *Asia Major*, 3rd ser., 11, no. 2 (1998): 14. Zhang and Rong's article is the most reliable history of Turfan available in English. In Chinese, see the timelines in Wang Su, *Gaochang*.

14. Wang Binghua, "New Finds in Turfan Archaeology," *Orientations* 30, no. 4 (April 1999): 58–64.

15. Zhang and Rong, "Concise History of the Turfan Oasis," 14–17.

16. Yamamoto and Ikeda, *Tun-huang and Turfan Documents*, 3A:3.

17. Linghu, *Zhou shu*, 50:915; Yu Taishan, *Xiyu zhuan*, 510–11.

18. Zhang Guangda, "An Outline of the Local Administration in Turfan," available online at http://eastasianstudies.research.yale.edu/turfan/government.html.

19. Valerie Hansen, *Negotiating Daily Life in Traditional China: How Ordinary People Used Contracts, 600–1400* (New Haven, CT: Yale University Press, 1995), 29–31.

20. Liu Xu, *Jiu Tang shu* (Beijing: Zhonghua Shuju, 1975), 198:5295.

21. Li Jifu, *Yuanhe junxian tuzhi* [Maps and gazetteer of the provinces and counties in the Yuanhe period, 806–814] (Beijing: Zhonghua Shuju, 1983), 40:1030.

22. Archeologists found some paper clothes for the dead in the northern district of the Dunhuang caves: a paper shoe (from cave B48) and a paper shirt. Peng Jinzhang and Wang Jianjun, *Dunhuang Mogaoku beiqu shiku* [Report from the caves in the northern district of Dunhuang Mogao caves] (Beijing: Wenwu Chubanshe, 2000–2004), 1:151–52; 1:177; 3:337.

23. Tang Zhangru, ed., *Tulufan chutu wenshu* (Beijing: Wenwu Chubanshe, 1992–96), 1:10; Chen Guocan, personal communication, April 10, 2006. The notes cite the four-volume set of Turfan documents and photographs, which is more reliable than the earlier ten-volume set.

24. Wang Su, "Changsha Zoumalou Sanguo Wujian yanjiu de huigu yu zhanwang" [Some remarks on the study of the slips of Wu of Three Kingdoms from Zoumalou in Changsha], *Zhongguo Lishi Wenwu* 2004, no. 1: 18–34, esp. 25; *Zhou Shu*, 50:915; Yu Taishan, *Xiyu zhuan*, 510–11.

25. Stein, *Innermost Asia*, 2:646.

26. Frank Dikötter, *Mao's Great Famine: The History of China's Most Devastating Catastrophe, 1958–1962* (New York: Walker, 2010), x.

27. This account is based on a conversation I had with the late Wu Zhen of the Xinjiang Museum, March 29, 2006.

28. The Xinjiang Museum published different brief excavation reports in *Wenwu* 1960, no. 6: 13–21; 1972, no. 1: 8–29; 1972, no. 2: 7–12; 1973, no. 10: 7–27; 1975, no. 7: 8–26; 1978, no. 6: 1–14. A fuller report of the Astana digs appeared in a special issue of *Xinjiang Wenwu* (2000, no. 3–4).

29. Hansen, "Turfan as a Silk Road Community," 1.

30. Tang Zhangru, "Xinchu Tulufan wenshu jianjie" [Recently discovered Turfan manuscripts: Presentation of texts and reediting], *Tōhō Gakuhō* 54 (1982): 83–100. Most of the Turfan documents have been published in the four-volume set of Tang Zhangru, *Tulufan chutu wenshu*. See also Chen Guocan, *Sitanyin suo huo Tulufan wenshu yanjiu* [Studies in the Turfan documents obtained by Aurel Stein] (Wuchang, China: Wuhan Daxue Chubanshe, 1995); Chen Guocan, *Riben Ningle meishuguan cang Tulufan wenshu* [Turfan documents held in the Neiraku Museum, Japan] (Beijing: Wenwu Chubanshe, 1997); Liu Hongliang, *Xinchu Tulufan wenshu ji qi yanjiu* [Newly excavated Turfan documents and studies of them] (Urumqi, China: Xinjiang Renmin Chubanshe, 1997); Rong Xinjiang, Li Xiao, and Meng Xianshi, *Xinhuo Tulufan chutu wenxian* [Newly obtained excavated documents from Turfan] (Beijing: Zhonghua Shuju, 2008).

31. Rong Xinjiang, "Kanshi Gaochang wangguo yu Rouran, Xiyu de guanxi" [The relations of the Kan-family rulers of Gaochang with the Rouran and Western Regions], *Lishi Yanjiu* 2007, no. 2: 4–14; Rong et al., *Xinhuo Tulufan chutu wenxian*, 1:163.

32. Jonathan Karam Skaff, "Sasanian and Arab-Sasanian Silver Coins from Turfan: Their Relationship to International Trade and the Local Economy," *Asia Major*, 3rd ser., 11, no. 2 (1998): 67–115, esp. 68.

33. Most of the coins from Gaochang City were found in three hoards of ten, twenty, and one hundred coins. See Skaff, "Sasanian and Arab-Sasanian Silver Coins," 71–72.

34. Tang, *Tulufan chutu wenshu* 1:143; discussed in Hansen, "The Path of Buddhism into China: The View from Turfan," *Asia Major*, 3rd ser., 11, no. 2 (1998): 37–66, esp. 51–52.

35. See the helpful chart in Skaff, "Sasanian and Arab-Sasanian Silver Coins," 108–9.

36. Yoshida, "Appendix: Translation of the Contract," 159–61.

37. Helen Wang, *Money on the Silk Road*, 34–36.

38. Skaff, "Sasanian and Arab-Sasanian Silver Coins," 68.

39. Helen Wang, *Money on the Silk Road*, 35.

40. Wang Binghua, personal communication, June 25, 2009; Li Yuchun, "Xinjiang Wuqia xian faxian jintiao he dapi Bosi yinbi" [Gold bars and a large deposit of Persian silver coins found in Wuqia county, Xinjiang], *Kaogu* 1959, no. 9: 482–83.

41. In 2006 Stephen Album was able to examine about a hundred of the Wuqia coins held in the Xinjiang Museum; he estimated that over one quarter were "contemporary imitations" of Sasanian silver coins, or "Peroz-style coins from Hephtalite mints." Stephen Album, conference paper presented at the International Symposium on Ancient Coins and the Culture of the Silk Road, Shanghai Museum, December 6, 2006. See also the photographs for each coin from the Wuqia find in *Silk Roadology* 19 (2003): 51–330.

42. Valerie Hansen, "Why Bury Contracts in Tombs?" *Cahiers d'Extrême-Asie* 8 (1995): 59–66.

43. Hansen, *Negotiating Daily Life*, 35, 43.

44. Tang, *Tulufan chutu wenshu*, 3: 517.

45. Luo Feng, *Hu Han zhi jian—"Sichou zhi lu" yu xibei lishi kaogu* [Between non-Chinese and Chinese: The Silk Road and historical archeology of China's northwestern regions] (Beijing: Wenwu Chubanshe, 2004), 147.

46. Luo Feng, *Hu Han zhi jian*, 117–120; François Thierry and Cecile Morrisson, "Sur les monnaies byzantines trouvées en Chine," *Revue Numismatique* 36 (1994): 109–45.

47. Helen Wang, *Money on the Silk Road*, 34.

48. The chart in Luo Feng, *Hu Han zhi jian*, 146, lists thirty-two genuine and fifteen imitation gold coins found in China. The Chinese-language literature about these coins is too extensive to list here. See Luo Feng's thorough notes instead.

49. Lin Ying and Maitelixi [Michael Metlich], "Luoyang faxian de Li'ao yishi jinbi kaoshi" [The gold coin of Leo I found in Luoyang city], *Zhongguo Qianbi* 90, no. 3 (2005): 70–72.

50. Five coins were found in the Northern Zhou tomb of Tian Hong; Luo Feng, *Hu Han zhi jian*, 118, items 21–24.

51. Luo Feng, *Hu Han zhi jian*, 96.

52. Wu Zhen, "'Hu' Non-Chinese as They Appear in the Materials from the Astana Graveyard at Turfan," *Sino-Platonic Papers* 119 (Summer 2002): 7.

53. Yoshida Yutaka, "On the Origin of the Sogdian Surname Zhaowu and Related Problems," *Journal Asiatique* 291, nos. 1–2 (2003): 35–67.

54. Yoshida Yutaka and Kageyama Etsuko, "Appendix I: Sogdian Names in Chinese Characters, Pinyin, Reconstructed Sogdian Pronunciation, and English Meanings," in Vaissière and Trombert, *Les Sogdiens en Chine*, 305–6.

55. In the sixth and seventh centuries, most of the Sogdians in Turfan were Zoroastrians, not Manichaeans. See Valerie Hansen, "The Impact of the Silk Road Trade on a Local Community: The Turfan Oasis, 500–800," in Vaissière and Trombert, *Les Sogdiens en Chine*, 283–310, esp. 299.

56. Kageyama Etsuko, "Higashi Torukisutan shutsudo no ossuari (Zoroasutā kyōto no nōkotsuki ni tsuite)" [The ossuaries (bone receptacles of Zoroastrians) unearthed in Chinese Turkestan], *Oriento* 40, no. 1 (1997): 73–89.

57. Zhang Guangda, "Iranian Religious Evidence in Turfan Chinese Texts," *China Archaeology and Art Digest* 4, no. 1 (2000): 193–206.

58. *Sabao* is the Chinese transcription of the Sogdian word, s'rtp'w, which was borrowed (maybe via Bactrian) from the Sanskrit *sārthavāha*, "caravan leader." Yoshida Yutaka, "Sogudogo zatsuroku, II" [Sogdian miscellany, II], *Oriento* 31, no. 2 (1988): 168–71.

59. Hansen, "Impact of the Silk Road Trade," 297–98.

60. Tulufan diqu wenwuju, "Xinjiang Tulufan diqu Badamu mudi fajue jianbao" [Brief report of excavations at the Badamu graveyard in Turfan, Xinjiang], *Kaogu* 2006, no. 12: 47–72.

61. Jonathan Karam Skaff, "Documenting Sogdian Society at Turfan in the Seventh and Eighth Centuries: Tang Dynasty Census Records as a Window on Cultural Distinction and Change," in Vaissière and Trombert, *Les Sogdiens en Chine*, 311–41.

62. The documents are not dated, but they contain the name of one man, Ju Buliu(lu)duo in Chinese, Parwēkht in Sogdian, whose name appears in another document that can be dated to 619. See Skaff, "Sasanian and Arab-Sasanian Silver Coins," 90n71.

63. Skaff, "Sasanian and Arab-Sasanian Silver Coins," 93–95.

64. Eight notations indicate that no tax was paid during the previous half month, meaning that no tax was paid for a total of four months during the course of the year.

65. The weight of the Chinese pound (jin) during the Gaochang period is not known because no weights from the time have been excavated. The Jin dynasty used the older system, and the Gaochang Kingdom adopted many measures from the Jin dynasty, so it seems most likely that the value of the jin in these documents was around 200 grams. Chen Guocan, personal communication, May 18, 2006.

66. Skaff, "Sasanian and Arab-Sasanian Silver Coins," 93.

67. Ronald M. Nowak, *Walker's Mammals of the World*, 5th ed. (Baltimore: Johns Hopkins University Press, 1991), 2:1357.

68. Discussed more fully in Valerie Hansen, "How Business Was Conducted on the Chinese Silk Road during the Tang Dynasty, 618–907," in *Origins of Value: The Financial Innovations That Created Modern Capital Markets*, ed. William N. Goetzmann and K. Geert Rouwenhorst (New York: Oxford University Press, 2005), 43–64; Arakawa Masaharu, "Sogdian Merchants and Chinese Han Merchants during the Tang Dynasty," in Vaissière and Trombert, *Les Sogdiens en Chine*, 231–42.

69. Éric Trombert, "Textiles et tissus sur la route de la soie: Eléments pour une géographie de la production et des échanges," in Drège, *La Serinde, terre d'échanges*, 107–20, esp. 108.

70. Trombert, "Textiles et tissus"; Michel Cartier, "Sapèques et tissus à l'époque des T'ang (618–906)," *Journal of the Economic and Social History of the Orient* 19, no. 3 (1976): 323–44.

71. Hansen, *Negotiating Daily Life*, 51–52.

72. Arakawa Masaharu, "The Transit Permit System of the Tang Empire and the Passage of Merchants," *Memoirs of the Research Department of the Toyo Bunko* 59 (2001): 1–21; Cheng Xilin, *Tangdai guosuo yanjiu*, 239–45.

73. Arakawa, "Transit Permit System," offers a full translation of the pass (8–10) and a sketch map of his route (11).

74. Skaff, "Sasanian and Arab-Sasanian Silver Coins," 97–98.

75. Tang, *Tulufan chutu wenshu*, 4:281–97.

76. Hansen, "Impact of the Silk Road Trade."

77. Wallace Johnson, trans., *The T'ang Code*, vol. 2, *Specific Articles* (Princeton, NJ: Princeton University Press, 1997), 482; Denis Twitchett, "The T'ang Market System," *Asia Major* 12 (1963): 245. The Turfan register, cited below, gives prices set two weeks apart.

78. Ikeda On ordered and transcribed the document in *Chūgoku kodai sekichō kenkyū* [Studies in ancient Chinese household registers] (Tokyo: Tōkyō Daigaku Tōyō Bunka Kenkyūjo, 1979), 447–62. Éric Trombert and Étienne de la Vaissière have provided extensive commentary as well as a full translation into French: "Le prix de denrées sur le marché de Turfan en 743," in *Études de Dunhuang et Turfan*, ed. Jean-Pierre Drège (Geneva, Switzerland: Droz, 2007), 1–52.

79. The second digit after the 20 is missing; it must be 7.

80. Arakawa, "Transit Permit System," 13.

81. Wang Binghua, "Tulufan chutu Tangdai yongdiaobu yanjiu" [Studies in the *yongdiao* tax cloths of the Tang dynasty excavated at Turfan], *Wenwu* 1981, no. 1: 56–62. Helen Wang kindly provided a copy of her forthcoming translation of this article.

82. Jonathan Karam Skaff, "Straddling Steppe and Sown: Tang China's Relations with the Nomads of Inner Asia (640–756)" (Ph.D. diss., University of Michigan, 1998).

83. Skaff, "Straddling Steppe and Sown," 224, 82n147, chart on 86; Du You, *Tongdian* [Encyclopedic history of institutions] (Beijing: Zhonghua Shuju, 1988), 6:111. Skaff's is the most recent and sustained effort in English, with detailed references to Chinese and Japanese works. See also Arakawa Masaharu, *Oashisu kokka to kyaraban kōeki* [The oasis countries and the caravan trade] (Tokyo: Yamakawa Shuppansha, 2003).

84. Skaff, "Straddling Steppe and Sown," 86, 244; D. C. Twitchett, *Financial Administration under the T'ang Dynasty*, 2nd ed. (Cambridge, UK: Cambridge University Press, 1970), 86.

85. Jonathan Karam Skaff, "Barbarians at the Gates? The Tang Frontier Military and the An Lushan Rebellion," *War and Society* 18, no. 2 (2000): 23–35, esp. 28, 33.

86. Twitchett, *Financial Administration*, 97–123.

87. Larry Clark points out the difficulties of determining the exact year in which the kaghan converted; he could have converted in 755–56, 761, or 763. See his "The Conversion of Bügü Khan to Manichaeism," in Emmerick, *Studia Manichaica*, 83–123.

88. Hans-J. Klimkeit, "Manichaean Kingship: Gnosis at Home in the World," *Numen* 29, no. 1 (1982): 17–32.

89. Michael R. Drompp, *Tang China and the Collapse of the Uighur Empire: A Documentary History* (Leiden, The Netherlands: Brill, 2005), 36–38; Zhang and Rong, "Concise History of the Turfan Oasis," 20–21; Moriyasu Takao, "Qui des Ouighours ou des Tibetains," 193–205.

90. Moriyasu Takao, "Notes on Uighur Documents," *Memoirs of the Research Department of the Toyo Bunko* 53 (1995): 67–108.

91. Nicholas Sims-Williams, "Sogdian and Turkish Christians in the Turfan and Tun-huang Manuscripts," in *Turfan and Tun-huang, the Texts: Encounter of Civilizations on the Silk Route*, ed. Alfredo Cadonna (Florence, Italy: Leo S. Olschki Editore, 1992), 43–61; Nicholas Sims-Williams, "Christianity, iii. In Central Asia and Chinese Turkestan," in *Encyclopædia Iranica*, Online Edition, October 18, 2011, available at http://www.iranicaonline.org/articles/christianity-iii; Sims-Williams, "Bulayïq," in *Encyclopædia Iranica*, Online Edition, December 15, 1989, available at http://www.iranicaonline.org/articles/bulayq-town-in-eastern-turkestan.

92. S. P. Brock, "The 'Nestorian' Church: A Lamentable Misnomer," *Bulletin of the John Rylands University Library of Manchester* 78, no. 3 (1996): 23–35.

93. For a full translation, see Hans-Joachim Klimkeit, *Gnosis on the Silk Road: Gnostic Texts from Central Asia* (San Francisco: HarperSanFrancisco, 1993), 353–56.

94. Klimkeit, *Gnosis on the Silk Road*, 40–41.

95. Zsuzsanna Gulacsi, *Manichaean Art in Berlin Collections* (Turnhout, Belgium: Brepols, 2001), 70–75.

96. Moriyasu Takao, *Uiguru-Manikyō shi no kenkyū* [Research in the history of Manichaeism under the Uighurs] (Osaka: Ōsaka Daigaku Bungakubu, 1991), 18–27, plate 1.

97. Werner Sundermann, "Completion and Correction of Archaeological Work by Philological Means: The Case of the Turfan Texts," in *Histoire et cultes de l'Asie centrale préislamique*, ed. Paul Bernard and Frantz Grenet (Paris: Éditions du Centre National de la Recherche Scientifique, 1991), 283–89.

98. Zhang and Rong, "Concise History of the Turfan Oasis," 20–21; Morris Rossabi, "Ming China and Turfan, 1406–1517," *Central Asiatic Journal* 16 (1972): 206–25.

99. Perdue, *China Marches West*.

CHAPTER 4

Étienne de la Vaissière, École Pratique des Hautes Études; Frantz Grenet, Centre Nationale de la Recherche Scientifique; the late Boris I. Marshak, Hermitage Museum; and Kevin van Bladel, University of Southern California, each went over earlier drafts of this chapter with meticulous care. The late Professor Marshak taught two classes at Yale during the spring of 2002; my discussion of Panjikent draws heavily on my notes from his lectures. Oktor Skjaervø, Harvard University, checked the translations against the Sogdian originals and made many helpful suggestions. I also want to thank Asel Umurzakova for her help in locating and reading Russian materials and Nikolaos A. Chrissidis for additional research assistance.

1. Shiratori, "Study on Su-t'ê," 81–145.

2. Huili and Yancong, *Sanzang fashi zhuan*, 27.

3. Arthur Waley, *The Real Tripitaka and Other Pieces* (London: George Allen & Unwin, 1952), 21.

4. Scholars are not certain which route Xuanzang took through the Tianshan mountains. One possible route crossed the Bedal Pass, which is not that high. The more likely route went directly north from Kucha to the heartland of the Western Turks, near Little Khonakhai in northern Xinjiang, and then due west to Lake Issyk-kul. See Xiang Da, "Rehai dao xiaokao" [A brief examination of the routes around Issuk-kul], *Wenwu* 1962, nos. 7–8: 35.

5. Beal, *Life of Hiuen-tsiang*, 25n80. The Chinese term for warm sea is *rehai*.

6. Xuanzang met Yabghu Kaghan Si, who succeeded his father, Tong, who was assassinated in 628 or the beginning of 629, as the leader of the Western Turks. Étienne de la Vaissière, "Oncles et frères: Les qaghans Ashinas et le vocabulaire turc de la parenté," *Turcica* 42 (2010): 267–78.

7. There were many ways to write the name of the Sogdians in Chinese. See the learned note by Ji Xianlin and his collaborators in Xuanzang's *Da Tang Xiyu ji jiaozhu*, 73–74.

8. Xuanzang, *Da Tang Xiyu ji*, 72; Beal, *Life of Hiuen-tsiang*, 27.

9. Liu, *Jiu Tang shu*, 198b:5310; Ouyang Xiu, *Xin Tang shu* [New Tang history] (Beijing: Zhonghua Shuju, 1975), 221b:6243–44.

10. Klimkeit, *Gnosis on the Silk Road*; Nicholas Sims-Williams, "Sogdian and Turkish Christians in the Turfan and Tun-huang Manuscripts," in Cadonna, *Turfan and Tunhuang*, 43–61.

11. Frantz Grenet, "Old Samarkand: Nexus of the Ancient World," *Archaeology Odyssey* 6, no. 5 (2003): 26–37.

12. Nicholas Sims-Williams and Frantz Grenet, "The Sogdian Inscriptions of Kultobe," *Shygys* 2006, no. 1: 95–111.

13. Ruins of both the house and tower appear in M. Aurel Stein, *Ruins of Desert Cathay: Personal Narrative of Explorations in Central Asia and Westernmost China* (London: Macmillan, 1912; repr., New York: Dover, 1987), figure 177.

14. Aurel Stein, *Ruins of Desert Cathay*, 2:113.

15. For the circumstances of discovery, see Stein, *Serindia*, 669–77, and map 74. For a general overview of the letters, see Vaissière, *Sogdian Traders*, 43–70. (The original book, in French, appeared in 2002, but I cite the English for the convenience of the reader.) See also Nicholas Sims-Williams and Frantz Grenet, "The Historical Context of the Sogdian Ancient Letters," in *Transition Periods in Iranian History, Actes du symposium de Fribourg-en-Brisgau (22–24 Mai 1985)* (Leuven, Belgium: E. Peeters, 1987), 101–22.

Nicholas Sims-Williams has posted translations of letters 1–3 and 5 on the Internet: http://depts.washington.edu/silkroad/texts/sogdlet.html.

The most recent and up-to-date translations of individual letters are as follows:

Letter 1: Nicholas Sims-Williams, "Towards a New Edition of the Sogdian Ancient Letters: Ancient Letter 1," in Vaissière and Trombert, *Les Sogdiens en Chine*, 181–93. Letter 2: Nicholas Sims-Williams, "The Sogdian Ancient Letter II," in *Philologica et Linguistica: Historia, Pluralitas, Universitas; Festschrift für Helmut Humbach zum 80. Geburtstag am 4. Dezember 2001*, ed. Maria Gabriela Schmidt and Walter Bisang (Trier, Germany: Wissenschaftlicher Verlag Trier, 2001), 267–80; Nicholas Sims-Williams, "Sogdian Ancient Letter 2," in *Monks and Merchants: Silk Road Treasures from Northwest China*, ed. Annette L. Juliano and Judith A. Lerner (New York: Harry N. Abrams with the Asia Society, 2001), 47–49. A summary of letter 3 can be found in Nicholas Sims-Williams,

"A Fourth-Century Abandoned Wife," in Whitfield and Ursula Sims-Williams, *Silk Road*, 248–49. Letter 5: Frantz Grenet, Nicholas Sims-Williams, and Étienne de la Vaissière, "The Sogdian Ancient Letter V," *Bulletin of the Asia Institute* 12 (1998): 91–104.

16. Nicholas Sims-Williams, "Sogdian Ancient Letter II," 261.

17. Either letters 3–5 were written between May 11, 313, and April 21, 314, or between June to December 313. Grenet et al., "Sogdian Ancient Letter V," 102; see also Vaissière, *Sogdian Traders*, 45n5.

18. Etienne de la Vaissière, "Xiongnu," in *Encyclopædia Iranica* Online Edition, November 15, 2006, available at http://www.iranicaonline.org/articles/xiongnu.

19. Pénélope Riboud, "Réflexions sur les pratiques religieuses designees sous le nom de *xian*," in Vaissière and Trombert, *Les Sogdiens en Chine*, 73–91.

20. Nicholas Sims-Williams, "Fourth-Century Abandoned Wife," 249.

21. This assumes that a vesicule has a value of 25 grams. Vaissière, *Sogdian Traders*, 53–55. For a general study of weights, see Boris I. Marshak and Valentina Raspopova, *Sogdiiskie giri iz Pendzhikenta/Sogdian Weights from Panjikent* (St. Petersburg: The Hermitage, 2005).

22. Nicholas Sims-Williams, "Ancient Letter 1," 182.

23. Grenet et al., "Sogdian Ancient Letter V," 100; Vaissière, *Sogdian Traders*, 53–54.

24. Grenet et al., "Sogdian Ancient Letter V," 101.

25. Étienne de la Vaissière, "Is There a 'Nationality' of the Hephthalites?" *Bulletin of the Asia Institute* 17 (2007): 119–32.

26. Frantz Grenet, "Regional Interaction in Central Asia and Northwest India in the Kidarite and Hephthalite Periods," in *Indo-Iranian Languages and Peoples: Proceedings of the British Academy*, ed. Nicholas Sims-Williams (Oxford: Oxford University Press, 2002), 220–21.

27. Vaissière, *Sogdian Traders*, 112–17.

28. For the most important publications about the site, see Boris I. Marshak and Valentina Raspopova, "Wall Paintings from a House with a Granary, Panjikent, 1st Quarter of the 8th Century A.D.," *Silk Road Art and Archaeology* 1 (1990): 123–76, especially 173n3. The current director of the excavations is Pavel Lur'e, head of the Oriental Department at the Hermitage Museum.

29. A. M. Belenitski and B. I. Marshak, "L'art de Piandjikent à la lumière des dernières fouilles (1958–1968)," *Arts Asiatiques* 23 (1971): 3–39.

30. Frantz Grenet and Étienne de la Vaissière, "The Last Days of Panjikent," *Silk Road Art and Archaeology* 8 (2002): 155–196, especially 176; Marshak and Raspopova, "Wall Paintings from a House with a Granary," 125.

31. Vaissière, *Sogdian Traders*, 190–94.

32. Vaissière, *Sogdian Traders*, 191.

33. Valentina Raspopova, "Gold Coins and Bracteates from Pendjikent," in *Coins, Art and Chronology: Essays on the Pre-Islamic History of the Indo-Iranian Borderlands*, ed. Michael Alram and Deborah E. Klimburg-Salter (Vienna: Österreichische Akademie der Wissenschaften, 1999), 453–60.

34. Boris Marshak, personal communication, February 7, 2002.

35. Raspopova, "Gold Coins and Bracteates from Pendjikent," 453–60.

36. G. A. Pugachenkova, "The Form and Style of Sogdian Ossuaries," *Bulletin of the Asia Institute* 8 (1994): 227–43; L. A. Pavchinskaia, "Sogdian Ossuaries," *Bulletin of the*

Asia Institute 8 (1994): 209–25; Frantz Grenet, "L'art zoroastrien en Sogdiane: Études d'iconographie funéraire," *Mesopotamia* 21 (1986): 97–131.

37. Boris I. Marshak, "On the Iconography of Ossuaries from Biya-Naiman," *Silk Road Art and Archaeology* 4 (1995–96): 299–321.

38. Raspopova, "Gold Coins and Bracteates," 453–60.

39. Boris I. Marshak and Valentina Raspopova, "Cultes communautaires et cultes privés en Sogdiane," in Bernard and Grenet, *Histoire et cultes de l'Asie préislamique*, 187–95, esp. 192.

40. Boris A. Litvinskij, *La civilisation de l'Asie centrale antique*, trans. Louis Vaysse (Rahden, Germany: Verlag Marie Leidorf, 1998), 182.

41. A. M. Belenitskii and B. I. Marshak, "The Paintings of Sogdiana," in *Sogdian Painting: The Pictorial Epic in Oriental Art*, by Guitty Azarpay (Berkeley: University of California Press, 1981), 11–77, esp. 20–23.

42. Marshak and Raspopova, "Cultes communautaires et cultes privés," 187–93.

43. Vaissière, *Sogdian Traders*, 163; Marshak and Raspopova, "Wall Paintings from a House with a Granary," 140–42, identify the deity as the God of Victory, but Frantz Grenet sees Farn, the deity of fortune, instead. "Vaiśravaṇa in Sogdiana: About the Origins of Bishamon-Ten," *Silk Road Art and Archaeology* 4 (1995–96): 277–97, esp. 279.

44. Marshak and Raspopova, "Wall Paintings from a House with a Granary," 150–53, figure 24 on 151.

45. Boris Marshak, *Legends, Tales, and Fables in the Art of Sogdiana* (New York: Bibliotheca Persica, 2002).

46. Vaissière, *Sogdian Traders*, 162, plate 5, illustration 1.

47. Varkhuman's name was transcribed in Chinese as Fuhuman. Liu, *Jiu Tang shu*, 221b:6244; Chavannes, *Documents sur les Tou-Kiue*, 135.

48. For a general introduction to the paintings, see Matteo Compareti and Étienne de la Vaissière, eds., *Royal Naurūz in Samarkand: Proceedings of the Conference Held in Venice on the Pre-Islamic Painting at Afrasiab* (Rome: Instituto Editoriali e Poligrafici Internazionali, 2006), 59–74. The essays in this volume present the most up-to-date analysis of the Afrasiab paintings. See also L. I. Al'baum, *Zhivopis' Afrasiaba* [Paintings from Afrosiab] (Tashkent, USSR: FAN, 1975); Boris I. Marshak, "Le programme iconographique des peintures de la 'Salle des ambassadeurs' à Afrasiab (Samarkand)," *Arts Asiatiques* 49 (1994): 5–20; "The Self-Image of the Sogdians," in Vaissière and Trombert, *Les Sogdiens en Chine*, 123–40; Matteo Compareti, "Afrāsiāb ii. Wall Paintings," in *Encyclopædia Iranica* Online Edition, April 14, 2009, available at http://www.iranicaonline.org/articles/afrasiab-ii- wall-paintings-2.

49. Grenet, "Self-Image of the Sogdians."

50. Frantz Grenet, "What was the Afrasiab Painting About," in Compareti and Vaissière, *Royal Naurūz in Samarkand*, 43–58, esp. 44–47 about the eastern wall.

51. Frantz Grenet, "The 7th-Century AD 'Ambassadors' Painting' at Samarkand," in *Mural Paintings of the Silk Road: Cultural Exchanges between East and West*, ed. Kuzuya Yamauchi (Tokyo: Archetype, 2007), 16; Vladimir Livšic, "The Sogdian Wall Inscriptions on the Site of Afrasiab," in Compareti and Vaissière, *Royal Naurūz in Samarkand*, 59–74.

52. Anazawa Wakō and Manome Junichi, "Afurashiyabu tojōshi shutsudo no hekiga ni mirareru Chōsen jin shisetsu ni tsuite" [Korean envoys on the mural painting from ancient Samarkand], *Chōsen Gakuhō* 80 (1976): 1–36.

53. Etsuko Kageyama, "A Chinese Way of Depicting Foreign Delegates Discerned in the Paintings of Afrasiab," *Cahiers de Studia Iranica* 25 (2002): 313–27.

54. One reconstruction of the missing top section of the wall, by the head of the Oriental Department of the Hermitage Museum in St. Petersburg, Boris Marshak, places the deity Nana, the supreme goddess of the Sogdians, in the throne above all the emissaries. See his "Sogudo no bijutsu" [Sogdian Art], in *Sekai bijutsu daizenshū: Chūō Ajia* [New history of world art: Central Asia], ed. Tanabe Katsumi and Maeda Kōsaku (Tokyo: Shōgakkan, 1999), 156–79. In contrast, Grenet, "Self-Image of the Sogdians," suggests that the throned Varkhuman occupied the same position, while Étienne de la Vaissière, "Les Turcs, rois du monde à Samarcande," 147–62, in Compareti and Vaissière, *Royal Naurūz in Samarkand*, proposes that the kaghan of the Western Turks was there.

55. The northern wall is illustrated in Compareti and Vaissière, *Royal Naurūz in Samarkand*, Plate 5, 27.

56. Marshak, "Le programme iconographique des peintures;" Grenet, "Self-Image of the Sogdians."

57. al-Bīrūnī, *The Chronology of Ancient Nations*, trans. C. Edward Sachau (Frankfurt: Institute for the History of Arabic Islamic Science at the Johann Wolfgang Goethe University, 1998; reprint of 1879 original), 201–4, 222.

58. Grenet, "Self-Image of the Sogdians," 132.

59. Grenet and Vaissière, "Last Days of Panjikent," 155.

60. The Mount Mugh documents have been published in three volumes: A. A. Freiman, *Opisanie, publikatsii, i issledovanie dokumentov s gory Mug: Sogdiiskie dokumenty s gory Mug 1* [Description, publications, and studies of the documents from Mount Mugh: Sogdian Documents from Mount Mugh 1] (Moscow: Izdatel'stvo Vostochnoi Literatury, 1962); Vladimir A. Livshits, *Iuridicheskie dokumenty i pis'ma: Sogdiiskie dokumenty s gory Mug 2* [Legal documents and letters: Sogdian documents from Mount Mugh 2] (Moscow: Izdatel'stvo Vostochnoi Literatury, 1962); M. N. Bogoliubov and O. I. Smirnova, *Khoziaistvennye dokumenty: Dokumenty s gory Mug 3* [Economic documents from Mount Mugh 3] (Moscow: Izdatel'stvo Vostochnoi Literatury, 1963). Recently, V. A. Livshits published a new edition of these documents: *Sogdiiskaia epigrafika Srednei Azii i Semirech'ia* (St. Petersburg: Filologicheskii Fakul'tet Sankt-Peterburgskogo Gosudarstvennogo Universiteta, 2008).

61. Ilya Yakubovich reports that the villagers mistook the Sogdian script for Arabic and believed that the document gave instructions for finding an ancient treasure. See his "Mugh 1.I Revisited," *Studia Iranica* 31, no. 2 (2002): 231–52.

62. This account is based on a conversation I had with Boris Marshak on March 25, 2000, at the University of Pennsylvania. Prof. Marshak knew Puloti personally, and Puloti told him this story. Livshits, *Sogdiiskie dokumenty s gory Mug 2*, gives a shorter version on 108–9 and reproduces a photograph of document 1.I facing 112.

63. Yakubovich, "Mugh 1.I Revisited."

64. This is the total number of documents as given in O. I. Smirnova, *Ocherki iz istorii Sogda* [Essays on the history of Sogdiana] (Moscow: Nauk, 1970), 14. The Mount Mugh documents are numbered according to the time at which they were found: document 1.1 was found in the spring of 1932; those documents with the Cyrillic letter B (= the English letter V) were excavated by Puloti in May 1933; A documents were excavated by A. Vasil'ev in the summer of 1933; those with the letter Б (= English letter B) were found

in November 1933 by the Freiman expedition; and the Nov. ("New") documents were given by Puloti in 1934. After the excavation had ended and the Freiman team returned to Leningrad, Puloti was pressured into handing over a group of documents that he had been given before Freiman's arrival: an upside-down basket that held six leather documents, including the longest documents found at Mount Mugh, a marriage contract, and the accompanying "bride's script."

65. A. S. Polyakov, "Kitaiskie rukopisi, naidennye v 1933 g. b Tadzhikistane," in *Sogdiiskii sbornik* [Sogdian miscellany], ed. N. I. Krachkovskii and A. A. Freiman (Leningrad: Akademii Nauk SSSR, 1934), 91–117, esp. 103, photograph on 99.

66. I. Y. Kratchkovsky, "A Letter from Sogdiana (1934)," in *Among Arabic Manuscripts: Memories of Libraries and Men*, trans. Tatiana Minorsky (Leiden, the Netherlands: Brill, 1953), 142–50.

67. For a translation of the letter, see Richard N. Frye, "Tarxūn-Türxün and Central Asian History," *Harvard Journal of Asiatic Studies* 14 (1951): 105–29, translation on 108–9.

68. David Stephan Powers, trans., *The History of al-Ṭabari (Ta'rīkh al-rusul wa'l mulūk)*, vol. 24, *The Empire in Transition* (Albany: State University of New York Press, 1989), 171, 177–78, 183.

69. Freiman, *Sogdiiskie dokumenty s gory Mug 1*, 7.

70. Krachkovskii and Freiman, *Sogdiiskii sbornik*, 29.

71. Bogoliubov and Smirnova, *Khoziaistvennye dokumenty*.

72. Krachkovskii and Freiman, *Sogdiiskii sbornik*, 29.

73. Documents Nov. 3 (the contract) and Nov. 4 (the groom's obligations) were originally transcribed and translated in Livshits, *Dokumenty s gory Mug 2*, 21–26. The most up-to-date translation is by Ilya Yakubovich, "Marriage Sogdian Style," in *Iranistik in Europa—Gestern, Heute, Morgen*, ed. H. Eichner, Bert G. Fragner, Velizar Sadovski, and Rüdiger Schmitt (Vienna: Österreichische Akademie der Wissenschaften, 2006), 307–44. See also the brief discussion in Ilya Gershevitch, "The Sogdian Word for 'Advice,' and Some Mugh Documents," *Central Asiatic Journal* 7 (1962): 90–94; W. B. Henning, "A Sogdian God," *Bulletin of the School of Oriental and African Studies* 28 (1965): 242–54.

74. Maria Macuch, *Das sasanidische Rechtsbuch "Mātakdān i hazār dātistān" (Teil 2)* (Wiesbaden, Germany: Kommissionsverlag F. Steiner, 1981).

75. Yakubovich, "Marriage Sogdian Style," surveys a wide range of marriage documents but finds only one other group of contracts—fifth-century BCE Aramaic agreements from the Jewish settlement in Elephantine, Egypt—that allow the wife to initiate divorce. He suggests two possibilities: perhaps Sogdian society afforded women more rights than many neighboring societies, or perhaps Cher was able to obtain unusually favorable conditions for his ward.

76. Scholars of Sogdian debate the meaning of this passage, with some contending that the phrase "by god Mithra" should be translated as "by God [that is, Ahura Mazda] and Mithra." Henning, "A Sogdian God," 248; Yakubovich, "Marriage Sogdian Style."

77. Document B-4 is transcribed and translated into Russian in Livshits, *Sogdiiskie dokumenty s gory Mug 2*, 56–58; see also the brief discussion in Gershevitch, "Sogdian Word for 'Advice,'" 84.

78. Document B-8 is transcribed and translated into Russian in Livshits, *Sogdiiskie dokumenty s gory Mug 2*, 47–48. Ilya Gershevitch revises the translation in his "Sogdians

on a Frogplain," in *Mélanges linguistiques offerts à Emile Benveniste* (Paris: Société de Linguistique de Paris, 1975), 195–211.

79. Gershevitch, "Sogdians on a Frogplain," 205–6, with Gershevitch's brackets removed to make the translation more readable. See also Frantz Grenet, "Annexe: Le contrat funéraire sogdien du Mont Mugh," in *Les pratiques funéraires dans l'Asie centrale sédentaire de la conquête Grecque à l'Islamisation* (Paris: Éditions du CNRS, 1984), 313–22.

80. See, for example, Paul Bernard's response in Grenet, "Annexe," 321–22.

81. Grenet and Vaissière, "Last Days of Panjikent," marks a genuine breakthrough in the clarification of these confusing events.

82. Vaissière, *Sogdian Traders*, 199–200.

83. Vaissière, *Sogdian Traders*, 161–62.

84. Yakubovich, "Mugh 1.I Revisited."

85. Frantz Grenet, "Les 'Huns' dans les documents sogdiens du mont Mugh (avec an appendix par N. Sims-Williams)," in *Études irano-aryennes offertes à Gilbert Lazard*, ed. C.-H. de Fouchécour and Ph. Gignoux, Cahiers de Studia Iranica 7 (Paris: Association pour l'Avancement des Études Iranniennes, 1989), 17.

86. A-14, A-9, Grenet and Vaissière, "Last Days of Panjikent," 168–69, 172.

87. Powers, *Empire in Transition*, 172–74; Grenet and Vaissière, "Last Days of Panjikent," 156.

88. E. V. Zeimal, "The Political History of Transoxiana," in *The Cambridge History of Iran*, volume 3, *The Seleucid, Parthian and Sasanian Periods*, ed. Ehsan Yarshater, part 1 (New York: Cambridge University Press, 1983), 259–60.

89. Richard Frye, "Tarxūn-Türxün and Central Asian History," 112–13; E. V. Zeimal, "Political History of Transoxiana," 259–60; Powers, *Empire in Transition*, 171, 177–78, 183.

90. Powers, *Empire in Transition*, 178. Powers renders Dēwāštīč's name in Arabic as al-Diwashini, the same name that Kratchkovsky read as Divashni. Powers inserts the word "Christian" in brackets before "burial place," but the Arabic original says *nāwūs* (Yakubovich, "Mugh 1.I Revisited," 249n31), so I have dropped the word here.

91. Yakubovich, "Mugh 1.I Revisited."

92. Document A-21, discussed in Polyakov, "Kitaiskie rukopisi."

93. Anna A. Ierusalimskaja and Birgitt Borkopp, *Von China nach Byzanz* (Munich: Bayerischen Nationalmuseum, 1996), item no. 120.

94. Elfriede R. Knauer, "A Man's Caftan and Leggings from the North Caucasus of the Eighth to Tenth Century: A Genealogical Study," *Metropolitan Museum Journal* 36 (2001): 125–54.

95. Hyunhee Park, "The Delineation of a Coastline: The Growth of Mutual Geographic Knowledge in China and the Islamic World from 750–1500" (Ph.D. diss., Yale University, 2008), 45.

96. Bloom, *Paper before Print*.

97. Grenet, "Self-Image of the Sogdians," 134.

CHAPTER 5

1. George F. Hourani, *Arab Seafaring in the Indian Ocean in Ancient and Early Medieval Times*, ed. John Carswell, rev. ed. (Princeton, NJ: Princeton University Press, 1995), 61.

2. Sun Fuxi, director, Institute of Preservation and Archeology, Xi'an City, personal communication, April 30, 2004.

3. Cheng Linquan, Zhang Xianyu, and Zhang Xiaoli, "Xi'an Bei Zhou Li Dan mu chutan" [A preliminary exploration on the Northern Zhou tomb of Li Dan in Xi'an], *Yishushi Yanjiu* 7 (2005): 299–308.

4. For an up-to-date survey of the most important finds and the extensive literature about them, see Judith Lerner, "Aspects of Assimilation: The Funerary Practices and Furnishings of Central Asians in China," *Sino-Platonic Papers* 168 (2005): 1–51.

5. Structures of this type are usually called "house-shaped sarcophagi" in the scholarly literature. Wu Hung suggests several possible precedents for these funerary structures, which were in use in earlier centuries and in regions some distance from Xi'an and the other cities with Sogdian graves, in his "A Case of Cultural Interaction: House-Shaped Sarcophagi of the Northern Dynasties," *Orientations* 34, no. 5 (2002): 34–41.

6. Juliano and Lerner, *Monks and Merchants*, 59.

7. There was a hole through the entry passage where a Tang-dynasty well had been dug. Shaanxi sheng kaogu yanjiusuo, *Xi'an Bei Zhou An Jia mu* [An Jia tomb of Northern Zhou at Xi'an] (Beijing: Wenwu Chubanshe, 2003), 12; Rong Xinjiang, "The Illustrative Sequence on An Jia's Screen: A Depiction of the Daily Life of a *Sabao*," *Orientations* 34, no. 2 (2003): 32–35.

8. Shaanxi sheng, *An Jia mu*, 61–62.

9. His mother's surname was Du, a family name not associated with foreigners.

10. Rong Xinjiang, *Zhonggu Zhongguo yu wailai wenming* [Middle-period China and outside cultures] (Beijing: Sanlian Chubanshe, 2001), 119.

11. Insufficient sources mean that we do not know the position of the sabao in the bureaucratic ranking (eighteen ranks existed, from a low of 9b to a high of 1a) of the Northern Zhou, but the next dynasty, the Sui, adopted its bureaucracy from the Northern Zhou. Under the Sui, the sabao of Yongzhou County (the capital) had a rank of 7b, while a sabao of rank 9a was appointed in every prefecture with a population of more than 10,000. Because the Sui adopted much of its bureaucratic structure from the Northern Zhou, it seems likely that the sabao of the Northern Zhou were similarly ranked. Albert E. Dien, "Observations Concerning the Tomb of Master Shi," *Bulletin of the Asia Institute* 17 (2003): 105–16, esp. 109–11.

12. Frantz Grenet, Pénélope Riboud, and Yang Junkai, "Zoroastrian Scenes on a Newly Discovered Sogdian Tomb in Xi'an, Northern China," *Studia Iranica* 33 (2004): 273–84, esp. 278–79.

13. Rong, *Zhonggu Zhongguo yu wailai wenming*, 32.

14. Grenet, "Self-Image of the Sogdians," 134–36; for an opposing view, see Lerner, "Aspects of Assimilation," 29n73.

15. Grenet, Riboud, and Yang, "Zoroastrian Scenes"; see also Yang Junkai, "Carvings on the Stone Outer Coffin of Lord Shi of the Northern Zhou," in Vaissière and Trombert, *Les Sogdiens en Chine*, 21–45. The best translation of the Sogdian epitaph is Yoshida Yutaka, "The Sogdian Version of the New Xi'an Inscription," in Vaissière and Trombert, *Les Sogdiens en Chine*, 57–71, while the best translation of the Chinese epitaph is Dien, "Observations Concerning the Tomb of Master Shi."

16. Another bilingual epitaph, in Chinese and Middle Persian, was dated 874 and found in Xi'an; see Yoshida, "Sogdian Version," 60.

17. Similarly, the Chinese text records that the three sons built a stone item for their father, but the word right after "stone" is missing. Yoshida, "Sogdian Version," 59, 68; bracketed material in Yoshida's translation.

18. Grenet, Riboud, and Yang, "Zoroastrian Scenes."

19. Arthur F. Wright, *The Sui Dynasty* (New York: Alfred A. Knopf, 1978).

20. Heng Chye Kiang, *Cities of Aristocrats and Bureaucrats: The Development of Medieval Chinese Cityscapes* (Honolulu: University of Hawai'i Press, 1999), 9.

21. For brief reports about the excavation of the Tang capital, see *Kaogu* 1961, no. 5: 248–50; 1963, no. 11: 595–611.

22. Twitchett, "T'ang Market System," 245.

23. Heng, *Cities of Aristocrats and Bureaucrats*, 22.

24. Edwin O. Reischauer, trans., *Ennin's Diary: The Record of a Pilgrimage to China in Search of the Law* (New York: Ronald, 1955), 333.

25. Wallace Johnson, trans., *The T'ang Code*, vol. 1, *General Principles* (Princeton, NJ: Princeton University Press, 1979), 252: chapter 6, article 48; Liu Junwen, *Zhonghua chuanshi fadian: Tanglü shuyi* [Chinese law codes for the ages: The Tang Code] (Beijing: Falü Chubanshe, 1999), 144; Liu Junwen, *Tanglü shuyi jianjie* [Commentaries on and interpretations of the Tang Code] (Beijing: Zhonghua Shuju, 1996), 478.

26. Liu, *Jiu Tang shu*, 37:961.

27. Xiang Da, *Tangdai Chang'an yu Xiyu wenming* [Tang-dynasty Chang'an and the civilization of the Western Regions] (1957; repr., Beijing: Sanlian Shudian, 1987), 28n8.

28. Rong Xinjiang, "The Migrations and Settlements of the Sogdians in the Northern Dynasties, Sui and Tang," *China Archaeology and Art Digest* 4, no. 1 (2000): 117–63, esp. 138.

29. Matteo Compareti, "Chinese-Iranian Relations, xv. The Last Sasanians in China," in *Encyclopædia Iranica*, Online Edition, July 20, 2009, available at http://www.iranicaonline.org/articles/china-xv-the-last-sasanians-in-china.

30. Rong, "Migrations and Settlements," 141.

31. James Legge, *The Nestorian Monument of Hsî-an Fû in Shen-hsî, China* (1888; repr., London: Trübner, 1966).

32. Pénélope Riboud, "Tang," in *Handbook of Christianity in China*, ed. Nicolas Standaert vol. 1, *635–1800* (Boston: Brill, 2001), 1–42. For a recent study of the Syriac inscription with a helpful line-by-line translation, see Erica C. D. Hunter, "The Persian Contribution to Christianity in China: Reflections in the Xi'an Fu Syriac Inscriptions," in *Hidden Treasures and Intercultural Encounters: Studies on East Syriac Christianity in China and Central Asia*, ed. Dietmar W. Winkler and Li Tang (Piscataway, NJ: Transaction, 2009), 71–86.

33. Valerie Hansen and Ana Mata-Fink, "Records from a Seventh-Century Pawnshop in China," in Goetzmann and Rouwenhorst, *Origins of Value*, 54–64.

34. Deng Xiaonan, "Women in Turfan during the Sixth to Eighth Centuries: A Look at Their Activities Outside the Home," *Journal of Asian Studies* 58, no. 1 (1999): 85–103, esp. 96.

35. For a sketch of the pots at the time they were found, see Helmut Brinker and Roger Goepper, eds., *Kunstschätze aus China: 5000 v. Chr. bis 900 n. Chr.: Neuere archäologische Funde aus der Volksrepublik China* (Zurich: Kunsthaus, 1980), 33. Like many Cultural Revolution finds, the Hejia Village site was never the subject of a detailed

site report. A preliminary report, which included a list of everything that was found, was published in *Wenwu* 1972, no. 1: 30–42, and I have published a short English article about the site that includes a table of all the finds, "The Hejia Village Hoard: A Snapshot of China's Silk Road Trade," *Orientations* 34, no. 2 (2003): 14–19. For the most thorough treatment in Chinese, see Qi Dongfang, *Tangdai jinyinqi yanjiu* [Studies of the silver and gold vessels of the Tang dynasty] (Beijing: Zhongguo Shehui Kexue Chubanshe, 1999). For a summary in English, see Qi Dongfang, "The Burial Location and Dating of the Hejia Village Treasures," *Orientations* 34, no. 2 (2003): 20–24.

36. Qi, "Burial Location," 202, figure 47.

37. Frédéric Obringer, *L'aconit et l'orpiment: Drogues et poisons en Chine ancienne et médiévale* (Paris: Fayard, 1997); Edward H. Schafer, "The Early History of Lead Pigments and Cosmetics in China," *T'oung Pao*, 2nd ser., 44 (1956): 413–38.

38. For photographs of the cup and details of its exterior and interior as well as line drawings of the exterior scenes, see Qi, *Tangdai jinyinqi*, 66–73.

39. François Louis, "The Hejiacun Rhyton and the Chinese Wine Horn (*Gong*): Intoxicating Rarities and Their Antiquarian History," *Artibus Asiae* 67, no. 2 (2007): 201–42, esp. 207–8.

40. Liu Xinru, *Ancient India and Ancient China: Trade and Religious Exchanges, AD 1–600* (Delhi: Oxford University Press, 1988), 160–61; Jens Kröger, "Laden with Glass Goods: From Syria via Iraq and Iran to the Famen Temple in China," in *Coins, Art and Chronology: Essays on the pre-Islamic History of the Indo-Iranian Borderlands*, ed. Michael Alram and Deborah E. Klimburg-Salter (Vienna: Österreichische Akademie der Wissenschaften, 1999), 481–98.

41. Li Jian, ed., *The Glory of the Silk Road: Art from Ancient China* (Dayton, OH: Dayton Art Institute, 2003), 208, catalog entry no. 116.

42. Louis, "Hejiacun Rhyton," 207–8.

43. Louis, "Hejiacun Rhyton," 210; Yao Runeng, *Histoire de Ngan Lou-Chan (Ngan Lou-Chan Che Tsi)*, trans. Robert des Rotours (Paris: Presses Universitaires de France, 1962), 81–84.

44. Liu, *Jiu Tang shu*, 8:171.

45. François Thierry, "Sur les monnaies Sassanides trouvées en Chine," *Res Orientales* 5 (1993): 89–139.

46. Charles A. Peterson, "Court and Province in Mid- and Late T'ang," in *The Cambridge History of China*, vol. 3, *Sui and T'ang China, 589–906, Part 1*, ed. Denis Twitchett (Cambridge, UK: Cambridge University Press, 1979), 474–86.

47. Rong Xinjiang, "An Shi zhi luan hou Sute huren de dongxiang" [The movement of Sogdians after the An Lushan rebellion], *Jinan Shixue* 2 (2004): 102–23.

48. Vaissière, *Sogdian Traders*, 220, 200n77; Yao Runeng, *Histoire de Ngan Louchan*, 238, 239, 254, 346.

49. Rong, "Migrations and Settlements," 138–39; Sima Guang, *Zizhi tongjian* [Comprehensive mirror for aid in government] (Beijing: Guji Chubanshe, 1957), 232:7493.

50. Edward H. Schafer, "Iranian Merchants in T'ang Dynasty Tales," in *Semitic and Oriental Studies: A Volume Presented to William Popper, Professor of Semitic Languages, Emeritus, on the Occasion of his Seventy-Fifth Birthday, October 29, 1949*, ed. Walter J. Fischel (Berkeley: University of California Press, 1951), 403–22, 411 ("wonder tale"),

409n58 (definition of "*hu*"). See also Francis K. H. So, "Middle Easterners in the T'ang Tales," *Tamkang Review* 18 (1987–88): 259–75.

51. Li Fang, *Taiping guangji* [Wide gleanings from the Taiping Era] (Beijing: Renmin Wenxue Chubanshe, 1959), 403:3252–53.

52. The decision is included in the anthology *Wenming panji*, preserved in Dunhuang document P3813. Liu Junwen, *Dunhuang Tulufan fazhi wenshu kaoshi* [An examination and explanation of documents about the legal system from Dunhuang and Turfan] (Beijing: Zhonghua Shuju, 1989), 444–45; Rong, *Zhonggu zhongguo yu wailai wenming*, 81; Rong, "Migrations and Settlements," 139.

53. Only one epitaph for a merchant survives. Rong Xinjiang and Zhang Zhiqing, *Cong Samaergan dao Chang'an—Suteren zai Zhongguo de wenhua yishu* [From Samarkand to Chang'an: Cultural traces of the Sogdians in China] (Beijing: Beijing Tushuguan Chubanshe, 2004), 137.

54. Axelle Rougelle, "Medieval Trade Networks in the Western Indian Ocean (8th–14th centuries)," in *Tradition and Archaeology: Early Maritime Contacts in the Indian Ocean*, ed. Himanshu Prabha Ray and Jean-François Salles (New Delhi: Manohar, 1996), 159–80.

55. The ancient name of Palembang was Bhoga.

56. The ancient name of this port was Tamralipti.

57. James Legge, trans., *A Record of Buddhistic Kingdoms: Being an Account by the Chinese Monk Fa-Hien of Travels in India and Ceylon (AD 399–414) in Search of the Buddhist Books of Discipline* (1886; repr., Delhi: Munshiram Manoharlal, 1991), 103, 37.

58. This passage has been variously understood by different scholars. Where Luo translates "sabao and merchants," others see "sabao" as an adjective, with the resulting translation "sabao merchants." Luo Feng, "*Sabao*: Further Consideration of the Only Post for Foreigners in the Tang Dynasty Bureaucracy," *China Archaeology and Art Digest* 4, no. 1 (2000): 165–91, esp. 178–79; Legge, *Fa-Hien*, 104, 38.

59. Legge, *Fa-Hien*, 111, 42.

60. Joseph Needham, *Science and Civilisation in China*, vol. 4, *Physics and Physical Technology*, part 3, *Civil Engineering and Nautics*, by Joseph Needham, Wang Ling, and Lu Gwei-Djen (Cambridge, UK: Cambridge University Press, 1971), 563–64.

61. Beal, *Si-yu ki*, xxxiv; *Da Tang Xiyu qiufa gaoseng zhuan*, in *Taishō shinshū Daizōkyō*, vol. 51, text 2066, 1–12b, esp. 11a.

62. Schafer, "Iranian Merchants in T'ang Dynasty Tales," 404n8.

63. See the very helpful discussion of this source in Park, "Delineation of a Coastline," 87–99.

64. Sulayman al-Tajir, *Ancient Accounts of India and China, by Two Mohammedan Travellers Who Went to Those Parts in the 9th Century*, trans. Eusebius Renaudot (London: Printed for Sam. Harding at the Bible and Author on the Pavement in St. Martins-Lane, 1733), 20 (list of goods), 21 (porcelain), 40 (later editor's views); available online through Google Books and the subscriber-only database *Eighteenth Century Collections Online* (http://mlr.com/DigitalCollections/products/ecco/), Range 1831.

For another partial translation, see S. Maqbul Ahmad, trans., *Arabic Classical Accounts of India and China* (Shimla, India: Indian Institute of Advanced Study, 1989).

65. Robert Somers, "The End of the T'ang," in Twitchett, *Cambridge History of China*, 3:682–789.

66. Park, "Delineation of a Coastline," 98.

67. Edward H. Schafer, "The Last Years of Ch'ang-an," *Oriens Extremus* 10 (1963): 133–79, esp. 157–58, citing Lionel Giles, "The Lament of the Lady of Ch'in," *T'oung Pao*, 2nd ser., 24 (1926): 305–80, poem on 343–44.

CHAPTER 6

Many colleagues have helped with this chapter, most notably Victor Mair of the University of Pennsylvania and Rong Xinjiang of Peking University. This chapter draws on two papers previously presented but never published: the first was coauthored with Valéria Escauriaza-Lopez, "The Negotiations for Cave 17: A Case Study in Archaeological Method," presented at "Dunhuang: Past, Present, Future—100th Anniversary of Sir Aurel Stein's Expedition," at the Department of the Far East, Eötvös Loránd University of Science (ELTE), Budapest, December 14–15, 2007; I presented the second, "Locating Dunhuang in a Broader History of the Silk Road," at a conference entitled "A Hundred Years of Dunhuang 1907–2007," at the British Library and the British Academy, London, May 17–19, 2007.

1. The International Dunhuang Project, available online at http://idp.bl.uk, gives the figure of forty thousand items in the cave. Victor Mair provides a breakdown of the number of manuscripts held in different places in "Lay Students and the Making of Written Vernacular Narrative: An Inventory of Tun-huang Manuscripts," *CHINOPERL Papers* 10 (1981): 95–96.

2. Mirsky, *Sir Aurel Stein*, 212–29.

3. Lilla Russell-Smith, "Hungarian Explorers in Dunhuang," *Journal of the Royal Asiatic Society*, 3rd ser., 10, no. 3 (2000): 341–61.

4. See the helpful chronology in Roderick Whitfield, *Dunhuang: Caves of the Singing Sands: Buddhist Art from the Silk Road* (London: Textile & Art Publications, 1995), 341–43.

5. Éric Trombert, "Dunhuang avant les manuscrits: Conservation, diffusion et confiscation du savoir dans la Chine médiévale," *Études chinoises* 24 (2005): 11–55.

6. Rong Xinjiang, "The Nature of the Dunhuang Library Cave and the Reasons for Its Sealing," trans. Valerie Hansen, *Cahiers d'Extrême-Asie* 11 (1999–2000): 247–75. Stein believed—erroneously—that Wang Yuanlu found the cave in 1905: *Ruins of Desert Cathay*, 2:164.

7. Lionel Giles, *Six Centuries at Tunhuang: A Short Account of the Stein Collection of Chinese Mss. in the British Museum* (London: China Society, 1944), 28.

8. The account of Stein's first trip to Dunhuang presented in this chapter draws on Stein, *Ruins of Desert Cathay*, 2:28–30, 159, 165, 798; Stein, *Serindia*, 2:805, 813, 825.

9. Donohashi Akio, "A Tentative Inquiry into the Early Caves of the Mo-kao Grottoes at Tun-huang: Questions Regarding the Caves from the Sui Dynasty," *Acta Asiatica* 78 (2000): 1–27, esp. 2. Ma De has sketched the cliff face at nine different points in time between the fourth and the ninth century: *Dunhuang shiku yingzao shi daolun* [An introduction to the history of the construction of the Dunhuang caves] (Taibei: Xinwenfeng, 2003), 119–50, figs. 1–9. For a chronology of how many caves were dug in each period, see Ma De, *Dunhuang Mogaoku shi yanjiu* [Studies in the history of the Mogao caves at Dunhuang] (Lanzhou, China: Gansu Jiaoyu Chubanshe, 1996), 43–46.

10. Mirsky, *Sir Aurel Stein*, 36–37.

11. Mirsky, *Sir Aurel Stein*, 280, citing Stein's letter to Allen dated October 14, 1907.

12. Paul Pelliot, "Une Bibliothèque Médiévale Retrouvée au Kan-sou," *Bulletin de l'Ecole Française d'Extrême-Orient* 8 (1908): 501–29; Stein, *Serindia*, 2:820.

13. Rong, "Nature of the Dunhuang Library Cave," 256.

14. James Russell Hamilton, ed. and trans., *Manuscrits ouïgours du IXe-Xe siècle de Touen-houang* (Paris: Peeters, 1986), ix.

15. Stein, *On Central Asian Tracks*, 211.

16. Asel Umurzakova, "Russian Archaeological Exploration of the Silk Road," paper for the seminar "The Social History of the Silk Road," dated April 30, 1999, citing S. F. Ol'denburg, *Russkaya Turkestanskaya ekspeditsiya (1909–1910 gg.): Kratkiy predvaritel'ny otchet* [The Russian Turkestan Expedition (1909–1910): Short preliminary report] (St. Petersburg: Imperatorskaya Akademiya Nauk, 1914).

17. Hodong Kim, *Holy War in China: The Muslim Rebellion and State in Chinese Central Asia, 1864–1877* (Stanford, CA: Stanford University Press, 2004).

18. Helen Wang, *Sir Aurel Stein in* The Times: *A Collection of over 100 References to Sir Aurel Stein and His Extraordinary Expeditions to Chinese Central Asia, India, Iran, Iraq and Jordan in* The Times *Newspaper 1901–1943* (London: Saffron Books, 2002), 147–51, appendix 2: "Meng Fanren's Preface to the Chinese Translation of *Serindia*."

19. Hao Chunwen, "A Retrospective of and Prospects for Historical Studies Based on Dunhuang Conducted this Century," *Social Sciences in China* 20, no. 4 (1999): 95–110. This is a translation of an article that appeared in *Lishi Yanjiu* in 1998.

20. Rong Xinjiang, "Zhongguo Dunhuangxue yanjiu yu guoji shiye," *Lishi Yanjiu* 2005, no. 4: 165–75.

21. Valéria Escauriaza-Lopez, "Aurel Stein's Methods and Aims."

22. Stein, *Ancient Khotan*, ix.

23. W. M. Flinders Petrie, *Methods & Aims in Archaeology* (London: Macmillan, 1904), 35 (baksheesh), 119 (publishing), 175 ("test of right"), 187 (government regulations).

24. Stein, *Ancient Khotan*, ix, citing Petrie, *Methods & Aims in Archaeology*, 175.

25. Rong, "Nature of the Dunhuang Library Cave," 247–75.

26. Rong Xinjiang, *Guiyijun shi yanjiu: Tang Song shidai Dunhuang lishi kaosuo* [Studies in the history of the Returning-to-Righteousness Army: An examination of Dunhuang's history in the Tang and Song dynasties] (Shanghai: Shanghai Guji Chubanshe, 1996), 3.

27. John C. Huntington, "A Note on Dunhuang Cave 17: 'The Library,' or Hong Bian's Reliquary Chamber," *Ars Orientalis* 16 (1986): 93–101; Imaeda Yoshirō, "The Provenance and Character of the Dunhuang Documents," *Memoirs of the Research Department of the Toyo Bunko* 66 (2008): 81–102. See also the cybercaves available on the ARTstor.org database (search "Dunhuang," "cave 16," and "QTVR").

28. Éric Trombert, *Le crédit à Dunhuang: Vie matérielle et société en Chine médievale* (Paris: Collège de France, Institut des Hautes Études Chinoises, 1995), 76; citing S2729, as explicated by Fujieda Akira, "Tonkō no sōni seki" [The registers of monks and nuns at Dunhuang], *Tōhō Gakuhō* 29 (1959): 293–95.

29. A partial translation of Document 0345 appears in Rong, "Nature of the Dunhuang Library Cave," 260; the full passage is translated by Stephen F. Teiser, *The*

Scripture of the Ten Kings and the Making of Purgatory in Medieval Chinese Buddhism (Honolulu: University of Hawai'i Press, 1994), 142–43.

30. Earliest text (S 797), Stein, *Serindia* 2: 821n2a; Shi Pingting, *Dunhuang yishu zongmu suoyin xinbian* (A new index to the lost manuscripts of Dunhuang) (Beijing: Zhonghua Shuju, 2000), 27. This is a very useful list of all the manuscripts in the Stein, Pelliot, and Beijing (but not Russian) collections. Latest text, see Rong, "The Nature of the Library Cave," 266.

31. For a discussion of one group of Dunhuang manuscripts not in the Buddhist canon, see *Cahiers d'Extrême-Asie* 7 (1993–1994), a special issue on Chan/Zen studies.

32. Victor Mair gives a breakdown of the number of student-copied manuscripts held in different places in "Lay Student Notations from Tun-huang," in *The Columbia Anthology of Traditional Chinese Literature*, ed. Victor H. Mair (New York: Columbia University Press, 1994), 644–45. See also Erik Zürcher, "Buddhism and Education in T'ang Times," in *Neo-Confucian Education: The Formative Stage*, ed. Wm. Theodore de Bary and John W. Chaffee (Berkeley: University of California Press, 1989), 19–56.

33. Giles, *Six Centuries at Tunhuang*.

34. Frances Wood and Mark Barnard, *The Diamond Sutra: The Story of the World's Earliest Dated Printed Book* (London: British Library, 2010). About the almanac (Dh 2880), see Jean-Pierre Drège, "Dunhuang and the Two Revolutions in the History of the Chinese Book," in *Crossing Pamir: Essays Dedicated to Professor Zhang Guangda for His Eightieth Birthday*, ed. Rong Xinjiang and Huaiyu Chen, forthcoming from Brill.

35. Jean-Pierre Drège, *Les bibliothèques en Chine au temps des manuscrits (jusqu'au Xe siècle)* (Paris: École Française d'Extrême-Orient, 1991).

36. Historians now date the Tibetan conquest of Dunhuang to 786—certainly not 781, and most likely not 787—as proposed by Yamaguchi Zuihō, "Toban shihai jidai" [Dunhuang under Tibetan rule], in *Kōza Tonkō 2: Tonkō no rekishi* (Lectures on Dunhuang 2: The history of Dunhuang), ed. Enoki Kazuo (Tokyo: Daitō Shuppansha, 1980), 195–232, esp. 197–98. My thanks to Sam van Schaik and Iwao Kazushi for this reference.

37. Rong Xinjiang, "Nature of the Dunhuang Library Cave," 251–54.

38. Stein, *Serindia*, 2:813.

39. Originally numbered Pelliot Hébreu 1; now Manuscrit hébreu 1412, Bibliothèque Nationale. Wu Chi-yu, "Le Manuscrit hébreu de Touen-huang," in *De Dunhuang au Japon: Études chinoises et bouddhiques offertes à Michel Soymié*, ed. Jean-Pierre Drège (Geneva, Switzerland: Librairie Droz, 1996), 259–91 (photo of document on 291). Photo available online at http://expositions.bnf.fr/parole/grand/018.htm.

40. For the Avestan prayer: K. E. Eduljee, *Scriptures Avesta*. Available online at http://www.heritageinstitute.com/zoroastrianism/scriptures/manuscripts.htm; for the sheet of paper showing the two deities, see Frantz Grenet and Zhang Guangda, "The Last Refuge of the Sogdian Religion: Dunhuang in the Ninth and Tenth Centuries," *Bulletin of the Asia Institute* 10 (1996): 175–86.

41. In the absence of census data from the ninth and tenth centuries, scholars round up from the pre-755 population figures from the revised official history of the Tang for Dunhuang: 16,250 people living in 4,265 households. Ouyang, *Xin Tang shu*, 40:1045.

42. Jason David BeDuhn, *The Manichaean Body in Discipline and Ritual* (Baltimore: Johns Hopkins University Press, 2000).

43. Peter Bryder, *The Chinese Transformation of Manichaeism: A Study of Chinese Manichaean Terminology* (Löberöd, Sweden: Bokförlaget Plus Ultra, 1985); Gunner B. Mikkelson, "Skilfully Planting the Trees of Light: The Chinese Manichaica, Their Central Asian Counterparts, and Some Observations on the Translation of Manichaeism into Chinese," in *Cultural Encounters: China, Japan, and the West*, ed. Søren Clausen, Roy Starrs, and Anne Wedell-Wedellsborg (Aarhus, Denmark: Aarhus University Press, 1995), 83–108; J. G. Haloun and W. B. Henning, "The Compendium of the Doctrines and Styles of the Teaching of Mani, the Buddha of Light," *Asia Major*, n.s., 3 (1952): 184–212. A partial translation of the Compendium gives the full English translation of the hymn scroll: Tsui Chi, trans., "Mo Ni Chiao Hsia Pu Tsan; 'The Lower (Second?) Section of the Manichæan Hymns," *Bulletin of the School of Oriental and African Studies* 11, no. 1 (1943): 174–219.

44. Mikkelson, "Skilfully Planting the Trees of Light," 87, a partial translation of S3969, P3884.

45. Mikkelson, "Skilfully Planting the Trees of Light," 93.

46. For the most up-to-date survey of these texts, see Riboud, "Tang," 4–7, who explains that some of the Christian texts are of uncertain origin, having been bought by Japanese buyers in 1916 and 1922, and others are forgeries.

47. A. C. Moule, *Christians in China before the Year 1550* (New York: Macmillan, 1930), facing p. 53, reproduces P3847; 53–55 gives the translation. See Riboud, "Tang," for references to other translations.

48. Jean-Pierre Drège, "Papiers de Dunhuang: Essai d'analyse morphologique des manuscrits chinois datés," *T'oung Pao*, 2nd ser., 67 (1981): 305–60.

49. Mair, "Lay Student," 644–45.

50. Hansen, *Negotiating Daily Life*, 50.

51. P3348, transcribed in Ikeda On, *Chūgoku kodai sekichō kenkyū: Gaikan, rokubun* [Research on ancient Chinese population registers: Overview and register texts] (Tokyo: Tōkyō Daigaku Tōkyō Bunka Kenkyūjo, 1979), 463–64.

52. Trombert, "Textiles et tissus," 111.

53. R. A. Stein, *Tibetan Civilization*, trans. J. E. Stapleton Driver (Stanford, CA: Stanford University Press, 1972), provides a charming introduction to the geography and history of Tibet.

54. Ouyang, *Xin Tang shu*, 216a: 6073.

55. Tsugihito Takeuchi, *Old Tibetan Contracts from Central Asia* (Tokyo: Daizo Shuppan, 1995); Takeuchi, "Military Administration and Military Duties in Tibetan-Ruled Central Asia (8th–9th century)," in *Tibet and Her Neighbours: A History*, ed. Alex McKay (London: Edition Hansjörg Mayer, 2003), 43–52. See the bibliographies of Prof. Takeuchi's works for detailed references, including the pioneering studies of the Hungarian scholar Géza Uray.

56. For the Chinese-language contracts, see Trombert, *Le crédit à Dunhuang*; for the Tibetan, see Takeuchi, *Old Tibetan Contracts*.

57. Ikeda On, "Tonkō no ryūtsū keizai" [The circulating economy of Dunhuang], in his *Kōza Tonkō 3: Tonkō no shakai* [Lectures on Dunhuang 3: Dunhuang society] (Tokyo: Daitō Shuppansha, 1980), 297–343, 316–17, citing P2763, P2654.

58. Yamamoto and Ikeda, *Tun-huang and Turfan Documents*, 13–18.

59. Takeuchi, *Old Tibetan Contracts*, 325; Yamamoto and Ikeda, *Tun-huang and Turfan Documents*, no. 257.

60. The Tibetan-language divination texts from Dunhuang that mention coins (P1055, P1056) use the Tibetan word *dong-tse*, a rendering of the Chinese word *tongzi*. See Takeuchi, *Old Tibetan Contracts*, 25–26.

61. Takata Tokio, "Multilingualism in Tun-huang," *Acta Asiatica* 78 (2000): 49–70, esp. 60–62.

62. Lilla Russell-Smith, *Uygur Patronage in Dunhuang: Regional Art Centres on the Northern Silk Road in the Tenth and Eleventh Centuries* (Leiden, The Netherlands: Brill, 2005), 22; Whitfield, *Singing Sands*, 318–26.

63. Ernesta Marchand, "The Panorama of Wu-t'ai Shan As an Example of Tenth Century Cartography," *Oriental Art* 22 (Summer 1976): 158–73; Dorothy C. Wong, "A Reassessment of the *Representation of Mt. Wutai* from Dunhuang Cave 61," *Archives of Asian Art* 46 (1993): 27–51; Natasha Heller, "Visualizing Pilgrimage and Mapping Experience: Mount Wutai on the Silk Road," in *The Journey of Maps and Images on the Silk Road*, ed. Philippe Forêt and Andreas Kaplony (Leiden, The Netherlands: Brill, 2008), 29–50.

64. Jacob Dalton, Tom Davis, and Sam van Schaik, "Beyond Anonymity: Paleographic Analyses of the Dunhuang Manuscripts," *Journal of the International Association of Tibetan Studies* 3 (2007): 12–17, available online at http://www.thlib.org/collections/texts/jiats/#jiats=/03/dalton/.

65. F. W. Thomas, "A Chinese Buddhist Pilgrim's Letters of Introduction," *Journal of the Royal Asiatic Society* (1927): 546–58; Sam van Schaik, "Oral Teachings and Written Texts: Transmission and Transformation in Dunhuang," in *Contributions to the Cultural History of Early Tibet*, ed. Matthew T. Kapstein and Brandon Dotson (Leiden, The Netherlands: Brill, 2007), 183–208; Whitfield, *Silk Road*, 126–27, photo on 127; Sam van Schaik and Imre Galambos, *Manuscripts and Travellers: The Sino-Tibetan Documents of a Tenth-Century Buddhist Pilgrim* (Berlin: De Gruyter, 2011).

66. Matthew T. Kapstein, "New Light on an Old Friend: PT 849 Reconsidered," in *Tibetan Buddhist Literature and Praxis: Studies in Its Formative Period, 900–1400*, ed. Ronald M. Davidson and Christian K. Wedemeyer (Leiden, The Netherlands: Brill, 2006), 23.

67. Takata, "Multilingualism in Tun-huang," 55–56.

68. Rong Xinjiang gives a year-by-year chronology, with relevant document numbers, for the period 848–1043. See his *Guiyijun shi yanjiu*, 1–43. In English, see the cogent summary of Dunhuang history in Russell-Smith, *Uygur Patronage in Dunhuang*, 31–76.

69. Victor H. Mair has devoted much of his scholarly career to studying transformation texts. His first book translated and copiously annotated four of these texts: *Tun-huang Popular Narratives* (New York: Cambridge University Press, 1983). His subsequent books have greatly expanded our understanding of storytelling traditions around the world.

70. Mair, "Lay Students," 5.

71. Mair, *Tun-huang Popular Narratives*, 169. Mair dates the text to between 856 and 870 (p. 11).

72. Southern wall of cave 156, shown in Ma De, *Dunhuang Mogaoku*, 4, figure 133; ARTstor.org offers a much sharper photo.

73. Whitfield, *Singing Sands*, 327, translation of P3720, a record of merit-making by Zhang Huaishen, as cited by Ma De, "Mogaoku ji jianyi," *Dunhuang Xue Jikan* 2 (1987): 129.

74. Ma Shichang, "Buddhist Cave-Temples and the Cao Family at Mogao Ku, Dunhuang," *World Archaeology* 27, no. 2 (1995): 303–17.

75. Sarah E. Fraser, *Performing the Visual: The Practice of Buddhist Wall Painting in China and Central Asia, 618–960* (Stanford, CA: Stanford University Press, 2004), 4 (the painting academy); 37 (donors' preparation); 18–19, figure 1.1 (position of donors' portraits in cave); Fraser, "Formulas of Creativity: Artist's Sketches and Techniques of Copying at Dunhuang," *Artibus Asiae* 59, nos. 3–4 (2000): 189–224.

76. Rong Xinjiang, "The Relationship of Dunhuang with the Uighur Kingdom in Turfan in the Tenth Century," in *De Dunhuang à Istanbul: Hommage à James Russell Hamilton*, ed. Louis Bazin and Peter Zieme (Turnhout, Belgium: Brepols, 2001), 275–98, esp. 287.

77. Rong, *Guiyijun shi yanjiu*, is the definitive work for the political history of Dunhuang in this period.

78. Moriyasu Takao, "Sha-chou Uighurs and the West Uighur Kingdom," *Acta Asiatica* 78 (2000): 28–48, esp. 36–40.

79. Rong, "Relationship of Dunhuang with the Uighur Kingdom," 275–98.

80. The document has not been studied extensively; Zheng Binglin analyzes document P3547 in his very useful article about trade at Dunhuang: "Wan Tang Wudai Dunhuang shangye maoyi shichang yanjiu" [A study of the mercantile trade and markets of Dunhuang in the late Tang dynasty and Five Dynasties periods], *Dunhuang Xue Jikan* 45 (2004): 108. See also Rong, *Guiyijun shi*, 8.

81. Rong, *Guiyijun shi*, 8, 11.

82. The Chinese word *jiu* is best translated as beer. Éric Trombert, "Bière et Bouddhisme—La consommation de boissons alcoolisées dans les monastères de Dunhuang aux VIIIe–Xe siècles," *Cahiers d'Extrême-Asie* 11 (1999–2000): 129–81.

83. P2629 and two related documents are reproduced and transcribed in Tang Geng'ou and Lu Hongji, eds., *Dunhuang shehui jingji wenxian zhenji shilu* [Photographs and transcription of Dunhuang social and economic documents] (Beijing: Shumu Wenxian Chubanshe, 1990), 3:271–76. Feng Peihong presents some of the information in a chart, which omits some visitors, in "Kesi yu Guiyijun de waijiao huodong" [Foreign relations between envoys and the Returning-to-Righteousness Army], in *Dunhuang Guiyijun shi zhuanti yanjiu xubian* [Continued studies on selected topics in the history of the Returning-to-Righteousness Army at Dunhuang], ed. Zheng Binglin (Lanzhou, China: Lanzhou Daxue Chubanshe, 2003), 314–17.

84. S1366 and S2474, discussed in Feng Peihong, "Waijiao huodong," 318.

85. Jacques Gernet, "Location de chameaux pour des voyages, à Touen-huang," in *Mélanges de sinologie offerts à Monsieur Paul Demiéville* (Paris: Institut des Hautes Études Chinoises, 1966), 1:41–51.

86. Gernet, "Location de chameaux," 45, French translation of document P3448.

87. Hao Chunwen and Ning Ke, *Dunhuang sheyi wenshu jijiao* [Collected collations of the club documents from Dunhuang] (Shanghai: Jiangsu Guji Chubanshe, 1997).

88. Ma De, *Dunhuang Mogaoku shi yanjiu*, 255–61.

89. Trombert, *Le crédit à Dunhuang*, 27, 190.

90. Rong Xinjiang, "Khotanese Felt and Sogdian Silver: Foreign Gifts to Buddhist Monasteries in Ninth- and Tenth-Century Dunhuang," *Asia Major*, 3rd ser., 17, no. 1 (2004): 15–34; the Chinese version of the article appeared in *Siyuan caifu yu shisu gongyang*, ed. Hu Suxin [Sarah E. Fraser] (Shanghai: Shanghai Shuhua Chubanshe, 2003), 246–60. The table on 31–34 in the *Asia Major* article is particularly useful; it lists all the commodities in each monastery and the documents mentioning them.

91. I thank my colleague Peter Perdue for this formulation.

92. Schafer, "Early History of Lead Pigments and Cosmetics," 413–38, esp. 428.

93. Zheng Binglin, "Wan Tang Wudai Dunhuang maoyi shichang de wailai shangpin jikao [A study of foreign commodities at the trade markets of Dunhuang in the late Tang dynasty and Five Dynasties period], in Zheng, *Dunhuang Guiyijun shi zhuanti yanjiu xubian*, 399.

94. *Corpus Inscriptionum Iranicarum*, part 2, *Inscriptions of the Seleucid and Parthian Periods and of Eastern Iran and Central Asia*, vol. 3, *Sogdian*, section 3, *Documents turco-sogdiens du IXe–Xe siècle de Touen-houang*, by James Hamilton and Nicholas Sims-Williams (London: Corpus Inscriptionum Iranicarum and School of Oriental and African Studies, 1990), 23; Takata, "Multilingualism in Tun-huang," 51–52.

95. Turco-Sogdian Document A (P3134), transcribed and analyzed in Hamilton and Nicholas Sims-Williams, *Documents turco-sogdiens*, 23–30.

96. Vaissière, *Sogdian Traders*, 328–30.

97. These have been translated by James Russell Hamilton in *Manuscrits ouïgours*.

98. Hamilton, *Manuscrits ouïgours*, 176–78.

99. Moriyasu Takao, *Shiruku Rōdo to Tō teikoku* [The Silk Road and the Tang Empire] (Tokyo: Kōdansha, 2007), 103–11.

100. Stein, *Ruins of Desert Cathay*, 2:38, 68, 99.

CHAPTER 7

Mathew Andrews, Kumamoto Hiroshi, Prods Oktor Skjærvø, Nicholas and Ursula Sims-Williams, Wen Xin, Yoshida Yutaka, and Zhang Zhan all graciously answered queries and provided unpublished materials.

1. For brief histories of Khotan, see Hiroshi Kumamoto, "Khotan ii. History in the Pre-Islamic Period," in *Encyclopædia Iranica, Online Edition*, April 20, 2009, available online at http://www.iranicaonline.org/articles/khotan-i-pre-islamic-history; *Corpus Inscriptionum Iranicarum*, part 2, *Inscriptions of the Seleucid and Parthian Periods and of Eastern Iran and Central Asia*, vol. 5, *Saka Texts*, section 6, *Khotanese Manuscripts from Chinese Turkestan in the British Library*, by Prods Oktor Skjærvø (London: British Library, 2002). Following scholarly convention, subsequent footnotes refer to this book as *Catalogue*.

2. Huili, *Biography of the Tripiṭaka Master*, 164; "Da Tang Da Ci'en si Sanzang Fashi zhuan" [Biography of the Great Tang Tripitaka Master from the Great Ci'en Monastery], in *Taishō shinshū Daizōkyō*, text 2053, 50:251a.

3. My discussion of the Shanpula site is based on a volume published by the Abegg Foundation in Switzerland, which contains extensive translations from Chinese sources and surveys all the earlier site reports in Chinese publications: Dominik Keller and Regula Schorta, eds., *Fabulous Creatures from the Desert Sands: Central Asian Woolen Textiles from the Second Century BC to the Second Century AD* (Riggisberg, Switzerland: Abegg-Stiftung, 2001); see 37, fig. 39, for the saddle blanket, and 50, fig. 48, for a diagram of a cleaver-shaped pit, mentioned below.

4. Stein, *Innermost Asia*, 1:127; 3:1022, 1023, 1027.

5. Angela Sheng, personal communication, June 28, 2010.

6. Elfriede Regina Knauer, *The Camel's Load in Life and Death: Iconography and Ideology of Chinese Pottery Figurines from Han to Tang and Their Relevance to Trade*

along the Silk Routes (Zurich: Akanthus, 1998), 110. The dimensions of the full tapestry are 7.5 feet (2.3 m) long, 19 inches (48 cm) wide.

7. Yu Taishan, *Xiyu zhuan*, 94–95; Ban, *Han shu* 96A:3881; Hulsewé, *China in Central Asia*, 96–97.

8. Following Joe Cribb, Helen Wang dates the Sino-Kharoṣṭhī coins to the first and second centuries CE: *Money on the Silk Road*, 37–38. Hiroshi Kumamoto, "Textual Sources for Buddhism in Khotan," in *Collection of Essays 1993: Buddhism across Boundaries; Chinese Buddhism and the Western Regions* (Taibei: Foguangshan Foundation for Buddhist and Culture Education, 1999), 345–60, notes that the kings' names do not match Chinese sources and dates them slightly later, to the second and early third centuries.

9. *Chu sanzang jiji*, 97a–b; Kumamoto, "Textual Sources for Buddhism in Khotan," 345–60, esp. 347–48.

10. This description of the site draws on Stein, *Ancient Khotan*, 2:482–506, and plate 40.

11. Rhie, *Early Buddhist Art*, 276–322. See also the discussion of the nearby Keriya site in Debaine-Francfort and Idriss, *Keriya, mémoires d'un fleuve*, 82–107.

12. Faxian, *Gaoseng Faxianzhuan*, 857b–c; Legge, *Record of Buddhistic Kingdoms*, 16–20.

13. Aurel Stein, *Sand-buried Ruins of Khotan: Personal Narrative of a Journey of Archaeological and Geographical Exploration in Chinese Turkestan* (London: T. F. Unwin, 1903; repr., Rye Brook, NY: Elibron Classics, 2005), 202.

14. Madhuvanti Ghose, "Terracottas of Yotkan," in Whitfield and Ursula Sims-Williams, *Silk Road*, 139–41.

15. Burrow, *Kharoṣṭhī Documents*, no. 661; in Stein's numbering system, E.vi.ii.1. Stein, *Serindia*, 1:276. For a photograph and succinct discussion, see Ursula Sims-Williams, "Khotan in the Third to Fourth Centuries," in Whitfield and Ursula Sims-Williams, *Silk Road*, 138. See also Thomas Burrow, "The Dialectical Position of the Niya Prakrit," *Bulletin of the School of Oriental Studies* 8, no. 2–3 (1936): 419–35, esp. 430–35. The document may be a copy of an earlier document: Peter S. Noble, "A Kharoṣṭhī Inscription from Endere," *Bulletin of the School of Oriental Studies* 6, no. 2 (1931): 445–55.

16. Skjærvø, *Catalogue*, xxxviii–xl.

17. Ursula Sims-Williams, "Hoernle, Augustus Frederic Rudolf," *Encyclopædia Iranica*, Online Edition, December 15, 2004, available at http://www.iranicaonline.org/articles/hoernle-augustus-frederic-rudolf.

18. A. F. Rudolf Hoernle, "A Report on the British Collection of Antiquities from Central Asia, Part 1," *Journal of the Asiatic Society of Bengal* 70, no. 1 (1898): 32–33; Ronald E. Emmerick, *A Guide to the Literature of Khotan*, 2d ed. (Tokyo: International Institute for Buddhist Studies, 1992), 6n19.

19. Skjærvø, *Catalogue*, lxx–lxxi.

20. R. E. Emmerick, ed. and trans., *The Book of Zambasta: A Khotanese Poem on Buddhism* (New York: Oxford University Press, 1968), order to Ysarkula (163), author's note (9), women's cunning arts (283), closing of chapter on women (285), palace of the gods (19).

21. Dao Shi, *Fayuan zhulin*, a Buddhist encyclopedia compiled in 668, contains a section on lay women. *Taishō shinshū Daizōkyō*, vol. 53, text 2122, 443c–447a. Koichi Shinohara, personal communication, June 25, 2010.

22. H. W. Bailey, "Khotanese Saka Literature," in *The Cambridge History of Iran*, vol. 3, *The Seleucid, Parthian and Sasanian Periods*, ed. Ehsan Yarshater, part 2 (New York: Cambridge University Press, 1983), 1234–35.

23. Skjærvø, *Catalogue*, lxxiii; Emmerick, *Guide*, 4–5; Emmerick, *Book of Zambasta*, xiv–xix.

24. Mauro Maggi, "The Manuscript T III S 16: Its Importance for the History of Khotanese Literature," in *Turfan Revisited: The First Century of Research in the Arts and Cultures of the Silk Road*, ed. Desmond Durkin-Meisterernst et al. (Berlin: Reimer Verlag, 2004), 184–90, 547; dating of earliest manuscript on 184.

25. The best account of this confusing period in English is Kumamoto, "Khotan."

26. Hedin, *My Life As an Explorer*, 188. In his first publications, Hedin referred to the site as "the ancient city Taklamakan"; later he used the name Dandan Uiliq. Stein, *Ancient Khotan*, 1:236.

27. Stein, *Ancient Khotan*, 1:240.

28. Stein, *Ancient Khotan*, 1:241.

29. Christoph Baumer, *Southern Silk Road: In the Footsteps of Sir Aurel Stein and Sven Hedin* (Bangkok: Orchid Books, 2000), 76–90.

30. Rong Xinjiang and Wen Xin, "Newly Discovered Chinese-Khotanese Bilingual Tallies," *Journal of Inner Asian Art and Archaeology* 3 (2008): 99–111, 209–15. The Chinese version of this article appeared in *Dunhuang Tulufan Yanjiu* 11 (2008): 45–69, in an issue devoted to Khotanese studies.

31. Rong and Wen, "Bilingual Tallies," 100, tally no. 2.

32. Yoshida Yutaka gives the most up-to-date translations for the Chinese and Khotanese names for grain grown in Khotan: "On the Taxation System of Pre-Islamic Khotan," *Acta Asiatica* 94 (2008): 95–126, esp. 118. This is the shorter English version of Yoshida's important Japanese book *Kōtan shutsudo 8–9 seiki no Kōtango sezoku monjo ni kansuru oboegaki* [Notes on the Khotanese secular documents of the eighth to ninth centuries unearthed from Khotan] (Kobe, Japan: Kobe City University of Foreign Studies, Research Publications, 2006).

33. Yoshida, "On the Taxation System," 104n19.

34. P. Oktor Skjærvø, "Legal Documents Concerning Ownership and Sale from Eighth Century Khotan," manuscript of a forthcoming article. For the dating of these texts, see Prods Oktor Skjærvø, "The End of Eighth-Century Khotan in its Texts," *Journal of Inner Asian Art and Archaeology* 3 (2008): 119–38, particularly 129–31. For a useful chart summarizing these texts, see table 44, "Contracts," in Helen Wang, *Money on the Silk Road*, 100.

35. Or. 9268A; translated in Skjærvø, "Legal Documents," 61, 63.

36. Or. 9268B; translated in Skjærvø, "Legal Documents," 65–66.

37. Helen Wang, *Money on the Silk Road*, 95–106, esp. table 46, "Payments Made Part in Coin Part in Textiles," 101. Yoshida thinks few coins were circulating in the 770s and 780s, the time of Archives no. 1 and no. 2: "On the Taxation System," 117n43.

38. Hoernle, "Report on the British Collection," 16; Helen Wang, *Money on the Silk Road*, 103.

39. The other archive at Dandan Uiliq is Archive no. 3, dating to 798, with several documents signed by an official named Sudārrjām whose rank was *tsīṣī spāta* (a higher position than simply a *spātā*), who signed documents with the Chinese character *fu* (literally "copy") serving as his signature. Yoshida, "On the Taxation System," 97–100.

40. The chronology of this period has still not been definitively established. See Yoshida Yutaka, "The Karabalgasun Inscription and the Khotanese documents," in *Literarische Stoffe und ihre Gestaltung in mitteliranischer Zeit,* ed. Desmond Durkin-Meisterernst, Christiane Reck, and Dieter Weber (Wiesbaden, Germany: Dr. Ludwig Reichert Verlag, 2009), 349–62, chronological chart on 361; Skjærvø, "End of Eighth-Century Khotan," 119–44; Guangda Zhang and Xinjiang Rong, "On the Dating of the Khotanese Documents from the Area of Khotan," *Journal of Inner Asian Art and Archaeology* 3 (2008): 149–56; Moriyasu Takao, "Toban no Chūō shinshutsu" [The Expansion of Tibet into Central Asia], *Kanazawa Daigaku Bungakubu Ronshū* (shigakuka hen) 4 (1984): 1–85.

41. Yoshida, "On the Taxation System," 100, 117.

42. Here I follow Yoshida, who explains the reasons for his view in "Karabalsagun Inscription," 353–54.

43. Yoshida, "On the Taxation System," 112–13n35.

44. Takeuchi, *Old Tibetan Contracts,* 118–19.

45. Yoshida, "On the Taxation System," 114.

46. Stein, *Ancient Khotan,* 1:282, 307–8.

47. Ursula Sims-Williams, "Hoernle."

48. Economic History Association: "Measuring Worth: Five Ways to Compute the Relative Value of a UK Pound Amount, 1830 to Present," using retail price index, available online at http://www.measuringworth.com/ukcompare.

49. D. S. Margoliouth, "An Early Judæo-Persian Document from Khotan, in the Stein Collection, with Other Early Persian Documents," *Journal of the Royal Asiatic Society of Great Britain and Ireland* (October 1903): 735–60, esp. 735–40, in which Stein explains the circumstances of discovery. Bo Utas has published the most accurate translation, "The Jewish-Persian Fragment from Dandān-Uiliq," *Orientalia Suecana* 17 (1968): 123–36.

50. W. J. Fischel and G. Lazard, "Judaeo-persian," *Encyclopaedia of Islam Three,* ed. Marc Gaborieu, vol. 4 (Leiden, The Netherlands: Brill, 2010), 308–13. Available online by subscription at http://www.brillonline.nl/subscriber/entry?entry=islam_COM-0400.

51. Zhang Zhan and Shi Guang, "Yijian xinfaxian Youtai-Bosiyu xinzha de duandai yu shidu" [A Newly-discovered Judeo-Persian Letter], *Dunhuang Tulufan Yanjiu* 11 (2008): 71–99. I thank Zhang Zhan for showing me his unpublished English translation.

52. Skjærvø, "End of Eighth-Century Khotan," 119.

53. P. Oktor Skjærvø estimated that cave 17 held over two thousand "individual pieces" in Khotanese. E-mail dated August 29, 2003.

54. Dalton, Davis, and van Schaik, "Beyond Anonymity."

55. S2736, S1000, S5212a1, Or. 8212.162, P2927; Skjærvø, *Catalogue,* 35–36, 44–45; Takata Tokio, *Tonkō shiryō ni yoru Chūgokugo shi no kenkyū* [A historical study of the Chinese language based on Dunhuang materials] (Tokyo: Sōbunsha, 1988), 199–227.

56. P5538; H. W. Bailey, "Hvatanica III," *Bulletin of the School of Oriental Studies* 9, no. 3 (1938): 521–43; updated translation by Skjærvø, unpublished manuscript.

57. P4640; Zhang Guangda and Rong Xinjiang, *Yutian shi congkao* [Collected studies on Khotanese history] (Shanghai: Shanghai Shudian, 1993), 112.

58. H. W. Bailey, "Altun Khan," *Bulletin of the School of Oriental and African Studies* 30 (1967): 98.

59. Rolf A. Stein, "'Saint et divin,' Un titre tibétain et chinois des rois tibétains," *Journal Asiatique* 209 (1981): 231–75, esp. 240–41.

60. Zhang and Rong, *Yutian shi congkao*, 110.

61. Valerie Hansen, "The Tribute Trade with Khotan in Light of Materials Found in the Dunhuang Library Cave," *Bulletin of the Asia Institute* 19 (2005): 37–46.

62. There is a very helpful list of these missions in Hiroshi Kumamoto, "Khotanese Official Documents in the Tenth Century A.D." (Ph.D. diss., University of Pennsylvania, 1982), 63–65.

63. *Song huiyao jigao* [The important documents of the Song], Fanyi [The Fan and Yi non-Chinese peoples] (Beiping, China: Guoli Tushuguan, 1936), 7:1b. The original text has Li Shengwen, presumably an error for Li Shengtian.

64. Hansen, "Tribute Trade," 42n5, gives the full references to the different documents about the seven princes and their translations. Scholars disagree about whether the documents date to the 890s or to 966.

65. They carried 600 *jin*, and each *jin* weighed about 600 grams. See "Table of Equivalent Measures," in Hansen, *Negotiating Daily Life*, xiii.

66. Kumamoto, "Khotanese Official Documents," 211–13.

67. P2786; as translated in Kumamoto, "Khotanese Official Documents," 122, and discussed on 197.

68. P2958; translated in Bailey, "Altun Khan," 96. James Hamilton suggests a possible date for the letter of 993: "Le pays des Tchong-yun, Čungul, ou Cumuḍa au Xe siècle," *Journal Asiatique* 265, nos. 3–4 (1977): 351–79, esp. 368.

69. Zhang and Rong, *Yutian shi congkao*, 18.

70. P2958; as translated in Bailey, "Altun Khan," 97.

71. Prods Oktor Skjærvø, "Perils of Princes and Ambassadors in Tenth-Century Khotan," unpublished paper.

72. IOL Khot S. 13/Ch. 00269.109–20; translated in Skjærvø, *Catalogue*, 514.

73. Khot. S. 13/Ch. 00269; as translated in Skjærvø, *Catalogue*, 512.

74. Kumamoto, "Khotanese Official Documents," 218.

75. Kumamoto, "Khotanese Official Documents," 225.

76. Or. 8212.162.125-b5; as translated in Kumamoto, "Khotanese Official Documents."

77. P2786; as translated in Kumamoto, "Khotanese Official Documents," 120.

78. IOL Khot. S. 13/CH. 00269; as translated in Skjærvø, *Catalogue*, 511.

79. P2958; as translated in Bailey, "Altun Khan," 98.

80. P2024; as translated in Kumamoto Hiroshi, "Miscellaneous Khotanese Documents from the Pelliot Collection," *Tokyo University Linguistics Papers (TULIP)* 14 (1995): 229–57. P2024 is translated on 231–35 and discussed on 235–38.

81. Kumamoto, "Miscellaneous Khotanese Documents," 230–31.

82. Kumamoto, "Khotanese Official Documents," 119, 150, 182.

83. Peter B. Golden, "The Karakhanids and Early Islam," in *The Cambridge History of Early Inner Asia*, ed. Denis Sinor (New York: Cambridge University Press, 1990), 354.

84. Andreas Kaplony, "The Conversion of the Turks of Central Asia to Islam as Seen by Arabic and Persian Geography: A Comparative Perspective," in *Islamisation de l'Asie Centrale: Processus locaux d'acculturation du VIIe au XIe siècle*, ed. Étienne de la Vaissière (Paris: Association pour l'Avancement des Études Iraniennes, 2008), 319–38.

85. H. W. Bailey, "Srī Viśa' Śura and the Ta-uang," *Asia Major*, n.s., 11 (1964): 1–26, translation of P5538 on 17–20.

86. *Song huiyao*, Fanyi, 7:3b; Kumamoto, "Khotanese Official Documents," 64.

87. William Samolin, *East Turkistan to the Twelfth Century: A Brief Political Survey* (The Hague: Mouton, 1964), 81.

88. Maḥmūd al-Kāsgarī, *Compendium of the Turkic Languages*, ed. and trans. Robert Dankoff and James Kelly, vol. 1 (Duxbury, MA: Tekin, 1982), 270.

89. Tuotuo, *Liaoshi* [Official history of the Liao dynasty] (Beijing: Zhonghua Shuju, 1974), 14:162.

90. Tuotuo, *Liaoshi*, 14:162.

91. *Song huiyao*, Fanyi, 7:17b–18a; Kumamoto, "Khotanese Official Documents," 64–65.

92. Cl. Huart, "Trois actes notariés arabes de Yarkend," *Journal Asiatique* 4 (1914): 607–27; Marcel Erdal, "The Turkish Yarkand Documents," *Bulletin of the School of Oriental and African Studies* 47 (1984): 261; Monika Gronke, "The Arabic Yārkand Documents," *Bulletin of the School of Oriental and African Studies* 49 (1986): 454–507.

93. Jürgen Paul, "Nouvelles pistes pour la recherché sur l'histoire de l'Asie centrale à l'époque karakhanide (Xe–début XIIIe siècle)," in "Études karakhanides," ed. Vincent Fourniau, special issue, *Cahiers d'Asie Centrale* 9 (2001): 13–34, esp. 33n64.

94. Map 2 in O. Pritsak, "Von den Karluk zu den Karachaniden," *Zeitschrift der Deutschen Morgenländischen Gesellschaft* 101 (1951): 270–300.

95. The best introduction to the history of Xinjiang between 1000 and the present is James A. Millward, *Eurasian Crossroads: A History of Xinjiang* (New York: Columbia University Press, 2007).

96. W. Barthold, *Turkestan Down to the Mongol Invasion*, 3d ed., trans. T. Minorsky (London: Luzac, 1968), 401–3; René Grousset, *The Empire of the Steppes: A History of Central Asia*, trans. Naomi Walford (New Brunswick, NJ: Rutgers University Press, 1970), 233–36.

97. Marco Polo, *The Travels of Marco Polo*, trans. Ronald Latham (New York: Penguin Books, 1958) 82–83. Quotations slightly modified for consistency.

98. Ursula Sims-Williams, "Khotan in the Third to Fourth Centuries," 138.

99. Frances Wood, *Did Marco Polo Go to China?* (London: Secker & Warburg, 1995); Igor de Rachewiltz, "Marco Polo Went to China" *Zentralasiatische Studien* 27 (1997): 34–92.

100. Thomas Allsen, "Mongolian Princes and Their Merchant Partners, 1200–1600," *Asia Major*, 3d ser., 3 (1989): 83–126; Elizabeth Endicott-West, "Merchant Associations in Yüan China: The Ortoγ," *Asia Major*, 3d ser., 3 (1989): 127–54.

101. Michal Biran, "The Chaghadaids and Islam: The Conversion of Tarmashirin Khan (1331–34)," *Journal of the American Oriental Society* 122 (2002): 742–52.

102. Morris Rossabi, "Ming China and Turfan, 1406–1517," *Central Asiatic Journal* 16 (1972): 206–25.

103. L. Carrington Goodrich, "Goes, Bento de," in *Dictionary of Ming Biography, 1368–1644*, ed. L. Carrington Goodrich (New York: Columbia University Press, 1976), 472–74.

104. Jonathan N. Lipman, *Familiar Strangers: A History of Muslims in Northwest China* (Seattle: University of Washington Press, 1997), 58–102.

105. Perdue, *China Marches West*.

106. James A. Millward, *Beyond the Pass: Economy, Ethnicity, and Empire in Qing Central Asia, 1759–1864* (Stanford, CA: Stanford University Press, 1998), 204–5.

107. Kim, *Holy War in China*; A. A. Kuropatkin, *Kashgaria: Eastern or Chinese Turkistan*, trans. Walter E. Gowan (Calcutta: Thacker, Spink, 1882).

108. Komil Kalanov and Antonio Alonso, "Sacred Places and 'Folk' Islam in Central Asia," *UNISCI Discussion Papers* 17 (2008): 175.

109. Hamadi Masami, "Le mausolée de Satuq Bughra Khan à Artush," *Journal of the History of Sufism* 3 (2001): 63–87.

110. Rahilä Dawut, "Shrine Pilgrimage among the Uighurs," *Silk Road* 6, no. 2 (2009): 56–67 available online at http://www.silk-road.com/newsletter/vol6num2/srjournal_v6n2.pdf.

111. Joseph Fletcher, "Les voies (turuq) soufies en Chine," in *Les Ordres mystiques dans l'Islam*, ed. Alexandre Popović and Gilles Veinstein (Paris: EHESS, 1986) 13–26, esp. 23.

112. Jane Macartney, "China Prevents Muslims from Hajj," *Muslim Observer*, November 29, 2007, available online at http://muslimmedianetwork.com/mmn/?p=1545; "Mapping the Global Muslim Population: A Report on the Size and Distribution of the World's Muslim Population" (Washington, DC: Pew Research Center, 2009).

Art Credits

COLOR PLATE SECTION

Plate 1: From Xinjiang Museum, ed., *Xinjiang chutu wenwu* (Excavated Artifacts from Xinjiang) (Shanghai: Wenwu chubanshe, 1975), plate 183. **Plate 2-3:** From Volume I of *China: Ergebnisse eigener residen und darauf gegründeter studien* (Berlin: D. Reimer, 1877–1912), facing p. 500. **Plate 4A:** © The Trustees of the British Museum, Stein IA.XII. cl AN 00031987001. **Plate 4B:** © The Trustees of the British Museum, Stein IA.XII.cl AN0012869001. **Plate 5A:** © The Trustees of the British Museum, L. A. I. 002, AN 00009325001. **Plate 5B:** From *Serindia* Plate XL. **Plates 6 and 7:** Wang Binghua. **Plate 8:** Xinjiang Museum. **Plate 9:** Author photo. **Plate 10:** From *Central Asia and Tibet*, facing page 106. **Plate 11A:** Museum fuer Asiatische Kunst, Staatliche Museen, Berlin, Germany, MIK III 4979 V. **Plate 11B:** François Ory. **Plate 12:** Bibliothèque Nationale de France, Manuscrits orientaux, hébrue 1412. **Plate 13:** From *Xinjiang Wewuer Zijiqu Bowuguan*, plate 34–5. **Plate 14:** From *Xian Bei Zhou An Jia Mu*, plate 42. **Plate 15:** From *Xian Bei Zhou An Jia Mu*, color plate 8. **Plate 16A:** Mathew Andrews, 12/11/08. **Plate 16B:** Mathew Andrews, 7/8/10.

INTRODUCTION

Page 2: Xinjiang Museum, Document #66TAM61:17(b). **11:** From *Xinjiang chutu wenwu*, plate 180. **16:** From Chang, *The Rise of the Chinese Empire*, plate 5.

CHAPTER 1

Page 25: Courtesy of the Board of the British Library. **31:** Courtesy of rock art archive, Heidelberg Academy of Sciences. **37:** From *Serindia*, figure 63, Courtesy of the Board of the British Library 392/27 (89). **39:** From *Xinjiang chutu wenwu*, plate 35. **40, 41:** Wang Binghua. **46:** From *Ancient Khotan*, Page 406, plate 72. **53:** Wang Binghua.

CHAPTER 2

Page 57: BNF, Manuscrits orientaux, Pelliot Koutchéen LP I + II. **62:** Courtesy of the Freer Gallery of Art and Arthur M. Sackler Gallery, Smithsonian Institution, Washington, D.C. **63:** From *The Art in the Caves of Xinjiang*, Cave 17, Plate 8. **67:** Takeshi Watanabe, 7/25/06.

CHAPTER 3

Page 84: From Aurel Stein, *Innermost Asia*, plate XCIII detail. **89:** Author photo. **105:** From Yan Wenru, "Tulufan de Gaochang gucheng," *Xinjiang kaogu sanshinian*, p. 137. **109:** From J. Hackin, *Recherches Archéologiques en Asie Centrale* (Paris: Les Éditions D'Art Et D'Histoire, 1931), plate I.

CHAPTER 4

Page 112: Courtesy of the Board of the British Library, Sogdian Letter #2 T.XII.A.II.2 Or.8212/95. **123:** Frantz Grenet. **124, 126:** Guitty Azarpay, *Sogdian Painting: The Pictorial Epic in Oriental Art*, University of California Press, 1981, the Regents of the University of California. **128:** © 2010 F. Ory-UMR 8546-CNRS. **131:** Frantz Grenet.

CHAPTER 5

Pages 140, 142: Xinjiang Museum (Chang'an diagram: Document #73TAM206:42/10). **145:** Cultural Relics Publishing House. **147:** From figure 4A, Yang Junkai, "Carvings on the Stone Outer Coffin of Lord Shi of the Northern Zhou," *Les Sogdians de Chine* (Paris: École française d'Extrême-Orient, 2005), p. 27. **150, 155:** Cultural Relics Publishing House.

CHAPTER 6

Page 168: From *Ruins of Desert Cathay*, p. 188. **172:** Courtesy of the Board of the British Library, 392/56 (690). **178:** From Wenwu, 1978, #12:23. **180:** Courtesy of the Board of the British Library, 392/27 (589). **189:** Amelia Sargent, detail from Dunhuang Cave 156. **193:** Amelia Sargent, detail from Dunhuang Cave 45.

CHAPTER 7

Page 198: BNF, Manuscrits orientaux, Pelliot V 5538. **203, 204:** Abegg-Stiftung, CH-3132 Riggisberg, inv. no. 5157. **205:** From *Ancient Khotan*, Figure 65. **206:** From *Ancient Khotan*, Figure 69. **208:** From Plate XLVII, *Ancient Khotan*. **213:** From Plate LXII, *Ancient Khotan*. **219:** From *Dunhuang tuwufan yanjiu*, Volume 11 (2008), colored plate #4. **223:** Amelia Sargent, detail from Dunhuang Cave 61.

CONCLUSION

Page 236: Courtesy of the Board of the British Library, Or. 8210/p. 2.

Index

Note: Page numbers in *italics* indicate photographs and illustrations.

Abbasid Caliphate, 138, 227
Abhidharma, 221
Abu Zayd, 165
Academy of Social Sciences, 130
Adams, Douglas Q., 72
adoption of children, 48,
    215
Aesop, 125
Afghanistan
    and Buddhist caves, 64
    Chinese trade goods in, 236
    and cultural exchange, 21,
        25, *26*
    and Hejiacun Village Hoard,
        156
    and Jewish-Persian documents,
        217
    and Kharoshthi script, 30
    and lapis lazuli, 194
    and Niya artifacts, 38, *39*, 50,
        52, 239
    and Silk Road routes, 27
    and Sogdians, 121
    and Tocharian language, 71–72
    and trading caravans, 196–97
    and Xuanquan documents,
        17–18
Afrasiab History Museum, 125
Afrasiab murals, 125, *128*, 129,
    138–39, *color plate 11B*
agates, 156, 194
Agnean language, 56–57, 70,
    73–75, 77, 82
Ahura Mazda, 98, 118, 123
Ajanta caves, 62
Akamatsu Akihiko, 47

Ak-Beshim, 114
Akhun, Islam, 217
Aksu River, 60
al-Biruni, 128–29
al-Diwashini. *See* Devashtich
Alexander of Macedon
    (Alexander the Great), 30,
    41, 48, 116, *color plate 13*
al-Harashi, Said, 136
Allen, Percy Stafford, 34, 174
al-Tabari, Muhammad ibn Jarir,
    130, 136
Aluohan, 149
amber, 194
Amgoka, 44
Amitabha Buddha, 182
Ammoniac Mountains, 122
Ancient Khotan (Stein), 176–77
An Jia, 143–46, *145*, *color plate 14*
An Lushan rebellion
    and Dunhuang cave
        documents, 183–85
    and economy of the Silk Road,
        237
    and Hejiacun Village Hoard,
        156–57
    and Khotanese legal system,
        215
    and retribution against
        Sogdians, 157–58
    and the Tang dynasty, 80–81,
        107–8, 137, 187
    and Tibetans, 184–85, 212
An Rokhshan. *See* An Lushan
    rebellion
anti-foreign sentiment, 159–60

Anxi Protectorate, 80
Anyang, 207, 235–36
Appian Way, 8
Arabic, 165, 228, 232
Aramaic, 117
Armenians, 231
arrowheads, 36
art. *See specific forms of art*
Arthashastra, 47
Ashoka, 200
Astana graveyard, *84*, *86*, 93–99,
    151, *color plate 1*
    and Sasanian coins, *color plate
    4B*
Atush, *color plate 16A*
Augustine, Saint, 182, *color plate
    11A*
avadana stories, 62
Avar confederacy, 75

Bactria, 14, *33*, 41
Bactrian language, 71
Badamu Village, 99
Bahudhiva, 209
Bai family, 66, 79
bamboo slips and documents, 14,
    15, 250n25
Bamiyan caves, 64
Ban Chao, 66
banditry. *See* robbers and bandits
bankruptcy law, 165
Bartus, Theodor, 60–61
Basra, 165
Battle of Talas, 137, 138
Baumer, Christoph, 212
Beijing Library Collection, 183

Beiting, 72, 108
Bezeklik, *109*, 110, *color plate 9*
Big Goose Pagoda, 151
bilingual texts, 220, 240
Blackmore, Charles, 9–10
Bodhi, 210
"The Book of Honor," 183
The Book of Zambasta, 210–12
Bosshard, Walter, 212
"Bound for Samarkand" (letter),
    112, 118
Bower, Hamilton, 10, 209
Bower Manuscript, 209
Boxer Rebellion, 169
Brahmans, 94, 143, 146, 161, 192
Brahmi script, 30, 53–54, 57, 70,
    209–10, 220
Britain, 233
Brough, John, 44
Buddhism
    and *The Book of Zambasta*,
        210–12
    and cataloging of documents,
        180
    and Chang'an, 150, 159–60
    and Dandan Uiliq, 12
    and dharma, 47
    and *The Diamond Sutra*, 24,
        179, 183, *236*
    and Dunhuang cave
        documents, 24, 167, 168,
        173, 181, 183, 188, 190, 241
    and education, 56
    Hinayana Buddhism, 68
    and immigrant populations
        from Gandhara, 21
    and Khotan, 199–200, 203–7,
        210–12, 221, 225, 227,
        228–29, 231, 240
    and Kroraina Kingdom, 26, 30,
        31, *33*–35, 47, 51–55, *53*
    and Kucha, 56–57, 66–70,
        76–77, 80
    and language studies, 221
    Mahayana Buddhism, 52,
        66–68, 69
    Maitreya Buddha, 61, 211
    and migrant populations, 4,
        239
    and missionaries, 240
    and Samarkand, 138
    and Sogdiana, 125
    and stupas, 30, *31*, *33*–35, *53*,
        61–62, *62*, 204–6, *205*, *205*,
        207
    and Tibetan rule, 186

    and Turfan, 85, 88, 90–92, 108,
        110–11, 231
Bühler, Georg, 173
Bukhara, 144
Bulayik, 108–9
burial practices
    and Buddhist stupas, 30, *31*,
        33–35, *53*
    coffins, 38–39, 41, *41*
    and coins, 123, *color plate 4A*
    funerary garments, *2*, *3*
    joint burials at Niya, *color
        plate 7*
    Khotanese, 201–2, *204*
    of Kroraina Kingdom, 38–42,
        41
    and *mazar* shrines, *color plate
        16A*
    Sogdian, 98–99, 143–46, *145*,
        147, 239–40
    and the Tang dynasty, 157
    tomb figurines, *140*
    and Turfan, 92–94, 98–99
Burma, 156
Burrow, Thomas, 43, 44
Burzil Pass, 27
Byzantine Empire, 20, 97–98, 123

camels
    and archeological expeditions,
        9, 11, 27, *33*, 38, 64, 94, 168,
        196, 212
    and caravans, *3*, 36, 79, 103
    and diplomatic envoys, 16–17,
        50, 191, 192, 222
    market for, 106, 148, 225
    and migrant populations, 48
    and religious artwork, 124, 128,
        144, *145*, *147*
    and sale documents, 209
    and tourism, 203
    and travel passes, 104
    and Xuanzang's travels, 113
Cao family at Dunhuang, *190*,
    191–92, 222, 227
Cao Lushan (Rokhshan), *2*,
    102–3, 148–49
Cao Yijin, 190, 222
Cao Yuanzhong, 186, 190
Capastaka, 225
capillary routes, 32
caravans
    and Bento de Goes, 231–32
    and camels, *3*, 36, 79, 103
    and Kucha trade, 77–82, *78*
    and local economies, 196–97

    and Sogdiana, 122, 239
    and Turfan, 88, 103–4, 232
    and the Western Market, 148
carbon 14 testing, 204
cataloging systems, 180, *180*
cattle
    and Kucha, 76
    and legal disputes, *3*
    and the Loulan garrison, 42
    and migrant populations, 48
    and Sogdian traders, 103
    and tax documents, 216
    and travel passes, 77–78, *78*
    and the Turfan market, 106
    and Xuanzang's travels, 114
Caucasoid groups, 13, 38
Chach, 127
Chaghanian Kingdom, 127
Chaghatai Khanate, 229, 231
Chang'an
    and the An Lushan rebellion,
        157–59, 185
    and anti-foreign sentiment,
        159–60
    and foreign merchants, 148–49,
        157–58
    and Han dynasty, 17, 34, 65,
        141, 143, 147
    and Hejiacun Village Hoard,
        152–57, *153*–*54*, *155*
    and the Huang Chao rebellion,
        165–66
    and Kumarajiva's travels,
        68–70
    and modern Xi'an, *142*
    and religious communities,
        149–51
    and sea travel, 160–65, *162*–*63*
    and Silk Road art, 239
    and Sogdians, 103, 143–47,
        145, *147*, 149–50, 157–59
    and Tang dynasty, 148–49, 191
    tombs found at, 22
    and Xuanzang's travels, 85, 141,
        144, 151
    See also Xi'an
Chat, 135
Chinese Communist Party, 93,
    233
Chinese language
    Dandan Uiliq documents, 215
    Duldur Aqur documents,
        81–82
    and Dunhuang cave
        documents, 180–81, *182*,
        185, 188, 195

and early European
geographers, 7
epitaphs, 143, 240
Faxian's writings, 55
and Khotanese government,
211, 214, 222, 227
and Kumarajiva, 56, 69–70
legal contracts, 81, 95
Mount Mugh documents, 137
and Qu dynasty, 91
Chinggis Khan, 229
Chinwad Bridge, 146
Christianity
and Chang'an, 149–50, *150*,
159–60
and cultural exchange, 4
and Dunhuang cave
documents, 167, 181, 183,
195, 241
and Huang Chao rebellion, 165
and Küchlük, 229
and the Tang dynasty, *150*
and Turfan, 108–10
Church of the East (Christian)
and Dunhuang cave
documents, 167, 181, *183*,
195
and Küchlük, 229
and migrant populations, 4,
149–50
and the Tang dynasty, 150, *150*
and Turfan, 109–10
clay figurines, 207, *208*
climate
and Chang'an, 151
and Dunhuang cave
documents, 175
and human remains, 13, 38, 39
Khotan, 199
Niya and Loulan sites, 38
of Samarkand, 116
Taklamakan desert, 10, 242
and Turfan, *11*, 21, 92–93
and Xuanzang's travels, 114
Coan silk, 19
coffins, 38–39, 41, *41*
coins
Arabo-Sasanian, 96
Byzantine coins, 9, 20, 97, 156
of Chang'an, 159, 165
of Dandan Uiliq, 215
and the Dunhuang cave
documents, 195, 215
gold, 9, 20, 48–49, 90, 93–98,
123, 153, 156, *156, color
plate 4A*

Greek types found in Gandhara
region, 48–49
of Hejiacun Village Hoard, 152,
153–54, 156–57
hybrid coins, 202
of Khotan, 202, 209
of Kroraina Kingdom, 35–36,
42–43, 48–50
of Kucha, 76, 79, 81–82
and legal disputes, 3–4
and local barter trade, 4
of Panjikent, 122–23
and payments to soldiers, 8–9
and port trade, 165
of Rome, 9, 20, 97
of Samarkand, 119, 132
of the Sasanian Empire, 3, 20,
75–76, 90, 93, 95, 97–102,
156, *color plate 4B*
silver, 3, 20, 49, 75–76, 90, 93,
97–102, 156, *color plate 4B*
Sino-Kharoshthi coins, 202
of Tang dynasty, 151–52,
159–60, 184–86, 193
and Tibetan rule, 185–86
and trade with Rome, 9, 20,
color plate 4A
of Turfan, 93–99, *100–102*, 103,
104, 106–7, 111
of Xuanquan, 15
colophons, 71
commodities, 99–102, *100–102*,
119, 239
Communist Party (China), 93,
233
*The Compendium of the Teachings
of Mani the Buddha of Light*,
183
Confessions (Augustine), 182
Confucianism, 144, 152, 182–83
Constantine, 97, **color plate 4A**
contracts
Astana graveyard documents,
94
and the Dunhuang economy,
192–94
and Karakhanid state, 228
and Khotanese documents, 209
marriage contracts, 133–34
and moneylenders, 96
and Niya documents, 45–47
and slavery, 3
and the Tang dynasty, 103–4,
192–93
and Tibetan rule, 185,
216–17

and wooden documents,
214–15
See also loan documents
coral, 194
corpses. *See* burial practices;
human remains
Cos (Greek island), 19
cosmopolitanism, 30, 83, *128*, 167,
181–82. *See also* Chang'an
cotton textiles, 38, *39*, 138, 195
court records, *2*, 3
craftsmen, 238
Crimean Peninsula, 229
Ctesiphon, 120
cultural exchanges, 5, 21, *25*, 26,
238
Cultural Revolution, 93, 94, 152,
175

Dandan Uiliq
Archive of Khotanese material,
286nn37, 39
Buddhist statues of, 12
Hedin on, 286n26
Judeo-Persian documents, *219*
and Khotanese documents,
199, 210, 212–13, *213*,
221–22
and Stein's excavations,
217–18
and tax documents, 215–17
Daoism, 80, 108, 169
"Daoist Wang." *See* Wang Yuanlu
Daozhen, 178–79
Da Qin, 18, 32
de Goes, Bento, 231–32, 242
Deng Xiaoping, 93
Devaputra, 187
Devashtich, 130, 134–36
dharma, 47, 55. *See also*
Buddhism
Dharmaguptakas, 52
The Diamond Sutra, 24, 179, 183,
236, 241
diao taxes, 152
diplomats. *See* envoys
divorce, 133
dmar, 185–86
Domoko, 199, 213
donkeys, *78*, 79, 83
Duldur Aqur, 79–80, 82
Dunhuang
and Buddhist pilgrimages,
221
cave 1, (see *library cave*
subentry below)

Dunhuang (*continued*)
 cave paintings, 24, 167–69,
  168, 172–79, *178*, 181, 186,
  188–90, *189*, *223*, 240
 and diplomatic envoys, 15, 188,
  191–92, 224–25
 and the Gansu Corridor, 9
 and the Han dynasty, 14,
  168–69
 and Hebrew documents, *color
  plate 12*
 and Khotanese documents, 24,
  181, 199, 210, 220, 226, 241
 library cave at, 24, 167, *168*,
  169, 173–75, 177–79, *178*,
  180, 181–83, 187–88, *198*,
  199, 218–20, 222, 226, 228,
  241
 location of, *170–71*
 and religious toleration, 241
 rulers of, *190*
 scope of documents at, 24
 and the Sogdian Ancient
  Letters, 116–19
 and Stein, 167–77, *172*, 180–81,
  196–97
 and the Tang dynasty, 184–85,
  186–88
 and tourism, 10
 Uighur conquest of, 216
Dunhuang Research Institute,
 172, *172*, 178
Du You, 107

earthquakes, 61
Eastern Market (Chang'an), *142*,
 148
Eastern Turks, 149
edicts
 and Buddhism, 47
 and Kharoshthi documents, 49
 and Khotan, *198*, 227
 and Qing dynasty, 232
 and Shanshan, 35, 250n25
 travel bans, 261n3
 and Xuanquan site, 15
education
 language education, 56,
  220–21, 240
 and spread of paper
  technology, 137–39
Elgin Marbles, 175
Endere, 35, 52, 199, 207, 209
envoys
 and the Afrasiab murals, 129,
  color plate 11B

and the An Lushan rebellion,
 157
and character of the Silk Road,
 238
documentary evidence on,
 50–51, 240–41
and Dunhuang, 15, 188, 191–92,
 224–25
and Gaochang Kingdom, 94
and Khotan, 16, 191, 192, 202,
 222–26, 241
and Kroraina Kingdom, *28–29*,
 49–50
epitaphs, 99, 143–44, 146, 240
ethnic diversity of the Silk Road,
 13, 136

fabrics. *See* textiles
Fadu, 32
fan ("foreign"), 194
Faxian, 55, 160–64, *162–63*,
 205–6, 240
Ferghana, 16, 136
fire altars and temples, 118, *123*,
 124, 144, *color plate 15*. *See
 also* Zoroastrianism
Forest of Steles (Beilin) Museum,
 149
Four Garrisons, 79, 211, 260n67
fragrances, 194
France, 167
frankincense, 20, 165
fraudulent artifacts, 97, 207, 217
Freiman, A. A., 130
frescoes, 212
Fu Hao, 13
funerary garments, *2*, *3*. *See also*
 burial practices
Furen Khi-vyaina, 225

Gandhara region
 and Hejiacun Village Hoard,
  156
 and house excavation, *37*
 and Kroraina Kingdom, 26–27,
  30, 32, 35, 37–38, 44–48,
  50–52
 and Kucha, 66
 and Kumarajiva, 56
 and migrant populations,
  50–51, 239
 and the Rawak statues, 205
 seals of, *46*
Gandhari language, 30, 32, 51, 56,
 66, 71, 209
Gansu Corridor, 9, 14, *59*

Gansu Province
 and business partnerships, 119
 and caravan trade, 232
 climate of, 13
 and coin shortages, 195
 and De Goes' expedition, 232
 and Shi Wirkak, 146
 and Stein's expeditions,
  167–68, 196
 and Tang rule, 107–8, 184, 237
 and Tibetan rule, 108, 158,
  185–86
 and Uighur rule, 111, 190, 196,
  220
 and Wuwei, 42, 68, 79, 85, 137,
  144, 146
 and Xiyu (Western Regions), 9
 and the Yuezhi, 32, 71
Ganzhou, 190, 192, 224–25
Gaochang, *89*, 89–95, 98–99,
 105, 108
Gao Juren, 157
Gaozong, Tang-dynasty Emperor,
 125
garbage pits, 15, 36, 131
Garuda, 61
gems, 155–56, 194
Genghis Khan, 229
Germany, 167
Ghafar, Abdul, 34
Ghurak, 135
Gilgit River, 32
Gilgit Road, 30
glassmaking, 122, 238
Global Positioning System, 212
Gobi Desert, 9, 55
Godfrey, S. H., 209
gold, 41, 48–49, 93, 96–98,
 100–102, *153–54*, 156, 165,
 205, 231, 239. *See also* gold
 under coins *entry*
Gongyuecheng, 103
Govind Kaul, 12
graffiti, 30–32, *31*, 76
grain, 132, 184, 194
graves, 201–2. *See also* Astana
 graveyard; burial practices;
 human remains
Greater Yuezhi, 32
Great Leap Forward, 93
Greek culture, 18–19, 46, 48, *color
 plate 13*
Grenet, Frantz, 138–39
Grünwedel, Albert, 65, 175
Guangzhou (Canton), 150, 161,
 164, 165–66

Guanyin, 88, 161, *193*
Guanyin Monastery, 151–52
guosuo. See travel passes
Guo Xin, 80

hajj pilgrimage, 232, 234, 241
Hami, 85, 88–89, 104, 107, 232
Han dynasty
    and Chang'an, 17, 34, 65, 141,
        143, 147
    and coins, 156
    and diplomatic envoys, 236
    and documents on the Silk
        Road, 14–18
    and Dunhuang cave
        documents, 14, 168–69
    and foreign influence in art,
        20–21
    and Khotan, 202
    and Kroraina Kingdom, 26, 32,
        34–37, 42, 55
    and Kucha, 65–66
    and military presence on the
        Silk Road, 8, 14–15, 236
    and trade with Rome, 20–21
    and Turfan, 83, 90
hang ("row"), 148
Hangzhou Silk Museum, 19
Han Wudi, 65
Hebei Province, 157
Hebrew, 31–32, 181, 217, 218–19,
    219, 241, *color plate 12*
Hedin, Sven
    and itinerant traders, 11,
        237–38
    and Khotan, 12, 13, 212
    and Kroraina Kingdom, 27
    and Kucha, 58–60
    Niya and Loulan excavations,
        38, 43
    and "Silk Road" term, 8
    and Taklamakan Desert, 11–12,
        242, *color plate 10*
Hejiacun Village Hoard, 152–57,
    153–54, 155, 239
Henan Province, 235–36
Henning, W. B., 71
Hephthalites, 75, 120–21
Heraclius, 156
herding, 132. *See also* cattle
Hermitage Museum, 122
Hinayana Buddhism, 68, 69
Hinaza Deva Vijitasimha,
    209
The History of the Han Dynasty,
    34, 35

The History of the Later Han,
    34, 40
Hoernle, Frederick Rudolf,
    209–10
Hongbian, 177, *178*
horses, 16, *78,* 80–82, 222–24
house excavations, *37,* 38
Huang Chao, 165–66
Huili, 85, 87, 88–89, 113, 114
Hulu River, 85, 86
human remains, 38–42, *41,*
    92–93, 201–2. *See also* burial
    practices
Huns, 117, 120–21
Huntington, Ellsworth, 212
Hunza River, 32
Husejnov, D., 130
Huvishka, 52

Ibn Hawkal, 122
Ibrahim (guide), 33–34
imperialism, 175
imported goods, 194, *233*
incenses, 194
India
    and An Jia, 143
    Buddhist missionaries, 66
    and de Goes' travels, 231
    and Dunhuang cave
        documents, 186–87
    funding for expeditions, 212
    gemstones of, 156
    influence in Kroraina Kingdom,
        25–26, 45
    and migrant populations, 200,
        236, 239
    and pilgrimage routes, *162–63*
    and religious art, 122, 125–27,
        126
    and Roman coins, 20
    and sea travel, 160–65, *162–63*
    and silk production, 19
    and Stein's expeditions, 174
    and Turfan, 94
Indus River, 32
International Dunhuang Project,
    176
inventory documents, 194
Iran
    and Chang'an, 150
    and Hejiacun Village Hoard,
        154, *155*
    and imported goods, 194
    languages of, 210
    and Manichaeism, *color plate 11A*
    and Sasanian refugees, 149

and the Sogdians, 113
    trade with Tang dynasty, 97
    and Zoroastrianism, 118, 181
Iraq, 165
Isai, Abdullah (Bento de Goes),
    231–32
Islam
    and coin designs, 97
    and Dunhuang caves, 175
    and the Huang Chao rebellion,
        165
    Islamic law, 228, 232
    and Khotan, 24, 199, 201, 218,
        226–34, 241–42
    and *mazar* shrines, 234, *color
        plate 16A*
    and Sasanian refugees, 149
    and Sogdiana, 116, 129, *131,*
        136–37
    spread with migrant
        populations, 139
    and Turfan, 95, 98, 111
    and use of paper, 138
Ito Toshio, 43

jade
    and de Goes, 231–32
    and diplomatic envoys,
        222–27, 241
    and earliest Silk Road trade,
        235–36
    and Xuanzang's travels, 207
Jade Gate, 85, 86
Jafar Sadik, Imam, 33
Japan, 167
jataka stories, 62–63, *63,* 73–74
Jesuit missionaries, *150,* 231–32
Jewish merchants, 31–32, 217–18,
    219, 231
Jiangsu, 164
Jiang Xiaowan, 169, 173–76, 180
Jiaohe, 91
Jiayuguan, 232
Jingjing, 183
Jingjue Kingdom, 35, 36, 40–41
jitumgha, 44
Jiumoluoshi, 70. *See also*
    Kumarajiva
Jiuquan, 119
Judaism, 165, 167, 241
Judeo-Persian language, *219*
judicial assemblies, 215
Jushi people, 90

Kabul, 231
Kageyama Etsuko, 98

Kaiyuan reign period, 156
Karakash River, 207
Karakhanids, 226–28, 241, *color plate 16A*
Karakhoja, 93
Karakorum Highway, *30, 31,* 31–32, 53, 218
karma, 164
Kashgar, 79, 218, 227, 234
Kashmir, 156
Keriya, *33*, 53
Khakhsar, 135
Khan, Sher Ali, 196–97
Kharoshthi script
    and Endere documents, 207–9
    and Kroraina Kingdom documents, *25*, 26–27, 30, 32–38, 42–43, 45–47
    and Kumarajiva, 57
    and Niya and Loulan documents, 202, 237
    and Sogdian documents, 117
Khoja Afaq, 232–33
Khorezm, 128
Khotan, *200–201*
    and Afghan caravans, 196
    and Buddhism, 199–200, 203–7, 210–12, 221, 225, 227, 228–29, 231, 240
    and diplomatic envoys, 16, 191, 192, 202, 222–26, 241
    and Hedin's explorations, 12, 13, 212
    and Islam, 24, 199, 201, 218, 226–34, 241–42
    and the jade trade, 235–36
    and Kroraina Kingdom, 48, 49–51, 54
    and *mazar* shrines, 234
    and the Tang dynasty, 79, 211, 226
    and Uighur population, 226, 233–34
Khotanese
    and Buddhist monasteries, 240
    and Dunhuang cave documents, 24, 181, 199, 210, 220, 226, 241
    and Islamic conquest, 199
    and legal contracts, 209
    and royal documents, *198*
    and Uighur language, 199, 211, 234
Khotan River, 11, 207
Khubilai Khan, 111

Khujand, 136
Khunjerab Pass, 32
Khusrau II, 156
Khvarnarse, 209
Kidarites, 120
Kirghiz, 108, 190, 216, 226
Kizil caves, 56–58, 60–65, *62, 63,* *67*, 77
Koguryo, 128
Kongque (Peacock) River, 27
Korea, 128, 147, 157, 165
Korla, 60, 75
Kratchkovsky, I. Y., 130
Kroraina Kingdom, *28–29*
    Buddhism in, 26, 30, *31,* 33–35, 47, 51–55, *53*
    burial practices, 38–42, *41*
    coins of, 35–36, 42–43, 48–50
    Gandhara immigrants, 26–27, 30, 32, 35, 37–38, 44–48, 50–52
    and Kharoshthi script, *25,* 26–27, 30, 32–38, 42–43, 45–47
    Stein's explorations of, 12–13, 25–27, 30, *32–38, 42–43,* 45–47, *53*–54
Kucha
    and Buddhism, 56–57, 66–70, 76–77, 80
    and Hedin's explorations, 58–60
    and the Kizil caves, 56–58, 60–65, *62, 67,* 77
    and Kumarajiva, 21
    political control of, 75–82
    religions of, 228
    routes through, *58–59*
    and the Tang dynasty, 79–82, 211
    and tourism, 10
    and trade, 76–82
    See also Kuchean language
Kucha caves, 10
Kucha River, 58
Kuchean language
    and Kumarajiva, 21, 56–57, 66
    and Pelliot's expedition, 65
    and Qu family rulers, 91
    scholarship on, 70–77
    and transformation texts, 188
    travel passes, *57*, 79, 80
    and Turfan, 82–83
    word for "coin," 259n58
Küchlük, 229
Kultobe, 116

Kum, 129
Kumamoto, Hiroshi, 226
Kumarajiva, 21, 56, 57, 66–70, *67*, 240
Kum River, 130
Kumtura, 61, 77
Kushan Empire, 18, 47–48, 52, 71, 202–3, 248n15
Kyrgyzstan, 90, 113

Lake Issyk-kul, 90, 113, 114
land deeds, 45–47
Lane, George Sherman, 72
languages of the Silk Road. *See specific languages*
Laozi, 182
lapis lazuli, 194
Late Khotanese, 210
Later Qin dynasty, 68–69
laws
    and archeology, 34, 143, 149
    and bankruptcy, 165
    and Buddhism, 47, 51, 61
    Islamic law, 136, 228–29, 232–33
    and land distribution, 92
    and moneylending, 151
    and raids, 49
    and silk as currency, 49
    and trade regulations, 165
    and travel restrictions, 17, 36
    See also contracts
lay associations, 193
leather documents, 132, 137
leather products, 227
Le Coq, Albert von, 12, 60, 61–62, 64–65, 110, 175
legal documents, 45–47, *46*, 228
Liangzhou, 85, 144, 184
Liangzhu, 19
Liao dynasty, 228
library cave. *See* Dunhuang
Li Cheng, 143
Li Guangli, 65
Li Mi, 157
Lingdi, Han-dynasty Emperor, 32
Li Shaojin, 148–49
Li Shengtian, 222
Lishi Yanjiu, 176
literature, 157–58
livestock. *See* cattle; horses
loan documents
    and diplomatic envoys, 192
    and Duldur Aqur documents, 81

and Khotanese legal system, 215
and monasteries, 194
and moneylender Zuo's tomb, 96
and pawn tickets, 151
and Sogdian merchants, 159
and Tang law, 103, 111
Lóczy, Lajos, 167–68
long-distance trade, 13
looting, 212
Lotus Sutra, 56, 69
Loulan
    abandonment of, 54–55
    and diplomatic envoys, 50
    and the Han dynasty, 34
    and Kharoshthi documents, 26, 237
    and Kroraina Kingdom, 27
    and migrant populations, 21, 236
    and the Shanshan Kingdom, 42–44
    and Stein's explorations, 35
    and trade documents, 42–44
    wooden artifacts of, 36–38, 42–43, 45
Lü Guang, 68
Luo Feng, 97
Luoyang, 17, 108, 117–19, 150, 157

Macartney, George, 209, 212, 228
The Mahabharata (Sanskrit epic), 52
Mahayana Buddhism, 52, 66–68, 69
Mahmud of Kashgar, 196, 227–28, 234
mail service, 112, 116, 196–97, 239
Maitreya Buddha, 61, 211
Malzahn, Melanie, 73
Manchus, 232–33
mandalas, 186
Manichaeism
    in art, 109, color plate 11A
    and Chang'an, 159
    and Dunhuang cave documents, 167, 181, 182–83, 241
    and immigrant populations, 4
    and Uighurs, 108–11, 109, 228
Marinus, 7
marriage contracts, 133–34
Mashik, 93, 95
Mauryan dynasty, 47

mazar shrines, 234, color plate 16A
Mazar Tagh, 216
medicine, 153, 154
Melikawat, 199, 207
Meng Fanren, 176
merchants
    and banditry, 193, 240
    Bento de Goes, 231–32
    caravans in the Zhou dynasty, 79
    in Caucasus region, 138
    in Chang'an markets, 148–49, 157–58
    and contract law, 103
    and Gansu Province, 85
    and Hedin's travels, 11
    Iranian, 2, 3, 159
    and jataka tales, 64
    Jewish, 31–32, 217–18, 219, 231
    Kharoshthi sources on, 50
    and local trade, 237
    misconceptions about, 82, 111, 184
    and the Mongol Empire, 231
    and Periplus of the Erythraean Sea, 18
    and precious stones, 194–95
    and Qing dynasty, 233
    regulation of, 37, 104, 237–38
    and sea travel, 160–65, 162–63
    and the silk trade, 49
    Sogdian traders, 43, 81, 104, 116, 119–20, 125, 136, 138, 157–59, 239
    and taxes, 99, 100–102, 102
    and Turfan, 96, 106
    and Zhang Qian's travels, 14
metalsmithing, 156
metalwares, 194
Methods & Aims in Archaeology (Stein), 176–77
Middle Khotanese, 210
Middle Persian, 71–72, 182, 210, 217
migrant populations, 47–48, 200, 235, 239, 240. See also nomadic people; refugees
military presence on the Silk Road
    economic impact of, 8–9, 107
    and the Han dynasty, 8, 14–15, 236
    and Kroraina Kingdom, 42
    and the Qing dynasty, 233

and Tang-dynasty payments to soldiers, 184, 215, 237
Minfeng, 33
Ming dynasty, 111, 151
Mintaka Pass, 32
Minway, 118–19, 239
Miran, 27, 53–54, color plate 5B
missionaries, 66, 150, 183, 238, 240
Mithra, 134
Mohoyan Desert, 85
Mongols, 110, 229, 231
monotheism, 118
Moshchevaia Balka, 137–38
Mount Ling, 113
Mount Mugh, 21, 129–39, 131
Mount Wutai, 186, 187
Muhammad, 129, 230
multilingual texts, 214
mummies. See human remains
murals, 125, 126, 128, 129, 138–39
Musakazim Mazar, color plate 16B
Museum of Indian Art (Berlin), 110
musk, 232
Muslim conquests. See Islam
mutual aid societies, 193
Muzart River, 58, 60

Nalanda, 240
Nana (goddess), 124, 126
Nanga Parbat, 27
National Library of China, 213, 217–18
naus structures, 123
Neelis, Jason, 32
negotiation for Dunhuang artifacts, 174–77
nephrite, 207
Nestorians, 110, 149
New Persian, 217, 219
Nisi Chilag, 218
Niya
    abandonment of, 54
    and banditry, 240
    and Buddhism, 51–54, 53, 61, 172, 206, 225
    climate of, 38, 199
    coins of, 48–49, 91
    and diplomatic envoys, 50, 94, 236
    and extent of Silk Road trade, 237
    and Gandhari-speaking residents, 32

Niya (*continued*)
  and Hedin's explorations,
    38, 43
  joint burials at, *color plate 7*
  and Kharoshthi script
    documents, *33*, 35, 40,
    42–44, *46*, 46–47, 51, 202
  and Khotanese documents, 199
  languages of, 56–57
  and migrant populations, 21,
    236–37, 239
  silk artifacts of, *40*
  and Stein's explorations,
    25–30, 33–38, *37*, 42–43,
    167, 173–74, 207, 209
  stupas, 33–35, 52–54, *53*, 205,
    color plate 6
  and travel passes, 36–37, 104
  wooden carvings of, 38
  and the Yuezhi, 71
nomadic people, 65, 73, 90,
  200–201, *203*. *See also*
  migrant populations
Norman Conquest, 210
Northern Liang dynasty, 172
Northern Qi dynasty, 143
Northern Wei dynasty, 55, 141–43,
  144
Northern Zhou dynasty, 143, 144,
  146–47

Ol'denburg, S. F., 175
Old Khotanese, 210
Ordam Padishah Mazar, 234
ossuaries, 98, 123, *123*, 143, 239
Ōtani Kozui, 12, 82
Ot-tegin, 133

padam face masks, *123*, 128, *145*,
  147
paintings
  An Jia's tomb, 144, *color plate*
    14
  Bezelik caves, *color plate 9*
  and Dandan Uiliq, *213*
  and Dunhuang caves, 24,
    167–69, *168*, 172–79, *178*,
    181, 186, 188–90, *189*, 223,
    240
  and Kizil caves, 61–65, *62*, *63*
  and Manichaeism, 111
  and Sogdian culture, 116, 121,
    124, 125–29, *126*, 138–39,
    154
  stupa at Niya, *53*, 53–54
Palembang, 164

Pamir Knot, 10, 27
Panchatantra (Indian tales), 125
Panjikent excavations, 121–26,
  124, *126*, 134–39, 154
paper
  early uses of, *16*
  and funerary garments, *2*
  and Khotanese envoys, 222
  in Kucha, 77
  and monastery schools, 179
  and Mount Mugh excavations,
    132
  reuse of, *2*, 3–4, 24, 83, *84*, 94,
    137, 151, 177
  in Samarkand, 137–38
  and Sogdian documents,
    117–18
  spread of, 15, 137–39, 238
  and trade product, 5–6
  and Turfan, 83, *84*, 92
  See also printing
Parthia, 202
Parthian language, 182
pawn tickets, *140*, 151
Pax Mongolica, 229
Pazyryk, *13*–14
pearls, 50, 151, 156, 159, 165, 194,
  196, 240
Pelliot, Paul
  and Duldur Aqur, 74–75,
    79–80
  and Dunhuang cave, 175–77,
    180, 183
  and Kucha, 65, 77
  and Xinjiang documents, 12
Pem, 230
Periplus of the Erythraean Sea,
  18–19
Persian language, 137, 217–18. *See*
  also Middle Persian
Petrie, William Matthew Flinders,
  176–77
petroleum, 75
Petrovsky, Nikolai, 211
Phema, 230
photography, 176
phrasebooks, 220–21, 240
pilgrimages, 221, 234, *color plate*
  16B
Pinault, Georges-Jean, 74, 78
pinyin, 70
plaid textiles, 13
Pliny the Elder, 19–20
poetry, 77, 188
Polo, Marco, 10, 229, 241–42
"The Polyglot Library," 181

porcelain, 165
posatha ceremonies, 51
pothi, 180
poverty, 118–19
"Praise of the World of Light"
  (hymn scroll), 182
precious stones, 194
prefectures, 79, 91
prenuptial agreements, 133–34
printing, 138, 179, *236*. *See also*
  paper
Protectorate General of Anxi, 91
Protvantak, 146
Ptolemy, 7, 19
Puloti, Abdulhamid, 129–30
Punyavan, 73–74

Qadir Khan, Yusuf, 227
Qarlups, 137
Qin dynasty, 19
Qing dynasty, 9, 111, 169, 232–33
Qinghai Mountains, 9
Qu family, 90, 91
Quianfodong caves at Dunhuang,
  172
Qutayba ibn Muslim, 129
Qu Wentai, 89, 91

raiding, 49–51, 185, 213. *See also*
  robbers and bandits
railroad lines, 8, *color plate 2–3*
Ramshotsa, 45–46
Rapson, E. J., 43
Rawak, 10, 199, 204, *205*, *206*
Record of Travels to the West
  (Xuanzang), 115
redistribution of land, 91–92
refugees
  and cultural exchange, 4
  and dispersal of technologies,
    239
  and Kroraina Kingdom, 26, 45
  Sasanian, 149
  Sogdian, 22–23
  Uighur, 190–91
  use of Silk Road routes, 238
  See also migrant populations
religious tolerance, 146, 181–82,
  241
retail trade, 122
Ricci, Matteo, 232
Richthofen, Ferdinand von, 6–8,
  235
  and "Silk Road" term, *color*
    plate 2–3
river travel, 58–60, 141–43

robbers and bandits
  artwork depicting, *193*
  and de Goes, 231
  and diplomatic delegations,
    225
  and Dunhuang caves, 188
  and Sogdian traders, 103
  use of Silk Road routes, 238
  and Xuanzang's travels, 113,
    192, 240
  See also raiding
rock crystal, 155
Roman Empire
  and diplomatic envoys, 18
  and Dunhuang documents, 197
  intermittent contact with
    China, 19–21
  and Kroraina Kingdom, 54
  Roman coins in China, 9, 20,
    color plate 4A
  and Shanpula graveyard
    artifacts, 202
  and silk production, 19
  and Turfan, 97
Rong Xinjiang, 176, 177, 228
Rouran confederacy, 55, 75, 94
Royal Asiatic Society of Bengal,
  209
royal orders. *See* edicts
royal silk, 49
rubies, 156
Ruins of Desert Cathay (Stein),
  173
Rulers of the Heavens, 169
Russia, 167, *233*
Rustam (Stein's assistant), 45, 125

sabao headmen
  An Jia, 144, *145, color plate 14*
  bureaucratic ranking of, 274n11
  etymology of, 265n58, 277n58
  Faxian on, 160
  and migrant populations, 239
  Shi Wirkak, 146
  and Sogdian religious
    practices, 118
  and Zoroastrian religious
    practices, 98
Samarkand, *115*
  and the Afrasiab murals, 125,
    128, 129, 138–39
  and diplomatic envoys, 127–29,
    128, 241
  and the horse trade, 81
  and Iranian merchants, 3
  languages of, 56–57

  and migrant populations, 239
  and the Mount Mugh letters,
    129–39
  Muslim conquest of, 22
  and the Panjikent excavations,
    121–26, *124*, 134–35, 138–39
  and popular perceptions of the
    Silk Road, 6
  and private mail, *112*
  and Silk Road routes, 10
  and Sogdian culture, 4–5, 31,
    43, 113–20, 121
  and Turfan, 83, 94, 98
  and Xuanzang's travels, 113–16,
    121
Sängim, 74
Sanskrit
  and birch bark documents, 10
  and Buddhism, 47, 56
  and Dunhuang cave
    documents, 174, 181, 187,
    240–41
  and Khotanese, 24, *203*, 210,
    211, 220
  and Kumarajiva, 56–57,
    69–70
  and languages of Kroraina
    Kingdom, 44
  The Mahabharata (Sanskrit
    epic), 52
  and Niya documents, 51–52
  and Stein, 12, 174
  and Tibetans, 184–85
  and Tocharian, 72
  and Turfan, 85
  word for "China," 19
  and Yijing's travels, 164
sapphires, 156
Sarvastivadin school of
  Buddhism, 52, 66
Sasanian Empire
  coins of, 20, 94–96, 122–23,
    156, *color plate 4B*
  refugees from Islamic conquest,
    149
  and Sogdian culture, 120
  and Turfan, 98
Satuq Bughra Khan, 226, 234,
  color plate 16A
scale fees, 99–102, *100–102*
scribes, 216–17, 220
*The Scripture of the Benevolent
  Kings* (Buddhist text), 90
sculptures, 212
seashells, 13
sea travel, 160–65, *162–63*

Second Central Asian Expedition,
  167, 168
Semireche, 196
Serindia (Stein), 35, 176
shamanism, 229
Shamasena, 52
Shan, Kingdom of, 41
Shandong Peninsula, 161–64
Shang dynasty, 13, 235–36
Shanpula, 199, 201, *204*
Shanshan Kingdom, 26, *28–29*,
  40, 42, 55. *See also* Kroraina
  Kingdom
Shatial site, 31
Shi Le, 117
Shi Pantuo, 85
Shi Randian, 104
Shiva, 122
Shi Wirkak, 143, 146, *147*
shizhong, 44
Shouchang, 185
Sidaka, 215–16
Siddhabhadra, 211
Sieg, Emil, 70–73, 211
Siegling, Wilhelm, 70–73, 211
silk
  and Dandan Uiliq painting, 213
  and diplomatic envoys, 225–26
  and Kroraina Kingdom, 38–40,
    40, 42–43, 49–51
  monetary value of, 96, 103,
    192–93, 225–26, *color plate
    5A*
  production of, 19–20
  "royal silk," 49
  and Samarkand, 138
  and the Sogdian Ancient
    Letters, 119
  spread of silk technology, 238
  and the Tang dynasty, 184
  and Turfan, 91
Silk Road, routes of, *color plate
  2–3*
  invention of the term, 6–8
  of Kucha region, *58–59*
  main Eurasian routes, *6–7*
  and pilgrimages to India,
    162–63
  popular perceptions of, 6–10
  of Taklamakan desert, 6, *22–23*
  of Turfan region, *86–87*
The Silk Road (Hedin), 8
Silla, 165
silver
  and Hejiacun Village Hoard,
    153, 155

silver (*continued*)
  ingots, 217
  tax biscuits, 152, 157
  See also silver *under* coins *entry*
Sims-Williams, Nicholas, 116
Skjærvø, Prods Oktor, 210
slavery, 3, 45, 48, 104, 183–84,
  224
Small Goose Pagoda, 151
Sogdians and Sogdiana, *115*
  and the Afrasiab murals, 125,
    128, 129, 138–39, *color plate
    11B*
  and An Jia's tomb, *color plate 14*
  and the An Lushan rebellion,
    157–58
  and anti-foreign sentiment,
    159–60
  and Chang'an, 103, 143–47,
    145, *147*, 149–50, 157–59
  and Christianity, 109
  and cultural exchange, 4–5
  and diplomatic envoys, 17
  and Dunhuang cave
    documents, 181, 182,
    195–96, 241
  and Hejiacun Village Hoard,
    154–55, *155*
  and the horse trade, 81
  and Karakorum Highway
    inscriptions, 31
  and Khotanese, 210
  and Kumarajiva, 56
  languages of, 56, 71–72, 113
  and Loulan documents, 43
  and migrant populations,
    22–23, 239
  and the Mount Mugh letters,
    129–39
  and the Panjikent excavations,
    121–26, *124*, 134–35, 138–39
  and Samarkand, 4–5, 31, 43,
    113–20, 121
  Sogdian Ancient Letters,
    116–20, *120–21*, 138, 160,
    173, 239
  and travels to India, 164–65
  and Turfan, 21, 83, 85–86, 91,
    98–99
  and Xuanzang's travels,
    113–16
Song dynasty, 94, 192, 222
Soviet Union, 130
Sri Lanka, 156, 160, 161
statues, 204–5, *206*
Steel Road, 113

Stein, Aurel
  and Astana graveyard site, *84*
  cataloguing of finds, 208
  and Dandan Uiliq, 217–18
  and the Dunhuang caves,
    167–77, *172*, 180–81, 196–97
  funding for expeditions, 212
  and itinerant traders, 237–38
  and Khotan, 176–77, 207,
    209, 212
  and Kroraina Kingdom sites,
    12–13, 25–27, 30, 32–38,
    42–43, 45–47, 53–54
  and Rawak, 204–5, *205*, *206*
  and the Sogdian Ancient
    Letters, 116
  and Turfan, *93*, 95
  and Xinjiang province, 233
  on Xuanzang's travels, 85
steles, 149, *150*
stupas
  of Karakorum Highway, 30, *31*
  at Kizil caves, 61–62, *62*
  at Niya, 33–35, 52–54, *53*, 205,
    color plate 6
  at Rawak, 204–6, *205*, 207
subsistence economy, 43, 79,
  197, 224, 237
Sufism, 232–34
Sui dynasty, 79, 85, 141, 147,
  168–69
Sumatra, 164
Supis, 49, 51, 54
Suvarnadeva, 77
Suzong, 107–8
Syrians, 231

Taizong, Tang-dynasty Emperor,
  125, 148, 151, 211
Tajikistan, 130
Taklamakan Desert
  and Dandan Uiliq, 212
  and de Goes' caravan, 232
  and distribution of languages,
    72, 75
  glacial rivers of, 58
  and Han dynasty trade, 18
  and Hedin's explorations,
    11–12, 242, *color plate 10*
  and Kroraina Kingdom, 27,
    33, 55
  and the Mongol Empire, 229
  and oasis towns, 8
  and Silk Road routes, 6, 9–10,
    22–23
  and Turfan, 82

withdrawal of Chinese military,
    160
Tamerlane, 231
Tamjaka, 47
Tamluk, 160, 164
Tang Code, 92, 96, 148,
  183–84
Tang dynasty
  and art trade, 21
  and Central Asian economy,
    107
  and Chang'an, 141–43, 147–59,
    166
  and contracts, 103–4, 192–94
  and Dunhuang cave
    documents, 184–85, 186–88
  and Gaochang City, *105*
  and Khotan, 79, 211, 226
  and Kucha, 79–82, 211
  military expenditures, 8
  monetary system, 184
  and moneylending, 151–52
  and Samarkand, 137
  and Sogdiana, 113, 116, 129
  "Tang Barbie," *color plate 8*
  and taxation, 184, 187, 214–16
  and trade disputes, 149
  and Turfan, 21, 82, 85, 88–89,
    91–92, 94, 96–98, 103–8,
    105, 111, 211
  and volume of Silk Road trade,
    237
  and Zhang-family rule at
    Dunhuang, 190
Tanguts, 190–91, 228
Tang Zhangru, 94
Tarim River, 58, 60
Tarxun, 135
taxation
  and the An Lushan rebellion,
    157
  cloth as payment, 106–7
  and coins, 95, 97
  and Dandan Uiliq, 214–17
  and Kroraina Kingdom, 48
  and Kucha, 77
  and Loulan documents, 43
  and payments to soldiers, 215
  and the Tang dynasty, 184, 187,
    214–16
  tax biscuits, 152, 157
  tax documents as evidence,
    238
  and Turfan, 91–92, 96, 99–102,
    100–102, 108
tea, 233

technology
  availability of Dunhuang
    documents, 176
  and locating sites, 212
  and migrant populations, 4,
    239
  paper-making technology,
    137–39, 238
  silk technology, 238
  technological transfer, 137–39
terra-cotta soldiers, 141
textiles
  cotton, 38, *39*, 138, 195
  and the Dunhuang economy, 195
  imported goods, 233
  and Kroraina Kingdom, 38, *39*,
    40, 41–43, 49–51
  of Mongols, 231
  nomadic themes in, *203*
  Shanpula burial garb, *204*
  and the Sogdians, 119
  and the Tang monetary system,
    184
  tax cloth, 106–7
  and Turfan markets, 106–7
  See also silk
Thailand, 156
Theodosius II, 97
Thierry, François, 76
Thousand Buddha
  (Quianfodong) site, 172
The Thousand-Character Classic,
  180
Three Realms Monastery,
  Dunhuang, 178–79, 181, 222
Tianshan Mountains, 113–14
Tibet and Tibetan Empire
  and the An Lushan rebellion,
    184–85, 212
  and Buddhist pilgrimages, 221
  challenge to Tang dynasty, 80,
    107, 108, 157
  collapse of, 216
  and diplomatic envoys, 192
  and Dunhuang cave
    documents, 169, 185–87
  and Khotan, 212
  and the Sogdian Ancient
    Letters, 119
Tibetan language, 180–81,
  186–87, 211, 240–41
Times of London, 8
Timur the Lame, 231
Tocharian language, 13, 44, 71–74
Tocharoi people, 71, 72
Tokmak, 114, 115

Tongzhou, Shaanxi, 144
topazes, 155–56
tortoiseshell, 20, 165
tourism
  and Astana graveyard, 93, 172
  and desert ruins, 10
  and Jiaohe ruins, 91
  and Khotan, 199, 233
  and the Kizil caves, 57–58
  and *mazar* shrines, 234, *color
    plate 16A, color plate 16B*
  and Melikawat ruins, 207
Tragbal Pass, 27
transformation texts, 76–77, 179,
  188
translations, 214
travel passes *(guosuo)*
  and diplomatic envoys, 17
  of Kucha, *57*, 77–80, *78*, 82
  at Niya, 36–37
  and sea travel, 165
  as source of evidence, 238
  and supervision of trade, 237
  and Turfan, 89, 103–4
tribute, 231
Trinkler, Emil, 212
Trombert, Éric, 82, 184
Turco-Sogdian, 195–96
Turdi, 212
Turfan
  and Astana graveyard site, *84*,
    86–87, 93–99, 151
  burial practices of, 92–94,
    98–99
  and caravan trade, 88, 103–7,
    232
  climate of, *11*, 21, 92–93
  coinage of, 99, *100–102*, 103–7,
    111
  coins of, *color plate 4B*
  and diplomatic envoys, 192
  foods of, 83
  and Gaochang city, *105*
  languages of, 72, 74–75
  religions of, 182, 228, 231
  and Sogdians, 21, 83, 85–86,
    91, 98–99
  and the Tang dynasty, 21, 82,
    85, 88–89, 91–92, 94, 96–98,
    103–8, *105*, 111, 211
  taxation in, 91–92, 96, 99–102,
    100–102, 108
  textile finds from, 14
  tomb figurines, *140*
  and tourism, 10, *color plate 9*
  and trade regulation, 237

and Uighur refugees, 190–91
and Xuanzang's travels, 83–91
Turgesh, 135–36
Turkic languages, 182, 233–34
Turkish kaghanates, 75, 79
Turks, 120, 127, 135, 226–27
Twgrhy language, 71–72, 211,
  257n30, 258n35

Uddyana Kingdom, 94
Uighur kaghanates, 108–11,
  190–92, 196, 216, 220, 222,
  224, 226
Uighur language
  and Dunhuang cave
    documents, 181, 195–96, 241
  and Khotanese, 199, 211, 234
  and Manichaeism, 108, *109*, 110
  and the Qing dynasty, 232–33
  spoken, 168–69
  and Tocharian, 71–74
  and Turfan, 108
  from Yarkand, 228
Uighurs
  and the An Lushan rebellion,
    157
  defeat of Tibetans, 218
  and diplomatic envoys, 191,
    192, 224
  and distribution of languages,
    73 (*see also* Uighur language)
  and Dunhuang, 168, 190–91,
    216
  and Khotan, 226, 233–34
  Kirghiz conquest of, 108, 190,
    216, 226
  and Kucha, 80
  and Manichaeism, 108–11,
    109, 228
  mercenaries, 108
  tensions with Han population,
    93
  and Turfan, 83, 108–10
  and Zhang Yichao, *189*
Umayyad Caliphate, 129
Urumqi Museum, 94

Vagiti Vadhaga, 209
Vaissière, Étienne de la, 119
Vajrayana, 221
Vandak, 85–86, *86–87*
Varkhuman, 125, 127, 129
vinaya law, 51, 79, 221
Visa Sambhava, 222, *223*, 227
Visa Sura, 227
Vreshmanvandak, 146

Wang Binghua, 41
Wang Fengxian, 104
Wang Mang, 36
Wang Pa-kyau, 225
Wang Yuanlu, 169, 173–74,
   177–78, 180
warlords, 233–34
Wei dynasty, 75
Wei River, 166
Wei Zhuang, 166
Western Jin dynasty, 44
Western Liao dynasty, 229
Western Market (Chang'an), 141,
   142, 148–49, 165–66
Western Paradise, 182
Western Turks, 88, 90, 114, 121
White Huns, 120–21
Wild Horse Spring, 88
willow branch documents, 132,
   134, 137
wonder tales, 157–58
woodblock printing, 138, 179, *236*
wooden documents
   and Buddhist texts, 52
   and burial practices, 99
   and Khotan, 207
   and Kuchean language, 70, 77
   legal documents, *46*, 214
   and Loulan site, 36–38, 42–43,
     45
   and Niya site, 21, *25*, 25–26,
     33–35, 46, *46*, 51–52
   requisition documents, *16*
   travel passes, *57*
   willow branch documents, 132,
     134, 137
   and Xuanquan site, 15, 241
wool, 13, 40, *41*, 50, 119, 196, 201,
   202, 239, 240
World War I, 64
Wu, Han-dynasty Emperor, 14
Wuhan University, 94
Wuqia hoard, 98
Wuwei, 85, 118, 119, 144
wuzhu coins, 36, 97, 250n30,
   255n90

Xi'an, *142*
   archeology in, 143, 152
   climate of, 151
   and Kumarajiva's travels, 68
   and railroad lines, 8
   and religious institutions, 150,
     182
   and Silk Road art, 239–40
   and Silk Road routes, 9

   tombs of foreign residents, 22
   tourist attractions, 141, 149
   and Xuanzang's travels, 85
   See also Chang'an
Xidir (Xizir) Khoja, 111
Xin ("New") Dynasty, 36
Xinjiang
   archeologists in, 93–94
   coins of, 82
   division of, 229
   and grasslands, 65
   and the Han dynasty, 37
   and the Kizil caves, 57–59
   and migrant populations, 50
   and the Qing dynasty, 233
   and Silk Road routes, 9
   and tax cloth, 107
   and Turkish conquests, 75
Xinjiang Museum, 38
Xiongnu confederation
   cooperation with Sogdians, 17
   and diplomatic envoys, 236
   and distribution of languages,
     73
   and the Han dynasty, 14
   and the Huns, 117
   and Kucha, 65, 73
   and Kushan migrants, 32
   and Loulan, 35
   and Turfan, 90–91
Xixia, 191, 228
Xiyu region, 9
Xuanquan, Dunhuang, 14–15, *16*,
   18, 241
Xuanzang
   account of travels, 83–91, 240
   and Chang'an, 85, 141, 144,
     151
   and Khotan, 200, 207, 211
   robbed, 192
   and Sanskrit, 85, 187
   and Sogdiana, 113–16, 121
   Stein's invocation of, 174, 176
Xuanzong, Tang-dynasty
   Emperor, 107, 157

Yaghnob Valley, 113
Yang Guifei, 107–8, 157
Yangzhou, 147, 164
Yangzi River, 141
Yanqi, 57–58, 70, 72–75, 79
Yanshuigou, 82
Yao Xing, 68, 69
Ya'qub Beg, 233
Yarkand, 59, 90–91, 228–29,
   231–32

Yarkand River, 59–60
Yarlung dynasty (Tibet), 184, 187
Yazdegerd III, 149
Ye Changchi, 169
Yijing, *162–63*, 164–65
Yingpan, 27, 40–42, *41*
Yizhou, 192
yong taxes, 152
Yoshida Yutaka, 98, 216
Yotkan, 199, 207, *208*
Ysambasta, 210
Ysarkula, 210
Yuan dynasty, 230–31
Yuezhi people, 14, *33*, 71
Yurungkash River, 203, 207

Zarathustra, 5, 30
Zerafshan River, 121, 130
Zhang Huaiding, 190
Zhang Huaishen, 188–89, 190, 191
Zhang Qian, 14, *33*, 236
Zhang Yichao, 187–88, *189*, 190,
   191
"Zhang Yichao Transformation
   Text," 188
Zhang Zhan, 218
Zhematvandak, 146
Zhi Qian, 32
Zhou dynasty, 79
Zoroastrianism
   and the Afrasiab murals, 128,
     128
   and An Jia's tomb, *color plate 15*
   and Chang'an, 149, 159
   and Dunhuang cave
     documents, 167, 181, 241
   and funerary practices, 118,
     123, *123*, 123–25, 143–46,
     145, *147*, 240
   and the Huang Chao rebellion,
     165
   and immigrant populations,
     4–5
   and Islamic conquest of
     Samarkand, 137
   and Kroraina Kingdom, 30
   and the Mount Mugh
     excavations, 134–35, 136–37
   and Sasanian coins, 95, *color
     plate 4B*
   and Sogdian migrants, 23
   spread with migrant
     populations, 139
   and Turfan, 95, 98, 108
Zou (moneylender), 96
zu taxes, 152